PLAYERS & PAINTED STAGE TOOK ALL MY LOVE

BUT NOT THOSE THINGS

THAT THEY WERE

EMBLEMS OF.

W.B.YEATS

TOWARD
A LARGER
THEATRE

7 Plays by
Mordecai Gorelik

UNIVERSITY
PRESS OF
AMERICA

Copyright © 1988 by

Mordecai Gorelik

University Press of America,® Inc.

4720 Boston Way
Lanham, MD 20706

All rights reserved

Printed in the United States of America

Library of Congress Cataloging-in-Publication Data

Gorelik, Mordecai, 1899–
Toward a larger theatre : 7 plays / by Mordecai Gorelik.
    p. cm.
Contents: Yes and no—Andrus, or, The vision—Rainbow Terrace—
The feast of unreason—Mrs. Disaster—The big day—Paul Thompson forever. I. Title.
    PS3557.0737T6   1988   812'.54—dc 19   87–35224 CIP
            ISBN 0–8191–6845–9 (alk. paper)
            ISBN 0–8191–6846–7 (pbk. : alk. paper)

All University Press of America books are produced on acid-free
paper which exceeds the minimum standards set by the National
Historical Publications and Records Commission.

TOWARD A LARGER THEATRE

It appears to be taken for granted that plays can be written by actors, directors, and even drama critics — but who ever heard that a play by a scene designer should be taken seriously?

These seven plays (four long, three short) are part of the collected dramatic scripts written by Mordecai Gorelik, internationally known designer whose career in the U.S. theatre now spans a period of 65 years. Much of his time has been devoted to stage production in the universities, among them the University of Southern Illinois, of which he is professor emeritus.

Although he was one of the first American adherents of Brechtian theatre (beginning in 1936), Gorelik has created his own kind of writing, joining tragedy to farce-comedy in a combination as animated as it is deeply felt — and on themes as diverse as the 13th century Inquisition, the religious war in Northern Ireland, the generations-gap in the American sixties, or the judgment of sin in the Life Hereafter. their author tells how the plays came to be written, and quotes some of the reactions, ranging from acclaim to insult, that they have received. Further of interest are his thoughts on the state of American theatre, current and recent.

Gorelik's study of the historic forms of staging, *New Theatres for Old* (1940) remains as a classic in its field. His adaptation of Max Frisch's *The Firebugs* has been accorded almost 550 separate U.S. stage productions to date.

iii

For

FRANCES

and

LORAINE

TOWARD A LARGER THEATRE

CONTENTS

ACKNOWLEDGMENTS

I am honored that you wish to allude to me as one of your "encouragers." For it is encouragement that theatre people need more than anything today. You, yourself, set a splendid example — daring to embark, Ulysseslike on a new voyage after the successful completion of so many others.

— Robert E. Lee.

Bob Lee, co-author with Jerome Lawrence, of so many contributions to a larger American theatre, had previously written me that my play, *The Feast of Unreason* "surely deserves production." He also told me that he was sending another of my plays, *Andrus, or the Vision*, to the American Playwrights Theatre (APT), of which he was then president; "Perhaps," he added, "they will make you an offer you can't refuse."

That the APT made no offer only emphasized, for me, the generosity of Bob Lee, who evidently did not consider that as a designer of stage settings I was just an intruder in the domain of playwriting.

But then, I was not of the school of scenic artists who designed a setting while painting it, starting at the upper left-hand corner of the drop cloth and finishing at the lower right-hand corner. I was one of a new breed who studied the dramatist's script with minute care in order to understand its style and purpose, to foresee the movements of the actors, to view the setting as "machine-for-theatre." That this could show in my drawings at the age of twenty amazes me when I think back on it — still more that it could have impressed someone of the caliber of Robert Edmond Jones, father of modern American scene design. From Bobby I inherited a reverence for theatre that I never have lost.

Nor did I encounter a narrower horizon as an apprentice to Norman Bel Geddes, who was as gifted in industrial design as in scenography. And it was Serge Soudeikin, designer for the *Chauve Souris*, who opened for me the world of Russian folk art. In those days designing for the stage was not taught in any classroom — a good thing, perhaps, in my case, for I learned it as a discipline and a backstage craft together with the whole meaning of theatre as a public experience.

Almost as soon as I entered the theatre I began writing about it. The leading magazine of "The New Stagecraft," *Theatre Arts Monthly*, edited by Edith J.R. Isaacs, liked my essays, and I wrote for that magazine very often during the following years. My writings have also appeared in *Contact Magazine* (San Francisco), *Drama Survey*, *Educational Theatre Journal*, *Quarterly Journal of Speech*, *Masque* (Sydney), *Meanjin* (Melbourne), *New Theatre and Film*, *New York Times*, *Players Magazine*, *Theatre Annual*, *Theatre Workshop*, *Tulane Drama Review*, *Theatre Crafts*, *Dramatics, The Cue*. Some of my articles have been published in Swedish, German, Czechoslovakian, and Russian periodicals, and I have contributed to Collier's *Encyclopedia*, the *Encyclopedia Americana*, and the *Encyclopaedia Britannica*.

I wish to acknowledge the use, in this volume, of any part of my essays borrowed from these publications. I am also obligated to the *Saturday Review*, the *Southern Illinoisan*, and the *Daily Egyptian* (the Southern Illinois University campus newspaper) for material that has appeared in their columns. I want, further, to express my gratitude to all who have written me their opinions of my playscripts, pro or con.

I treasure the recognition given to my dramatic writings, whether in play contests, publications, or onstage. I owe heartfelt thanks to those people who have transcribed my playscripts into print or brought them to the stage:

A tryout of *Paul Thompson Forever*, under my direction, was made possible by Mary Tarcai at the Actors Laboratory Theatre, Hollywood, California, in 1947. The script was published by Walter Baker & Co., Boston, in 1950.

A production, under my direction, of *The Annotated Hamlet*, my treatment of Shakespeares's play, at Southern Illinois University (Carbondale), was made possible by Archibald McLeod, chair, Department of Theatre, S.I.U., 1961.

My adaptation of Max Frisch's *Biedermann und die Brandstifter (The Firebugs)*, was published by Hill and Wang, New York, in 1963, and listed after 1968 by Samuel French, New York. It has also appeared in anthologies by Random House, Crown Publishers and Harcourt Brace Jovanovich. Several scenes from this script were tried out, under my direction, at the Actors Studio, New York City, in 1959. Its first full-stage productions, also directed by me, were at California State College (San Jose), in 1964 and at S.I.U. in 1965. There have since been 548 productions* of my playscript in the United States alone.

A number of scenes from *Rainbow Terrace*, with Frederick O'Neal heading a cast of black players, was also tried out under my direction at the Actors Studio, New York, 1959. The full-stage premiere of this play, directed and designed by me at S.I.U. in 1966, was made possible by Dr. McLeod. In 1983, at Ghost Ranch, New Mexico, I directed a staged reading of the script at the invitation of Wilma Ringstrom and Dr. Norman J. Fedder, of the ECDA (Ecumenical Council for Drama and Other Arts.)

The Big Day was published in *The Best Short Plays* series, 1977 edited by Stanley Richards.

---

*<u>Productions</u>, not performances.

A tryout of *Andrus, or the Vision* at the Purple Masque Theatre, Kansas State University (Manhattan, Kansas), under the direction of Joel Climenhaga, was made possible by Climenhaga and Dr. Norma D. Bunton, chair, Department of Speech, 1977. The subsequent full-stage premiere of this play, directed by Dr. Marilyn Hylland at the Act 2 Community Theatre, Ada, Oklahoma, with the cooperation of Oklahoma East Central University, was made possible by Dr. Hylland, 1979.

A staged reading, with music, of a scene from *Andrus, or the Vision*, was directed by Christian Moe at the Unitarian Fellowship, Carbondale, Illinois, in 1978.

A cast reading of *Yes and No*, with Dr. McLeod as Don, was directed by me at S.I.U., 1969.

A brief cast reading of a scene from *Rainbow Terrace*, taken from *Wrestling With God*, an anthology of religous plays in preparation by the Anchorage Press (New Orleans), was directed by Wilma Ringstrom at the American Theatre Association meeting in New York City, 1982.

A cast reading of *Rainbow Terrace* was made possible by John Gulley, under auspices of the Asolo State Theatre, Sarasota, Florida, 1985.

The Feast of Unreason, in a reader's theatre presentation with action, music and sound recording, was staged by Theatre-in-the-Works, Orlando, Florida, under the direction of Edward Dilks, at the Black Box Theatre of Central Florida University, 1985.

I acknowledge herewith the use of lines from the following songs:

In Yes and No: *I Want to Hold Your Hand*. Words and music by John Lennon and Paul McCartney, Copyright 1963 by Northern Songs Ltd., London, England. Sole selling agent Duchess Music Corp., New York, New York. All rights reserved. Used by permission.

Gallant Men. Copyright 1965 and 1966 by Chappell & Co., Inc. International copyright secured. All rights reserved. Used by permission.

MacArthur Park, by Jimmy Webb. Copyright 1968, 1973 Canopy Music, Inc. All rights reserved. Used by permission of Warner Brothers Music.

Swinging on a Star. Copyright 1944 by Burke and Van Heusen, Inc. Copyright renewed and assigned to Bourne Company and Dorsey

Brothers Music, Inc. All rights reserved. Used by permission of Bourne Company.*

We Shall Overcome. New words and musical arrangement by Zilphia Horton, Frank Hamilton, Guy Carawan and Pete Seeger. TRO.**

The words of *The FAC Rides Forth To Battle*, in *Yes and No*, appeared in an article, "G-Eye view of Vietnam," by Joseph B. Treastor, in the *New York Times Magazine* of October 30, 1966. The *Times* Rights and Royalties Department has been unable to locate any copyright owner.

I did my best to learn if any of the Irish songs in *The Feast of Unreason* were under copyright. Evidently they were not. In this quest and in other matters I had the help of Brendan McMahon, vice-consul of Ireland at San Francisco, and his successor, Thelma M. Doran. Further contacts were Waltons Musical Galleries, Ltd., the National Library of Ireland and the Association of Music Publishers in Ireland, all of Dublin, as well as the Linen Hall Library, Belfast. I am grateful for all the courtesy these Irish people and institutions have shown me.

In checking up some of the American songs for *Yes and No*, I was aided by the Music Division of the Library of Performing Arts, New York. The same Library's Research Center and its Billy Rose Theatre Collection were also helpful. I am indebted, further, to Ann Hammil, of the Huntington Beach Library, California; Anne Mochedlover, of the Public Library of Los Angeles; and the Macmillan Co., New York, for the quotations from the Irish poet William Butler Yeats.

Finally I want to thank Lorin Brennan, of the Los Angeles Lawyers for the Arts, and Kenneth D. Werner, of the Dramatists Guild for their advice; my cousin, Jacob Gorelik, for his information on the *stetl* of Shchedrin; and my dear wife, Loraine, for her loving assistance and support in making this book a reality.

I can't say I've made it easy for producers or play agents by writing scripts that call for a single domestic interior and two actors each. However, the Kansas showing of *Andrus* proved that it could be put on for less than the well-known shoestring. Besides, I have no objection to readers' theatre productions or even a script-in-hand cast reading of any of the plays.

---

* Bourne Co. must be contacted for permission to use the song in any stage production.
** 1960 and 1963 by Ludlow Music, Inc., New York, New York, Used by permission.

All of the playscripts in this books are prefaced by a very short outline of their plots. This ought to prove useful to playreaders accustomed to making snap judgments. For those with more patience, who may want to know how — or even if — my longer plays can be staged, I will be happy to supply, without charge, a set of Production Notes for any of the longer scripts. Meanwhile, notes on casting follow each of the longer playtexts.

MORDECAI GORELIK

INTRODUCTION

I must have been eleven years old when my grammar school class at P.S. 70, Manhattan, was given a home assignment: to get acquainted with a branch of literature known as drama. We were to read a play — any play — and to report on it next day in class.

By some instinct I found on the shelves of our local library a small volume whose pages, entirely in the form of clipped dialog, told how a young bank clerk made an error in judgment that led to his arrest, prosecution, imprisonment, and the increasing madness of his encounter with the stony bureaucratic mind of the law.

The compassion of this account, its controlled indignation, its exposure of the inhumanity of human beings, were laid bare as by a skilled surgeon; every word counted in the mounting intensity of this frightening story. I had stumbled on a stage piece named *Justice*, by an already famous English novelist named John Galsworthy. Not least impressive about the writing was the seeming remoteness with which the evidence was presented. I was already acquainted with Dickens' romantic picture of the bygone underworld of London. Galsworthy's England was cold-blooded and modern; his defense of the victimized seemed to come of an upper class outraged by the hardened cruelty of its own servants. Unlike Dickens, who came of the lowest, poverty-ridden middle class, Galsworthy, as I learned afterward, was a son of an old English family, educated at Harrow and Oxford.

It is now considered proper to speak of Galsworthy as oldfashioned — in a theatre that is itself out of date. His dramas are as "old-fashioned" as the most recent case of murderous racism and as the latest outbreak of blood-drenched war. My admiration for this English master deepened in the following years. In 1920, when I entered the backstage of a theatre for the first time in my life, it was my good fortune to be on hand when one of Galsworthy's plays was going into rehearsal. The play was *The Mob*, and it remains as newsworthy, to my mind, as any demonstration that is going to be put on tomorrow morning against nuclear war.

Victim of *The Mob* is Stephen More, a young member of the British Cabinet, who opposes Britain's invasion of a small, still independent country. His idealism outrages the patriotic mob; he loses his friends and relatives; his wife deserts him, taking their little daughter with her, and the mob finally catches up with him, ending his life.

Written in 1914, the play did so well at its debut in Manchester that it was being readied to open in London. I have never learned if it did so and was immediately withdrawn, or if the project was abandoned. With true Galsworthian irony, World War I broke out at this juncture, leaving no room for antiwar sentiments onstage.

TOWARD A LARGER THEATRE

The opening of *The Mob* at the attractive little Neighborhood Playhouse, on Grand Street in downtown New York, may have been the first showing anywhere of this play after the war. I had been given permission to be useful to the show's designer, Warren Dahler, and so could watch its production. The dramatist himself came to New York and was given an informal, awed reception. He looked exactly as I had imagined him: a tall, elegant, and courteous patrician to whom I dared not address a word; just having seen him was a reward for my unimportant work backstage.

*　　　*　　　*

I had become friendly with some of the cast of *The Mob*, surprised to find that actors could be literate; they argued over George Bernard Shaw, read *Theatre Arts Monthly* and books by Hiram K. Moderwell, Sheldon Cheney, and Huntly Carter about the New Stagecraft in Europe. A couple of the male actors informed me that the Playhouse was a "sissy outfit" supported by the wealthy Lewisohn sisters, managed by Helen Arthur, and stage directed by Agnes Morgan. I ought to try the Provincetown Players, who were "for real," with a hit play, *The Emperor Jones*, by a new dramatist named Eugene O'Neill, already transferred to Broadway.

Supplied with a recommendation from Robert Edmond Jones, who had become my mentor, I journeyed to Macdougal Street, in Greenwich Village, where I met the Provincetown's founder, George Cram Cook, and Eugene O'Neill's stage director, Jimmy Light. I felt at home immediately. Not only actors and dramatists but poets, painters, sculptors, anarchists, and other free spirits loved the ramshackle little theatre imbedded in a street of small red-brick houses. Here, with young Cleon Throckmorton, designer and technical director, as my boss, I continued to learn my trade as a stage carpenter and scene painter. There was plenty of unpaid scenic work to do for the bills of new one-acts that were constantly being tried out. O'Neill's *Glencairn* series and other of his plays were in repertory; and, on one unforgettable occasion, came the premiere of Theodore Dreiser's *The Hand of the Potter*. (This piece, about a child molester on the lam, almost ended in disaster. Someone had neglected to hang a gas jet on the wall of the last-act setting so that the sex fiend could commit suicide by gas.)

*　　　*　　　*

I have often thought there would be no such thing as theatre if it were not for all those people — some with talent, some without — who choose to enter it, leaving home and any rational future behind them. Theatre is not a profession but a lifelong adventure. And there is no telling, either, where it will pick up its recruits, of whom I was one.

2

My family name, pronounced Gorel'ik, is of Russian Jewish origin; my first name is biblical (*Book of Esther*). I am known to my friends as Max — a name bestowed on me by an Ellis Island inspector when I arrived in this country at the age of five and a half. I was just in time to start grammar school at P.S. 70, in Manhattan. And I was not over seven when I began working for my father, who owned a newsstand at the corner of Second Avenue and 72d Street. Torn out of my dreams every morning by a double-belled alarm clock, I folded newspapers at daybreak, then delivered them, falling asleep afterwards at the school's morning assembly. Home life was no easier. My family lived in a tough neighborhood, mainly Irish Catholic, where I was continually made to pay for having nailed Our Savior to the cross.

This introduction to the New World was phased out for me at thirteen, when my father at last gave up his newsstand in favor of a partnership in a small lumber yard in Brooklyn. When this venture failed almost immediately he opened an equally small yard of his own, the Williamsburg Lumber Co., where I functioned as lumber salesman, truckman and bookkeeper — as well as general secretary, since Pop could not write English.

I was still in high school when I decided, to the consternation of my parents, that I did not look forward to inheriting my father's business and chose instead to attend Pratt Institute Art School in the hope of becoming a book-illustrator.

My work at the yard continued after school hours, and at times I was called away from nude "life-class" in order to truck lumber from the Bushwick freight yards with the help of two hired horses. If my parents still thought I would return to my senses, that notion vanished, one day, when a schoolmate at Pratt called my attention to the art of scenic design — something I may never have heard of before. A young man named Robert Edmond Jones had made U.S. stage history by designing, in new-wave "symbolist" style, the settings for a play by Leo Tolstoy called *Redemption*. Broadway was only a subway trip away; a visit to the Plymouth Theatre opened my mind to the startling combination of design and drama.

I have written elsewhere of my subsequent meeting with Bobby Jones and his kindness to a raw Brooklyn twenty-year-old.[1] It was he who advised me to learn my trade at places like the Neighborhood Playhouse and the Provincetown; he wrote to both, introducing me in terms much better than I thought I deserved. My work backstage was not paid for, but it was not charged for either, as at school — a net gain.

Meanwhile things were becoming decidedly uncomfortable at home. Pop reminded me that he was under no obligation to keep supporting me at my age, and Mom added that if this Mr. Jones thought so highly of me, why wasn't he giving me a job?

3

At length, again on Bobby's glowing recommendation, I was taken on by the Messrs. Golden and Kessler, of the Novelty Scenic Studio, located in the West 40's in a street known as Tin Pan Alley on account of its piano-accompanied rehearsals and song tryouts. Novelty specialized in vaudeville and burlesque backdrops; these I designed in the sewing-room, with a wardrobe trunk as a worktable. I earned enough to share a ramshackle joint on the second floor above the Provincetown with two "at liberty" actors; we each owned a cot to sleep on, and had a merry time on weekends with visiting girl friends and other companions.

However, it was not my particular way of life, and it changed when I began designing settings for Mrs. Clare Tree Major's School of the Theatre, located above a Loewe's Movie House uptown at Lexington Avenue and 50th Street. I rented an inexpensive but pleasantly furnished room nearby, and even found time from my duties to try my hand at writing a one-act play.

The title of that script is gone from memory; nor can I think what it contained, but I seem to remember dimly that it was about a white goddess of an African tribe, or something like that. Evidently the effect of Galsworthy had faded from my mind, replaced (temporarily) by the dreamy melancholy of O'Neill and by the exotically romantic novels of H. Rider Haggard, whom I had also discovered.

That summer, in 1922, I was in Germany, on a trip that my very meager finances could afford only because of that country's economic breakdown after the war. I wanted to see for myself why the German expressionist staging had caught the attention of American commentators. Bobby Jones, who had once studied with Max Reinhardt, was also in Berlin, collaborating with the drama critic Kenneth Macgowan on what became the beautiful book of the *Continental Stagecraft*. I accompanied Bobby, Kenneth, and two U.S. journalists, Lincoln Steffens and Sam Spewack, to a showing at the Volksbühne of Ernst Toller's *Massemensch* (later called *Man and the Masses* in a New York Theatre Guild version). As directed by Jürgen Fehling and designed by Hans Strohbach, this tragedy of the class war that followed Germany's lost war of conquest exploded on the Volksbühne stage "like a single outburst of passion — and of grief."[2] I could never again look at theatre as the home only of family problems.

For the rest of my brief stay in Berlin I was haunted by the visible evidence of ruined Germany's defeat, depression and defiance. The Fatherland awaited only the right kind of Führer to lead it into another and even more spectacular world conflagration.

*   *   *

4

In the early 20's the world war that established the U.S. as a superpower was followed by a national prosperity without equal, perhaps, in all history. With it came a surge of more sophisticated drama and staging, as exemplified by the Theatre Guild, in New York, and by "little theatres" that spread across America, while our universities began to give classes in theatre and even built playhouses to stage their productions.

I was now serving full time at my apprenticeship. As one of Norman Bel Geddes's assistants, I encountered, at first reluctantly, the exactness of working-drawings. At Stony Point, not far upstate, I and two other young scene painters carried out, full scale, the backdrops designed by the gifted refugee Russian artist Serge Soudeikin for the Metropolitan Opera's *Petrushka*. At the Cornish School in Seattle, one summer, I entered on the teaching career that was to occupy a large part of my life. And I was one of the first "new" designers who were obliged to join the United Scenic Artists, Local 829, a labor union affiliated with the Painters Brotherhood, A.F. of L. This was a turn of events that many of us, including myself, bewailed at the time but have since found necessary in a trade as unstable as the theatre.

By 1924 I was getting a surprising amount of attention. Elizabeth B. Grimball, who had an acting school in Greenwich Village, unexpectedly offered to let me try out any play I cared to direct as well as design. I chose Leonid Andreyev's *King Hunger*, and arranged to direct it at Jasper Deeter's Hedgerow Theatre (Moylan, PA). The play was a social-minded fantasy, and Deeter, gaunt and raspingly sarcastic, was perfectly cast as Hunger. The production opened at the Plays and Players Club in Philadelphia, to favorable reviews, but nothing further happened except for my realizing that a theme on the consequences of starvation would not be profitable on Broadway or anywhere else. That should have taught me something about my wrong choice of stories for stage production, but it never did.

On the other hand the experience of directing actors in a play gave me a closer look at the problems of dramatic composition — a study that lingered in my mind from then on during my whole career in the theatre. I wondered also why I had chosen a play like *King Hunger*. I had been attracted by the fantasy of the Russian author and his compassion for "the masses," realizing only later on that his theme was a political one as well — at a polar remove from anything written by Chekhov.

In the following year I made a lifelong friend of John Howard Lawson with my designs for his *Processional*. Jack had won attention with his expressionist drama *Roger Bloomer*. His new play was a hilarious takeoff, in jazz rhythm, of some of the dizzier aspects of the American scene, with the Ku Klux Klan as a comedy menace. When I learned that *Processional* was to be staged in burlesque style, I lost no time meeting its author, who let me borrow the script. The drawings that I submitted for it delighted him. In the meantime, however, he had lost his would-be producer, with no other prospect in sight — until, very surprisingly, the Theatre Guild bought the play and, with it, my designs (1925).

The success of my work on *Processional*, which made me a Broadway scene designer, gave me at the same time a foretaste of what Broadway would be like as a source of livelihood. Any "Main Stem" manager whose office I visited praised the *Processional* designs, then informed me that he had no play for which I would be suitable. The "come-down" was terrific.

But my depression began to lift when I was asked to design a Yiddish comedy, Ossip Dymov's *The Last Love*, for old Rudolph Schildkraut's little playhouse in the Bronx (1926) and for David Pinsky's *The Final Balance*, a Yiddish play, in English, at the Provincetown (1928). For the Yiddish Art Theatre and its famous actor-manager, Maurice Schwartz, I designed Jacob Gordin's *God, Man and Devil* (1928) and Sholom Ash's *Uncle Moses* (1930), as well as a multiple setting for Schwartz's touring production of scenes from Shakespeare.

Another happy experience of those days was the beginning of my friendship with the young dramatist Em Jo (later Em Jo Basshe), who liked to relate that he was the son of a London banker and a Russian peasant woman. When I first met him he was a Village character and Provincetown Players actor; he had an appealing, simple quality, and he did look like a Russian mujik, although his original name was Emanuel Jochelman. Our temperaments were not alike: he was then writing curiously unreal plays with titles like *The Bitter Fantasy* and *The Drum Major's Beads* — works that would have been perfect for the absurdist theatre of thirty years ahead; and he jeered at my enthusiasm for H.G. Wells' amazing novel, *The War of the Worlds*. Still it was Em, I think, who suggested that we write a play together — a collaboration that started with discussions and got nowhere fast.

In 1925 Em's tragedy, *Adam Solitaire*, about a character forever pursued by bad luck, was put on at the Provincetown, where it was seen by Otto Kahn, a millionaire theatre patron. Kahn found this story so heart-warming that when its author came up with an idea for a playhouse to be managed by a group of young dramatists, Kahn made it financially possible. As inaugurated at a small meeting-house on West 52nd Street, the executives of the New Playwrights Theatre consisted of Em Jo himself, Jack Lawson, Francis Farragoh, John Dos Passos, and Mike Gold, who, incidentally, was a featured writer for the Communist newspaper *The Daily Worker*.

To the somewhat pained amusement of the New York drama critics, the New Playwrights survived for two years. It considered itself a champion of the working class and the underprivileged, very few of whose members showed any interest in its dramas. Its benefactor remained unconcerned even when, for its second season, it moved

6

downtown and flew a red flag outside its new home, the Cherry Lane Theatre in Greenwich Village. Em Jo, suddenly attaining an impressive new realism, was represented in both seasons by *Earth*, a study of Negro life in the South, and *The Centuries*, a history of the East European Jewish immigrants in New York.

I thoroughly enjoyed the burlesque humor of Lawson's *Loud Speaker*, which I designed for the New Playwrights, but Jack's increasing radicalism, did not convey much to me. As a matter of fact he was so harshly critical of the Communist line of the *New Masses* magazine that I was amazed when, without warning, he turned around and became a Marxist disciplinarian — in the process alienating Dos Passos, who had been one of his closest friends. With the breakup of the Playwrights, Lawson left for Hollywood, where he had been preceded by Farragoh and where, besides becoming a leading film writer, he organized and became the first president of the Screen Writers Guild. Dos went back to his novels and Mike to his column in *The Daily Worker*. Em Jo also had a turn at the movies, evidently without success. Except that he married a lovely Southern girl and that they had a baby girl whom they called "Topper," I know nothing of Em's later history. He died very suddenly in 1939.

* * *

It must have been some time in 1930 when Harold Clurman, who was organizing the future Group Theatre, asked me to accompany him to an interview with Sidney Howard, author of *They Knew What They Wanted*, *The Silver Cord*, and other plays that had established him as a leading Broadway dramatist. I don't know why I was invited to be present except that I had been put on the Group's advisory board, but I listened with interest to Clurman's outline of what the Group would be.

Howard finally asked, "Will your theatre be Marxist?"

"We are not going to be constricted by Marxism," Clurman assured him.

To which the dramatist replied, "Marxism is a pretty roomy philosophy, Harold."

The meaning of Marxism and Communism (two separate categories confused then as now in the minds of people alarmed by both) was being fiercely debated by many of my friends in the theatre. Karl Marx had taught that private capitalism was subject to alternative periods of prosperity and depression, "boom" and "bust." In the twenties, following a world war that established the United States as a superpower, the nation was enjoying a prosperity without equal in its history. That period ended overnight in 1929 with the crash of the Wall Street stock market, followed by the kind of devastation that had fallen upon Germany less than a decade before.

TOWARD A LARGER THEATRE

The Great Depression shook the whole economy of the United States with the impact of an atomic bomb. Banks, businesses and factories closed down; farms were auctioned off; in cities like New York, millions of unemployed workers found themselves in the streets, on lines for handouts of bread or soup, waiting their turns for a bed in flophouses, or sometimes sleeping on subway platforms in New York. President Hoover, known as "the Great Engineer" when he was elected, assured the country that the problem would cure itself; all that was needed was patience. But the trouble did not cure itself; instead, antigovernment and anticapitalist demonstrations and riots taxed the power of the police in American cities, large and small.

What was more, the temporary downward plunge of America coincided with the rise of a new order in Russia. Emerging from civil war, armed foreign intervention, plague and famine, that country, under a Communist dictatorship, was being transformed from a backward agricultural region into an industrial state where unemployment was unheard of — all without benefit of private capitalism. For many hopeful onlookers, the Soviet Union shone forth as the first example of a new, enlightened and humanitarian world. And for stage people there was a vista of sweeping away of the picture-frame stage and a return to the vigorous theatricalism of the historic stage platform. At least this was what interested me when I visited the theatres of Moscow and Leningrad in 1932 and again as a Guggenheim Foundation Fellow four years later, when an official Soviet theatre festival attracted stage people from all over the globe.

During the Soviet civil war Vsevelod Meyerhold, one of Russia's leading directors, organized groups of working-class actors, the Blue Blouses, for agitprop (agitation-propaganda) work across the nation. Under Communist guidance, these mobile troups, playing to audiences of workers and peasants, commented on topical events, using a form of mass chants — a method as simple as it was effective with their particular audiences. In the thirties, this kind of theatre spread to Germany and from there to the United States, where it made its initial appearance in New York with a German-speaking group, the Proletbühne. It was soon copied in other American cities, whose acting companies united in 1935, as the Workers' Drama League.

By then I had become familiar with a leading New York agitprop group of amateur players known as the Theatre of Action, whose method of performance was a distinct advance over mere chanting. It used individualized stage characters and a variety of groupings and stage actions. Its productions were aimed directly at its audiences, in abandoned factory lofts, at union meetings, or in the streets. Its head-on attack on social injustice was so startling that people came down from Broadway to see its performances. I was invited by Edith J.R. Isaacs, editor of *Theatre Arts*, to write an article about this type of amateur theatre; entitled *Theatre is a Weapon*, my essay appeared in January 1933. The new movement continued to expand, developing more experienced companies and issuing a magazine, *New Theatre and Film*, to which I contributed a number of articles including one on *Soviet Scene Design*.[3]

In 1933 workingclass drama in the American theatre rose to a professional level with a new organization, the Theatre Union (T.U.), located in a crumbling old playhouse on West 14th Street in New York, where it offered a program of full-length plays. It was more effectively organized than its predecessor, the New Playwrights; its executive board was shared by liberals and trade union representatives and by Communists and Socialists working peacefully together (for once). It sold subscription tickets to union groups at a discount and gave free tickets to the unemployed. The T.U. earned the grudging respect of the newspaper critics, and during its four-year existence it even scored some hits. Nevertheless it, too, failed to enlist a following large enough to give it any security. It also failed to develop many new "proletarian" authors and had to eke out its programs with imported dramas, among them Friedrich Wolf's *The Sailors of Cattaro*, which I designed.

Meanwhile I had begun to write boy-and-girl one-acts with no distinction about them except, perhaps, that they were somewhat more ironic than the favorite "youth" plays at the booksellers. In spite of the kind of education I had been getting at the New Playwrights and the Theatre Union, it was not until 1935 that I acquired a new outlook in my dramatic writing. The change was evident in a wry comedy about some young people caught in the web of unemployment. I called it *Song of the Whippoorwill* because whippoorwills don't sing — they shout.

By then I had begun work for the Group Theatre, designing its second play, *1931—*, followed by my designs for *Success Story, Big Night, Men in White, Golden Boy, Casey Jones, Thunder Rock, Rocket to the Moon*, and *Night Music*. How the Group, an independent acting company of leftist persuasion, managed to survive on Broadway for ten years has never been more clearly summed up than by Karen Malpede Taylor:

> The Group Theatre solved the problem of an establishment approach to social questions. They took what was most potent (and commercially attractive, as it is today) from the radical theatre — moral outrage — and grafted it into a drama structured by the belief that neither human nature nor society can be fundamentally changed. They did this with an acting method that limits the actor to the portrayal of his own emotional past.[4]

If this was the unstated and, in fact, unaware strategy of the Group, it worked not only by means of the company's inspired ensemble acting but because of the devotion and tenacity of its three directors, Harold Clurman, Lee Strasberg, and Cheryl Crawford, and by the development of one of its actors, Clifford Odets, as a leading American dramatist. Cliff became the authentic voice of an endangered and radicalized middleclass.

TOWARD A LARGER THEATRE

The familiar diagram of the social strata, upper, middle and lower, marked off from each other by an invisible line, does not allow for tremors or convulsions. In the Depression, the lower middleclass became alarmingly aware that the line between it and the workingclass below it was not holding, and the same disaster was reaching for them both. Understandably the Group's second production was a play of social protest. Written by Claire and Paul Sifton, and named *1931* —, it told the grim story of a young unemployed worker, ending with a scene that showed, high above the stage, guardsmen ready to take action against demonstrators demanding relief. The metropolitan drama critics who had hailed the Group's first production, Paul Green's *House of Connelly*, with unqualified praise, turned away from *1931* — with distaste, and it closed in nine days. But this was not before its constantly sold-out balconies and empty orchestra seats suggested, at least to some members of the Group, that a new kind of audience was being born.

This experience taught the Group directors to be less challenging, but it did not stop others, Odets among them, from producing, on their own, a short play of Cliff's, *Waiting for Lefty*, in the Theatre Union's old quarters. In sympathy with a hard-fought taxi strike in New York, the play depicted a labor union meeting where a decision to strike was being put to a vote. Directed at a hectic pace before an audience containing real hackmen, the stage action at the end erupted into thunderous shout of "Strike! Strike! Strike!" in which the audience excitedly joined. With *Lefty* a sensational hit, the Group eventually took it uptown for special performances.

*   *   *

In 1936 came another event that contributed to my stage education. Two years after its successful *Sailors of Cattaro*, the Theatre Union decided on another foreign drama, *Mother*, by Bertolt Brecht. *Mother* (not the same as the later *Mother Courage*) was a treatment by Brecht of a novel by Maxim Gorky. I was again called in as designer.

I had known of Brecht as the author of a play with music by Kurt Weill, *The Threepenny Opera* (1928), generally acknowledged as one of the modern classics of European theatre. (I knew, too, that when the *Opera* was produced on Broadway in 1933, it met a swift end.) I also had heard that Brecht and his likewise famous actress-wife, Helene Weigel, were now refugees from Hitler's Germany and were living in Denmark. That Brecht was a convert to Marxism was news to me, and I was even less prepared for his theories concerning "Epic theatre" and the "learning-play."

When the German dramatist and his fellow refugee, the composer Hanns Eisler, arrived in New York to attend rehearsals, I quickly became aware of Brecht's temperament, for he declared war at once on the Theatre Union's directors — a conflict whose raucousness still echoes after almost half a century.[5] Brecht asserted that someone, without his

10

permission, had translated his learning play into melodramatic trash, that the director and conductor chosen for the production were incompetent, and finally that the proposed settings by Mordecai Gorelik were "bourgeois."

Learning that I spoke German fluently, the harassed T.U. directors delegated me to have a talk with that "madman." I did so and have described that interview elsewhere.[6] It resulted in my fascinated interest in the Brechtian views on theatre and in a lasting friendship with Bert himself.

Brecht told me he had no use for the established theatre, which he labeled "confectionery," no matter if its style was naturalistic, symbolic or theatricalist. It is a means of titillation, he said — overwhelmingly and sentimentally emotional at the expense of thought; its themes are sex, family anxieties, and an inane idealism, and its well-made play structure is especially useful in "pumping up" the emotions of an audience, giving the audience no chance to think. His own kind of theatre, which he called "Epic," believes in clarifying life, not in evading reality by means of emotional hypnotism. In short, the contemporary theatre, whether in America or in Soviet Russia, is decapitated. "We must put its head back on its shoulders."

Brecht added that he had written a number of short "learning-plays" for school use, teaching the difference between present-day theatre and the Epic theatre of the future. *Mother*, he pointed out, was not intended as an emotional or sensational appeal to its audiences but as a lesson and an explanation. Its story, laid in Tsarist Russia, is about a peasant woman who had barely learned to read and write. She knows nothing about political matters and is bewildered when her son becomes a revolutionary. It is then shown how she learns, step by step, about the Marxist class war, and we last see her holding up the red flag of Socialism.

I told Brecht, "I have been taught the definition by Aristotle that "catharsis," the purging of the spectator, is the basis of drama. Where does that fit in with your learning-plays? Or have you no use for catharsis, either?"

B.B.: "Epic is opposed to catharsis as the *sole purpose* of drama. It is not enough for the playgoer to leave the theatre feeling better. He should come away more informed, wiser, and more capable."

I described Odets's play, *Waiting for Lefty*, and asked, "Would you consider it an Epic play?"

B.B.: "I would consider it just the opposite."

"Even though we are shown why some of the new union members decide to vote for the strike?"

B.B.: "No play is ever 100 percent Epic — not mine or anyone else's. And even the most idiotic emotional play or melodrama teaches a few things — if only stupid banalities. But what does *Waiting for Lefty* teach? From your description the taxi union appears to consist of middle-class people who have joined the union entirely as a personal gesture. I am sure that the union's general membership does not consist of such people. The play should tell us what issues are involved in the strike, what attempts, if any, have been made to avert it, and the respective strengths, resources, determination, and tactics of each side."

When I reported this interview to the Theatre Union, its directors — or some of them — thought they understood, at last, what Brecht was after, but they were far from enthusiastic. However, they consented to have me design *Mother* as a learning-play, with functional settings, visible lighting equipment, a projection screen above the actors, and visible scene changes on a small turntable. The whole thing made a very interesting stage production, but I was as certain as the rest of the Theatre Union that its audience would only be puzzled and bored. Or even worse — resentful at being made to undergo a whole evening of primary-grade lectures. And so it turned out.

As very often happens, a pioneer in any field thinks it necessary to emphasize the difference between his views and those that have already been accepted. I consider that Bert's learning-play obsession did him no good; it would have served him better had he left that theory (and *Mother* as an example of it) on paper, or in readings for discussion. Deprived of his radical Berlin public and with the need to reach out to middleclass audiences during his years of exile, he must at length have given up bringing abstract theory into his script; instead he wrote integrated plays that dealt with issues, events, and human characters on a plane that made them his masterpieces.

I never agreed with Brecht's attack on the "well-made" play, for I saw no reason why a play of real merit should not be well organized in its presentation. My differences with Bert on that score came up repeatedly — in New York, in Denmark, and finally in Santa Monica, where he quite lost his temper and threatened to throw me out the window. From the start his instinctive way of writing took the form of the chronicle play, which was good enough for Shakespeare — why did Brecht have to defend his own use of it? I suspect that some of his detractors — and he had plenty of them — may have taunted him because he did not write in the tightly knit Scribe-Sardou form.

When peace was once more established between us at a pleasant dinner prepared by Helli herself, I asked B.B., "Isn't it true that each of the separate scenes in your plays has suspense, climax, and resolution?"

"Is *that* what you mean?" he exclaimed. "Of course they have! That's not worth discussing!"

*   *   *

After the Group Theatre folded, some of its leading actors came to Hollywood, where they rented a small local playhouse around the corner from Schwab's legendary drugstore. The Actors' Laboratory, as it was called, had many first-class programs to its credit, including a one-act by Tennessee Williams, *Portrait of a Madonna*, in which Jessica Tandy gave a wonderful performance. She was perfectly cast, later, as Blanche Dubois, when Williams expanded his short play into *A Streetcar Named Desire*, but the Lab was given no hand in that production. The most successful Lab offering in terms of box office as well as of stage achievement was Ben Jonson's *Volpone*, in the version by Morris Carnovsky. Morris also directed, with great gusto, humor, and imagination. The only people who were displeased with the show were the neighbors of the theatre, who were assaulted every night with the echoes of onstage yells of "Rape!" and general bedlam in Act II, Scene 4.

Perhaps in return for my having designed the settings and costumes of *Volpone*, the Lab, in 1947, allowed my short comedy, *Paul Thompson Forever*, to take the stage for two performances under my direction, with a makeshift setting and a few properties. *Thompson* pleased its audiences much more than it did the Lab executive board, as I judged by the reaction of its chairman, Roman (Bud) Bohnen. Bud told me with distaste that the character of Thompson was like a man in a straitjacket. What he meant by that, evidently, was that I showed no admirable side to Thompson's character and there was nothing to be said for the man's behavior except the single occasion of the holiday outing. It was not the first time anyone has disagreed with me about what is comic onstage.

Brecht, whom I was visiting often, came to see the play. He was delighted with it — the only time I ever knew him to laugh out loud. The next day he sent his photographer, Ruth Berlau, to take some pictures of the production. I still have those photos.

After seeing *Thompson*, Brecht even proposed that we write a play together about an American worker. We started to do so, under the title of *Nothing but the Best*, but after a few sessions, during which I did all the writing, he gave it up, saying he could not understand the psychology of the U.S. working class. The "bourgeoisified" American worker was, in fact, a different species from the German Communists who had been Bert's favorite audience in Berlin. Furthermore, he may have realized, or had it conveyed to him, that anything less than a heroic image of the proletariat, whether in the United States or anywhere else, could alienate his familiar public in Europe. *Nothing but the Best* never resulted in anything with B.B., but *Thompson* contributed, later on, to the theme of *Rainbow Terrace*, another of my plays.

Incidentally, I had kept after Bert to give a talk on Epic theatre at the Lab. He reluctantly agreed to do so, but when I told Mary Tarcai, who was the Lab's conscientious general manager, she said, "It won't do. We go by Stanislavsky, and it would only confuse our actors." I

13

described this episode almost twenty years later, to the New Theatre, Australia's best-known radical stage group, who thought it was one of the funniest stories they ever heard.

My work at Southern Illinois University began in 1961 with a production of *The Annotated Hamlet.* (Not in the present collection.) Annotated, directed, and designed by me, the script made use of a commentator and of projection slides to accompany a "regular" staging of the play. In an interview by Robert Hethmon, of UCLA, I pointed out that this treatment of a script can be especially useful for school productions, not only of *Hamlet* but of any other world classic, adding clarification while in no way distracting from the play itself.[7]   Ben Gelman, drama reviewer of *The Daily Southern Illinoisan* (May 21, 1961), called *The Annotated Hamlet* production "an intelligent innovation":

> An innovation in its approach to Epic theatre — which endeavors to relate a story in its true relation to historic background. The production features a commentator, a stage manager who speaks lines, and projected slides . . . The careful, scholarly probing into the mystery of the character of Hamlet lends a rather clinical atmosphere to the proceedings. And yet the acting itself, more than capably performed by a cast of fifty SIU students, has its moments of high drama, humor, pathos, and just plain excitement.

"In fact the performances were so good," the reviewer added with some asperity, "that Gorelik should not have cautioned the audience not to expect a 'high voltage' performance from the student actors."

Actually I was concerned, not about the ability of the cast, but whether the "asides" from the commentator and the stage manager, together with the overhead projections, might upset the actors, and annoy the audience. I need not have been anxious — both actors and audience took the whole thing in their stride. So did an elderly professor who, on being introduced to my wife, Frances, before the play began, asked rather crossly why Shakespeare had to be "annotated." He assured her, afterward, that he had no criticism: the production was "a wonderful experience."

I offer my thanks, herewith, to Dr. McLeod as commentator, Charles Zoekler as stage manager, Will Gay Bottje for his original period music, and to everyone in the notable cast headed by Victor Cook, who "projected a youthful, vital, yet emotionally hamstrung Hamlet."

THE ANNOTATED HAMLET

Shakespeare's *Hamlet*, annotated, directed and designed by Mordecai Gorelik. Performance accompanied by "asides" from a commentator and by projection-slide illustrations. An example of "learning theatre" adapted to the staging of the world classics of drama. Southern Illinois University, 1961.

TOWARD A LARGER THEATRE

* * *

On a visit to Paris in 1980 I was interviewed by Thomas Quinn Curtiss, of the *International Herald Tribune*, under the heading of "At Age 80, Gorelik Changes His Act."[8]

This may sound like some magical transformation overnight, but as already noted I wrote my first one-act play in 1922, and I have been writing — and revising — plays ever since. Some have been produced, some published. In trying to get them accepted I have sometimes met with a special kind of handicap. An actor, a director, even a drama critic, can become a playwright without being told that a shoemaker ought to stick to his last. The notion that a scene designer can write a play worth taking seriously recalls Dr. Samuel Johnson's dour opinion that a woman preacher is "like a dog walking on its hind legs. It is not done well but you are surprised that it is done at all."

But in fact I have never viewed scene design apart from its relation to the dramatic script, nor have I been barred from acquiring any of the expertise of other contributors to the work onstage — beginning with that of the playwright. When I design a play I must study it with the utmost care until I know its salient qualities, its characters, its construction, its action, its style, its way of confronting an audience.

Actually I doubt very much if any of my plays have been discounted because they were "composed" by a designer. Far more to the point, they do not belong in the current category of possible stage hits.

In *Mrs Disaster*, an early one-act, I had written what I thought was a typical domestic comedy, but it troubled some of the people who read it. I did not know why, until I realized that the young father of a family was cracking up not merely because he was ridiculously short-tempered but because he had met with a bad reversal on his business trip. This was an infusion of reality that changed the story, in spite of its humor, into something more serious than a situation comedy.

After that experience it became clear that anything I wrote, even if it was otherwise comic, had a context of tough realism that could not be ignored. Religious judgment is the theme of *Paul Thompson Forever*. In *The Big Day*, industry and trade unionism provide the setting for a character study of two men. Of the longer plays, *Yes and No* is a political cartoon of the American Fifties and Sixties centered on the issue of the Vietnam War. *The Feast of Unreason*, for all its Irish humor, is a lament over the ferocity that, worldwide, has replaced any rational political discourse. *Andrus, or the Vision*, compares the faiths of science and religion. In *Rainbow Terrace*, a wheeler-dealer businessman attempts to create a God in his own image.

At a time when the best of films and TV deal impressively with social and political realities, our theatre, and its vanguard as well, have turned escapist. But its playgoers live under pressures, material and spiritual, that the stage can no longer regard as none of its business.

THE LONG PLAYS

YES AND NO

1957-1975

A straw vote shows only which way the hot air blows.

— O. Henry:
Rolling Stones

21

During my twelve years at Southern Illinois I conducted a seminar in *The Scenic Imagination*, and also directed and designed seven plays, including my own script, *Rainbow Terrace*, my adaption of Max Frisch's *The Firebugs*, and *Pagnol's Marseilles*, in which Frederick O'Neal, at my invitation, took the leading part. In the same period, as guest professor, I staged productions at three other universities.

My final years at SIU coincided with the outbreak of the student "upsurge" against the Vietnam War — an issue that soon widened to include a barrage of protests against school regulations considered irksome or unfair. The increasing disorder caused many universities to shut down.[9] Southern Illinois remained open but suspended all classes and instead called for a student-teacher discussion in every Department. Our theatre students won, among other concessions, the right to take part in the choice of plays for production. But when they chose my very timely script, *Yes and No*, it was vetoed immediately by the Administration. I was told, however, that I could put on any other play I cared to present.

I decided on Ansky's *The Dybbuk*, which I had twice directed successfully — at Brigham Young University (1961) and San Jose State College (1965). This masterpiece of the practically unknown Yiddish drama, strange, exotic and fervent, was unusual fare for any academic theatre, but it had proved impressive each time. I can only add that at Carbondale, for a variety of reasons, it was a dismal failure.

Pronounced "unacceptable" in 1971, *Yes and No* has remained unacceptable ever since. It deals with one of the most crucial eras in modern American history: the conflict in ideologies between right and left over the humiliating war in Vietnam, the Joe McCarthy hysteria, the student rebellion in the universities, the spread of "live-together" communes, the disillusionment of the American liberals with the Soviet dictatorship, and, not least, the so-called generations-gap between parents and their offspring.

OUTLINE

Time: toward the end of the Vietnam War. Don Taylor, a lawyer who owns a little shack in a New Jersey summer community, was once a radical, but his diminishing clientele and the illness of his wife, Ruth, have taught him caution. Ruth still dreams of a radical future and is meanwhile carried away by an obsession about pure food. The vitality of their seventeen-year-old son, Larry, is overlaid, at his age, by callowness, adolescent bravado, and the confused political and philosophical cliches he has learned on working with a so-called commune in the neighborhood — a group that is rehearsing a *Peace Ballet*.

When Don, on a contingency basis, takes on Mrs. Crain, a reactionary, tough-talking client who is suing for big money, he may finally be in luck — except that he must hide Larry's connection with the commune. But Mrs. Crain learns about the show and insists on attending a rehearsal. A little gang of "patriotic" hoodlums also comes to the rehearsal and starts beating up the members of the cast. The violence abates when the local police chief, although fed up with the activities of the commune, orders the gang to leave. Larry, one of those injured, joins his friends, who are now more than ever determined to put the *Ballet* on stage. Don, regaining some of his courage, will demand a citizen's arrest of the hoodlums. Thus the differences between Larry and his father are papered over, but Larry is "out of the nest," and Don is left with only a faint hope of winning back Mrs. Crain as a client.

CHARACTERS

Ruth Taylor
Don Taylor
Larry Taylor, *also* Joe Blow
Judge Olroyd
Murchison
Margie Dale
Shirley Crain
Cathy Clark, *also* Tambourine Girl
John Ambruster, *also* Ringmaster
Ed
Scorpy
The Scorpions
A Waiter (*or* Waitress)

Time: 1971.

ACT I

Scene 1

House lights fade. In the dark, a voice, testifying.

FIRST VOICE: . . . Old men, women, children and a baby, standing and kneeling in the ditch, screaming and crying . . . . There was a pile of bodies in the ditch . . .

SECOND VOICE: Two thousand years ago they crucified a man named Jesus. Now they're out to get a man named Brownie Corby because he wore his country's uniform! Stand tall, Lieutenant Corby! You wasted those gooks like you're supposed to!

Song

My name is Brownie Corby, I'm a hero
 Of this land,
A soldier brave and upright,
 One to bet the band,
But they've told me I'm a bastard
 And refuse to shake my hand . . .

Voices fade.   Curtain rises on the Taylor's cottage at Tidewater, New Jersey — the living room, dining room, kitchen and stairway to the bedrooms, of an unpretentious frame house.   Sunday noon of a late summer's day.   The shades are drawn and a cool light filters into the room.   The quiet sound of the surf near by can be heard with the occasional clang of a bell-buoy farther off; the sounds harmonize with a radio broadcast of a church hymn.   RUTH TAYLOR, in a sunsuit, is doing sitting-up exercises combined with deep breathing.   She is fifty-one, a pretty, friendly woman.

RUTH: One — two — three — four —
(Slows up and stops, painfully recovering her breath.   Resumes.)
 Five — six —
  (A cat is heard yowling outside.)
 Seven — eight — nine —
  (She goes to the back door, calls)
 Go away!   Poor little thing you!
  (Returns, snaps off the radio, continues exercising.)
 Ten — eleven —

(She stops, gasping, falls into a chair, then gets up unsteadily at the sound of footsteps on the wooden walk outside.   DON TAYLOR appears in the doorway.   He is a contemplative man of fifty-five, in the full panoply of a surf fisherman.   He carries a surf-rod.)

RUTH: Happy birthday!   Happy day!   *(Kissing him.)*   Oh, Don, isn't it a beautiful summer day, just for you?   Air like clear springwater!

27

DON *(hanging up his surf-rod)*: Summer's almost over.

RUTH: You *must* have caught some fish today!
    (He starts putting away his equipment.)
    Not even on your birthday? You'll be burning up — all the rest of the weekend!

DON: Did Jimmy Leonard call from Trenton? He said he'd know by Friday how the Rodriguez case was going. Now it's Sunday.

RUTH: You'll hear from him.

DON: Is that so?

RUTH: You will, darling. And from Mrs. Crain, too. *(She begins setting the table.)* She probably gets up late on Sunday.

DON: You think I want her here? It was a great mistake asking her.

RUTH: You said I could.

DON: I must have lost my mind. That impossible woman —

RUTH: No one's impossible. People are people.

DON: Not some people!

RUTH: Everybody. No exceptions.

DON: How do *you* describe that witless mob at the Town Hall yesterday?

RUTH: They have their convictions.

DON: What good are their convictions? A little army officer who butchered at least twenty-two civilians! What is he? A hero? *(stripping off his waders)* And the President himself intervenes for him, and soon he'll go scot free! That's the sort of country we've turned into — morally downhill ever since 1776 !

RUTH: Every time you fish you come home in a tantrum. Why do you go on fishing?

DON: Only because I'm the kind of damned fool who has to keep on trying until Kingdom Come, amen. *(feelingly)* This morning Hans Jorgensen and Davy Elder had seven fish between them. I bought all this equipment and haven't caught anything in at least four years!

RUTH: It's because you expect to fail. Your vibrations go out to the end of the line.

DON *(throwing down his waders)*: Quite right. The fish know I'm an underachiever. *(Changing)* You're really annoyed with me, Ruth.

RUTH: Yes I am.
(He kisses her.)
At a time when all doors will be opening for you — ever since you went to your class reunion —
(Phone rings.)

RUTH *(answering it)*: Oh, Mrs. Crain! How nice! Did Donald give you all the directions? He's somewhere around; wait a second — *(She covers the mouthpiece of the phone.)* Don! We're delighted she's coming! — Don!

DON *(at phone)*: Hello, Shirley. We're delighted you're coming.

RUTH: Can you catch the 1:40 and bring a sunsuit or something? Naturally we will . . . 'Bye.
(Hangs up.)
How can you be so ungracious? . . . We'll show her a nice day at the beach —

DON: What else is there to show her? This shack? I told you her opinion of my office.

RUTH: It's true you have that one-room office, and this house can use repairs, and the town isn't much, and neither is the beach; but with her troubles she's not going to notice whether we're plain or fancy; she's coming for your advice.

DON: So far she's had it for nothing. I still haven't got her retainer.

RUTH: You'll get it! Why do you let everything get you down?

DON: Because I've had a lifetime of crawling through a tunnel.

RUTH: The light is straight ahead of you, dear. Can't you see it?

(Sound of an asthmatic old car stopping outside.)

LARRY (offstage): Thanks, Cathy.

CATHY (offstage): As long as this rattle-mill holds out. I'll try to get you on my way back, Junior.

(Car goes off.)

RUTH: Larry! I thought he was in bed!

(LARRY enters. A *handsome boy of seventeen, with a guitar.*)

LARRY: Good morning, folksies. Lovely morning!

DON: It's almost afternoon.

LARRY: You know I never get enough sleep? I was setting up the stage lights till now — tomorrow night's the dress rehearsal.

RUTH: Now go to bed.

29

LARRY: Dad, you know your Lieutenant Corby idea turned everybody on? "Not so bad for an old geezer," everybody said. Cathy wrote in the new lines and the cast went over them all night.

DON: The old geezer thanks you. Let your show give this town of Tidewater a little taste of truth.

LARRY: Right on. They all said it's the answer to the Town Hall demonstration. (*Yawns.*) I'm beat. Have to set my alarm, they'll be coming back for me very soon.

RUTH: Go on upstairs, darling.
             (LARRY *exits upstairs.*)
He's so much like you, Don! Dedicated!

DON: Like me. Full of idealism and confusion. Giving his all to that crude little amateur show —

RUTH: You don't fool me, Don Taylor. You think you act tough, but it's just a put-on.

DON: Not me. Gall and wormwood! At my age a man ought to show something for his life. What have I got? Cheap landlord-tenant cases, living from fee to fee —

RUTH: You have your integrity and always have had, no matter what it's cost you. What more could anyone have? And there's Larry and me. Don't we count?

DON (*taking her in his arms*): Sure you do. A wife who is a healthnut, a son as mixed-up as his mother is simpleminded —

RUTH: You're the one who's perfect.

DON: Not so perfect that I can't see I'm getting my last chance. Don't worry — I'm *not* giving up on Shirley Crain!

RUTH: Because your time has come, darling! "Donald Taylor, representing Mrs. Shirley Crain !" Your name in all the papers coast to coast, an uptown office and a private secretary, a Park Avenue apartment for the family —

(*Light fades. Song, recorded: "O Alma Mater Fordham." Hum of voices, tinkle of glasses. Light rises on two comfortable armchairs and a small table downstage right. DON, JUDGE OLROYD, a WAITER. Flashback*)

Scene 2

OLROYD: What'll it be?

DON: Nothing for me, Ed.

OLROYD (*to* WAITER): Make mine a double scotch. Whiskey sour for my friend.

WAITER: Yes, sir.

(Exits.)

OLROYD: Florence won't let you drink?

DON: Florence?

OLROYD: Your wife.

DON: Ruth.

OLROYD: Of course, Ruth. On the health kick — sunflower seeds or something. How long is it since I've seen you? Almost thirty years?

DON: Since my marriage.

OLROYD: First reunion of our class that you've come to in all that time. Bet the little woman made you do it: you'll meet all the Establishment big shots. Me, for instance . . .

DON: She and I both realized I was getting bogged down.

OLROYD: You mean you've got nothing to show for your career. The reward of virtue!

DON *(stiffly)*: I own a summer home on the beach in New Jersey.

OLROYD: Bet it's a mosquito-ridden shack and you're losing it — Don't answer that. Cigar? You don't smoke . . . You must be pushing fifty-five or fifty-six by now . . . a crummy little office, life beginning to close in on you —

(WAITER *brings drinks.*)

DON: I don't drink.

OLROYD: Let it stand.

(WAITER *exits.*)

They tell me you had offers, years ago. Fox, Landesman & Di Grandi. You said they represent the Mafia.

DON: Don't they?

OLROYD: Among their other clients. What was wrong with Tallens & Judson?

DON: Corporation counsel.

OLROYD: Still carrying a torch for the working class, sore at the capitalist exploiters? Ready to take a two-dollar case to the Supreme Court, citing precedents no judge ever heard of or would listen to?

DON *(getting up)*: I don't care for your line of kidding.

OLROYD: Sit down, Don. I don't mean anything, it's just a legal habit.
(DON *slowly sits.*)
Something's on your mind. What made you came here tonight?
— Raise your right hand!

DON· Ruth has a heart ailment. She may be dying.

OLROYD: These days, with proper treatment, a woman of her age?

DON: She needs an operation. I had to force her to get a diagnosis two months ago. She said afterward the doctor was an alarmist. She refuses to see any doctor again.

OLROYD: By God, man, if she were *my* wife —

DON: What could you do? *(Glumly)* I talked with the doctor. He said an operation or else: he wouldn't give her more than four years.

OLROYD: I can see what's coming: quack practitioners, a wheelchair, nursing around the clock at a hundred dollars a day. Years of it. No health insurance, of course — against her principles —

DON: I fought with her. She says nothing can happen — she's God's perfect child.

OLROYD: Say no more. Plaintiff rests. *(After a pause)* I remember a book you wrote, Don.

DON: What book?

OLROYD: On inheritance cases. *Probate* something.

DON: *Probate Proceedings and the Common Law.* That was school dissertation, not a book.

OLROYD: I remember it, though . . . It's a providential thing you came here tonight — we're looking for someone to take care of a client, Mrs. Shirley Crain. We can't take her case — conflict of interest. You'll be in the Big League, Don.

(WAITER *comes back with a charge slip as they get up. Light fades.*)

(In the dark)

A WOMAN *(off stage)*: I don't care how many demonstrations you hold or how many draft dodgers attend them — when you read out the war dead of New Jersey, don't read the name of my son, Robert T. Murray, killed in action May 7, 1969. He died for his country and his sacred memory is mine, not yours.

(Blackout)

Scene 3

Light rises on the Taylor cottage. DON *is taking books out of the bookcase, tossing them into a paper carton.*

DON: Nikolai Bukharin: *Historical Materialism* . . . Materialism — That's un-American.

RUTH: Materialism doesn't explain everything.

DON: Yes and no. It explains a lot. *(picking up more books)* Friedrich Engels, Plekhanov —

RUTH: You haven't read any of those books in thirty years.

DON: Mrs. Crain looks for Communists under her bedsprings every night. If she notices any books like these —

RUTH: Communism is a dead issue.

DON: If it is, it doesn't know enough to lie down. It's not dead with Shirley Crain. *(tossing down a book)* Or with the citizens of Tidewater.

RUTH: What's wrong with them?

DON: Two hundred percent red-blooded American sheep. Bring back a spoiled grapefruit to Cully's Market, ask the Acme Laundry to pay for a lost shirt, and you're a Communist s.o.b. Give them a flag, a brass band, and somebody to hate — Reds, Kikes, Niggers — and the wolves run howling.

RUTH: What are they, sheep or wolves?

(Sound of a car stopping outside)

DON: Both.

RUTH *(going to the window)*: The Chief of Police, and a woman with him, coming this way.

DON: What for?

(He shoves the carton under the table. RUTH *admits* MURCHESON *and* DALE. MURCHISON *is a ruddy-faced man of forty-six, in uniform.* MARGIE DALE *is a Tidewater native, thirty-seven.)*

RUTH: Don, you know Mr. Murchison.

MURCHISON: Mr. and Mrs. Taylor. And this is Margie Dale.

RUTH: Do sit down, please.

MURCHISON: Margie is handling the Art Festival the town is getting up for you vacationers. It was her idea in the first place.

RUTH: And it's a wonderful idea.

MURCHISON: She's woman poet, printed almost every Friday in the Woman's Page of the Jersey *Citizen.* I'm helping her out with the Festival, supervising the *artistes.*

DON: Is that a police duty?

MURCHESON (*to* DALE): Making fun. I told you — have to watch out for these city folks. (*to* DON) Mr. Taylor, sir, you've been here every summer for about eight years; you know Tidewater's always been a quiet, orderly sort of place —

DON: Yes, that's what we thought when we moved here.

DALE: Well, it isn't like that any more.

RUTH: Oh, dear. What's gone wrong?

DALE: The commune that's living together in the old, tumbledown Collins place —

RUTH: Yes. Such freethinking young people.

DALE: Freethinking?

RUTH: The Off-Limits, I believe they call themselves.

DALE: Mrs. Taylor, I believe you know they've declared themselves in on the Festival. And the way they're doing it, they're putting on a show they call *The Peace Ballet*, so they can pour their poison into the bloodstream of New Jersey.

RUTH: Surely not!

DALE: Preaching free love, taking dope and plotting anarchy —

RUTH: That's a wild exaggeration.

DALE: Your son is in that show, Mrs. Taylor. Evidently with your approval.

RUTH: Wait a minute, Miss Dale —

MURCHISON: That bunch wants straightening out.

RUTH: By you?

DON: All right, Ruth. (*To* MURCHISON.) We'll talk with Larry when he gets up. He's sleeping.   ,

MURCHISON: Then we'll leave it in your hands.

DON: Yes and no. It's Larry's decision. He's the one who decides what concerns him.

DALE: This is getting nowhere.

DON: I said I'll talk with him.

MURCHISON *(getting up)*: You know the folks in town ask me, "How come these city people are so peculiarly inclined?"

RUTH: Liberal, I guess you mean. We can all learn a few things even after we leave school, don't you think so?

34

MURCHISON: Speaking for myself, ma'am, I don't think of things I don't think about, because I have all the necessary information to live and die by. (*To* DON.) I doubt if you know all about that Off-Limits gang. They're distributing propaganda to the soldiers in the Veterans Hospital in the next town — just think *that* over!

DON: What propaganda?

MURCHISON: Anti-government, anti-war —

DALE: Telling the soldiers they were fools to fight for America — excusing the draft-evaders —

DON: Still —

DALE (*picking up a magazine*): This the kind of magazine you people subscribe to?

DON: What about it?

DALE: The kind of reading matter you find in these vacationers' houses! All the literature that's listed in the newsletter I get every week: *Civil Liberties Bulletin, American Report, Saturday Review* — I don't know what all!

MURCHISON: Got to move on, now. Jeep's waiting.

DALE (*tossing down the magazine*): I've lived in Tidewater all my life, and my parents before me — upstanding Americans! Suddenly this raggle-taggle crew out of nowhere, whiskers and sandals, sitting on the floor, holding hands with those blackamuffins and kissing them — (*She is unable to finish.*)

RUTH: We're sorry you're upset, Miss Dale.

(MURCHISON *and* DALE *exit.*)

DON: I forgot about that magazine. (*throwing it into the carton*) I forget everything, these days — can't remember names, telephone numbers . . .

(*The cat screeches.*)

RUTH: Couple of bigots!

DON: It's getting more messy than I thought. Did you know about the Veterans Hospital?

RUTH: Not about the Off-Limits group trying to give shows there. I stopped in at the hospital once, going by . . . Oh, Don, it's so pathetic: young soldiers, crippled, blind —

(*Pause*)

DON: The land of the brave and the free, where they tell you what you can think and what you can't. This ass-hole of Tidewater: a preview of tomorrow's America.

35

RUTH: Where could we go?

DON: With the small equity we'd get out of selling this place — even if anyone wants to buy — where could we move to?

(He goes to the refrigerator.)

RUTH: What are you looking for?

DON: Milk for the cat.

RUTH: Put that away. We can't go on feeding her or she'll adopt us for good and all. Let her go elsewhere, poor little mother; she'll find a home.

DON: Where? Almost every house out here is closed now for the season. *(Puts back the milk.)* Why does Larry have to bring that cat here for his parents to take care of?

RUTH: Larry's so good-hearted.

DON: Only he'd show it more if you didn't have to pick up after him; he drops his shoes and shirts and pants anywhere on the floor —

RUTH: He's a little careless.

DON: Only a little? When he gets up —

RUTH: What then?

DON: I'll have to have a talk with him. He's so spoiled and lazy —

RUTH: He's only seventeen, Donald.

DON: At seventeen I was earning my own living. Our noble son is a bit infantile, Ruth. His room is a rat's nest — old underwear, sand all over, tin cans, a chewed-up tennis racket . . . He painted half of one wall in his room and left the can of paint and dirty brushes in the middle of the floor, walked around them for the next three months when I didn't go up there to clean up the place —

RUTH: You're jumping on him suddenly.

DON *(a little startled)*: You're right — he's just a kid.

(Stage lights dim out quickly. LARRY's voice, recorded, sings)

> *I'm up the creek without a paddle*
> *Getting nowhere up or down,*
> *Up or down or here or there*
> *Nothing left for me but prayer.*

Scene 4

Light returns. The Taylor cottage. DON is carrying the carton of books to the pantry.

RUTH: Why don't you eat? A hungry man is an angry man. Look — a wonderful fresh salad —

DON: For breakfast?

RUTH: With wheat germ and sunflower seeds. You just have time for it before we go to the station.

DON: No. *(Puts down the carton.)*

RUTH: No what?

DON: No sunflower seeds! When a man's been fishing since the break of day — even if he's caught no fish — he's entitled to bacon and eggs and coffee. I'll eat in town — Gavenmeyer's Luncheonette.

RUTH: All right — goodbye!

DON: Is that what you're going to feed Shirley Crain — Health Hygiene food?

RUTH: How do you know she won't appreciate it?

DON: She lives on steak, and you'd better have some for her, with plenty of delicatessen, besides. And whiskey.

RUTH: Whiskey?

DON: Straight Scotch.

RUTH: Straight poison!

DON: She's of age, and if she wants to poison herself, that's her privilege.

RUTH: Is there anything else we have to supply?

DON: She'd like some romance, meaning sex.

RUTH: Sorry! Some things I don't share!

(LARRY *appears on the stairs in his pajamas.*)

LARRY: What's all the row? Can't a man have some sleep in his own home?

DON: If you'd get to bed on time and get up on time, like other people —

LARRY: If I did, we'd never get the show on, so give me a break, folks.

DON: Larry, we just had a visit from the Chief of Police about the show. He said the town is antagonized. In fact he raised hell about the whole commune.

LARRY: Screw him!

RUTH: Larry, please!

37

DON: He had someone with him. A Miss Dale —

LARRY: That old bag! She spies on people and writes poems.

DON: Writing poems is not reprehensible.

LARRY: About how the young men of this village are young freedom's eagles, or something like that.

DON: What eagles?

LARRY: She means the Scorpions, that little gang of plumber's helpers, garage mechanics, and barber's assistants — the ones who've been breaking the windows of the Collins house. *(with indignation)* Why doesn't that pig of a Murchison get after them instead of us? And what right does he have to come here, anyway? You must have told him off real good, Dad!

DON: Yes and no. You can't just hit a man over the head when everybody agrees with him. We have to go now — let's talk about it when we get back.

LARRY: Yeah, Dad. Only —

RUTH: Get your sleep in, dear. We have to meet Mrs. Shirley Crain at the station. If you can wait till then for your brunch —

LARRY *(astounded)*: Is *that* one coming here —

RUTH: She'll only stay until tomorrow morning. I know how considerate you can be — wonderfully helpful —

LARRY: Don't put me on, Mom! Nobody asked *me* about inviting her —

DON: Did we have to?

LARRY: I don't understand, Dad. After everything you said about that rich bitch —

DON: Try to be reasonable, will you, Larry? Mrs. Crain has been victimized; she may have a personality problem but she's entitled to legal help, like anybody else. We're not asking you to entertain her — just keep out of her way.

LARRY: Who wants to go near *her*? If I had to explain somebody like her to the commune —

DON: Since when does my business have to be explained to them?

RUTH *(to* LARRY*)*: We'll discuss it later. Please, dear!

(RUTH *and* DON *exit.* LARRY *stands quietly burning for a moment, then starts upstairs. Light fades. In the dark, voices of* LARRY *and* CATHY, *recorded:*)

LARRY: Cathy, you want a date-and-tunafish sandwich? I'm on a new diet, dates and tunafish. Dr. Ellenbogen gave me a list of the right things to eat, and all that gunk —

CATHY: Who's Dr. Ellenbogen?

LARRY: Mom's chiropractor. So I picked the dates and tunafish out of the list.

CATHY: I thought you don't eat meat. Tuna is meat.

LARRY: I know, and Mom is always landing on me because I keep bringing home pizza and crap like that. Only meat contains this certain poison called echnon, which is necessary for my mind-development as a stimulant, but otherwise I shouldn't have it.

CATHY: Don't get overstimulated, will you, dear?

(Blackout)

Scene 5

Back room of the Off-Limits Club. Recording of hard rock can be heard as the light rises on the rehearsal of The Peace Ballet. *A long and narrow platform against the back wall, on which is hung a bedsheet. In a dim work-light a few rickety chairs are seen in front of the platform.* JOHN AMBRUSTER, CATHY CLARK *and* LARRY *hold typed parts, and are not in costume.* JOHN, *twenty-eight, tall, dark glasses, is the* RINGMASTER; CATHY, *twenty-six, pert and pretty, is the* GIRL WITH THE TAMBOURINE. LARRY *is* JOE BLOW.

CATHY: Places!

(From now on the lights on the platform will keep changing, sometimes dim and focused, sometimes bright and flooded, and in various colors. CATHY *comes forward as the* TAMBOURINE GIRL.)

GIRL: Ladies and gentlemen, and others: we present for your delectation and edification *The Peace Ballet!* *(She bangs the tambourine.)* Here is Joe Blow!

LARRY *(as* JOE, *enters with guitar, reading a comic book)*: This here hero in this here book is exactly like me, just a nice young average feller rollin' along singin' a song . . . *(Sings)*

Rollin' home, rollin' home,
By the light of the silvery moon . . .

GIRL: Here he is, Joe Blow, average citizen, not a care in the world, but care is coming his way, don't you worry —

JOE *(singing):*

Rollin' along, singin' a song. . .

(Spot on JOHN, *as* RINGMASTER.)

RINGMASTER: Where you goin', Bud?

39

JOE: Joe. Name's Joe Blow.

RINGMASTER: Joe . . . Not a care in the world, have ya? Not worried by nothin'?

JOE: Well, sir, yes, sir. This dastardly villyun is got the fine, upstandin' hero an' the sweet l'il heroine tied up with ropes onto the railroad tracks, an' there ain't a Superman or Batman in sight —

RINGMASTER: Put that there comic book away, boy. You got somethin' real, not fiction, comin' your way, son.

JOE: Somethin' bad?

RINGMASTER: Somethin' real, low-down mean. A hellish conspiracy is goin' on, boy, an' y'don' even know it.

JOE: Whadzzat?

RINGMASTER: I mean the Reds, boy. The Comm*yune*-ists.

(GIRL *does a scared pirouette.*)

JOE *(wide-eyed)*: Yeah?

RINGMASTER: They're fixin' to take all of Asia away from us.

JOE: No! I didn't know we owned it, even!

RINGMASTER *(sobbing)*: Y'gonna let 'em?

JOE: I dunno, mister. They ain't done nothin' to me.

RINGMASTER: So far.

JOE: An' if they did, I forgive 'em.

(*He starts to amble along again. The* RINGMASTER *gives a shrill whistle, catching* JOE *by the seat of his pants as he passes.*)

RINGMASTER *(bellowing)*: Aggression!

(GIRL *bangs tambourine;* JOE *does a somersault. A cartoon of little yellow Mongols, grinning, armed to the teeth, flashes on the screen. Red sickles and hammers.*)

RINGMASTER: L'il yaller Reds!

GIRL *(banging tambourine)*: Red Peril!

JOE: Wow!

(*He does another somersault as he ducks in fear. The word "Aggression" echoes from all directions and appears on the screen in quivering red letters. The* RINGMASTER *shoves toward* JOE *a broom-handle representing a gun with bayonet fixed.* JOE *shies away.* RINGMASTER *grabs him by the collar.*)

GIRL: American way of life! Christian cause! Red, white, and blue! George Washington! Statue of Liberty!

(She bangs the drum each time, ends with a rattle of the disks. Machine guns. Light fades.)

Scene 6

Light rises on the Taylor cottage. DON *and* RUTH *usher in* SHIRLEY CRAIN, DON *carrying her suitcase.*

SHIRLEY CRAIN, *forty-five, is an overweight, fretful woman with too much makeup.*

RUTH: You know your train actually arrived two minutes early? I hope you enjoyed your trip.

SHIRLEY: It was great, if you enjoy a steam bath, all the way here. That train ride after a bad night! You know what I dreamt of, all last night? Lions and tigers!

RUTH: Carnivores.

SHIRLEY: Can you imagine? And I'm just a helpless capricorn — that's a goat.

RUTH: Mrs. Crain, dear, with Donald in charge, you'll be rested and relaxed.

SHIRLEY: I can't think where I got the idea that Tidewater was some sort of beach resort. It's just a little shantytown on the ocean.

RUTH *(determinedly)*: May I fix you a drink, dear? We have some lemonade, not very cold, I'm afraid —

SHIRLEY *(not believing her ears)*: Lemonade?

DON *(to* RUTH's *astonishment)*: It's all right, Ruth, we have some Scotch — picked it up in town yesterday, just in case.

SHIRLEY: On the rocks. Just a thimbleful.

RUTH *(giving up)*: Could you take it with water, Mrs. Crain? Unfortunately our refrigerator suddenly defrosted, this morning.

SHIRLEY *(with a shudder)*: Not just water! I'll take it straight while I'm here. The doctor said to watch out, on account of my kidneys, but since it's an emergency —

RUTH: It may be less poisonous if it's not chilled.

DON *(pouring* SHIRLEY *a drink in a tumbler)*: Ruth's joking. We don't usually drink.

SHIRLEY: Pour one for yourself. You're not going to make me into a lone drinker this weekend, old buddy.

(She takes out a pack of cigarettes. DON brings matches.)

RUTH: We don't smoke, either — not with the possibility of lung cancer. In fact —

SHIRLEY *(looking around)*: What made me imagine you had some sort of scrumptious beach house?

RUTH: We like to think it's a snug little place.

(Drops of water drip from the ceiling.)

SHIRLEY *(startled)*: What is that?

DON: Only our son Larry, having his shower with the curtains outside the tub, as usual.

RUTH *(going to the stairs to call)*: Larry!

DON: He never answers. Must be on the toilet by now; he sits there for hours, practically lives there.

RUTH: Don, if you don't mind —

SHIRLEY: Believe me, it's a very disappointing generation. What do the young fellows know, besides plunking their guitars, sniffing dope, and making trouble for their elders? *(She settles down to her drink.)* As for their dopey little girl friends — *(To DON)* I'll have another thimbleful after this. You, too.

RUTH *(resolutely)*: Mrs. Crain, after you have a nap, let us show you the beach. It's glorious; you can get a suntan and watch Don go surf-casting —

SHIRLEY: I'm here on business, madam, and we'd better get started.

DON *(with no visible enthusiasm)*: That's right.

RUTH: We'll have an early dinner, then you'll both have time to talk.

SHIRLEY: Early suits me, with a nibble to tide us over. The doctor said no between meals, but since it's only over the week-end —

RUTH: Aren't you well most of the time?

SHIRLEY *(resentfully)*: What do you mean?! I've only got asthma — outside of that I'm as solid as a fifteen-year-old. Just feel that. Go ahead!

(She presents her front. RUTH feels it.)

RUTH: At least, if you don't take any medicines —

SHIRLEY: My doctor is a top man. If you need any kind of assistance, use a top man — you can't go wrong.

RUTH: When it comes to doctors, what difference does it make? You know the saying: "God heals and the doctor takes the fee."

SHIRLEY: They take the fee, all right! . . . The asthma is not my main headache, Mrs. Taylor —

RUTH: Ruth.

SHIRLEY: My main headache is the law profession. The sort of money they want for taking a case on contingency! I told Judge Olroyd I've had enough experience with big-shot lawyers. "Nothing doing, Judge," I said. "If they're not hungry, then put me on to someone who *is* hungry."

DON: I see what you mean, Shirley.

SHIRLEY: Sure you do.

DON: On speculation other attorneys would charge you at least a third of your claim. All we arranged for is ten percent.

SHIRLEY: That isn't hay for horses, is it — ten percent? Especially when I'm asked to hand over $300 just for disbursements, before anything even happens?

DON: Four hundred dollars. I haven't received that check yet.

SHIRLEY: It's in the mail; I mailed it yesterday. Or else it's all signed, on my desk. I came here about my case, not about that check.

DON: Just let me look for your papers . . .

(He exits upstairs.)

RUTH: Don has been working so hard on your case!. He's simply indignant about the unfair way you've been treated!

SHIRLEY: Unfair is not the name for it, my dear!

RUTH: I know — I read about it in the papers.

SHIRLEY: To say the least, I am entitled to inherit one-third, the widow's mite, according to state law. . . With your husband grabbing off ten percent — that's about $55,000, no less — they'd still have to hand over a check for $675,000 as I figure it —
(She looks up as DON comes back empty-handed.)
Where are those papers?

DON: Can't seem to lay hands on them at the moment. They're misplaced somewhere —

RUTH: Have you really looked? *(To SHIRLEY.)* Please excuse me.

(She goes up to the bedrooms.)

SHIRLEY: Can't find my papers?

DON: They'll turn up. I know what's in them.

SHIRLEY: I don't.

DON: In the meantime we can discuss the possible court expenses.

SHIRLEY: You mean your share of my money . . . Don't tell me about lawyers — they say you've got a sure thing until they get hold of your retainer, then they advise you to settle in a hurry because you haven't got a chance. What I need is somebody who goes in there and fights. I have my doubts about you, but never mind, I'm getting tired of shopping around. I'll see my business adviser tomorrow and if he approves I'll write you out that check.

DON: I'm sure he'll have no objection.

SHIRLEY: He investigates everybody I deal with, and I know he wouldn't like the looks of Tidewater.

DON: You mean he's coming here?

SHIRLEY: I mean a dump like Tidewater is no place for a reputable attorney. *(taking out a torn circular)* You know some insolent little tart handed me this thing at the station just as I got off the train? *(reading)* "All out against war! Come one, come all! *The Peace Ballet!"* *(acidly)* This whole country is crawling with Reds! Everywhere you go, these days, nothing but junky talk against America! In some of the most exclusive places you ever heard of! No more patriots left in this goddam country!

DON *(wearily)*: I've tried to tell you, Shirley: if people can't learn to respect each other's opinions —

SHIRLEY: Are you my lawyer or aren't you? If you're so picky and choosy, why are you trying to represent me in the first place?

DON: Mrs. Crain, I tried to oblige you with the incorporation outline for your project. It bothered me when I wrote it.

SHIRLEY: I could see that, all right! You turned all my ideas into a wishy-washy compromise! *(Takes several pages of a scrawled memorandum out of her bag.)* And that isn't all: you left out everything I had in here about Lieutenant Corby — and he's the whole reason why I thought up this project!

DON: I thought we discussed that at the office, Mrs. Crain. A foundation just to glamorize someone like Corby is a mistake. According to his court-martial —

SHIRLEY: Don't tell *me* what to do with my own money! A genuine American fighting man who risked his life for his country — and you want to cover him up! *(indignantly)* I spent the whole rest of this week putting back all the gutsy expose you left out! You'll have your office girl type this up — *(reading)* "The Shirley Crain Foundation . . ."

DON: Can you keep your voice down, please? I'd rather my wife didn't hear you.

SHIRLEY: I want everybody in the U.S.A. to hear me — why should she be left out? When my Foundation gets through proving how the subversives and the bleeding hearts are ruining this country, some people are going to get a little lead in the head!

(RUTH appears on the stair landing.)

DON: We'll talk about it later!

RUTH (*coming down; to* SHIRLEY): I can usually locate anything Donald leaves around, but this time. . . Those papers are in his briefcase and we haven't found it yet. . . Meanwhile, why don't you lie down, Mrs. Crain, and relax after your trip?

SHIRLEY: It might do me some good, at that.

RUTH: Your room is in the back, dear, the corner one; I'll come up there in a minute. Tonight we're having a steak dinner for you and Don. Don says he's a captive audience when he eats at home, because I'm a strict vegetarian; but since you are a special guest — *(hopefully)* Have you ever tried a salad with sunflower seeds?

SHIRLEY: Sunflower seeds? To *eat*?

RUTH: They are very important for health. You know they are given to every soldier in the Red Army, regular rations?

SHIRLEY: I'll take the U.S. Army.

DON: Ruth —

RUTH (*unheeding*): That's one reason why the Soviet Army is so strong. Look at what our people are eating instead! Dead meat! *(warming up)* The human digestive system is not the same as a dog's, a cat's, or a lion's, who have a simple stomach for digesting meat. We have more like the apes' digestion, who have complicated intestines for digesting fruit —

SHIRLEY: Excuse me, I don't swing from trees. And I know what else those monkeys eat — off each other: I saw it in the zoo. I'll take steak with onions and fried potatoes, Mrs. Taylor. You can take the statistics. *(freezingly, to* DON) And while I'm at it, I want my papers.

DON: I'm still looking.

SHIRLEY: Don't look! Find! *(She starts upstairs, taking her drink with her.)* Sunflower seeds!

(Exits.)

RUTH: What's become of her papers?

DON: I ate them.

RUTH: You what?!

45

DON: I put things down and can't find them again; I must have swallowed them whole. I'm getting senile.

RUTH: At fifty-five? Mrs. Crain is cracking you up. Why didn't you tell me what she's like? Mrs. Meat-packer, baloney and salami! Snorting about Reds from the minute she came here. Why don't you drop her?

DON: Why do you refuse to listen to a doctor?

RUTH *(sharply)*: What has that to do with it?

DON: Nothing.

RUTH: Something's happened since that class reunion, Donald. What is it?

DON: What's happened is that I'm a fish on the hook for Shirley Crain. She's the last crazy hope of my misdirected career.

RUTH: Misdirected?

DON: Who wants a lawyer too high-minded to represent one crook suing another crook? A radical lawyer who defended people instead of property — can I ever live that down? There isn't a judge or an employer who'll give me the time of day! If I'd had a grain of sense, thirty years ago, I'd have minded my own business instead of taking civil rights cases without pay!

RUTH: You had to be your kind of man. You still are. If you weren't, I'd leave you.

DON: Where would you go, Ruth? Back to the picket lines where I found you? Under the hoofs of the police horses?

RUTH: Maybe! "A better world's in birth!" I haven't forgotten!

DON: You've been asleep for forty years! Still back before they found Stalin was insane — before China and Russia started trading threats and bullets — before Soviet tanks rolled into Hungary and Czechoslovakia —

RUTH: You're hurting me!

DON: I'm sorry, Ruth. *(Embracing her.)* You're right. Something's happening to me, and I can feel it: I'm trying to hold on to my integrity while losing it. They don't open the gates of the Establishment free of charge.

RUTH *(remorsefully)*: I shouldn't have spoken the way I did. That was wild and stupid.

DON: Don't say that.

RUTH: We have to see this thing through and come out on the other side. You need this chance; you need it. Mrs. Crain may be your last chance. Just because she's a little batty —

46

(SHIRLEY *comes downstairs.*)

SHIRLEY (*to* RUTH): I've thought it over. I'm not staying.

RUTH: But why?

SHIRLEY: You know your husband had the nerve to tell me my case makes him want to throw up?

DON: When did I say that?!

SHIRLEY: If you didn't say it, you meant it! So don't tell me —

(CATHY CLARK, *tambourine in hand, enters at the screen door in a rush.*)

CATHY: Larry still here? (*to* RUTH) Are you his mother? I'm Cathy Clark.

RUTH (*introducing*): Larry's father. . . Mrs. Crain. . .

CATHY: Greetings! *(At the stairs, she shouts, rattling her tambourine.)* Sonny-boy! Rehearsal!! Will you get your butt in gear? We're a whole hour late!!

SHIRLEY *(furiously)*: She's the one who shoved that circular at me at the station!

CATHY: So I did! Hello again and welcome! Seats at the box office, madam — *(banging tambourine) The Peace Ballet!*

SHIRLEY: I'm in the middle of the Red Network! *(She grabs her suitcase.)* Out of my way!

(LARRY *appears on the stairs, dressed, and with his guitar.*)

LARRY: May I ask the meaning of this hullabaloo? *(coming down; elaborately)* Is this *the* Mrs. Crain herself, in person? Please to accept my apologies, madam, for the uncouthness of your reception in our home.

DON: What sort of vaudeville is that?

SHIRLEY *(hesitating; to* LARRY): Are you the son of the house?

LARRY *(bowing)*: Lawrence T. Taylor, no other!

CATHY: The Taylor family treasure! (*to* LARRY.) Are you going or staying? Come on!

(She exits.)

SHIRLEY: Slut!

LARRY *(grandly)*: Duty calls. I trust, madam, you will excuse my departure for the nonce? We shall meet again.

(SHIRLEY *follows him, entranced, to the door.*)

SHIRLEY *(returning)*: Such lovely manners, that boy. And so nice-

47

SHIRLEY *(returning)*: Such lovely manners, that boy. And so nice-looking! Your son has got to be saved! That draggle-tail has him in her clutches!

RUTH *(reaching for her suitcase)*: Why don't you think it over, Shirley, about leaving? It's so hot in the city; we have a nice, cool beach —

SHIRLEY: Don't I know I get a little squiffy sometimes? I could use more self-control. And I'd be better off eating vegetables — I'd still have a 24-inch waist instead of a 38 and asthma. The way I indulge myself is a sin and a shame!

(Light fades. Soft dance music. SHIRLEY'S *voice, recorded, speaks,)*

SHIRLEY'S VOICE: A part-time cashier in one of the finest cafeterias in Granite City, Colorado. That's what I was when that bastard of a Raymond Crain picked me up. The Prince of Packers, they called him, and he sure did a wholesale job on me! Married eleven years, and he admitted from the start he was never blown off better in his life — but he had to have somebody with a mind, he said! An old rooster like him, wallowing in money, handing it out in fistfuls to every charity racket you ever heard of! And the older he got, the worse it was! Suddenly he flies off, gets a phony Mexican divorce, and marries this trollop of a school librarian full of half-baked, un-American, bleeding-heart ideas . . .

The papers don't tell you a Mexican divorce is illegal if the wife doesn't appear! Entirely and thoroughly illegal in any state in the Union! He was living illegally with that woman until suddenly he deceases, last year, and the relatives claim *she's* his wife, by God!
(Furiously)
I'll show the old S.O.B. wherever he is, now — I've got a mind, all right! His money's going to a *real* worthy cause, this time upholding the name of a great American, by God!

Scene 7

Light rises on the rehearsal. Sound of machine guns. On screen, silhouettes of tired soldiers climb a hill at dusk.

RINGMASTER: Looka them poor, tired, wornout sojers of democracy protectin' their beloved, democratic homelan' against the maraudin', murderin' Red hordes! *(Bugle call. Proudly)* Do not despair, gallant sojers of democracy! Not while the military might of U.S.A. is rushin' — I mean hastenin' — to your side!

(Sound: airplane revving up, loud and louder. On screen: jet plane taxiing to a landing with the lettering United States of America *on its side. Cheers and deafening applause.)*

JOE *(wildly)*: Wow! To the rescue! Here come the good guys!

48

(*He is loose by now and, with supposed gun and bayonet, is sprinting madly in a circle. On screen: hammers and sickles turn like a pinwheel, then give way to a projection of huge black dominoes falling in a succession of crashes.*)

RINGMASTER, GIRL (*together*): FALLING DOMINOES!

RINGMASTER: Yahoo!

(JOE *is still jabbing, but the* RINGMASTER *now has him by a rope around the neck.*)

Give 'em hell! Give 'em peace! Give 'em gas!
(GIRL *gasps and chokes.*)
Sorry about that. That ain't gas, just a lachrimatory agent.

GIRL (*pirouetting gaily*): Peace!

RINGMASTER: Negotiate or we escalate!

GIRL (*crooning*): Peace, kiddo! B Girls, V Girls. "Hey you, Number One, I love you too much. You like make boom-boom? (*sexy*) Venereal disease, one G.I. out of five —

RINGMASTER: Par for the course! You can't fight no immaculate war! (*Explosion and machine-gun fire. A jerky picture of American troops advancing toward an Asian hamlet. Light fades. Rock recording.*)

(*Blackout and curtain*)

ACT II

Scene 1

The stage is dark. Then voices, recorded; hard rock under.

DON'S VOICE: Luis Rodriguez, an old workman, picketing, has his leg crushed in the street by his boss's truck; has to have an amputation.

RODRIGUEZ'S VOICE: Judge, Your Honor, I have suffered with this leg.

JUDGE'S VOICE: Your suffering is not in question. . . Case not ready — dismissed with prejudice!

DON'S VOICE: My key witness out of town and sick. Case dismissed with prejudice by that bastard of a Judge Kroger! After three years of work on contingency we leave the court empty-handed!

(*Voices fade. Light rises on the Taylor cottage,* LARRY *and* CATHY *enter at the screen door.*)

LARRY (*as they enter*): I heard you, Cathy. Don't scold.

CATHY: We can't tell if you're with us or if you're off by yourself. Sometimes you show up when you're needed, sometimes you don't —

49

LARRY: Just because I live at home, you and John think I'm some kind of baby!

CATHY: Don't take my head off, Junior! — Where are your folks and Mrs. Crain?

LARRY: Must be on the beach somewhere or upstairs, sleeping. You need them?

(Sings)

Ha, ha, come away
Ha, ha, go away —

(Breaks off.)

Call me Junior just once more, you want your head busted! Didn't I stay up all last night, helping you? And who's been delivering the copies of *The Peace Bulletin* out to the hospital, if not me?

CATHY *(concerned)*: You shouldn't go there alone. If the Scorpions lay hands on you —

LARRY: Fuck the Scorpions. *(Sings)*

Looka here, Sister
You got to treat soul food
Like it's food for your soul —

(Breaks off.)

I need somebody in my corner. All I have is my parents, and I couldn't care less. Mom is all gush, Dad is corrupt —

CATHY: Didn't you say the F.B.I. once came after him? You ought to be proud.

LARRY: He used to be with the Civil Liberties Union, long ago — so what? All he says, now, is "Yes and no, and don't make waves" and, "Why is Lieutenant Corby any worse than his superiors?" They're all getting let off.

CATHY: That, too, now?

LARRY *(making himself a sandwich)*: I'm an unloved person with no one to talk to in the world.

CATHY: You had Susie Platt — such a sweet, modest little thing. What became of *her*?

LARRY: Nothing — I just don't see her any more. That kind of thing either is or it isn't, so don't bring up Susie.

CATHY: That's typical. If you love men, they leave you. And if they love you and you don't love them back, they're insulted.

LARRY *(suddenly)*: I'm not coming around tonight.

CATHY *(alarmed)*: You don't mean that! We open tomorrow night — how could we replace you in time? Please don't talk like that — you've been such a pest, lately, for no reason —

50

(LARRY *tries to grab her.)*
Don't!

LARRY: All you care about is your boy friend! What's that old moose got that I haven't got twice of?

CATHY: Twice your age and ten times your experience. You don't know John: he takes no nonsense from anybody — cops, thugs, or anyone else.

LARRY: You told me — the two of you in Chicago, beat up by Mayor Daley's police. Who can't demonstrate? Or get beaten up, either?

CATHY: Can't I make you understand something? John is my man. I love him.

LARRY: What for?

CATHY: Because that's how it is, Larry, just like you said.

LARRY: Just self-indulgence! What are you, a little child or something, giving in to your emotions?

CATHY: Did anybody ever tell you you're a nuisance?

LARRY: I don't like your legs. They turn in.

CATHY *(going to the door)*: I'll fix them. *(Coming back)* Little lost boy!

(She kisses him, exits. LARRY remains wedged against the door, hand on the knob. Light dips. LARRY'S voice, recorded, sings.

*I want to hold your hand,
And when I touch you,
I feel happy inside.
It's such a feeling
That my love I can't hide.
I can't hide,
I can't hide . . .*

(Light returns. The phone rings.)

LARRY *(opening the door, shouts)*: Goddam you!

(RUTH appears on the stair landing.)

RUTH: Larry? What's wrong, precious?

(He runs out. She comes down, gripping the stair-rail; opens the screen door to look out; comes back, becomes aware of the phone and picks up the receiver.)

RUTH: Mrs. Taylor . . . Yes . . . *(Long pause)* Yes, of course . . . Thank you so much, Jimmy.

(She hangs up, shaken, pulls herself together as DON enters from the back porch, holding a briefcase.)

51

DON: Wasn't that the phone just now?

RUTH: Wrong number.

DON: I've got to hear from Jimmy. He's covering the Appeals Court for his newspaper.

RUTH: Yes . . . He'd know how things look.

DON: Why doesn't he call? He thinks Rodriguez will have a sure thing on appeal.

RUTH: No news is good news. *(Changing; quickly)* You found your briefcase!

DON: On a chair on the back porch; I must have left it there Friday night when I came home.

RUTH: I knew it would turn up!

DON: Freudian! Trying to forget Mrs. Crain's whole existence! *(He takes a soiled and folded letter out of his briefcase.)* Just listen to this: on the letterhead of J. R. Crain, dated a week before his demise! *(Reads)* "To whom it may concern: This is to certify that I, J. Raymond Crain, divorced my wife, Shirley Mulhall Crain, illegally, because I bribed the judge and jury."

RUTH *(startled)*: Why, it cracks the case wide open! All you have to do —

DON: Is to get old Crain out of his mausoleum and have him sign this before a notary and witnesses. There's no signature. I don't know where she got it; she must have typed it up herself. That won't prevent her from ordering me to win the case with it. Who needs this insane paper? She's had a deal so raw that there's not the slightest doubt she'll win — if I can keep her from ruining her own case in court.

RUTH: Poor thing! She's so upset by her troubles! She's resting, now; I hope she's getting some sleep.

DON *(putting away papers)*: She needs it, after two pounds of steak washed down with all that Scotch! And she's going to want more liquor when she wakes up — that means another trip to town.

RUTH: I'll go with you. We'll walk along the beach.

DON: Are you up to it, Ruthie? You look so tired. . .

RUTH: Donald, Larry was here just now. In and out, like a small explosion looking for a place to happen.

DON: That boy again — he's never out of your mind! Why must you let him get you like that?

RUTH: You've shaken him up. I don't think he'll ever be the same again.

DON *(confounded)*: What did I do to him?

RUTH: He doesn't know what to think of you any more. Ever since you started criticizing *The Peace Ballet* —

DON: Did I ever take it one hundred percent? How do I, or you, know what that show of theirs is going to look like when they put it on?

RUTH: You never said that before. Now you tell him you have nothing against the commune, but they ought to locate somewhere else — the ballet is all right, but it ought to be postponed to a more appropriate time —

DON: You don't imagine that I excuse that dismal Corby episode, do you? I even suggested that they use it for *The Peace Ballet*. But if Larry expects me to start applauding in advance —

RUTH: He needs your approval, Don; he needs it badly. You've always given him that, up to now.

DON: Then it's time he realized that if he wants approval he has to earn it.

RUTH: Give him a chance. He's not ready for that lesson. *(with feeling.)* Can't you see the child is suffering? A wonderful boy who doesn't drink, doesn't use LSD, doesn't mug anybody —

DON: That ought to make us happy as the day is long! *(tartly)* He's wasting away! All he has is a room for himself, a bathroom, clothing, four meals a day if he wants them. *I* was brought up in the Depression, happy if I could eat and had a pair of shoes!

RUTH: "Not by bread alone," Don.

DON: He ought to go to work, the way I did at his age. It could do him a world of good.

RUTH: He *is* working. At the commune.

DON: That's not work — that's self-indulgence.

RUTH: And he thinks about things. That's work, too, isn't it?

DON: Maybe, if you say so. I once asked him what he thinks about. He said, "About what one fly tells another fly when they meet on the sugar bowl." *(ruefully)* I don't want to be unfair to him, Ruth. It's just that we can't reach him anymore. Something happened to him at the age of thirteen: he went into a closed room and we haven't seen him since.

RUTH: You've forgotten the agonies of adolescence.

DON: You're right. Maybe I ought to get him laid, like they did in the old days — father takes son to a whorehouse!

RUTH: Do you have to be so crude, Don?

53

(She sways. DON catches her.)

DON: What'll I do with you? The doctor said to come back and see him. Are you waiting to crack up?

RUTH: I won't go near the medical gentry again! I told you: those medical monopolists —

(Light fades. DON'S voice, recorded; music under.)

DON'S VOICE: The war was this country's watershed — it'll never be the same again. The war! It was what this country wanted, and never mind all protest. Who could have stopped it? Not even Congress! Who could have stopped a Lieutenant Corby from killing all those people? We wallowed in the righteousness of the biggest mistake we ever made — and we'll pay for it with the ruin of everything the U.S.A. ever meant to the world and to itself . . .

(The rest is obliterated by a different voice, loud, triumphant.)

VOICE: U.S.A.! Take it or leave it!

(Sings)

Stand tall, America,
Let nobody pass you by!
Let them know you're strong, America,
Lift your sword up high!

ACT III

Scene 1

Light returns to the cottage. A moment, then the piteous cat is heard. SHIRLEY descends the stairs majestically in her wrapper, holding her bottle of Scotch. Finding no one present, she goes to the screen door to look out, then to the back door, which she opens.

SHIRLEY: Scat, you!
(She slams the door shut, goes to the refrigerator, where she finds a chicken leg. She crosses to the radio, turns it on.)

RADIO VOICE *(crooning)*:

. . . There have been men
Who have died
That others might be free
And even now
They do it still . . .

(She sits down comfortably to listen.)

Brave, gallant men
Know that someone must

And so they will.

Gallant men . . .

(LARRY *enters, letting the screen door bang shut. His mood has not improved.)*

LARRY: You mind if I end the suffering?

(He switches off the radio.)

SHIRLEY: What was the suffering?

LARRY: Is that my drumstick you have there?

SHIRLEY: Oh, is it yours?

LARRY: Never mind, I shouldn't be eating it, according to Mom. All these chickens get hormone injections to make them grow faster, and it poisons the human system when you eat them. Besides, when the chickens are murdered the shock gives them waste matter in their circulations. *(depressed)* Confidentially, though, I eat meat only because I'm used to it, that's all. When you believe in the principles of health hygiene to the degree that I do — which is the highest degree — it makes it all the harder to live up to. Know what I mean?

SHIRLEY: Surely. I have no will power, either. We're the same. *(She looks him over greedily.)* You have probably never thought how many things younger and older people have in common. Especially when they are opposite sexes.

LARRY: That's a new philosophy on me, Mrs. Crain.

SHIRLEY: You can call me Shirley.

(The cat screeches.)

You look a little downhearted. Are you? You could use somebody's caressing hand to wipe that frown off you, child.

LARRY: Somebody's caressing hand better not try it. I've got far, far too much on my mind as it is. *(He goes to the refrigerator, takes out a carton of milk.)* You hear that cat crying? Dad put all her kittens in a paper bag and threw them in the ocean. Is that genocide or isn't it? If you can take Dad and Mom you're a better man than I am, Gunga Din.

SHIRLEY: What's the matter with them?

LARRY: Not *with* it. They had some guts once upon a time, maybe; but now Dad is backing away from it all, and Mom is so hopped up with all those cliches and platitudes —

SHIRLEY: I agree with you, but you should be ashamed to talk that way about your parents.

LARRY: If I had charge of this family they'd have to face up, that's all.

SHIRLEY: I think you are a very brash young man.

LARRY *(pouring milk into a bowl)*: Very possibly, very possibly. You know they never bother to feed that cat? It's always left up to me.

SIIIRLEY: You spend a lot of time out here?

LARRY: All summer doing nothing, according to Dad. *(He opens the back door, sets milk outside.)* I started college last fall, but I'm not going back. They were supposed to teach me wisdom, but they only wasted a year of my life, so I'm suing them.

SHIRLEY: Have you got a lawyer?

LARRY *(singing):*

God gave Noah the rainbow sign
No more water but fire next time —

SHIRLEY: What are you going to do now, look for work?

LARRY *(impressively)*: I am not even considering outside employment, because I am writing a book called *Going My Way on This Remarkable Planet*: the philosophy of pessimistic realism, from the vegetarian point of view, in which I make the point that man will be a success if he can only avoid failure. It'll take seven years to write, but it'll be worth it — don't say it won't.

SHIRLEY *(sitting near him)*: Am I saying it?

LARRY *(moving to another seat)*: Furthermore it will advise people not to wear leather shoes made from suffering animals. I am against the killing of anything that has life.

SHIRLEY: How about roaches and bedbugs?

LARRY: I am taking that problem under advisement.

SHIRLEY: You're a deep one, besides being handsome.

LARRY *(shrugging)*: Just consider when the atom bombs start dropping. That's no roach powder, killing 65 million people in this country, official estimate.

SHIRLEY: What can you do about that?

LARRY: Not a thing, if you talk the way Dad does, only I don't accept his kind of self-image. You ever hear of Zarathustra?

SHIRLEY: She's a belly-dancer?

LARRY: He, not she. *(He sprawls on the sofa.)* Zarathustra was a philosopher. He believed in the superior being. Me, too.

SHIRLEY: Aha! You're a superior being?

LARRY: Independent, at least.

SHIRLEY: Selfish, you mean. Is that good? I can think of better things than being selfish. Like being comfy-cozy with somebody else instead of being so lonesome and wrapped up in yourself. Somebody who is all wrapped up in himself makes a very small package. You're different from me. I don't believe I ever had a selfish thought in my life.

LARRY: Well, that's very commendable, I'm sure. Only you can *afford* it — living the life of the Upper Register —

SHIRLEY *(still closer)*: A lot you know, lovey! Have you ever noticed how many people, even if they have money, spend all their lives sitting around, alone, on bar stools?

LARRY: You mean it? Why?

SHIRLEY: You get old enough so nobody phones you any more and you'll learn why. Just fill up this glass for me, will you, like a good boy?

LARRY: Don't you know it's bad for you?

(He gets up, fills her glass.)

SHIRLEY: And one for yourself, lover-boy. Nobody drinks alone.

LARRY: *You're* going to drink alone.

SHIRLEY: Oh, dear, a cave-man! You can come closer. You don't think, do you, that I'm anything like that little chippy who's got you tied up in knots? You're much too good for an unfeeling little doll like her. *(patting his hand)* Such sensitive fingers! Let me see the palm of your hand.

LARRY: Are you into palm-reading? I think it's a lot of crap, but I have an open mind. Don't tell me something bad — I have enough bothering me already.

SHIRLEY: Sit nearer — nobody's going to bite you. *(She examines his palm.)* Mmm — those lines. Trouble. Woman-trouble, of course. A heartbreaker like you — but then, you're at the age when you have no idea what a truly understanding woman could do for you. *(Her hand crawls up his leg.)* Someone who knows the right places —

LARRY *(escaping)*: Never mind, I can do a good enough job myself. My trouble is with Dad. He said not to rap with you, and I don't know how I got into it at all.

SHIRLEY *(setting down her glass; caustically)*: You're beginning to irk me! Where does your father get his nerve, telling you not to talk to me? I've made inquiries about him; at least four people told me he's no lawyer and never will be.

57

LARRY *(seriously)*: Look, man, I may not agree with Dad's outlook on life, because he doesn't know where he's at, anymore, but I don't like to see him run down; I'll bet he knows his business inside out as a lawyer.

SHIRLEY: A *good* lawyer?

LARRY: You mean, can he scream, lie, and put on an act?

SHIRLEY: In my opinion your father is a red-hot Communist.

LARRY: You have to be kidding — he's nothing but one of those do-nothing liberals. If he was into anything real like Communism, it was far away and long ago, and he'd like to forget about it. *(He goes to the pantry, brings back several books.)* Look at this: books by all kinds of radicals. I found them hidden away.

SHIRLEY: Radical, liberal, Communist, they're all the same.

LARRY: The hell they are, but I'll give Dad credit for one thing, at least: I'll bet he could have been a corporation lawyer if he wasn't so anti.

SHIRLEY *(getting up)*: I'm getting convinced you're just as anti as he is.

LARRY: Right on! It's a good thing they stopped the draft; I could have gone in and killed a few Commies for Christ, but what for, if the army is just as Communist?

SHIRLEY *(outraged)*: Communist? The Army?

LARRY *(returning books to the pantry)*: Gad, lady, you realize all that regimentation, welfare-statism and big-brotherism, and a lack of private initiative that's almost total?

SHIRLEY: Where do you get all those words? From your friends? Who's going to defend our country if they're all like you? We have to protect our way of life, don't we?

LARRY: Are you going to shove your way of life onto the Asiatic peasant? What the futz does the Asiatic peasant care about the Shirley Crain way of life? You let some little jag-off in a uniform go out there and commit genocide, like this so-called Lieutenant Corby, and the President says it's no big deal! Who is the President, for cripe's sake? Was he anointed, or only elected?

SHIRLEY: So now you're with the gang that's stabbing our President in the back! Red propaganda!

LARRY: You said it! Subversive as all get-out, Shirley!

SHIRLEY: Tearing down a patriot like Lieutenant Corby, one of the finest men of all time — *(Glacially)* When does the next train leave for New York?

LARRY: You mean right now? Mom thought you were staying till tomorrow.

SHIRLEY: She couldn't be more wrong!

LARRY: There's no more trains to New York today. You'd have to get a taxi. Forty-five dollars — that's cheap for somebody in your bracket.

SHIRLEY: Cheap! I wonder if you're all there!

LARRY (seriously): Not demonstrably, and neither are you. Like, who knows if you or I exist? Can you prove it? Like, it may look like you're sitting on a chair when you're sitting on it, but maybe you're only a thought and that chair is only a prayer.

SHIRLEY (alarmed): Junk!

LARRY: Don't say junk! It's a high thought in Zen, maybe even in Za-Zen!

SHIRLEY: Instead of thinking high thoughts, you ought to be out working — I fully agree with your parents about you! (acidly) When is this ballet going on? Today?

LARRY: Only a dress rehearsal. Why?

SHIRLEY: Because I am going to inspect it and report it to the proper authorities.
(DON and RUTH enter with packages.)
And after that I'm leaving this place! Fast!

(She exits upstairs.)

DON (to LARRY): What did you say to Mrs Crain? I asked you not to go near her!

LARRY: Don't yell — I can hear you.

DON: Answer me!

LARRY (singing):

MacArthur Park is melting in the dark
All that sweet green icing flowing down —

(Breaking off)

I don't like your tone, Dad — it's not respectful. Don't think you and Mom can keep ordering me around like you've been doing all my life! Just because you're after that big legal fee —

DON: Who's been ordering you around?

RUTH: Larry, dear, I don't know what you're holding against Dad and me. We are no different from any other parents. We raised you in love and hope, and even if we made mistakes, you should learn to forgive them.

59

DON *(bitterly)*: Not him! He worries over every stray dog and cat in the street, but he's vicious to his father and mother!

LARRY: What the futz do I have to care if you win the rat race? Even if you win, you're still a rat!

(Sings)

Someone left the cake out in the rain,
And I don't think I can take it,
'Cause it took so long to bake it —

(DON *grabs the guitar out of* LARRY'S *hands. There is a struggle.*)

RUTH *(with a cry)*: Stop! Stop it!

(She snatches the guitar from DON, *gives it to* LARRY. SHIRLEY *appears on the stairs.*)

LARRY *(to* DON): You shouldn't let go at me like that, Dad — you're liable to lose a son. Besides, you're an old man. I could hurt you.

DON: Get out with that thing! And don't come back! I'm writing you off!

(LARRY *exits.*)

RUTH: Oh my God! What made you say a thing like that to your son? You hate him!

DON: No. I only can't stand him.

(Blackout. A voice.)

VOICE:
From the Prosecutor of the Corby trial
To the President of the United States

Sir:

It is unlawful for an American soldier to summarily execute unarmed and unresisting men, women, children and babies. For the nation to condone the acts of Lieutenant Corby is to make us no better than our enemies.

Your intervention has, in my opinion, damaged the military judicial system and lessened any respect it may have gained as a result of the proceedings . . .

(*The* VOICE *fades. Light returns to the Taylor cottage.* RUTH *and* SHIRLEY *are at the stairs.*)

Scene 2

RUTH: Please listen, Mrs. Crain. You're overexcited.

SHIRLEY: *You're* overexcited. I am cool as an iceberg.

DON *(entering at the screen door)*: There's no sign of him — must have run on to town.

SHIRLEY: A real loony-bin you have here! And I came near sewing myself up with you — imagine! Except that I don't mind telling you I'm sorry for your wife Daddy as she is, That health hygiene! She needs to gorge on some steak!

RUTH: Never mind about me, Mrs. Crain. Try to be fair to Don: he's stayed up nights looking through your papers; the poor man hasn't slept, thinking of ways to fight for you in court —

DON: And that's the truth.

SHIRLEY: Don't tell *me*! I was brainwashed when they told me to hire you! You want my money, but you won't get it! You can try — why not? Everybody else does — because I'm nothing but a pushover! Wipe your feet on Shirley!

DON: Who's pushing you over? Or wiping his feet on you?

SHIRLEY *(with a rush of overwhelming self-pity)*: I used to be Shirley Mulhall, pretty as a picture, a little kewpie-doll with a waist you could span with your two hands, a little girl with a song and a laugh . . .

RUTH *(compassionately)*: You were a lovely girl, I'm sure.

SHIRLEY *(harshly)*: I was a born trollop! By the time old Crain came along I wasn't giving a damn — handing myself out free of charge to any man who'd treat me to a picture show or a double rum cola. A rag doll with the stuffing running out — never knew in whose room I would wake up, and didn't care, as long as I could still crawl to work in the morning! *(with contempt)* Only why am I talking to a crazy like you? No wonder your husband never got to first base! With something like you around his neck —

DON: Leave my wife out of this! *(fiercely)* My Ruth — a good woman in an evil world! The one good fortune I can count on, now and forever!

SHIRLEY: You can have her, and welcome! *(picking up her suitcase)* I'm going to have a look at the Communist show your son is helping to put on, so I can report it. And you'd better find my papers, or I'll have you up before the Bar Association and every investigating committee going, so help me God!

DON *(taking a large envelope out of his briefcase)*: Here you are, Shirley — and goodbye!
(She grabs the envelope from him and exits. The screen door bangs behind her.)
And good riddance! *(To RUTH)* If she hadn't been insulted by that son of yours —

61

RUTH: *Our* son! A fine boy, only he's hanging on to his childhood!

DON: Could it have been so bad if he's hanging on to it? The way he treats us both — and especially me —

RUTH: Why should he care about you, if you don't care about him, anymore? You've failed him. He needs a committed model of integrity, not a committed model of compromises full of whereases and aforesaids, where everything is yes and no!

DON: That doesn't sound good, does it?

RUTH: No, it doesn't.

DON: It's easy to tell me I've failed him. I'm in the middle of a war with life every day of the year, and he just sits there and criticizes. Why do I have to succeed, he wants to know. Has he ever tasted failure? You don't exist as a human being in this country unless you succeed, no matter how or why! And you don't get there by antagonizing people! *(with feeling) Any* people! Do you want to fight it out with the town of Tidewater? This little shack lets us escape, a few weekends a year, from the noise and rush and the grime and crime of the city. Are you ready to have the Tidewater tax board raise the taxes on this house — to have the sanitation inspector find things wrong with the cesspool — to get police summonses twice a week for this and that —

RUTH: You can take those things to court.

DON: A full career for an indignant lawyer! . . . The kind I was, once upon a time — when everything that was wrong with the world was waiting for me to come and fix it. Not anymore! I'm not a kid like Larry; he can do without those things he thinks he despises — he can roam the country in a pair of faded Levis . . .

RUTH: You hate him.

(She staggers.)

DON *(supporting her, alarmed. Taking her to the sofa)*: How do you feel? You need a doctor.

RUTH: No! No doctor! And don't keep asking me how I feel! I'll be all right in a minute if you'll let me alone! *(agonized)* We've got to find Larry. He's our son!

(Quick fade. A voice singing joyously.)

VOICE:
We don't spit on the flag in Pocahoxie,
We don't flake out on pot or grass,
We don't burn Bibles up on Main Street,
We don't say "fuck" or "shit" or "up your ass."

Scene 3

Light jumps on at the Off-Limits. It is 7:00 p.m. JOHN *and* CATHY *are on the platform with* ED, *a young black in overalls.* JOHN *is wearing a red stovepipe hat spangled with stars, and a bright blue tuxedo with gold epaulettes; he has a whip and two pistols in holsters.* CATHY *is in a Columbine costume.*

ED: (*giving* JOHN *a framed gelatin*): Amber, number 22. I'm going back on the light-board.

JOHN: Right, Ed.

(*ED exits.*)

Larry's quit the show.

CATHY: He promised he wouldn't.

JOHN: Last sequence, and where is he?

CATHY: Something may have happened to him. We're so hated now, anything's possible. (*ruefully*) We shouldn't have ordered our bunch to stay away: they're a nuisance around rehearsals, but they could have kept an eye on things outside . . . When that Margie Dale character came sniffing around here, this afternoon — poet laureate of the town delinquents —

JOHN: Professional jealousy!

(*He holds her to him.*)

CATHY: She told me they're going to hang a legal sign on the Collins house: "Fornication, assignation, and lewdness prohibited."

JOHN: That sign belongs on the two motels in town.

CATHY: I'm frightened, John. Those louts who tried to drag Phoebe into their car last night . . . Not to mention the broken windows, the torn-out plumbing, the local stores who won't sell us anything anymore —

JOHN: We should have involved the city people this summer, instead of letting them cop out. They didn't like the way the town behaved, but they were strictly minding their own business.

CATHY: Anyway, come winter, there'll be no place to stay in Tidewater. We'll have to hit the road.

JOHN: That would be a relief, if we knew where we were going. (*He calls*) Ed?

ED (*offstage*): Ready to go.

CATHY: Okay. From "Students protesting . . ."

(SHIRLEY *enters with* MURCHISON. *Everything stops.*)

MURCHISON: I'll leave you here, ma'am. If they give you any trouble —

SHIRLEY: I can handle them, officer, don't worry. I'll give you a full report.

MURCHISON: Appreciate it.

(He salutes and exits.)

CATHY: It's Mrs. Crain; I met her at Larry's house today.

JOHN *(to SHIRLEY)*: How did you get in here?

SHIRLEY: The door was open, Smarty; and I had a police escort, that's how.

JOHN: Madam, this a private rehearsal — will you be good enough to leave?

SHIRLEY *(sitting down next to the platform and folding her arms)*: Try and move me. You don't know Shirley Crain!

CATHY *(after a pause)*: Right we don't know Shirley Crain . . . We've got an audience, John — may as well get an audience reaction; let's go on.

JOHN *(calling)*: Eddie . . .

(Lights change on the platform.)

CATHY *(as the TAMBOURINE GIRL)*: Students protesting, mothers protesting, ministers and senators protesting —

JOHN *(as the RINGMASTER)*: Comm*yune*-ists!

(SHIRLEY scribbles industriously.)

GIRL: Buddhists no like, Japanese, French, Swedes, British, no like. United Nations no like, Pope no like —

RINGMASTER: You think *I* like?

(LARRY enters.)

SHIRLEY: He's here, the young gentleman — all flustered __

CATHY *(calling)*: Hold everything! *(To LARRY.)* Where were you?

LARRY: You want me to rehearse or you want me to walk out? I got delayed at the hospital, that's all. That tight-ass superintendent yelled at me, then I saw the Scorpions laying for me outside. I had to duck back to the wards, then went through the back alleys, out of sight.

SHIRLEY: You'd better have stayed away!

JOHN: That noisy dowager out there —

LARRY: An ex-friend of ours. Howdy, Shirley. Stick around and get an education. (*To* CATHY.) What's my cue?

CATHY: If you feel up to it, Larry . . . Never mind your costume.

(JOHN *hands* LARRY *a gun with a fixed bayonet. Light changes on the platform.*)

Take it from "United Nations no like, Pope no like — "

RINGMASTER: You think *I* like? Screw 'em!

(LARRY, *as* JOE, *starts to wander off.*)

Where you hikin' off to, boy? Back to work!

(*He pulls* JOE *up short.* JOE, *with a little white flag attached to his bayonet, starts tearing around in a circle.*)

JOE: Give 'em peace! Give 'em hell! Falling dominoes!

(*He does a spectacular double somersault over his gun. On screen: bombs fall; U.S. troops are seen wading through swamps. Shots of whirly-birds, native villages burning, frightened and napalmed peasant women and children. The platoon of American soldiers previously shown is seen again, led by an undersized lieutenant, this time with panic-stricken villagers backing away from the advancing troops.*)

GIRL: Unarmed civilians, splinter-bombed, fried in napalm.

RINGMASTER: Sorry about that. Heathens, though, the big majority of 'em: barbecued Buddhists.

GIRL (*sings or recites*):

The FAC rides forth to battle, a warrior without match,
In his monogrammed flak jacket and his F-100 patch,
Put napalm on a hamlet and burned the whole thing flat,
Got a thousand noncombatants and he's sorry about that . . .

American boys dead, dead, dead. Thousands, fifty thousand!

RINGMASTER: Sorry about that, but it ain't nothing at all compared with the Commie body count. We got to be sad and steady, like ole Abe Lincoln.

GIRL (*huskily*): This tragically cruel war, waged for the liberation of mankind . . . (*crooning*) Brave boys, wonderful American boys. They gave their last full measure of devotion . . .

SHIRLEY: Hussy! *You* ought to be fried and frazzled!

RINGMASTER: We're gonna save the lives of our American boys by makin' this war bigger an' better, an' at the same time practicin' restraint. We don't aim to scuttle an' run, none. *(Sings)*

We're there because
We're there because
We're there —

(The word PEACE roars out. On screen: missiles rain down. An explosion, then screams, darkness, in which a little diagram of an atom is seen whirling.)

RINGMASTER *(with tremendous solemnity)*: My fellow Americans, at this here solemn moment, lemme make one thing puffickly clear: long as we got the moral burden of safe-guardin' the world, we aim to save it even if we got to destroy it in the process. At this very moment, as I speak to you from this nation's capitol in Wash'non, D.C., our bombers, without escalatin' any more than necessary, are a-hoverin' over well-selected targets over enemy territory on this Christmas Day, givin' them l'il bastards a pastin' they'll never forget!

GIRL *(in a little, childish voice)*: Sock it to 'em, tear 'em apart! Peace!

(On screen: a mushroom-shaped cloud rises and grows, turning into a blinding red glare followed by strangled screams, blackness and silence. As the light returns, the RINGMASTER is seen holding JOE by the collar. All three players make their bows. The light, still rising, discloses that the SCORPIONS have infiltrated the Off-Limits. Their leader, SCORPY, applauds, Ed Sullivan style.)

SCORPY: Wonderful, wonderful . . . great, great performance . . .

(He signals the gang, who applaud likewise. There are six or eight of them, teenage and over, dressed like their führer, in black leather jackets a la Hell's Angels. All are superheated patriots.)

SHIRLEY: Lowlife! Applauding a Red, un-American show —

SCORPY: Who's this old bag? *(To SHIRLEY.)* I follow your thought, but you've got me wrong, lady — I'm on your side. *(He takes out a small American flag.)* Watch this. This brother is gonna do us a star-spangled encore. *(He dances up to JOHN.)* You ever seen this flag, brother?

JOHN: Under fire — where you never saw it, brother.

SCORPY: Right, so you gotta love it, brother, and you're gonna show us how much. You're gonna kneel down and kiss this sacred flag!

JOHN: I'll kneel down and kiss your sacred flag when you kneel down and kiss my sacred ass, brother.

(This elicits a howl of rage from the SCORPIONS. CATHY *calls to* ED, *the electrician.)*

CATHY: Get the police, Ed!

SCORPY: What have we here? A guffy guy! All right, guffy guy —

(There is a wholesale onslaught on JOHN, *who goes down fighting as* SHIRLEY *cries out.)*

CATHY *(trying to reach him)*: John! Let him alone, you animals!

(She is slapped in the face and hurled back as they drag JOHN *out.)*

LARRY: Is that a right thing, hitting a woman?

CATHY: Larry, don't say anything!

SHIRLEY: She's bleeding! *(To the* SCORPIONS.*)* No-good bums! You think you're all so patriotic, why don't you enlist?

SCORPY: Who asked you, you old twat? Stay outa this and keep your trap shut!

(He shoves her violently into her seat.)

A SCORPION: Wanna label her, Scorpy? Say it!

SCORPY: Shut up!

SCORPIONS *(indicating* LARRY*)*: How about this one? We've got him, now!

SCORPY: Lay off — I like to hear him! *(To* LARRY.*)* Talk, shit-head!

LARRY: Thank you. *(choosing his words, earnestly)* Like, what I stand for, you evidently do not consider to be creditable, and on the other hand I do not consider to be creditable the things which you might expect me to stand for. Right? Now, I am searching for an understanding which will cancel the situation in which I find that our divergent views of the situation — *(Prolonged hooting from the* SCORPIONS. DON *hurriedly enters with* RUTH.*)* In other words we could all look groovy in a well-fitting soldier suit, but on the other hand, I have this thing that everybody is a part of the human family, also the enemy. Right?

DON: Suddenly he's full of family spirit! Even learned how to think yes and no!

RUTH: I'm so frightened! He's bleeding, Don! Get him out of here!

LARRY *(continuing)*: Naturally I know we are the most free, moral, right-thinking, law-abiding people sitting at the right hand of God Almighty —

SCORPY: You got the goddam nerve to mention God?

(There is an indignant outburst from the SCORPIONS.*)*

67

DON: Come down, Larry!

    (He tries to reach the platform.)

A SCORPION: Who the hell are you?

    (SCORPION *shoves* DON *violently back.*)

CATHY (*to* LARRY, *blood dribbling from her mouth*): Don't talk to them anymore, Junior! Don't be a Roman holiday for a mob of dropouts!

SCORPY: I'll mob you, you frigging — (*To* LARRY) Go on! Talk!

LARRY: She's right. I've got nothing more to say.

    (He tries to leave the platform. The fury of the mob vents itself in an animal roar and the smashing of chairs as LARRY *is attacked.* RUTH *screams.*)

DON *(shouting)*: Let him go!

    (He is knocked down. A police whistle is heard as MURCHISON *and* DALE *enter.*)

MURCHISON: Break it up! You, Scorpy! *(There is an abrupt quiet.)* You hear me? Out! We don't want this kind of advertising!

SCORPIONS *(cheerfully)*: Okedoke, Chief! Sure, Mr. Murchison!

    (They leave, grinning but subdued.)

DON *(panting)*: Mr. Murchison, I want those thugs under arrest.

SHIRLEY: I'm shaking all over! A criminal element —

MURCHISON *(walking away. To* CATHY.*)* Your boyfriend is in the next room. He may need a hospital.

    (CATHY *runs out.*)

DON: Did you hear me, Mr. Murchison? People have been beaten and bloodied. Will you attend to your police duty, or must I make a citizen's arrest?

MURCHISON: I would not advise you to try any arresting, Mr. Taylor; the people of this town won't like it.

SHIRLEY: Won't they? Then they can lump it!

DON (*to* MURCHISON): I guess you're right: they won't like to see it in court or in the newspapers. But they ought to learn that if someone has an opinion he has a right to state it — without being assaulted by hoodlums!

MURCHISON (*to* SHIRLEY): I'm surprised at you, ma'am. You'd better be civil. (*To* DON) And I don't need a lecture from you. We never had riots before you outsiders came here.

DALE: Tidewater was a neighborly place!

MURCHISON: We can do without the vacationers and freaks! Take young hopeful with you and find somewhere else for your summers!

DON: We'll stay right here, without a passport. And if Larry wants to be in this ballet, that's his privilege — and maybe his duty to this town!

DALE: Then don't be too surprised if you get midnight phone calls and letters shoved under your door! Or maybe something even more, my dear Mr. Taylor! Because there's a limit to what people will take!

MURCHISON: And that goes double, Mr. Taylor, sir.

DALE: One of these days we'll get back not only this town but this whole land of ours out of the hands of the betrayers who are destroying this nation under God!

(DALE *and* MURCHISON *exit.*)

SHIRLEY: So this is Tidewater, New Jersey, where they talk like patriots, but don't care if you're murdered!

DON: Didn't you ask for this violence?

SHIRLEY: *I* did? *(furiously)* That's what I can expect for coming to a place like this! Accused and lied to at every turn — *(indignantly)* If I have to walk every mile on foot to New York City I'll do it, and when I'm there I'll tell every waiter, cop, and bartender about Tidewater and the kind of shows they put on here! *(loudly)* As for you and your screwy family —

DON: Haven't you had enough for one day, Mrs. Crain?

SHIRLEY: You bet I have! I'm going — I wouldn't stay in this dump another minute, not if you begged me on your bended knees!

(She departs in regal disdain.)

RUTH: At least *that's* over!

LARRY *(nursing his bruises)*: That was real boss, Dad, the way you cut down those two buzzards.

DON: You've got to be looked after. You're all bloody.

LARRY: Think nothing of it. My friends got it worse. And there's kids my age who got zapped in the swamps and jungles — the least I can do for them and me is to take a bloody nose.

DON: You still want this show to go on?

LARRY: You don't think we'll close it on account of this beating-up? If that gang thinks they're done with us, they're mistaken. *(With raised fist)* Power to the people!

69

DON: What people? The Tidewaters? The Scorpions will burn this place down to the ground while the town applauds them. There's nothing worse than the cold ferocity of the self-righteous when they're shown a picture of themselves.

RUTH: Yes, that's how it is.

(The light dims. Spot on DON.)

DON: I'm getting old and frightened; the integrity I once had is eroding. In my twenties I held down two jobs at a time, went to night school because I had a dream about the law. In that dream I saw myself in a courtroom with marble columns, where facts and logic were respectfully heard. The time for a rational world hasn't come yet. The tribal drums and rumbling, everybody howling and stamping his feet. Only a crazy man tries to be sane.

(The light returns.)

DON: I'll be at the Town Hall tomorrow to swear out a warrant for those hoods.

LARRY: Good for you, Dad!

DON: Don't cheer! You don't see the consequences.

RUTH: He sees them. So do I. Come home with us, Larry. We'll have supper.

LARRY: I've got to see how my friends are. I'm out of the nest, Mom.

RUTH: Don't say that!

*(*LARRY *exits.)*

He's gone, Donald. He's gone.

DON: You look white and exhausted.

RUTH: I'm all right. I'm sorry you lost Mrs. Crain.

DON: I should have known they don't hand out prizes to people like me. You said let her go, and you were right.

RUTH: You let her go when we couldn't hold her anymore. But we'll live, just the same.

DON: And we'll still own ourselves.

RUTH: Yes!

DON: The Appellate Court decision won't bring in very much, but at least our heads will be above water — we'll still pay the installment on this house, the rent on my office —

RUTH: Don — that phone call this afternoon: it was Jimmy, not a wrong number. It wasn't good news, dear. Some technical points of the law, he said . . . I meant to tell you at a better time, but it's been too great a strain, holding off. Forgive me.

DON *(after a silence)* I'll call Mrs. Crain tomorrow morning. She's an excitable woman, but she has an eye for bargains, and I can be had cheap. There may still be a chance — if I get down on *my* knees.

RUTH: Oh, Don!

DON: I'm not the stuff that heroes are made of. It's going to be tough enough to take on what the landlord, the mortgage company, and the Tidewater rowdies will do, without leaving ourselves any alternative whatever. Do you agree?

RUTH: I must. *(taking his hand)* When we get home, Donald, go fishing. Get into your waders.

DON: Maybe, if *you* feel all right. It's getting dark; the fish will be coming inshore, now . . .

RUTH: You'll be just in time, dear.

(Light fades. Rock recording.)

CURTAIN

CASTING

This play looks like an attempt at family drama, but one that is not likely to find a place in the soap opera department. Don Taylor isn't much of a hero, his wife Ruth is a rather pitiful heroine, and their seventeen-year-old son Larry is pretty insufferable. But in fact *Yes and No* is a cartoon of our America of the sixties, with a focus on the Vietnam War and the generation gap. Mrs. Shirley Crain is its villainess; other villains are the Town Poetess, the Chief of Police, and the Scorpions. Just the same, don't try to direct it as straight burlesque. There is grimness and pathos in it.

RUTH TAYLOR. Eager, friendly, and physically fragile, not yet cured of her enthusiasm for causes.

DON TAYLOR. A loser and knows it.

LARRY TAYLOR. At seventeen, thoroughly mixed up, but if you look hard enough you'll find vitality and even some judgment there. Also he is capable of putting on an act, as he does at his first meeting with Shirley.

SHIRLEY CRAIN. Tough, full of her own opinions, glib and self-pitying, with a violent sense of humor. She could even be played by someone in drag.

MARGIE DALE. The Town Poetess, a vestal of patriotism and a worrybird.

MURCHISON. The Tidewater Police Chief, respected by the town. Impressive and deliberate.

CATHY CLARK. The Tambourine Girl. Quick, reserved, not yet fully experienced in standing up to the "pigs."

JOHN AMBRUSTER. The Ringmaster. A war veteran in his early thirties, seasoned and hard-knuckled.

JUDGE OLROYD. Probably in his sixties, prosperous and relaxed, searching but not intentionally unkind.

ED. Young and businesslike.

SCORPY. A prancing little hoodlum.

AUTHOR'S POSTSCRIPT

I am under no illusion that *Yes and No* will please audiences wholesale. This picture of the erosion of morale in America is not one to celebrate the two hundredth anniversary of American independence. It may not even satisfy those liberals who like to think of their liberalism as "passionate and stirring in its hatred of oppression and its love of the indomitable battlers against tyranny."*

There is no single-minded "indomitable" purpose in any of the leading characters of *Yes and No*: they are, more or less, ordinary citizens. The lawyer, Don Taylor, is a tired radical; he has paid a heavy price for his integrity, which has begun to wear thin. His diminishing clientele and the serious illness of his wife have taught him caution and left him unsatisfied with the virtue that is supposed to be its own reward. Besides, at age fifty-five, he is ashamed at having nothing to show for his professional life. And once entrapped into taking on Mrs. Crain as a client, he begins to lose, rapidly, the little that remains of his earlier defiance of the Establishment. Even when the Establishment is nothing more than that of a backward little beach community.

His wife, Ruth, appears foolishly carried away by the faddism which she has retained from her own period of radical idealism; and she continues to live in her dreams of the "better world in birth," although her life at present is centered on her husband and her son.

If there is any promise of "indomitable" resistance in this story, it is in the vitality of the seventeen-year-old Larry, whose strength is hidden, at his age, by callowness, self-pity, adolescent bravado, and the confused political and philosophical cliches derived from his parents and from his elders in the commune. His sufferings, however, are real enough, and so is his contempt for his parents, a contempt they do not altogether deserve.

The commune, hated by the natives of the town, is openly defiant, but not all its members are free of apprehension. The hostility of the town chief of police and the local poetess is measured by their fear of the unorthodox. Even the fire-eating Mrs. Crain is so unnerved by her experiences that, in the end, she indignantly disclaims having made any threats. Only Scorpy and his little band of vigilantes are confident, untroubled by doubts. Are they the wave of the future?

It is the case of Lieutenant Corby, killer of unarmed Asian villagers, that precipitates the conflict in the Taylor family. Don is not alone in viewing that case as a watershed of American morality. But there is only a very limited discussion of it in forensic style by the

---

* Judy Klemesrud, "Wertmuller: the Foremost Woman Movie Director" (*New York Times*, Feb. 9, 1975).

members of the family. Most of it is conveyed in the crudely partisan amateur show put on by the commune, and in intervals between the scenes of *Yes and No.*

The play comes to no neat conclusion about anything. We are not told what will ultimately happen to the commune or the village of Tidewater. We do not learn if a doctor's prognosis of Ruth's condition will prove correct. Don realizes he must take action, but he worries about the consequences; and he abhors Mrs. Crain but must go on trying to interest her. Between him and Larry there is a reconciliation that is only a papering-over of their differences: Larry's real place, for the time being, at least, is with the commune: he is "out of the nest."

THOUGHTS ON *YES AND NO*

To date, this play has never been staged and has never before been published. It was, however, given a cast reading at SIU under one of its former titles, *Megan's Son.* The views expressed by the student audience were diverse:

The characters are real.
The characters are stupid, grotesque cartoons and I detest them all.
The boy is charming.
The boy doesn't add up and is an insufferable, priggish little bastard.
The Don-Ruth relationship is a moving love story.
The Don-Ruth relationship is a long whimper.
Mrs. Crain is nothing but a comic-strip cartoon.
Mrs. Crain is the realest, most interesting character in the play, a perfect example of a Bircher.[10]

The perceptive Ben Gelman, of *The Daily Southern Illinoisan,* who also attended the reading, wrote afterwards:

The fact that Larry Taylor's parents in *Yes and No* are the revolutionists of another generation rather than conservative types all their lives, makes a special case of the relationship between Larry and his parents — because left-wing types have always been a small minority in this rich country. But at the same time it sharpens the conflict between the age groups, because they are poles apart — at least until the physical clash between the *Peace Ballet* cast and the Establishment's hoodlums.[11]

Robert E. Lee, co-author of *Inherit the Wind* and of many other justly famous scripts, wrote me after reading *Yes and No:*

The men and women of *Yes and No* are clearly flesh and blood. The problem of the aging liberal touches a nerve. I share your passion and disgust over the [Lt. Corby] matter — and I think you have translated it obliquely and expertly to the stage. And you need not apologize for inconclusiveness! I am suspicious of all answers!

From Prof. Van Phillips, Purdue University (West Lafayette, Indiana)

All the people who decide on season read *Yes and No* and a great deal of excitement was generated in it as a possible production.

A discussion of *YES AND NO* followed a reading of the script at a New York apartment in September 1969. I quote from some of the comments, using invented names for the speakers:

Sue: I don't know what the play is about.
I: The basic idea is that it is difficult to be rational in a world that is increasingly insane.

Ralph: I don't see how that is shown. Don is not a good sample of a rational man.

I: Who says Don is rational? In my view he is as crazy as all the other characters. At first he equates idealism with rationality. Finally he tells Larry, "Only a crazy man tries to be sane."

Ralph: The Rodriguez case ought to be the reason why Don changes from idealism to "hiding" and opportunism.

I: Not the reason, only the last straw. Don is so boxed in that he has the simple problem of surviving. The Rodriguez case marks him as desperate.

Ralph: Shirley Crain ought to have a demand that will destroy him.

I: I fully agree. And it is already in the play.

Ralph: I don't see how the audience can feel sympathy for Don.

I: I was told the same thing about Vern in *Rainbow Terrace*. I don't accept that criticism. The audience will both like and dislike him. The same with Larry.

Ellen: I am entirely for Larry, in spite of his faults.

Everybody: Yes.

Lucy: That is what is so good about this play. It sees people as they are, good and bad at the same time.

Ralph: We ought to know what made Larry rebellious between thirteen and seventeen.

Ken: Why must we know everything?

I: I don't know why, and a whole set of psychoanalysts may never find out. At adolescence sex arrives and a lot of things begin to follow. The "girl with the tambourine" is a beatnik like Larry; she loves him in her perverse, impatient way, calls him "little lost boy."

From Dr. Louis E. Roberts, University of Massachusetts (Boston):

Yes and No — the title has the spirit of a dramatized lament. The phrase is used several times. I hear it as a satiric song — rock — a beating refrain throughout much of the play. Don is dramatically appealing because his strength lies in his weakness. He bears an untragic, unimportant futility about him that makes him a challenging and workable character. He and Larry deserve each other, as most fathers and sons do. I like *The Peace Ballet* very much and think it could be a focal point of the show, maybe mingling its refrains with yes-and-no. Every Tidewater has its projections work well as climactic counterpoint to the middle class throughout. It is a sad ballad, but it is funny, too. Heavy direction will kill it. I see more human comedy, more Brecht than Odets.

To Louis Roberts:

"You are correct about the differing levels of reality in *Yes and No*. Every character in the story is hung up in some way. Shirley is the most violent, next to the Scorpions. Saddest is Don, whose trouble is that he tries to keep sane. And I agree with you about Murchison and Dale: they are more remote than they are vicious — mildewed leftovers of the past."

From Gil Lazier, Florida State University (Tallahassee).

I especially enjoyed *The Peace Ballet* in *Yes and No*. It is evocative, theatrically exciting, and very potent. It enriches the play.

The motivations and interactions of the Taylors, the way they express their reactions to the world, ring true. And the situation in which they find themselves is plausible.

On the other hand I had trouble with some of the less developed way I found Margie Dale, Murchison, and to a certain extent Shirley Crain, too blunt and direct in revealing their true opinions. I am not questioning that such people exist. But their expressions are too direct at times in revealing their prejudices for my tastes. My suggestion is that you make these characters a little smarter, a little more diplomatic, while preserving their basic values.

To Dr. Lazier: You are not the only reader of *Y&N* who has been repelled by some — or all — of its characters. Not long ago I left a copy of *Y&N* with the chairman of the theatre department of a California university after seeing his excellent production of *The Three-Penny Opera*. My script was returned with the following comment:

I am not sufficiently arrested by *Yes and No* to commit it to production here. It is good, solid drama, but I am not compelled by the characters. The villains particularly — for me what is most egregious about such people is their talent at being ingratiating. Or worse, inspirational.

I: A competent director is well aware that starting work on a script without fully recognizing its atmosphere, ambience, point of view — in short, it style — is off on the wrong foot. In the case of a play that has already been successfully produced, not only once but many times, its style has long since been evaluated. Brecht's *Threepenny Opera* (1928) is a cheerfully satirical inversion of capitalism, with funny mobsters and cheap whores in it, and a stylishly romantic crook like Macheath as its protagonist.

The humor of *Yes and No* is more abrasive than the genial burlesque of the *Opera*. If its style must be listed as a fault, the fault lies
in the nature of its material. Following the bestiality of World War II,
Hiroshima and the Holocaust, it is no longer possible to write with the
good-natured kidding of Brecht's masterpiece.

Yes and No is funny but it is not easy-going funny. The members
of the commune are outsiders whose way of life unsettles the little town
of Tidewater, while Don Taylor, his wife, Ruth, and their unpredictable
son, Larry, are soulsearching innocents who run into an opposition as
brutal as a concrete wall.

Nor do I agree that the "villains" are one-dimensional. Mrs. Crain,
the Chief of Police, the Town Poetess, are mildewed clowns, and must be
played as such; and Scorpy is a prancing little kook who goes in for
machismo to make himself feel superior.

Shirley Crain, in particular, has been singled out for criticism.
"She is too powerful for the other characters," observes one playreader.
But she is as foolishly confused and self-pitying as she is vicious, no
less a "lifelike" than many of the other crazies we meet in the
newspapers or next door. (Her line about "a little lead in the head"
comes straight from the Governor of a southern state.)

The world is overflowing with aggressive and opinionated Shirleys;
they cannot be ignored, and I think they lend themselves to the sort of
portrayal that can be appreciated by a general audience.

Too often a playreader, especially a humorless one, fails to notice
the *style* in which a play takes on life. Reading a play automatically in
terms of "realism" can do violence to its whole meaning and structure.

What is said in a play — or anywhere else — depends on the intention or circumstances behind it. An identical combination of words in a
sentence or phrase can be joyous, ominous, casual, depressing, stern,
flighty, savage, hilarious, wise, foolish, crazy or challenging, or it may
have any of a thousand and one other implications. Stanislavsky's
well-known principle of the *subtext* is just as true of the quality of a
whole play as of any line in its dialog. The plays in this book contain
elements of tragedy and of farce; some of them have even been called
"disturbing." Essentially they are *ironic tragi-comedies*; to view them in
terms of simple naturalism is to distort them.

The ability to misread a whole script, when not due to incompetence,
depends on a reader's pattern of thought, which may be miles removed
from that of the author. After translating Frisch's *The Firebugs* I tried
to find someone to produce it. It was not easy going, but at last one
possible backer turned up who told me with enthusiasm how much this
fine tragedy impressed him.

It isn't a tragedy, I told him, "It's a sardonic fable."

That ended his interest in *The Firebugs* and my interest in him.

As an associate member of the Actors' Studio in New York, I was permitted to direct several scenes of the Frisch play as a tryout. The performance, with the marvelously gifted Zero Mostel in the lead as Biedermann, surprised some of the audience of stage professionals who watched it. Accustomed to the method of Stanislavsky, they were fascinated by the play and performance — "unlike anything I ever saw before, "as Geraldine Page described it. But it bothered others, who found its story unreal. (How could all those barrels of gasoline have been brought up to Biedermann's attic with no one noticing?)

Lee Strasberg, as usual, was the adjudicator of the performance. Since he was the foremost U.S. advocate of Stanislavsky I had reason to dread what he would say. Instead he not only took the play in his stride but proceeded to give the Studio members a brief introduction to commedia and vaudeville. "There is a stage category," he said, "that is not naturalism but is infused with the life of the stage itself." He gave as an example a juggler captivating an audience with dexterity alone.

(Curiously, *The Firebugs*, my translation-adaptation of Max Frisch's *Biedermann Und Die Brandstifter*, which failed at least three times when put on in New York, has received 548 productions in the U.S. to date.)

ANDRUS, 22

ANDRUS, OR THE VISION

1970-1979

A Fable of the Middle Ages

*Spunteranno le ali.**

— Leonardo da Vinci

*There shall be wings.

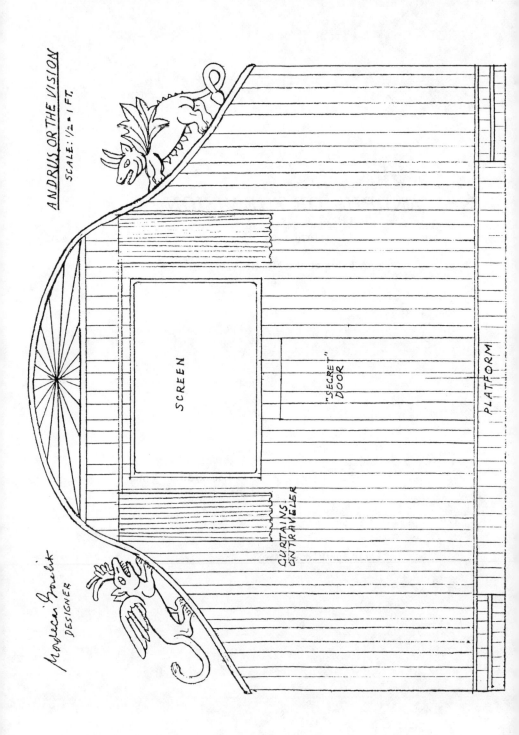

ANDRUS OR THE VISION

SCALE: ½ = 1 FT.

SCREEN

"SECRET" DOOR

CURTAINS ON TRAVELER

PLATFORM

Mordecai Gorelik
DESIGNER

A day-dream of someone of the Middle Ages suddenly confronted by today's world stirred my boyhood imagination. This fantasy finally became the dramatic image of *Andrus, or the Vision*, but it was not until the play was actually staged that I guessed why the idea had haunted me ever since I could remember. I was born in Tsarist Russia, in the prairie village of Shchedrin, in the province of Minsk.[12] This little ghetto town, or *stetl*, surrounded by pine and birch forests, with its rutted roads, well-sweeps, log-hut barns and outhouses, its oil lamps and wood-burning ovens, was founded in 1842; it would not have looked very different seven centuries earlier. For someone like myself, transported as a child to the city of New York, the experience must have been like stepping straight from the 13th Century into the 20th.

So far, *Andrus, or the Vision* is the only one of my plays that has had two productions, one in Kansas, one in Oklahoma. It is also noteworthy for receiving no reviews in the local press each time — perhaps because the orthodox members of our two leading faiths, the church and science, could both have found it disquieting.[13] I am not religionist, and while I have a very great admiration for science, I do not ignore its dangers. Modern science has performed miracles in preserving life, but its misuse has also created machines for destroying life wholesale — capable, in fact, of ending all existence on this planet in just a few minutes. I do not consider *Andrus* to be anti-scientific; it only warns that science must not be used for evil purposes.

83

OUTLINE

Europe, thirteenth century. Belial, the demon of unbelief and secular knowledge, inherits Andrus as a son by contract with Andrus's father, an alchemist, in return for a promise to keep Andrus from being "entrapped by the faith in God." Andrus, grown up, is a coal-miner, a devout Christian, a non-thinker and ridiculously honest. To pry him out of his religious faith, the demon sends him visions of a future Paradise created by man himself. These visions, which give Andrus a sense of joyous hope, are hailed by his fellow-miners as a sign of the second coming of Jesus, descending to take Christianity away from the Roman Pope. Alarmed, the Inquisition orders Andrus to renounce his visions or be burned alive. He remains unshaken until a final vision, a nightmare of future violence, fills him with horror. Recanting, he is sentenced, as a penitent, to spend the rest of his life in prison — a fate from which he is rescued when Belial arms the miners. The demon has found Andrus no bargain. He takes away the gift of vision, leaving Andrus to "the comfort of his orthodox superstitions."

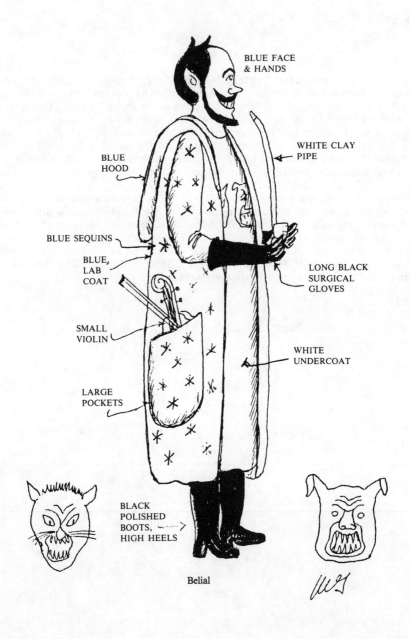

BLUE FACE
& HANDS

WHITE CLAY
PIPE

BLUE
HOOD

BLUE SEQUINS

BLUE,
LAB
COAT

LONG BLACK
SURGICAL
GLOVES

SMALL
VIOLIN

WHITE
UNDERCOAT

LARGE
POCKETS

BLACK
POLISHED
BOOTS,
HIGH HEELS

Belial

CHARACTERS

Andrus (*at fourteen*)
Andrus (*at twenty-two*)
Belial, the Demon
Carla, *Andrus's sister*
Ludwig, *a young lout*
Janette, *andrus's wife*
Mattias ⎫
Ignace ⎬ *coal miners*
Anselm ⎭
Father Jerome
Father Simon
A Notary
Captain Bernard
Duke Roderick
Guards
Miners

CARLA

ACT I

Scene 1

Stage light fades. Europe, thirteenth century, the town of Marienburg. Indication of an alchemist's laboratory. A small cot in the foreground. ANDRUS, at the age of fourteen, is sitting up in bed, his attention concentrated on the door, upstage. The door is closed except for a crack, out of which light spills. Silence. Then ANDRUS gets stealthily out of bed, tiptoes to the door, peers in. He stifles a cry as he backs away, covering his face with his hands as though blinded. Suddenly a figure, robed and hooded, steps into the room out of a blaze of fire and smoke. THE FIGURE advances toward ANDRUS, who retreats from him in horror.

THE FIGURE: Do not run away from me, Andrus, my son.

ANDRUS (*terrified*): Who are you? The Heresiarch? The Anti-Christ?

THE FIGURE: My name is Belial.

(*He throws off his hood and opens his cloak, revealing himself as the Demon, blue and sparkling from head to foot. He has a pleasant face with deep-set eyes, and two more faces in his chest. The extra faces are those of a snarling cat and a panting dog.*)

(*Blackout.*)

Scene 2

A light picks up BELIAL, center stage. He has closed his robe, but has not put back his hood. He speaks to the audience in a voice that is crisp and authoritative.

BELIAL: You all know me: Belial, the eternal enemy of the so-called True Faith. I am not pleased at Andrus's refusal to accept me; but then, Gregor, his father, never told him he is mine. . . . Besides, the boy is in a state of shock after looking into his parents' room, for there he saw that his father had cut open the dead body of his mother. (*Pause*) His father has always had my affection and regard, from the beginning, as a small boy. Gregor was inquisitive by nature. When other boys tore off the wings of houseflies, he did, too, but not out of idleness or malice. Even then he had a notebook. One like this. (*Shows it.*)

He noted the puzzled behavior of the fly, which he afterwards placed gently in a spider's web, carefully noting the maneuvers of the spider. A few years later, while other boys played games, he roamed the countryside, taking his notebook with him, making

observations of every tree, bush, and flower, every animal, bird, reptile, and insect. It was Gregor who dug into a hillside with his spade and pick, and there found the remains of shellfish and insects dead a million years before. It made him think hard about the six-day schedule of Genesis . . . . He managed to have himself apprenticed to an alchemist, and in time became an alchemist himself, engaged, unsuccessfully, in trying to transmute the strange base metal, mercury, into gold. But that was only one of his experiments; he began to work on a certain noxious powder that . . . I can't tell you any more about it — it is top secret.
(*Puts away the notebook.*)
I told you Andrus belongs to me. He does. He became my property by contract. This contract. (*He shows it.*) Written in Gregor's blood by Gregor himself when he summoned me to the bedside of his dying wife. No, it was not to save his wife or himself that he gave me the gift of his son — he knew that was beyond my power. He asked only for my help in keeping his son true to the heretical Faith in Man, to keep the boy from being entrapped by the Faith in God. I agreed, of course, to do my best, although I had serious doubts whether Andrus would prove to be a bargain. A non-thinker, and ridiculously honest! (*angrily*) And so it has turned out! He's a reaction against everything that was admirable in his father!

(*Spotlight reveals ANDRUS kneeling, telling his beads. It is eight years later and ANDRUS, at the age of twenty-two, is wrapped up in his meekness like a grub in a cocoon. Dirty, emaciated, ragged, and resigned, he has his mind fixed on the reward in Heaven promised him by the Gospel of the True Faith.*)

BELIAL (*as ANDRUS vanishes*): Always on his knees! If something isn't done about him, that contract I showed you won't be worth the blood it was written in!

(*Blackout.*)

Scene 3

A war-ravaged hut, Trimar. It has a door of rough boards, a shuttered, unglazed window, a makeshift, broken-down bed, a rickety table and some stools. The place is empty, but after an instant the door is opened tentatively from outside. CARLA peers in, then sidles into the room, followed by LUDWIG. CARLA is pretty and appealing, but wan, dirty, ragged, barefoot — and obviously pregnant. LUDWIG is a town hoodlum.

CARLA: Go away, you lout! You ought to be ashamed, following me into my brother's house!

LUDWIG: Nobody's here, can't you see? (*easily*) I know Andrus, and his wife, too. They work in the mines. They won't be here before dark.

CARLA: And what's more, in my condition —

LUDWIG: I love big bellies. Why did you roll your eyes at me if you didn't want me?

CARLA: Because I couldn't help it. It comes over me any time I see a man — any man — even a thing like you!

LUDWIG: This is my lucky day! A bitch in heat!

(*He presses against her.*)

CARLA (*sullenly*): What will you give me?

LUDWIG (*shoving her toward the bed*): Get in there, draggle-tail, and I'll give you all you can take — up your rear end.

(*The room darkens out as they thrash under the bed-cover.* BELIAL *appears. Unseen by those in the room, he walks toward the bed, considers what is going on, then moves off to the side of the pro-scenium, where he resumes his speech to the audience.*)

BELIAL: An enjoyable exercise, invented by the Lord thy God Himself. Bestial but enjoyable. Andrus's sister Carla is sixteen. She's spent a good part of her life tramping the roads, and starving. After his father was arrested and Andrus was ordered to wear the yellow crosses on his clothes, she lost all her young friends. In fact she was left with no friends at all until she reached the age of thirteen and discovered sex. After that, she no longer lacked for temporary playmates, with whom she played when no one was looking.

Something told her it would be better not to let Andrus or Janette know about those fondlings and cuddlings. Instead she developed a secret self-reproach of sin and disgrace, and became irritable and insolent. Her moods were resented by Janette, if not by Andrus. When Janette began to question her, she simply disappeared and could not be found. She was given up for dead, like so many other waifs and strays of the endless roads.

Now, with her sinful misery, her belly, and her compulsive appetite for fornication, she is returning to the only shelter she can think of — her brother's shanty. (*Pause*)

If Andrus can be changed — if there is any chance of prying him out of that pious chastity of his — the time is now. Get ready with your Christian charity, my son Andrus!

(BELIAL *disappears, and the light rises dimly in the room as* ANDRUS *and* JANETTE *come to the door.* ANDRUS *holds a lamp.*)

JANETTE: Someone is here!
>   (ANDRUS *raises his lamp.*)
>   There's someone in the bed!

(LUDWIG *gets out of the bed, hitching up his pants. He walks indolently past* JANETTE *and* ANDRUS, *and exits.*)

JANETTE: There's someone else!

ANDRUS (*pulling back the bed cover*): It's Carla! Carla is back!

>   (CARLA *sits up in the bed with knees drawn up, trembling.*)

JANETTE: Who was with you?

CARLA: Nobody. Nobody was with me.

JANETTE: Stupid liar!

ANDRUS: She's back after two years!

CARLA: And no welcome . . .

JANETTE: Who invited you to come back, you dirty little slut?

ANDRUS: Stop it. Janette!

JANETTE: Soiling our bed!
>   (CARLA *starts to cry.* JANETTE *slaps her.*)
>   Out of the bed!
>   (JANETTE *drags her out by the hair.*)

ANDRUS: Janette, she's just a child!

JANETTE: Old enough to crawl under the covers with anyone in pants!
That's how she was, and that's how she is! Look at that belly!

>   (CARLA *cowers against the wall.*)

ANDRUS: Let her alone!

(*He tries to intervene.* JANETTE *throws him off.*)

CARLA (*whimpering*): I'll never do it again.

JANETTE (*to* ANDRUS): "I'll never do it again!" How many times did
we hear that, before she finally disappeared — and good riddance!
She told you lies about me — she told me lies about you — tried to
drive us apart —

ANDRUS: Can't you see you're being as un-Christian as the neighbors?
Treating her the way they've treated us — with no understanding or
forgiveness —

JANETTE (*wildly*): The neighbors had no reason to treat us the way they
have. We have good reason to be rid of her! Not only her
mischief! Another mouth to feed, when we can't feed ourselves —

ANDRUS: She'll go to work.

JANETTE: Where? There's only the mines. What will she do there with her swollen belly? That's why she came back! So we will take care of her — and look after that brat of hers, too, when it gets here!

ANDRUS: She's managed by herself up to now.

JANETTE: By spreading her legs under every Tom, Dick, and Harry! That dog's son who just walked past us is going to make it known all over: we're a whorehouse! Is that what you'd like?

ANDRUS (*faintly*): No.

JANETTE: Then don't talk like a ninny! By tomorrow afternoon every clod in town — and his father and his uncle — will know they can line up outside this door, ready to be served! (*savagely*) There is no room in this house for both her and me! If she stays, I leave! (*Tears spring to her eyes.*) She or I! Make up your mind, you — Christian!

(*Blackout. Spotlight again picks up* BELIAL *at the proscenium.*)

BELIAL: That was a month ago. After Carla was thrown out of the house, Andrus could not sleep because of the thoughts that gnawed at his conscience and oppressed his mind. Thoughts not only of his sister, but of the whole world's helplessness, callousness, and sin. He felt despair, and not only his own despair: suffering was visible in the drawn faces of his neighbors, in the hunched shoulders of the laborers in the mines . . . (*briefly*) Today, at work, he suddenly felt exhausted. Before the day was over, he came home, alone.

(*The hut, in a very dim light, as* ANDRUS *opens the door. He staggers back in horror.* CARLA's *body is hanging from a roof beam. Blackout, except for a spotlight on* BELIAL.)

BELIAL: It will take weeks before he can work again. Then he will be ready for his first vision.

(*Spotlight off.*)

Scene 4

A tunnel in a coal mine, dimly lit, narrow, and lower than head height. ANDRUS, *his wife* JANETTE, MATTIAS, *and other* MINERS, *including children, are at work. All are black with coal dust.* MATTIAS, *a giant of a man, wielding a pick, dislodges a heavy block of coal, which* ANDRUS *smashes with a sledge hammer.* JANETTE *picks up the pieces in a basket. As* ANDRUS *bears down with his hammer for the second time, he lurches forward and falls. The others, alarmed, drop their tools and run toward him. Blackout.*

TOWARD A LARGER THEATRE

FIRST VISION

A film documentary shows travelers at an airport desk, then going out to a plane, which they enter. Interior: hostesses show them to their seats. Exterior: the plane takes off.

(*Blackout.*)

Scene 5

The tunnel. JANETTE *is on her knees beside* ANDRUS. *The other* MINERS *crowd around them,* MATTIAS *holding up a lamp.*

JANETTE (*frightened*): Andrus!

IGNACE: It be the falling sickness!

ANSELM (*terrified*): Nay, the coal-damp!

MATTIAS: Neither. His face is calm, and the air whistles chill through the tunnel. Stand away!

ANSELM: He wakes!

(ANDRUS *struggles to sit up.*)

JANETTE: What overcame you, my husband? (*She puts her hand to his heart.*) Are you ill?

ANDRUS: I am very well. A vision passed before my eyes — a fair vision.

IGNACE: A dream?

ANDRUS: A vision! A great concourse of people in fine clothing, in a room of tremendous size, shining with light from above. The people carried strange bundles, like boxes, and they formed lines before very long tables attended by clerks with whom they spoke, in speech like ours, but with many strange words . . .

IGNACE: So many rich people, all of the nobility? Princes, merchants and coal-masters?

ANDRUS: No, no! Ordinary people — men, women, children —

MATTIAS: Go on, Andrus!

ANDRUS: They passed through doors that opened of themselves, and came to a field of great white ships —

ANSELM: Ships, on land?

IGNACE: In a dream anything can be.

94

ANDRUS: I followed the people into one of the ships. Inside, there were seats arranged in rows, and beautiful young women helped everyone to be seated. Then came a sound of thundering, the ship rolled over the ground —

MATTIAS: Into water?

ANDRUS: Into the sky!

(There are cries of astonishment.)

MATTIAS: The ship flew?

ANDRUS: Into the sky!

IGNACE: A strange vision indeed! Where was this sailing into the sky that thou sawest?

ANDRUS: In the future.

IGNACE: In what future? *(harshly)* When will it be, this Paradise, when people will fly like the holy angels?

ANDRUS: I do not know, but I have seen it.

IGNACE: If wishes were horses —

MATTIAS: Silence, thou! This be no dream! It be the sign, surely!

ANSELM: The sign?

MATTIAS *(violently)*: Of the day of the Redeemer at hand! When we and our children shall not hunger and go in rags! When the masters shall not ride on our backs or the priests leave us in ignorance while we die of starvation, plagues, and war! We shall be witnesses of the Second Coming of Jesus and the days of miracles: people shall no more be as sick worms crawling on the ground or under it! People shall fly! *(in a thunderous voice)* I say amen!

IGNACE *(awed)*: Then I say so, too. Amen!

MATTIAS *(ecstatically)*: He comes who is the first and the last! With his sharp sword of two edges! With his hair white as snow! With his eyes as a flame of fire!

(All except JANETTE)
Amen!

(A piercing whistle is heard. All quickly return to their work.)

JANETTE: Andrus, I am afraid.

(Blackout. BELIAL reappears in a red spotlight. He is thoughtful as he takes out a long clay pipe and stuffs it with tobacco.)

95

BELIAL: Andrus was fourteen, his sister Carla no more than eight, on the night when the bailiffs, on orders from the Inquisition, came for Gregor. (*With a click of his fingers he produces a flame with which he lights his pipe.*)

A very persistent type, Gregor. Months earlier, when the plague struck, and when, each morning, the carts came to collect the dead, he would inspect the bodies thoughtfully. He went from house to house, talking with the sick and dying, asking about their symptoms and the remedies they had tried. He himself became ill, but he did not pause in his inquiries. Everyone told him the plague was caused by the accursed Jews, who had poisoned the wells at the behest of Satan. Led by his perverse curiosity, he traveled to the nearest ghetto, where he learned that the Jews, too, were dying — no doubt because their crude conspiracy had miscarried.

(He pulls up a stool and sits.)

He filled several bottles with water drawn from wells in various neighborhoods, and staggered home with them. Through a glass of his own invention he examined minutely every specimen of the well-water, but found nothing unusual in any of them.

Meanwhile, with trembling fingers he noted, daily, the increasing virulence of his own illness and that of his wife, Andrus's mother, who was showing the familiar symptoms and was worsening even more rapidly than himself.

He had learned, in the course of his research, that the most reliable remedy against the plague, though its usefulness could not be assured, was a mixture of snail's blood, the testicles of a he-goat, barley, and the early-morning bowel movement of an orphan, all well compounded and seasoned with salt, vinegar, and hot pepper. After some hesitation he applied this remedy, and was not surprised when it made him throw up and turn sicker than before. There was nothing left for him but bloodletting — a task with which his wife could not help him, for she now lay dead. He managed, by himself, to fill a quart jar with the blood from one of his veins. This left him feeling extremely weak but still with no change for the better . . . . Just the same he went on, even more relentlessly, with his experiments. I can tell you that he finally began to recover, although being obliged to swallow boiling oil while undergoing torture in prison, did not prove beneficial.

(He becomes attentive.)

I can look back and see the three men who are entering Gregor's laboratory to arrest him on a charge of desecrating a human body. His illness, and the death of his wife, has unhinged him, destroying the balanced mind with which he had interviewed those who were dying. He was determined to find the source of the plague — some elusive little animal, perhaps, that dried up the organs of the body of his wife. He found nothing.

(BELIAL *rises and taps out his pipe against the stool on which he has been sitting. The stool blazes up.*)

I see the bailiffs leading him out, now, as little Andrus looks on, terrified. Gregor's active mind was bound to lead him, sooner or later, straight into disaster. And not only Gregor. His children as well.

(*Blackout.*)

Scene 6

The hut. It is raining, outside, and the rain drives through the roof and walls. The parish priest, JEROME, *is quizzing* JANETTE. JANETTE *is toilworn, her face and hands seamed with black grime.*

JEROME: You are new to this parish.

JANETTE: Yes, father.

JEROME: It is not the town's wealthy district. My parishioners are plowmen or coal miners.

JANETTE: Yes, father. My husband, Andrus, and I both work in the mines. Andrus is strong; he breaks up blocks of coal with his sledgehammer. I collect the pieces and throw them into a basket.

JEROME: Have you children?

JANETTE: We had a little girl, Giselle. She died.

JEROME: Do not grieve, my daughter.

JANETTE: She was an innocent child, not two years old. She died in my arms, on the road.

JEROME: You must not go on mourning. She is with the Heavenly Father.

JANETTE: Yes. Now we are alone in the world, Andrus and I. Andrus had a sister, Carla, who came with us on the way here —

JEROME: On the way from where?

JANETTE: From Marienburg, where Andrus was born. We had to leave there when the war broke out. Our cow and chickens were stolen and slaughtered by our own troops. We protested to the army chaplain, and when the soldiers heard that we had complained, they threw us out of our cottage.

JEROME: Such are the hardships of war.

JANETTE: We joined the other refugees on the roads. From one town to the next. Sometimes we found work, but not often; then we again took to the roads. Most of the time we starved.

JEROME: Your history is not unusual in wartime.

JANETTE: The war never seems to end.

JEROME: It starts and stops, and new wars arise. Some wars are Godless, but not this one. Our Duke Roderick is waging a just war, in spite of anything you may hear.

JANETTE: Yes, father.

JEROME: Certain malicious outsiders, who come here from other towns, are inflaming our population, saying the war is causing all their hardships — as if their sins had nothing to do with their plight. What brought you and your husband here?

JANETTE: We came because we heard there is work underground, in the mines. And we found this war-ruined cottage, which the owners had abandoned.

JEROME: Why did your child die?

JANETTE: One day she closed her eyes and never opened them again.

JEROME: And your sister-in-law?

JANETTE: Died, too.

JEROME: Be comforted, my daughter.

(ANDRUS *enters, with a gust of rain. His face, hands, and clothes are black with coal dust.*)

JANETTE: Andrus, the good father of the parish is visiting us. Father Jerome.

ANDRUS: I ask your blessing, father.

(ANDRUS *kneels.* JEROME *makes the sign of the cross over him.*)

JEROME: *In nomine Patris et Filii et Spiritus Sancti* . . . Be seated, my son.

ANDRUS: Thank you, father.

JEROME: My son, do you have a sickness?

JANETTE (*quickly*): Oh no, father, he is well and strong.

JEROME: Some of my flock have told me he has spells of illness.

JANETTE: What do they say?

JEROME: They say your husband sometimes falls down and stares into distant space.

ANDRUS: That seldom happens.

98

JEROME: They say you rave about unheard-of things. They say you see visions.

ANDRUS: That is true, father.

JANETTE: Just dreams, when his thoughts carry him away.

JEROME: Frightening dreams?

ANDRUS: No, no, not frightening, and almost always the same dream.

JEROME: Indeed? And what is the dream about?

JANETTE: It is nonsense, like all dreams.

ANDRUS: The father is asking me, Janette, not you. I see people flying.

JEROME: Flying?

ANDRUS: Peacefully and happily.

JEROME: People, flying?

ANDRUS: Yes, father. People like us. And I, too, feel happy as long as the vision lasts.

JEROME: Why does that vision make you feel good?

ANDRUS: Because those people do not crawl underground breaking out coal. I have a revelation of people who have good food and good clothes, and who fly.

JEROME: People!

ANDRUS: Yes, father. (*ecstatically*) People who fly!

JEROME: Not angels?

ANDRUS: No, father, people like you and me.

JEROME: What sort of wings do they have?

ANDRUS: They do not have wings.

JEROME: Then how do they fly?

ANDRUS: They go into something like a ship but that is also like a great bird.

JEROME: All that is very interesting.

ANDRUS: Yes, father.

JEROME (*bursting out*): Most interesting! The angels of Heaven fly! Not the miserable sinners of this earth! Your revelations are those of the devil!

ANDRUS: No, no! Surely not!

JEROME (*taking hold of* ANDRUS's *shirt*): And here is proof! On this shirt I see the faded outlines of two yellow crosses.
(ANDRUS *gets up, alarmed.*)
Those visions of yours must be reported.

JANETTE (*anguished*): Father Jerome!
(JEROME *stalks out.*)
Andrus, you talk too much!

ANDRUS: What did I say? Only that some day men will fly.

JANETTE: Some day? Were you deaf, my husband, when Mattias shouted that the day of miracles is at hand? Not some day! Now!

ANDRUS: Janette, you must allow for the wildness of people like Mattias, who have never known anything but working underground. More than all others they deserve our compassion.

(*Blackout*)

Scene 7

A room in the local Holy Office. A large crucifix hangs on the wall. FATHER SIMON *and* FATHER JEROME *are conducting a formal examination of* JANETTE. FATHER SIMON *is an elderly Dominican monk, a member of the Inquisition. A* GUARD *remains in the background.*

SIMON: No, it is not easy to work underground. I can see, my daughter, how the black dust of the coal has eaten into your face and hands, yours and those of Andrus, your husband. And you are lucky if the coal-damp does not come and strangle you while you work.

JEROME: It was ordained that man must earn his bread by the sweat of his brow.

SIMON: Father Jerome, some work is easier than other work. Unlike the miner and the plowman, neither you nor I work by the sweat of our brows. And in the case of coal miners it often happens that the coal dust enters and cakes the lungs, making it hard to breathe and causing premature death. (*To* JANETTE.) Tell us, my daughter, the circumstances of the death of your dear sister-inlaw.

JEROME (*to* SIMON): Let her tell us exactly, holding nothing back. A messenger has been sent to Marienburg for the report of what happened there. The report from the Marienburg office of our Holy Inquisition will be compared with her own; therefore it will be best for her to give us the facts simply and completely.

JANETTE: Reverend fathers, I will tell nothing but the plain truth. (*She sobs.*)

SIMON: Compose yourself, my daughter.

100

JANETTE (*after a moment*): Father, I have sworn on the Bible, I have repeated the catechism. We are orthodox — my husband, especially —

SIMON (*gently*): It is not permitted for a wife to testify in favor of her husband . . . . Continue.

JANETTE: With the times as hard as they are, we were greatly burdened — all the more because Andrus wore the yellow crosses of penitence on account of his father. People chased us away when we begged for work or bread; they set their dogs on us, their children threw stones —

SIMON: You must realize that the sufferings of your neighbors incite them to cruelty. They, too, labor under privation and are left with little charity in their hearts for others. They are not aware of their own wickedness. Our Lord said, "Father, forgive them, for they know not what they do."

JEROME (*with some impatience*): Brother Simon, you were asking about Carla.

JANETTE (*in a low voice*): She dreamt of finding a husband and having children, but no reputable young man, seeing the crosses her brother wore, would go near her. At last she gave herself to the devil. She wandered away from us and turned into a harlot lost to all shame.

JEROME: Accursed and damned, and responsible for the damnation of those who had lewd intercourse with her.

JANETTE: She had moments of repentance. In the end she was found hanging from a roof beam.

SIMON: Many times damned, poor girl! Her soul extinguished forever.

JEROME: Driven forever from God's mercy. What excuse is there for the destruction of His handiwork?

SIMON: Brother Jerome, let us remember that there are others who also destroy God's handiwork, yet are granted God's mercy. I speak of those who make use of weapons of war.

JEROME: In the line of their duty.

SIMON: True. And often they are made to kill at the command of unscrupulous seigneurs.

JEROME (*sharply*): Brother Simon, do you speak of our Duke Roderick?

SIMON: I speak of no one in particular.

JEROME (*abruptly, changing the subject*): Brother Simon, there are certain questions that remain to be asked of this woman. If you will allow me —

SIMON: You have my permission.

JEROME: Very well. Sister Janette, you must know that sometimes there are swearers who come to us with rumors and accusations which afterward prove to be groundless. All such testimony is suspect, for it may be caused by envy or malice. Thus the testimony of a wife is all the more valuable in establishing the truth. Do you understand?

JANETTE: Yes, as long as it is not favorable to the husband.

JEROME: Precisely. Tell us, now: is it not true that Gregor, the father of your husband, Andrus, was a necromancer?

JANETTE: A necromancer?

JEROME: One who practices the black arts, including traffic with the dead.

JANETTE: I know nothing for certain about Andrus's father.

JEROME: But you must have asked your husband why he was obliged to wear the yellow crosses?

JANETTE: He never wished to talk about his father.

JEROME: Was it not because his father had relations with the emissaries of Satan?

JANETTE: I know nothing about that.

JEROME: I think you *do* know. Surely it had come to your ears that the infamous Gregor, the father of your husband, was tried by our Holy Office? And that he was imprisoned as a contumacious heretic?

JANETTE (*faintly*): I heard rumors that he was accused.

JEROME: He was accused and tried, and his offense was proven.

SIMON (*interrupting*): I must correct that impression, Brother Jerome. I believe our records show that Gregor died before his formal trial.

JEROME: We shall know, soon, if that is so. I await the messenger, sent posthaste to Marienburg, for the original records.

JANETTE: Yes, father.

JEROME: Sister Janette, would you have us believe you know nothing of the wild fabrications that are spreading in this town?

JANETTE: For what cause, father?

JEROME: Do not dissemble! Because of the visions so glibly described by your husband! It is claimed by a conspiracy of miners that our Lord Jesus is about to descend to earth in order to disavow His own Church and to bid men rise against their natural masters!

JANETTE: Believe me, Father Jerome, my husband Andrus had no such intention.

JEROME: I warn you for the second time that you are not to favor your husband!

SIMON: The witness is overstrained, Brother Jerome.

JEROME: She must remain for the confrontation. (*To the* GUARD) Next witness.

GUARD: Yes, sir. (*Exits.*)

SIMON: Sister Janette, we know you are heavy of heart and sorely afflicted because of your misfortunes. Consider your duty. And take counsel of the Son of God, who suffered for us all: let Him be always with you. Above all, beware of those who pretend to sympathize with you in order to mislead you from your Faith.

JANETTE: Yes, father, I am content in Jesus.

(JANETTE *is obviously alarmed as the* GUARD *enters with* ANSELM.)

JEROME (*to* ANSELM): Do you know this woman?

ANSELM (*reluctantly*): She is the wife of Andrus.

JEROME (*to* JANETTE): Do you know this man?

JANETTE: He is a coal miner.

JEROME: Who has worked with you and Andrus.

JANETTE: Yes.

JEROME (*to* ANSELM): Repeat before this woman the testimony which you have given to Father Simon and myself.

ANSELM (*after a moment*): Your Reverence, I —

JEROME: You heard a denunciation of our Mother Church, did you not? And you came before us of your own free will to tell of a conspiracy of the miners. Did you not describe that criminal conspiracy and its origin? Yet now you are tongue-tied! (*curtly*) Was your testimony a lie? If it was, there is a cure for such lying.

ANSELM (*frightened*): I told what I saw . . .

JEROME: Yes, and heard! But you have not yet named the leader of this Godless revolt. Name him!

ANSELM: Sometimes one, sometimes another . . .

JEROME: This vagueness will not do.

SIMON: My son, no one ordered you to testify. You came to us yourself, to offer your help.

ANSELM (*miserably*): It is as I said, sometimes one, sometimes another . . .

JANETTE (*taking heart*): Tell them, Anselm, so I can hear you!

ANSELM: I feared for the Church, and they threatened me. With horrible swearing.

JANETTE: Who threatened you? Did my husband ever threaten you?

(ANSELM *is silent.*)

Would my husband ever harm anyone?

JEROME (*to* JANETTE): That will do! You are not in charge here! (*To* SIMON) This man did not know he would be confronted. Now he pretends to be an idiot. (*To the* GUARD) This witness is to be held until he is enabled to recover his wits. And make certain no one speaks with him.

SIMON (*to the* GUARD): We are ready for the prisoner Andrus and the notary. Please to bring them in.

GUARD: Yes, sir.

(*Exits with* ANSELM.)

JEROME (*to* JANETTE): For your presumption, you are not to remain in this room during our interview with your husband. You will be held elsewhere until your examination is completed.

JANETTE: Father Jerome, let me stay!

JEROME: We must have discipline!

(ANDRUS *and* NOTARY *are brought in, attended by* BERNARD, *Captain of the Guard.*)

(*To* BERNARD) Remove this woman, Captain, and hold her for further orders.

JANETTE (*to* ANDRUS): Do not insist on your visions, Andrus! If I, or our dead child, or your dead sister, have any meaning for you, do not insist!

(JANETTE *is taken out by* BERNARD.)

JEROME (*to* ANDRUS *and the* NOTARY): Take your seats. (*To* ANDRUS.) Your words will be recorded by the notary. They will be officially recorded; take care, therefore, that they are words of truth.

ANDRUS: Yes, father.

SIMON: Are you exhausted?

ANDRUS: I have been given only bread and water for six days and nights.

SIMON: The bread of tribulation and the water of affliction.

ANDRUS: Shared by the rats swarming in my cell. I have not been allowed to sleep.

SIMON: You must bear with us, my son. You have remained obdurate under questioning. All this has been done to help you become more responsive. When an immortal soul like yours is endangered, it becomes necessary to reach you through your mortal body.

ANDRUS: Yes, father.

JEROME: Look up when you reply. I ask you, now, did you not witness the vile experiments conducted by your father? You were not blind! Yet you told no one, made no protest —

ANDRUS: I did not think the experiments were evil.

JEROME: Not even the dismemberment of the body of your mother? Not even that?

ANDRUS: It was not meant as a sacrilege. My father was seeking a way to overcome the plague.

JEROME: You still defend him.

ANDRUS: He was my father.

JEROME: And for you, evidently, the defense of your father comes before your Christian duty to your Church.

SIMON (*to* ANDRUS): Has it not occurred to you that the plague may be God's means of testing and purifying His creatures? By what sin of pride did your father think to oppose God's great design? (*As* ANDRUS *struggles with his thoughts.*) We come now to something even more serious, if possible. It has been reported to us that, among your other claims, you have seen in one of your visions our holy father, the Supreme Pontiff himself, and that you heard him disavow our great task, the Inquisition, as a grievous and inexcusable error.

JEROME (*angrily*): The Supreme Pontiff indeed! An Anti-Christ, crowned and mitered, grinning and posturing before a congregation of devils!

SIMON: An apex of calamity. (*visibly moved*) My son, should not that fantasm alone have warned you of the dreadful nature of your obsession?

ANDRUS: Father, I am confused.

JEROME: Do you deny having made so abominable a charge?

ANDRUS: I do not deny having reported it, but I have not said I approved it.

JEROME: Evasion and deceit!

105

SIMON: Brother Jerome, I propose that we leave for later the subject of his visions. Let us first dispose of the simple facts of his behavior.

JEROME: Very well. They are damaging enough. (*To* ANDRUS.) After the imprisonment of your father, and because you had made no report of his heresy, were you not ordered to wear the yellow crosses?

ANDRUS: My mother was dead, and I was not allowed to speak with my father. Carla and I were children who knew nothing of the canon laws. I was fourteen, Carla was eight —

JEROME: At fourteen you, at least, were legally responsible.

ANDRUS: So I learned later.

JEROME: Later, at any rate, you knew that the crosses must be worn to the end of your life in token of your penitence and remorse. Why did you remove them from your garment?

(*Suddenly* BELIAL *appears. Unseen by any others in the room, he seats himself on a stool at the side of* ANDRUS *away from the* interrogators. *Now* ANDRUS *begins to speak like a puppet, his face blank and his lips moving mechanically. His voice is that of* BELIAL.)

BELIAL: Reverend fathers, I do not wish to add to the list of my sins, but I confess, to my sorrow, that when the crosses wore out, I did not have the few pennies necessary to replace them. Besides —

JEROME: What has happened to your voice?

BELIAL: I am hoarse after answering so many questions.

JEROME: Speak distinctly.

SIMON: My son, those crosses were meant to help you in your pursuit of salvation. It is indeed an additional sin that they were not replaced, but perhaps that sin is mitigated in view of your extreme poverty.

BELIAL: Reverend Father Simon, our home was requisitioned after my father was taken. Carla and I were left without food or shelter, dependent on the charity of our neighbors, few of whom dared to help us in any way, for fear they would in turn be suspected. And no one would let me work for them as long as I wore the crosses.

SIMON: It was sinful on the part of those who were afraid to employ you. But that does not wipe away your own sins.

BELIAL: Yes, father, if you say so.

(*Crowd noise erupts, joined by bells tolling alarm.*)

BERNARD (*suddenly entering, in haste*): Fathers, I bring you shocking news. The Cathedral of Santa Isabel has been desecrated!

SIMON (*horrified*): By whom?

BERNARD: A great crowd, led by coal miners, shouting of the second coming of Jesus — invading and looting the nave during the saying of the Mass. Our guards are already on their way.

(*He exits*)

JEROME (*to* ANDRUS): This is not your concern — is that it?

SIMON (*grimly*): Waste no time, Brother Jerome. Put him to the questions.

JEROME (*to* ANDRUS): Repeat after me: "I believe in all those things that a true Christian should believe."

BELIAL: I believe what you and the other good doctors tell me to believe.

JEROME: You are not ordered to believe! And those whom you call "the good doctors" are heretics and blasphemers, the masters of your sect! You have not repeated my words!

BELIAL: I willingly believe, if what you teach is good for me. I am simple and ignorant.

JEROME: If you are simple, answer simply, without distortions and lies! Will you swear that no one has ever taught you anything contrary to the Gospels of the True Faith?

BELIAL: If I am ordered to swear, I willingly do so.

JEROME: Your answers are not to the point. And again I tell you you are not being ordered!

BELIAL (*after a moment*): I humbly beg your pardon, father. I will answer simply and directly.

JEROME: Once more, repeat after me: "I believe in the Trinity of God the Father, Jesus His Son, and the Holy Ghost."

BELIAL: I do not believe in the Trinity or in any other part of your filthy superstitious swindle.

(JEROME, SIMON *and the* NOTARY *rise in consternation.*)

There is no God the father. Jesus never existed — He is a pious invention. And the Holy Ghost is nothing but theological garbage.

SIMON (*in a shaking voice*): You are possessed!

BELIAL: Yes, reverend father.

SIMON (*to the others*): Leave him! Lock the doors!

(*They exit, hurriedly.*)

BELIAL: My son, your enemies are scattered.

(*Blackout*)

SECOND VISION

Exterior: the plane. It passes over mountains, meadows, lakes and rivers, towns and cities. Interior: the pilot's compartment; a panel of complex instruments; instructions come over the airwaves. Exterior: the plane circles over an immense city with a view of great ships and smaller craft in harbor, then out over the ocean.

Scene 8

The stage is dim. Separate beams of light pick out BELIAL *and* ANDRUS.

ANDRUS: Demon, I did not summon you.

BELIAL: You must learn to trust me.

ANDRUS: To trust you, who bring blasphemy, insurrection, strife, and crime? The Cathedral sacked by raging mobs, its golden chalices trampled and stolen, its sacred vestments torn to rags! And for all this I am held to be the cause.

BELIAL: And are you?

ANDRUS: When I see the visions, I feel the joy of salvation. But afterward I am infected with unbelief and tormented with doubt.

BELIAL: Do you doubt the foolish fables you have been taught? Adam and Eve thrust out of Paradise for eating an apple? Jonah living undigested inside a whale —

ANDRUS: Only those who are desperately wicked have doubts! (*wretchedly*) More and more I find myself becoming like the miners — cut off from God, and darkened even in prayer.

BELIAL: You are indeed infected. And confused.

ANDRUS: Thanks to you! (*He goes to his knees before the crucifix.*) Kind Jesus, protect me! Oh Thou, the Crucified, pity me — wash me in the blood of Thy wounds!
(*The crucifix begins to swing.*)
Let my anguish merge with thine, let me merit Thy divine compassion —

BELIAL: What a mean, suffering idol you kneel to, Andrus! I begin to see why Gregor was so willing to let me own you!

ANDRUS: Begone, you enemy of the Lamb of God!

(*The crucifix falls with a crash and breaks.*)

108

BELIAL: There's a task for you, my suffering son. Pick up those pieces.

(ANDRUS *scrambles to pick them up. The heavy iron door of the room is swung open, and* JEROME, SIMON *and the* NOTARY *enter, accompanied by two* GUARDS *armed with pikes.*)

SIMON: The cross fell from the wall. It lies in pieces.

JEROME: Courage, Brother Simon! We are met with a demon, but he shall know the power of our Faith! (*to* ANDRUS) Leave off that task, Andrus, or whoever you may be, and attend to our questions.

BELIAL (*As* ANDRUS, *once more a puppet, returns to his seat*): I am ready, Father Jerome.

(*Still invisible to the others,* BELIAL *takes a violin and bow out of his robes, and with one foot on a stool, begins to play a mysterious, sustained, sighing melody.*)

SIMON: I hear a dim, distant sound, as of the sigh of a soul condemned.

JEROME: I hear no sound, Brother Simon, except the echo of the riot in the Cathedral Square. (*to* ANDRUS, *grimly*) Tell us of your visions.

BELIAL: They come upon me at almost any time of night or day, whether I am asleep or awake.

JEROME: As in a trance?

BELIAL: Yes, and when they appear I am overcome with happiness.

JEROME: Are you, indeed?

BELIAL: Yes. The visions show what men can accomplish.

JEROME: God made the world as it is, not as you'd like it to be. Your visions are a mirage conjured by Satan.

BELIAL: They are the visions of future science.

JEROME: Of what?

BELIAL: Of science! They show what men can do in the light of knowledge.

SIMON: Vain images! The revelations of the Anti-Christ! (*recovering*) Do these visions of yours show our Lord Jesus, our Holy Mother Mary, our Dove of the Holy Ghost?

BELIAL: They do not.

JEROME (*To* SIMON): Brother Simon, with all due respect: can it make any difference whether the sacred images have appeared in his visions? Those visions, on their very face, are a snare and a delusion fabricated by the devil. Is it not known that Satan can quote scripture for his purpose? Why, then, can he not use our holy images to mask his evildoing, if he so determines?

BELIAL: Reverend fathers, does it make any difference what I reply?

JEROME. Brother Simon, whatever God chose to give them was not intended to encourage their willful and presumptuous misconduct! Blasphemous indeed is the suggestion that men can fly into the heavens, there to intrude on the abode of God, His Son, and the blessed company of the saints!

BELIAL: In my visions —

SIMON: What are those visions, illuminated by your "science," as you call it? At their best they can shed no more light than a feeble candle compared with the radiance of the Heavenly Spirit! You would have us believe in a man-made Paradise! But imperfect man can create no Paradise — the Kingdom of God surpasses any false Eden conceived by His poor creatures!

BELIAL: Men will fly!

SIMON (*sorrowfully*): You do not listen.

JEROME: Andrus, the demon who possesses you will not serve you any longer. I hold in my hand the reports carried here from your native town. Here is the record of the family of the heretic and necromancer, Gregor, and of his wife and offspring, who, in defiance of the canons of our Holy Church, kept secret that he had met the demon Belial, not once but several times. Heinous, particularly, was your father's sin in dismembering a human body in contempt of the laws of God and man. When your father died during interrogation —

BELIAL: Under torture, you mean.

JEROME: There is no reference to any form of torture in these reports.

BELIAL: There never is.

SIMON: We will not continue this vain discussion with the demon — perhaps Belial himself — who has taken possession of the body and soul of Andrus, son of Gregor. (*with great earnestness*) Andrus, you have been lured to the abyss. Pray Heaven to save you in time.

JEROME (*to the* GUARDS): Tie the hands of the prisoner and conduct him to his cell.

ANDRUS (*returning to himself as his hands are tied*): What are you doing to me? Ah! merciful Savior!

(*He is dragged out.*)

110

SIMON (*tiredly*): There are times when this whole procedure begins to weary me to the marrow of my old bones. If it is in fact true that a demon has taken hold of this poor innocent —

JEROME (*startled*): Why do you say "If it is true"? Are you of two minds, suddenly, whether the man is possessed? How could it be more obvious! Only a moment ago, you yourself cried out —

SIMON: Yes, I know. I spoke without second thought, and for that I am sorry. (*remorsefully*) Heaven protect us, Brother Jerome, from judging anything to be obvious! I have learned that in the search for truth few things are what they appear to be at first glance and it behooves us all to proceed with caution. All we know for certain is the existence of God, His Son, and the Holy Writ; beyond these there is a veil of mystery no man can penetrate.

JEROME: Perhaps no man can draw aside the veil you speak of, but a demon can do so! Consider what "this poor innocent," as you call him, has reported to us: not only ships that fly, but houses so tall they scrape the heavens, wagons that race with lightning speed and without horses to draw them, machines that speak in human language —

SIMON: But does not the Book tell us of marvels even more amazing? And what is more mysterious than the future? (*troubled*) What if the visions are not false — even if it is a demon who presents them? Andrus tells of multitudes of future churches, great congregations of the faithful —

JEROME: Churches of Hell! A future Pope himself deserving of the rack! I wonder, Brother Simon, that you can be so swiftly undermined!

SIMON (*sharply*): I have not been undermined, Brother Jerome! And I wonder, in turn, at the excess of zeal with which you pronounce judgment. You seize upon a suspected wrongdoer with all the satisfaction of a cat pouncing on a helpless mouse. It is not our duty to carry a flaming sword but to inquire with patience and compassion into each case that comes before us. Else we may indeed stand condemned in the eyes of generations to come!

JEROME: Those are the very same sentiments uttered by Andrus — at the behest of Satan! (*with indignation and dismay*) I fear for the wasting away of our purpose! It is a wrong done to God and man to remain undecided when Unbelief stares us insolently in the face! Are we to release an infected sheep, allowing him to spread pestilence through the whole flock? We have a sworn and sacred duty, Brother Simon. Heresy cannot be destroyed unless heretics are destroyed; and heretics cannot be destroyed unless their defenders and dupes are destroyed. This is no time for mild preachment! The Cathedral pillaged, the Mass profaned by a howling mob —

(*The stage begins to darken as the* CHURCHMEN *exit, leaving only* BELIAL *in a flickering light. Then blackout.*)

CURTAIN

ACT II

Scene 1

A dungeon cell in the monastery of Trimar. BELIAL *is no longer present but his music remains under the scene, now loud, now almost inaudible.* ANDRUS, *in a dirty loin cloth, sags agains the wall. His arms are chained to the wall above his head.*

ANDRUS: Almighty God! Lord Jesus! (*He rattles his chains.*) Save me! I am innocent!

(*He faints.* CAPTAIN BERNARD *enters with* JANETTE, *who stumbles forward.*)

BERNARD (*to* JANETTE): Your time is short. Do your best.

JANETTE: I fear to wake him. Is he still controlled by the demon?

BERNARD: He has been speaking in his normal voice. The demon has left him.
                    (ANDRUS *stirs.*)
He is your husband again.
                    (*He exits.*)

JANETTE: Andrus!

ANDRUS: You are here, Janette! My prayers have been heard!

JANETTE: Andrus, my husband, they have asked me to speak to you to persuade you —

ANDRUS: I have been chained like this for more days than I can remember. No food, filthy water to drink — my arms have turned to ice — (*Agonized*) What sort of people are they? More cruel than the wild beasts, and all in the name of the meek Lord Jesus!

JANETTE: You give them no choice. Reason and prayer have not moved you: only torture is left. Listen to me, my dear husband! They do this for your sake, to save your soul from everlasting torment in the Hereafter. You must not madden yourself with raging thoughts, or your demon may return.

ANDRUS: I need no demon to tell me what some of these righteous people are like . . . . They have not even left my dead father in peace! (*wildly*) Is it true what they say — that he has been dragged out of his grave? Answer me!

JANETTE (*unwillingly*): His trial, that was suspended at his death, was resumed. They found him guilty of everything that was charged against him.

ANDRUS: And so?

JANETTE: They threw his bones on the fire in the public square in Marienburg and burnt them to ashes.

ANDRUS: My father!
                        (*He weeps.*)

JANETTE: You told me he never loved you. A stern and heartless man, you always said —

ANDRUS: So I thought. Interested only in his alchemy, with no belief in the Faith. . . . What right have I to judge him? They imprisoned him and tormented him to his death — took away his cottage —

JANETTE: The cottage has been torn down by decree of the Inquisition. The ground it stood on is accursed and strewn with garbage.

ANDRUS: My parents and their home — vanished from the earth! (*bitterly*) Who defended my father at his trial? No one? (*anguished*) Christ Jesus is our defense, they tell us. But his ministers commit crimes in his name and tremble for fear he will come back to see what they are doing.

JANETTE: Dear husband, you've turned so bitter and vengeful!

ANDRUS: You have been tortured.

JANETTE: No, no. They only told me —

ANDRUS: All your fingers are bruised.

JANETTE: They said you are an unrepentant heretic — that you —

ANDRUS: Will be burnt alive.

JANETTE: Andrus, your burning will make a feast day for the town. This afternoon there was a procession carrying the image of Saint Isabel, begging her to save us from the contamination of the Second Coming, which is spreading like another plague. (*Breaking down*) Why must you have your own way at such a terrible cost? In times like these, when everyone's nerves are strained by the war, when every wild rumor is believed, when everyone accuses his neighbor . . . . All the young men have been called to arms; the mines are shut down and filling with water; there is no way to earn one's bread. . . .

ANDRUS: Such are the dreadful days in which we live — filled with suffering and crime. Including our own crime — driving Carla to her death!

JANETTE (*vehemently*): Call it *your* crime, if you like! And treasure your remorse but don't ask me to share it! I did what had to be done! And anyone else in my place —

ANDRUS: Would have done the same. Guilt lies on our whole generation!

JANETTE: Only you alone want to pay for it!
(BELIAL's *music ends as the demon himself reappears, unseen by* ANDRUS *or* JANETTE.)
It's all so unnecessary! Why can you not let the priests have their way? If you will only agree that your visions are false —

ANDRUS: You're so changed, Janette! You were all of kindness, once, whose heart went out to me when all other women fled from my yellow crosses —

JANETTE: Do not punish me further, Andrus! When our child went into her grave she took a part of me with her.

ANDRUS: Would you pretend now that it does not matter whether she lived or died? Woman, do not drive me deeper into sin! My visions reveal that God loves us and will redeem us! All of us! Here on earth and not in some Hereafter! (*Suddenly, in a different, half-strangled voice,* ANDRUS *speaks with the voice of* BELIAL.) I will not deny my visions! They are not false!

(JANETTE *reels back, astonished.*)

BELIAL (*as* ANDRUS, *savagely*): Why do you come here to serve my jailers? What did you tell them about me when they pressed your fingers? That when I saw my mother cut open I ran away and told no one? That I owe my visions to a demon but will not confess it? That I begin to ask why we are punished with hunger, want and serfdom only because we are born?

JANETTE (*running from him with a scream*): The demon owns you!

(BERNARD *swiftly opens the door to let her out.*)

ANDRUS (*to* BELIAL, *as the door slams shut*): Demon! What right had you to terrify that woman?

BELIAL: She betrayed you. Doesn't that matter?

ANDRUS: She could not hold up under torture.

BELIAL: She was sent here to help break your courage. Doesn't that matter?

(ANDRUS *turns away, anguished.*)

(*Blackout.*)

THIRD VISION

Interior of the control tower of an airfield. Its operators are giving information over their phones. Through the windows, planes are seen circling and passing. Exterior: a plane is coming in for a landing. Interior: hostesses announce the landing. Exterior: plane taxies on its roadway, then comes to a stop and a passenger-bridge extends to meet it. Interior: passengers rise from their seats, pick up their belongings, and begin to file out. Interior: the airport waiting room. As the passengers emerge from the gates, they are greeted and kissed by friends.

(*Blackout. BELIAL reappears.*)

BELIAL: How can Andrus — even if he wanted to — deny the marvelous future I've revealed to him? Honest as he is, he will affirm to the last the truthfulness of his visions. In fact he is now so deeply convinced of them that he invites them himself, and I don't have to supervise them any longer. A good thing, too!
(*He takes out a scroll.*)
With all the crimes, disasters, misfortunes, and mistakes that call for my attention elsewhere, I am a very busy demon. Just look at this list!
(*He shows it.*)
Longer and longer as the centuries go by, and the incidents always bigger and uglier. Not just items like setting fire to damp bath towels, rattling dresser drawers, or causing beds to levitate! Such antics are left to our imps, who are happy when they can taunt a priest or two into exorcising them.
(*Rolls up the list.*)
I'll be back here as soon as I'm needed.

(*Blackout*)

Scene 2

The cell. Through the small window, high up, snow can be seen whirling past. ANDRUS, still chained to the wall, lies inert. The room is lit by a single candle, and is still. CAPTAIN BERNARD enters, shaking the snow from his clothes. With him comes the sound of hammering, which ceases as the door is closed.

BERNARD: Andrus! Still with us?
(ANDRUS *stirs feebly.*)

Good. We have a dozen carpenters in the snow and cold, building your platform and the dignitaries' stand for tomorrow. The whole town will be there in the morning. What a shame it would be, wouldn't it, if your soul had flown away, unshrived, before we could roast you? (*He removes his coat.*) You know you could almost call it cozy in here compared with outside? I have time off duty, and I've come to spend it with you before you leave us. It's true I've known you only a few weeks, but it's as though we're in this thing together — in a way.

(*He takes a key from his belt, unfastens ANDRUS's chains. ANDRUS'S arms drop to his sides.*)

How does that feel, eh? Better? If I hadn't done this for you, now and then, whenever the good fathers were not on their rounds, you might have departed from us long before now. Sit up, Andrus, here's your cup of good cheer; it's only dirty water, still it's something to drink . . .

(*He puts the cup to ANDRUS'S mouth. ANDRUS gulps some of the water; the rest spills down his chest.*)

Not only are the carpenters here, blowing on their fingers to keep them from freezing; there are two dozen guards to make sure the carpenters keep working in this weather. (*sardonically*) With the enemy pushing closer each day, and the coal miners idle and misbehaving, we need every one of my men for the front lines and for keeping order in our streets at home — but here they are, instead, in your honor . . . Orders from the Inquisition, backed up by documents from the Pope himself. We, the secular authorities, must look after you until we burn you, because the churchmen mustn't soil their hands with you. Only why can't they wait a little? They won't get a good turnout of citizens for the ceremony if this weather doesn't let up.

(*A knock at the door. BERNARD admits a GUARD holding a brazier. The GUARD sets down the brazier, salutes and exits. BERNARD places the brazier at his feet.*)

Now, that's something like!

(*He stretches out in his chair.*)

About the ceremony. Those citizens who stay home will get a tongue-lashing from Father Jerome next Sunday. Some will even be written down as suspects — inciters of heresy, they're called. . . . (*With real curiosity*) Andrus, I can't understand your type — you'd rather sizzle than change your mind and behave like other people. And there's more and more like you all the time — you're the fourth one this year, in this town alone. Don't think *I* enjoy it — after the last burning I couldn't eat steak for a week. (*almost pleadingly*) Come, now — why do you heretics let the devil rule your tongues? Especially when some of you are so nimble-brained and so much better informed about everything than the rest of us? You, however, except for those visions of yours, are not much of a heretic, in my opinion. You're not at all clever. The last one

116

we had here was Father Molinari — he was still called "Father," because once a priest you're forever a priest, even if you're unfrocked, as he was . . . . The way he talked made you shudder to hear him. (*wryly*) "Who is His Holiness the Pope," he says to me, "but the Anti-Christ himself? Chief of the banditti," he screeched "decked out in silks and velvets, ribbons and jewels, stuffing himself like a pig, fornicating and breeding so-called nieces and nephews! Did Christ Jesus lead that sort of life?" He raves on, "His holiness has a good thing going for him with the farce of the Inquisition — it keeps him and his familiars swilling at their troughs!"
(ANDRUS *stirs uneasily.*)
"I don't know why I listen to a creature like you," I told him. "Are you trying to say that the Dominicans or the Franciscans are part of what you call a farce? That anyone like Father Simon, for instance, who owns nothing but his robe and his sandals — who is devoted to no one but God and the Savior — who asks nothing but to rescue the souls of abandoned heretics like yourself — are in the secret pay of Rome?"
(ANDRUS *sits up feebly.*)
"I don't care how holy or poor the Inquisitors are," this Father replies with scorn, "They are the tools of the Roman Uncleanliness, all the more because the common people respect them. They are owned," he says, "the same way you are owned by your master, the Duke." (*shrugging*) It must be admitted — he had a point there. Where would I be if I didn't serve Duke Roderick? Where would we *all* be? Not that the Duke is getting too well served. Very poor morale in the ranks! Our Duke has been biting off chunks of the town common land for himself, and the town hasn't liked it — to say the least. Now he has his eye on the mines — even the mines that run under Count Norbert's land — that's why there's this war . . .
(ANDRUS *begins to speak.*)

ANDRUS: In the mine . . . the roof fell in . . . . Forty-three of us working underground . . . . I alone escaped . . . with a torn leg. God's miracle.

BERNARD: What became of the other forty-two? And their families?

ANDRUS: "Whom God loveth He chasteneth."

BERNARD: You heard that from Father Simon. God must love us all a great deal, for we die like flies — and not only in the mines. In the streets, of the plague. And after every battle, dogs devour our corpses in the mud of the fields. (*After a pause*) Count Norbert will win this war; that's certain, the way it's going. Duke Roderick never imagined that Count Norbert would be supported by the Prince de Fraise. We have all had more than we can take, Andrus — with no vision to console us.

117

ANDRUS: People will fly.

BERNARD (*deliberately, after a moment*): How?

ANDRUS: Men must not pry into God's secrets.

BERNARD: You echo Father Simon's words like a parrot. I wonder why he wants to burn you, since you've learned your lessons so well.

ANDRUS: I will not testify that my visions are false and of the devil — that is why! People will not always crawl as they do now. I see them in the future, free as the birds of the air. And that is not all I see and hear. They speak to each other across whole oceans. Their homes are as bright by night as by day; water, cold and hot, comes straight out of the walls of their rooms, which can be heated or cooled invisibly at their command. And in those rooms they can eat fresh strawberries in the middle of winter; they listen to music that comes to them out of the air, or look upon moving, colored images that appear to them out of boxes. Everywhere there are great churches and hospitals and libraries. . . . I cannot begin to tell you what other strange and wonderful things I see in my visions!

BERNARD: Is it the life of God's blessed Paradise that you see?

ANDRUS: No, it is the daily life of the common people who will learn to have all these things.

BERNARD: Then why do you talk like Father Simon and declare that flying is God's secret, which people have no right to learn? (*angered*) I begin to see why that mocking Father Molinari told me, "Your God is an Old Man in the sky, who orders you never to think! Did not the true God give us the gift of minds to think with, so that we are not like the dumb brutes? And have we not made use of that gift, as God intended? Have we not learned how to build homes and cathedrals? To sail ships? To use fire for our hearths? To tame horses, oxen, dogs and cats, pigs and chickens? Have we not invented wagons and their wheels, spades for digging, hammers and axes, and a hundred thousand other things that were never on this earth before we thought of them?"

ANDRUS: I do not know how to answer you. I who cannot even read or write, was never taught to be clever, like that heretic priest.

BERNARD (*suddenly changing his tone*): Andrus, when you see people flying — what sort of wings have they? How do they flap their wings?

ANDRUS: I have answered that many times. They do not fly by themselves. They enter a kind of ship that flies.

BERNARD: A whole ship that goes into the air? With people inside it?

ANDRUS: A great many people — sometimes a hundred or more.

BERNARD (*rising*): I must be turning as crazed as you are, but somehow I want to believe you.

ANDRUS: All of what I say is true, with no falsehood whatever.

BERNARD (*solemnly, but with suppressed excitement*): You can leave this cell a free man if you will answer what I ask you. I myself will free you, and leave the priests to grind their teeth. Duke Roderick will support my action to the limit! To be able to fly over the enemy — (*eagerly*) Tell me, how does one build that kind of ship?

ANDRUS: I do not know.

BERNARD: You can see it clearly?

ANDRUS: Very clearly, and I can hear the language of the passengers.

BERNARD: Well, then: what material is the ship made of?

ANDRUS: I don't know. Maybe silver,

BERNARD: A ship, all of metal?

ANDRUS: It shines . . .

BERNARD: How is it steered? By what?

ANDRUS: Dials. A great many clocks.

BERNARD (*losing patience*): What kind of sails does it have?

ANDRUS: No sails. It has wheels.

BERNARD: Wheels on a ship? A great metal hulk that would sink immediately, even in water? Steered by clocks, running on wheels in the sky? (*curtly*) What could hold a monstrous thing like that in the air?

ANDRUS (*helplessly*): I am not a builder, Captain; I am not an engineer — not even a master mechanic. I can only tell you they build everything with the help of their techni — techni something — technology.

BERNARD: I never heard of it. What is it? Where is it?

ANDRUS: I only know that it's a part of their science, their knowledge.

BERNARD: Is that all? (*bitterly*) Forget I asked you!

(*He raises* ANDRUS's *arms, chaining them again. There is another knock at the door.*)

Enter!

(*The door is opened by the* GUARD, *admitting* FATHER JEROME, *who carries a package.*)

Wild weather, Father Jerome, in which to be out.

119

JEROME: We each have our duties. Mine is to make sure all is in order for tomorrow. (*With a glance at* ANDRUS.) Nothing new?

BERNARD: Nothing. The prisoner is alive and conscious.

JEROME: And with no change of heart.
> (BERNARD *shrugs.*)
I have brought him his shirt for tomorrow. (*He opens his package, disclosing a long shirt with an all-over pattern of black demons.*) Let him be clothed.

(BERNARD *unchains* ANDRUS's *arms once more. He and the* GUARD *slip the shirt over the head of* ANDRUS, *who struggles desperately.*)

JEROME (*bending forward with his crucifix and making the ˌsign of the cross over* ANDRUS *as the prisoner is again chained up*): Andrus, it will soon be morning, but it is never too late. *Cor contritum —* a contrite heart —

ANDRUS (*in a choked voice*): Wild beasts!

> (*He rattles his chains. Blackout.*)

FOURTH VISION

Exterior: a bombing plane is being loaded. Planes dropping bombs, hitting villages and cities; antiaircraft guns reply. Cities are enveloped in smoke, house timbers fall on terrified people; children run to escape napalm and machine guns; a child is hit, stumbles, falls, and goes up in flames.

> (ANDRUS *cries out in his nightmare.*)

> (*Blackout*)

Scene 3

The cell, morning. A few last snowflakes drift past the little window. Still chained, and in his ceremonial shirt, ANDRUS *lies gasping and moaning in contorted sleep.* DUKE RODERICK *enters attended by two* GUARDS *and by* SIMON, JEROME, BERNARD *and the* NOTARY. *Church bells toll above a confused shouting in the square outside the monastery walls.*

BERNARD (*to* DUKE RODERICK): The guards have been doubled, sire, since last night, and our archers have arrived.

RODERICK: We'll need them. I was hooted at and threatened as I rode across the square. One grime-faced ape even tried to seize the horse's bridle before I trod him down.

JEROME: Coal miners. Godless and desperate men.

BERNARD: Filtering in here in packs last night and this morning from the neighboring towns.

SIMON: Sire, these ruffians are far outnumbered by our pious citizens — men, women and children who come to attend the ceremony.

RODERICK: Yes, I know. They come because they must, I wish you would carry out your own ceremony, as you call it. If our civil magistrates were not under strict orders from Rome —

SIMON: The Church must shed no blood. You are doing God's work, sire. We of the Holy Inquisition have no other purpose.

RODERICK: Maybe not the Holy Inquisition, but some of your unholy Inquisitors. Like those three rascals who were caught trying to blackmail a chaste and honorable lady, married to my cousin Cyril, of Touraine.

JEROME: The occasion was scandalous. Those thieves were stripped of their credentials and ordered back to their monastery, subject to discipline.

RODERICK (*wryly*): Indeed! (*as the noise outside grows in volume.*) May I abjectly offer the opinion that your Holy Office accomplishes more harm than good? These burnings at the stake may entertain some, and terrorize others, but they spread resentment and disobedience, as well, throughout this region. Why must we have the coal miners versus your upright citizens at a time when the enemy is upon us and we need unity as never before? (*Grimly*) Proceed with your circus: wake up that wretch and lead him out to his fate. You will be safe from those grime-blackened, hate-filled faces: our troops surround the square. (*To* BERNARD) Archers to the forefront — and await my order!

BERNARD: Yes, sire.

(*He salutes and exits.*)

RODERICK: Are we ready?

(ANDRUS *is prodded awake by* JEROME.)

JEROME (*To* ANDRUS): Heretic, outcast of men! On this, your last day on earth, you are still offered the grace of the Eucharist. (*He recites*) *Absolve, Domine, animas fidelium ab omni vincule delictorum* —

(ANDRUS, *awakened, cries out in a trembling voice.*)

ANDRUS: I repent! I have indeed known and trafficked with the demon Belial!

(JEROME *steps back, shaken.*)

Reverend fathers, brothers and sisters in Christ — forgive me and receive me!

VOICES: The prisoner recants! He is redeemed!

ANDRUS: I should have known from the beginning that I was mired in evil! With each step I sank deeper! Yet, possessed by arrogance and blindness, I thought to know more than the God-ordained ministers of the Church! (*Racked by sobs*) Now, from the depths of my soul, I renounce the visions of the Anti-Christ! Let me be cleansed!

SIMON (*kneeling beside* ANDRUS, *in tears*): Oh, God be praised for His goodness!

VOICES: Halleluia! A miracle! A miracle!

SIMON: Once more the Lord our God triumphs over the prince of darkness! (*To the* NOTARY, *as the church bells now ring out jubilantly.*) Go! Read at the top of your voice the message of the recantation!

(NOTARY *exits. The confused shouts of the square rise abruptly while the door is open.*)

RODERICK: *There's* a miracle worth having! Unchain the prisoner.

(ANDRUS, *released by the* GUARDS, *is brought forward, supported by* SIMON *and* JEROME.)

(*To* ANDRUS, *who kneels before him.*) Fellow, if yours is a true repentance, you have benfitted more than yourself. You may help to undo some of the mischief you have created up to now.

(*There is a renewed outburst from the streets outside.*)

But that's not all cheering!

BERNARD (*entering hurriedly*): Sire, the miners are enraged and not convinced. Some are throwing stones, and they have driven off the notary.

RODERICK: Let them send someone in to hear Andrus himself.
                    (BERNARD *exits.*)
Reverend fathers, it's just as I have told you: these exercises of yours serve less and less to keep the peace; on the contrary, you embitter our whole countryside.

JEROME: Sire, the bitterness is of the times. We work for our Mother Church, which has never failed to give you her support.

RODERICK (*impatiently*): Well, well, priest, the matter can be debated.
                    (BERNARD *returns with* MATTIAS.)
What is this man called?

BERNARD: Mattias, sire.

RODERICK: And what is his complaint?

MATTIAS: We do not allow to be tricked, sire.

RODERICK: Forebear that sullen look when you answer me! Tricked by whom?

MATTIAS: The clericals would pretend the man Andrus has recanted.

RODERICK: You see him on his knees. Ask him yourself.

MATTIAS (to ANDRUS): Do that the truth? Thou hast seen no visions!

ANDRUS: I have seen them. They were sent me by the devil.

MATTIAS: The visions were of free men! Were thy visions true or no?

ANDRUS: They were true visions.

MATTIAS: Ah!

JEROME (astounded; to ANDRUS): What words are these? Do you perjure yourself once more?

ANDRUS: True visions, shown to me by God's enemy, whom I curse and abhor.

MATTIAS: True visions of Christ's coming and of hope for us all — but shown to thee by Satan? What clerical trickery hast thou been taught?

JEROME: Enough of questions! Your limited understanding —

MATTIAS: I understand that he think it painful to be burnt alive!

SIMON: How! You will not be satisfied unless he merits to be burnt? So that you can go on believing his former lies, which he has now foresworn?

MATTIAS: Indeed, if thou do free him —

JEROME: Free him? No indeed! He shall not be returned to the company of the Godless! There will be no burning, but neither shall he ever see again the outside of these walls! For the remainder of the life God grants him, he shall abide in fasting and prayer in this cell, that his piety may at last admit him to salvation!

MATTIAS (to ANDRUS): Is it for this thou hast belied thy vision?

(MATTIAS strides to the door, thrusts aside the startled GUARD, and exits.)

RODERICK (to BERNARD): Damnation! He will arouse them all, and at once!
    (There is a vast roar from the crowd.)
Give the order! And bolt all doors!
    (Blackout, as iron doors clang shut.)

Scene 4

The light picks out BELIAL *in his gown with hood thrown back. He has opened out a slender tripod, on which he lays a crude tube-shaped instrument. Outside, there is an uproar of mingled pain and rage. It is muted as he speaks to the audience.*

BELIAL: I'm sure you're ready to reproach me for having been absent so long while my son Andrus was in trouble. But I knew he was in no real danger, heavenly-minded as he is. He suffers from a bad conscience, and was bound to repent and recant. *(troubled)* Just the same, I should not have let him go on summoning his visions by himself. That was worse than carelessness on my part, and I'll catch Hell for it, as you folks like to say. It's excusable only because I have something truly worthwhile to show for the time I've been away. *(with quiet enthusiasm)* For several months now, I've been occupied with the local coal miners. They are a truly headstrong lot, and what is more, they are men of action, people after my own heart. It was obvious that Duke Roderick would one day set his archers on them. Several of those miners are already lying stretched out, dead, in the square outside, with arrows in their backs; others have only been hit and are shrieking out their agony.

They can now retaliate. You remember about that extraordinary powder my old friend Gregor was compounding before he was torn away from his work? It is a powder that explodes at the slightest provocation. For centuries to come, there will be nothing more devilish on earth than this powder, which our miners have perfected with my help. They tested it in blasting coal in the mines, but now it is ready for even more important work.

For instance it can be inserted at the end of a tube like this one *(showing it)* which can then be aimed in any direction you please, with just a spark to let it send injury and destruction on its way. When used in this tube it is called *gun powder.* The tube itself is a *gun,* and I can only apologize for its unwieldy appearance. Right now it is heavy and clumsy, but its possibilities for the future are stupendous.

(Blackout)

Scene 5

The cell. ANDRUS, DUKE RODERICK, BERNARD, SIMON, JEROME, *and* GUARDS. *The shouting in the streets is no longer heard, but there are bursts of minor explosions that sound like the crackling of dry branches.* BERNARD *up on a stool, is straining to look out of the window.*

BERNARD: I see flashes of fire. The archers are breaking ranks; they are falling back! So are the guards! (*stunned*) They're panicked, sire, running away!
(*The explosions continue.*)
The miners have scattered them.

RODERICK: Scattered my troops? The miners?

BERNARD: The miners are carrying machines of some kind. Weapons of war.

RODERICK: What machines? This is idiotic! Get down, let me see for myself!

(*As he starts toward the window, he is stopped by a heavy explosion that shakes the room and everyone in it.*)

A VOICE (*as fists pound the door from outside*): Make open!

BERNARD: What shall we do, sire?

(*A second explosion, even more powerful, tears the iron door from its hinges; smoke floods into the cell. MATTIAS enters, attended by two other MINERS carrying crude guns.*)

MATTIAS: Let fall thy weapons!

(*The GUARDS drop their pikes; BERNARD drops his sword.*)

RODERICK (*drawing his sword*): Scum, all of you!

(*He is shot down.*)

SIMON: Do you raise your hands against your masters? Murderers and blasphemers —

(*He begins the Excommunication.*)

MATTIAS (*punching SIMON in the face*): Hold thy foul tongue, priest! (*To the others.*) Hands behind backs! Move out!

(*Those in the room file out, BERNARD and the GUARDS with the body of RODERICK. JEROME supports SIMON. The armed MINERS follow them. ANDRUS is waved back.*)

MATTIAS: We care nothing for thee. Thou canst stay — we will settle with the others.

ANDRUS (*frightened*): Mattias, what will you do with them?

MATTIAS: What is it to thee that they will meet their fate?

ANDRUS: Will you add killing to killing? God preserve you from it! Besides, they will surely be avenged —

MATTIAS: Thou art a cowardly fool, and they have addled thy wits with starvation! Be grateful for thy life!

(He flings ANDRUS *to the ground, and exits. Tongues of flame lick the walls of the room, which darkens to blackout.)*

Scene 6

The light returns. BELIAL, *a book under his arm, stands before* ANDRUS, *all three dreadful heads exposed.* ANDRUS *looks up, startled.*

ANDRUS (*weakly*): Demon, are you still here? Close your robe — I cannot bear to look!

BELIAL (*closing his robe*): You pious people are so squeamish!

ANDRUS: And leave me!

BELIAL: Not before we understand each other. (*without emphasis*) You are ungrateful, Andrus, after what I've done for you and your coal-mining friends. You were about to be burnt alive by a pair of sadists.

ANDRUS: They were holy men of God, innocent people, and you've sent them to their deaths.

BELIAL: Innocent? Those two executioners?

ANDRUS: They pitied me for my sins. They tried to save me —

BELIAL: From the deadly sin of using the mind your God is supposed to have given you! Compassionate, were they? That's true. They could have flayed you alive, broken your limbs on the wheel, and torn out your fingernails and your tongue. Instead they only kept you in chains and even fed you mouldy bread and muddy water. Have you forgotten you called them wild beasts? You're much too ready to forgive, dear Andrus.

ANDRUS: Even wild beasts should not be slaughtered.

BELIAL: Where does it say so in this Holy Book you're so fond of quoting? Did your Almighty permit His faithful servants, Jerome and Simon, to be chastened because He loved them? By God's grace to suffer annihilation!
    (ANDRUS *covers his ears.*)
By the way, could He not have created people out of something more durable than flesh and blood, while He was at it? How about iron, or granite?
    (ANDRUS *tries to get up, falls.*)
You need help: you've been brutalized and tormented. You live in a savage world, Andrus, a world *I* did not create. A world where everything that lives must eat everything else to go on living. "The lions roaring after their prey do seek their meat from God," it says in this book. (*dourly*) What a marvelous creative inspiration of your God — to make life depend on killing! He also created evil, as I find when I read this book: for how else would your

126

ancestors have found me in His garden disguised as a snake? (*He tears several pages out of the book, crumples them up and throws them into the flames.*) Why did He, the Omniscient, plant the tree of knowledge, so that His creatures would eat of its fruit and be damned forever? Why did He send His only begotten Son to this miserable earth, moving people like pawns in a sordid game, toward the day of crucifixion? (*harshly*) You're right — the miners' victims will be avenged. How long do you think it will be before the seigneurs learn all about gunpowder and guns? Mattias and his friends will pay doubly for their recklessness — with writhing bodies and screaming flesh. Then *they* will be avenged in turn . . . and so on, *etcetera* and *ad infinitum*, through the ages, because that's how the world was created — by your God, not by me!

ANDRUS: It is not for me to know His divine purpose. He is far greater than you think.

BELIAL: Yes. He may have created me just to keep Himself from going completely mad in His unbridled creative passion! It has been my task, ever since the beginning, to help make this world a little more rational than He planned it.

ANDRUS: Saint Belial, patron saint of improvement! Men flying, with your help, carrying death and destruction on their wings!

BELIAL: I will go on helping them to fly. They will fly to the moon and walk on it. With my help they will send their recording instruments to distant planets across infinite space. There will be no limit to the assistance I will give them —

ANDRUS: If they pay for it.

BELIAL: You surprise me, Andrus — you've been learning sarcasm, lately. It doesn't become you.

ANDRUS: Why does blood have to keep running forever through this world? There's another way! In peace, in brotherhood and sensible agreement! If people learned to love instead of hating —

BELIAL: When will that be, in your world of fangs and claws? When the Saviour comes again? There will be no Second Coming! Forget those miracles dreamed up by wailing Jewish rabbis and pitiful Christian saints! (*violently*) There will be no miracles! Only a long, steep road ahead, with each step of the way attended by massacre and terror! Because that's how it must be, even though the book of your Father God doesn't say so: "By the bloody sweat of thy body shalt thou pay for thy improvements!"

(He tosses the book at the feet of ANDRUS, *who seizes it, holding it reverently in his arms.*)

You are unworthy of me, Andrus. You won't see me again. I disown you, and my gift of vision is withdrawn.

(*In farewell*)

Commodo superstitionum tuarum te reliquo. I leave you to the comfort of your superstitions.

(*The stage darkens swiftly, to the accompaniment of a heavy rumbling noise and a great burst of flames into which* BELIAL *vanishes. Blackout and silence, then the light returns, revealing* ANDRUS *and* JANETTE *on their knees in prayer; behind them is a stand of votive lights in red tumblers.*)

Scene 7

ANDRUS
     } (*together*):
JANETTE

O thou my Saviour, who gavest for my sake Thy precious blood —
From the perils that lie in my way,
Kind Lord, defend me,
From the snares of the Evil One,
Lord, guide Thou my feet aright . . .

(ANGEL VOICES *intone the Dies Irae. From far off comes the rasping laughter of* BELIAL.)

CURTAIN

Andrus imprisoned

CASTING

The acting space is the whole downstage area, including the stage apron, as well as the steps on either side of the proscenium leading to the stage. Belial's speeches are almost always delivered "straight across the footlights," but the whole cast is encouraged to feel a close rapport with the audience, and they can also speak their thoughts to the audience when opportunity offers. They are emphatically *not* asked to use an allegedly Brechtian unemotional declamatory style. Brecht never intended anything of the sort. The delivery of the Brechtian actor is clearly articulated and audible; he is keenly aware of what he is saying and why he is saying it; he may even be surprised at what he is saying. What Brecht criticized was (a) schmaltz, (b) bombast, (c) mugging. In other words, he wanted good acting and redefined what good acting consists of.*

ANDRUS. Compassion is his salient quality, together with his abiding trust in Jesus, Lamb of God.

BELIAL. His playful cynicism has a sinister charm of its own.

JANETTE. Her harshness and irritation are in complete contrast to the meekness of her husband, but her love for him is never in doubt.

CARLA. Pathetically desperate.

LUDWIG. A swaggering hoodlum of the streets.

MATTIAS. His authority is as impressive as his size and as imaginative as his quotations from Scripture.

IGNACE. He is interested in the vision but nowise inclined to believe in it.

ANSELM. He didn't know what he was in for when he reported on his fellow-miners.

FATHER JEROME. One of the more unmerciful members of the sacred Inquisition.

FATHER SIMON. The thoughtfulness of this good man is always lost on Jerome, but neither of them hesitate when the Faith is met with violence.

NOTARY. A simple clerk of court.

CAPTAIN BERNARD. An army officer, who thinks and speaks like one.

DUKE RODERICK. A patrician accustomed to awed respect.

---

*See Mordecai Gorelik, "On Brechtian Acting," *Quarterly Journal of Speech* (October 1974).

THOUGHTS ON *ANDRUS, OR THE VISION*

Cleveland Playhouse, play reader's report:

> *Andrus, or the Vision* is a most intriguing script.

Thomas Edward West, Asolo Theatre, Tallahassee (Florida):

> *Andrus* and *The Feast of Unreason* are both excellent, vibrant works and it was a special pleasure to read them.

Gil Lazier, Florida State University (Tallahassee):

> *Andrus, or the Vision* is the most exciting, imaginative and striking of the three scripts by Gorelik that I have read. I was carried away by the first act, fascinated by its theatricality, its power. The direct address devices, the "visions" of the future, the entire medieval context with its bluntness but its parallels to our own world, add a theatrical power to the piece.

Anta West, play reader's report:

> I don't think it is a play at all — just an undigested mass of material. The author has failed to translate this material into playable dramatic form. Instead, he has characters going into long monologs telling us things that should either be eliminated or dramatized. I found it very hard to read through, and I can't imagine an audience responding to it in the theatre. Besides that, the play presents production problems that are staggering for a one-act play.

To Anta West:

I: I find this comment on *Andrus, or the Vision* merely insulting. The play, which has already proved itself onstage, left no one in its audiences angrily bewildered, as it did your reader. Incidentally, in its tryout at Kansas State University it managed with a single, permanent setting, makeshift costumes off the racks, no properties except a few stools, no lighting effects, and no projections. Moreover, *Andrus* is not a one-act play.

From Louis E. Roberts, University of Massachusetts (Boston):

> Andrus is more sinned against than sinning, a victim of his father's deal with Belial, a passive agent, thus hard to focus on unless universalized.

You make diabolic possession credible. For all his fireworks, Belial is as real as any other character, suitably amoral, and ultimately seen as a victim himself of a screwy morality. Although you seem to make Belial an independent agent, where does the demon originate? Your Belial is not an effective power in his own right. He is to God as Andrus is to Gregor, both disappointments as children. I'd like to see that emphasized in production.

The airplane image is effective. We may be builders, while Andrus was only a visionary, but we can't control our creation any more than Jehovah can His.

Hauptmann would love your crowd scenes. The crazed crowd, not understanding anything but their own desperation, could be terrifying. As for the scenic effect, which you toss off lightly, I think you should be around to light all the fires — and put them out.

Arthur Miller, dramatist:

I must confess that the devil as the technical dreamer and man's helper is a congenial thought . . . (John Proctor, according to one tradition, was a farmer with a talent for inventing labor-saving devices and this was what drew suspicion on him as in league with the devil)

I feel the play's central paradox is too readily grasped to sustain interest, however. The lesson emerges, as it were, too soon for the mind to continue digesting it in its motivations, these being insufficiently various. This is of course my own reaction.

But I must mention that another audience than now exists (the coal miners?) might be moved by the *kind* of sophistication with which it approaches the social split. I needn't tell you, however, that the oppressed themselves do not see it with their own eyes and rarely have, here — or perhaps in Europe either. So a play must, I think, create a different bridge not only toward social reality, but at the same time inwardly, between their own experience with life and their illusory expression of it. I don't feel the play really does this. Its objectivity would, I think, leave Americans on the outside of its world, despite some good sharp scenes and telling passages. — I am absolutely certain that I could be mistaken.

Dear Arthur [Miller],

I am confused by the reference to a new audience "of coal miners, perhaps," which could be "more moved by the *kind* of sophistication with which it approaches the social split." I was far from trying to write a class-conscious proletarian drama of the thirties. I am pretty sure that no Communist theatre would like *Andrus*, which does not square with "revolutionary optimism."

There is certainly oppression in the play, not only of the miners but of all the people of the town. Andrus himself is a miner because he can't help it; he does not talk like one, and his outlook is philosophic, not socially militant. As the son of a professional (an alchemist) he is less troubled by social conditions than by the problems of his religious faith.

What I am trying to deal with primarily is the question of where science and technology are taking us. The dramatists of the expressionist period of the 20's were very pessimistic about that. I have always disagreed with them, but I am not as naively optimistic about science and progress as I used to be, in spite of my continuing great admiration for both. I still think improvement is possible in man's lot, but evidently it has to be paid for in blood.

RAINBOW TERRACE

1956-1983

Woe unto him who strives with his Maker, an earthen vessel with the potter! Shall the clay say to him that fashioneth it, what makest thou?

Isaiah 45:9

The idea of a street called Rainbow Terrace located in the Afterlife came to me not long after the death of both my parents. (My father died in 1951, and my mother in 1955.) In fantasy I saw them living in a suburban cottage in a district in Long Home, a place that recalled the quiet streets of Fire Island or one of the better middle-class neighborhoods around Los Angeles. Once that fantasy was established, the Angels arrived, and so did the theme of an Afterlife judgment.

Much earlier I had written a one-act play, PAUL THOMPSON FOREVER, about a works foreman who embarrasses his wife and daughter by returning immediately after his funeral, accompanied by an Inspector from the Beyond. It was up to his family to prove that Paul had originally been made in the image of God. With the help of his wife's recollections and untruths, he passes inspection and is admitted to a type of Afterlife existence as futile as himself.

PAUL THOMPSON, published by Walter Baker in 1950, was given a brief tryout three years before by the Actors Lab Theatre in Hollywood. At that time Bertolt Brecht was living in Santa Monica, where I was seeing him often, and I invited him to the play. The story delighted him — the only time I ever knew him to laugh out loud. Next day he sent his photographer, Ruth Berlau, to take some pictures of the production. I still have those photos.

Brecht even proposed that we write a play together about an American worker, and we started to do so, under the title of NOTHING BUT THE BEST, but after a few sessions he gave it up, saying that he just could not understand the psychology of the U.S. working class. (The "bourgeoisified" American worker was, in fact, a different species from the German Communist workers who had been Bert's favorite audience in Berlin. Furthermore he must have realized, or had it conveyed to him, that any less than a heroic image of the "proletariat," whether in the U.S. or anywhere else, could alienate his familiar public in Europe.) But if NOTHING BUT THE BEST did not result in anything with Brecht, its quality came to mind as I went on developing RAINBOW TERRACE.

By 1957, with the play ready for copyright, I felt that RT could be especially suited to a black company. In New York I sounded out one of my friends, Fred O'Neal, about doing a scene or two of the play with a black cast. Fred, whom I directed afterwards in a production of MARSEILLES at Southern Illinois University, liked the suggestion, and the project was carried out at the Actors Studio, of which I was an associate member. Fred made a superb Vern Falkimer.[14]

Nothing further happened until 1965 or 1966, when, as research professor and director at Southern Illinois University, I urged a production of the play at our new theatre. In the regular open discussion of plays that were being nominated for the coming season, our Department chairman, Dr. Archibald McLeod, who always refrained, on principle, from stating his own opinion, said, of RT, "I must tell you that I do not like this play." That fall I was away from SIU, teaching at San Jose State College, where I received a letter from Colgate University asking for RAINBOW TERRACE as its first production in its new theatre. I wrote to Mac asking for a four-week release to direct the play there.

He wrote back at once, telling me sternly that the play must be done at SIU. I answered that I would be happy to have it done there, only I wondered why his offer was in the form of an ultimatum. I must add that, once resigned to the play's being staged at our own theatre, Mac gave it his full support. A professional actor, Paul Mann, was invited to do Vern, and the main-stage production, under my direction and with my designs for the setting and costumes, was given a warm welcome by the faculty, students and townspeople alike.

OUTLINE

After Vern Falkimer, a dynamic businessman, and his wife, Della, are killed in an auto accident, they find themselves in a cottage in the suburb of Long Home, a modern purgatory in the Afterlife. Here they encounter two others who have preceded them: Vern's girl friend, Lottie Aldrich, and the Falkimers' son Danny, who was killed in action in Korea. Vern not only resumes his affair with Lottie but insists that he has been mistakenly assigned to Long Home instead of to Glory Above, where he belongs. Meanwhile, against all odds, he seeks to establish a branch agency in the Afterlife for Viogen, his phony tonic.

The task of evaluating someone like Vern deepens the political split between the fundamentalist and the liberal Angels of the Long Home administration and leads to serious rioting by Long Home's inhabitants. Vern is finally sentenced to be dispersed forever in the Angels' "fading machine."

CHARACTERS

Belle Falkimer
Danny Falkimer
Vern Falkimer
Tony Kellog
Joe Merwin
Fred
Sister Guthrie
Brother Anstice
Pip*
Brother Morias
Brother Finch
Sister Cheswick
Lottie Aldrich
Mrs. Bianco
John Perry
Steve
Norman Falkimer
Neighbors*

*The role of Pip can be played by a boy or a girl, or can be omitted. The Neighbors can be omitted if no porch is shown.

ACT I

Scene 1

*The Falkimer cottage on Rainbow Terrace, a side street in the garden
suburb of Long Home. The setting resembles a Hollywood, California,
bungalow, as it might have looked to a Fra Angelico or a Jan van
Eyck. We see the interior and a little of the exterior, including the
porch, which has a walk leading up to it and a hedge of poplar trees
beyond it. The entrance door of the house is downstage right, in the
wall between the porch and the cottage; the door has a glass panel in
it. There are two windows in the upstage right corner of the room.
Upstage left is the stairway to the bedrooms; doors to the kitchen and
the cellar are under the stairs and are not visible. A writing desk,
littered with notes, and containing a kit of test tubes, stands next to
the window; there is a buffet against the back wall, a round table and
some chairs, center. The makings of a fruit punch are on the table.
Against the left wall there is a couch with an armchair and a floor lamp
beside it and a mirror above it. A rocking chair is on the porch.*

*At rise, DANNY lies sprawled on the couch, with BELLE standing over
him. BELLE FALKIMER is a plain and sturdy woman of fifty-two. Her
son DANNY is an idealistic, morose kid of seventeen.*

BELLE: Will you get moving, Danny? We've got to know what they'll do
to your father! If you can't imagine what sort of disaster he's
heading for —

DANNY: He's headed for something, all right. He's so burned up at
being sent here, he's ready to turn the place inside out! How can
we hold him back? He thinks he's got God on his payroll!

(*He turns over.*)

BELLE: Don't talk like that around me!

DANNY: Okay, skip it.

BELLE (*shaking him*): Do as you're told — run to the Atonement Office,
find out what's going on!

DANNY (*getting up*): I'm going, I'm going. Don't shove —

BELLE: And come right back, you hear me?

(VERN FALKIMER *enters from the cellar. He is in shirt sleeves. He is
fifty-four, vigorous, impressive, a man of great natural dignity and
cultivated warmth.*)

VERN: That's speed — the jet age! (*To* DANNY.) Where are you bound
for?

DANNY: Nowhere.

VERN: There's a printer's on Redemption Avenue, Danny, corner Epiphany. They have a package for me — Viogen circulars.

BELLE: You've got the printers in with you now, on the q.t.?

VERN (*ignoring her*): Get it for me, Danny?

DANNY (*sullenly, after a moment*): I'll get it.

VERN: Good lad. (*putting on his jacket.*) You don't have to be so mopey about it, do you, just because you're doing me a favor for once? Get me a paper while you're out, will you? (*He puts his hand in his pocket.*) I'll never get used to it — no money.

DANNY: And no newspapers, no stock quotations. Nothing to live for!

(*Exits.*)

VERN: A real bundle of charm, that kid; never a pleasant word. If we only had Norman here instead of him —

BELLE: You don't mean that, dear.

VERN (*a little startled*): No, of course not. Only I can't help thinking of Norman — a boy with a head on his shoulders, always bright, helpful, and willing. Couldn't be more different from his brother. (*going to the table*) Danny gets up on the wrong side of the bed every morning. So do you. So do I, and everybody else in this town. Because there's not a damn thing to do here, and all the time in the world to do it in.

BELLE: Can't you realize the business life is over? Over and done with! If you'd only try to find some satisfaction here instead of tormenting yourself and us —

VERN (*slicing an orange*): What satisfaction? You know these Long Home oranges taste like cotton? We've got food here that doesn't taste, sunshine that doesn't warm, so-called fresh air that doesn't cool —

(*A sky-blue envelope comes flying through a mail slot in the wall.*)

VERN: What's that letter?

BELLE (*opening the letter and reading*): "Registration for the spring term of the Process now going on."

VERN (*indicating the wastebasket*): File it.

BELLE: It's that school they have here.

VERN: All the mail we ever get is that official advertising.

BELLE: We ought to consider registering for those courses; that's what we're urged to do.

VERN: What for? To drum up trade for their teachers? Belle, will you save it, please? I'm going to have my hands full with Kellog and Merwin. They started out with zip and vinegar, and now —

BELLE: Are they coming here again? (*bitterly*) I want an end to what you're cooking up with them! And I *mean* cooking up! In the cellar, with all those figs and my best saucepans —

VERN (*with restraint*): I told you — I have a job to do here! As God is my helper, I'm going to bring some businesslike sense and order into this place before we leave!

BELLE (*startled*): Before we leave?

VERN: That's right. Before we leave! You know I never discuss things before I'm ready. Just hold on to your girdle, lady.

BELLE (*vehemently*): It's useless! I can't talk to you any more — I can't reason with you, I can't reach you — you're so wrapped up in yourself, so completely selfish —

VERN: Always building me up!

(*He exits to the kitchen. Trumpets are heard in the near distance. BELLE stands for a moment rigid with frustration. The doorbell rings, and she goes to answer it.*)

KELLOG: Peace, ma'am.

(*TONY KELLOG is a small man with a salesman's bright professional eye. He is accompanied by JOE MERWIN, a more stolid version of the same type.*)

BELLE: Vern is not in! (*feelingly*) Who needs you in our existence, Mr. Kellog? Why do you come here?

KELLOG: I'm starting to wonder about that myself.

BELLE: Stop wondering and make up your mind to keep away from this house!

(*VERN comes back with a bottle of Viogen and drinking glasses.*)

VERN: Cut that, will you, hon?

BELLE: I won't "cut that!" Thirty years your wife and business partner —

VERN: All right, all right, lady —

BELLE: And now I'm shut out while you plot and plan with those two characters —

(*She is unable to continue; exits to the kitchen.*)

KELLOG: Characters! How *about* that! She's gonna bust in on us again, like she did last time. And it ain't only her. Your son Danny, always needling us —

VERN: He's not so bad, just a boy with a chip on his shoulder. You're not going to put yourself on his level? Forget it — get down to

143

business. (s*ternly, as they sit down*) Gentlemen, I have to talk to you seriously. The kind of reports you've been bringing me this week simply will not do, and I want to know the reason.

KELLOG: I hate to say it, Vernie, but Merwin and me have just about hit bottom. You know we can sell. We can even sell what we ain't got — which is exactly what we are doing — and it ain't that there's no interest . . . (*He takes a bundle of orders out of his pocket.*) Just one day's work. We give them a look at these order blanks and they've got their tongues hanging out, ready to sign. Because they all heard of the product —

MERWIN: All these years, that historic slogan: "Viogen, the time-tested tonic for tired tissues."

KELLOG: Nevertheless and still and all they ain't convinced, even while they're signing up. You ought to hear some of these foxy customers: "Falkimer's playing it close to the vest," they says. "There's no money in Long Home," they says, "so what's he trying to sell?"

VERN: And you let that bother you! Because a project like this was never tried here before, does that mean it must never *be* tried?

KELLOG (*uneasily*): You've got to admit the whole setup here is so cockeyed and lopsided —

VERN: And you're accepting that state of affairs as normal! (*proudly*) Gentlemen, we're selling something! So what? Is there anybody in the world who isn't? Only we are the professionals! Who else has the enterprise, the independence, the courage and carefulness, of the man of business? The man of business makes the world go round! Everywhere he goes he's building up the wealth and resources of the world! Nobody's closer to the One Above than a businessman of national reputation!

MERWIN (*impressed*): It couldn't be said better!

KELLOG (*protestingly*): You know we're with you, ninety percent at least, Vern. Still and all —

VERN: A ninety percent effort is not a business effort, you know that, Tony. Not ninety or ninety-five or ninety-nine and nine-tenths percent, either! A distributor of your experience —

KELLOG: I *am* experienced. Twenty-two years with Lowney Brothers, Standard Brand Insecticides — roaches, bedbugs, centipedes, moths, and so forth.

VERN: For a tonic like Viogen you've got to have the old up-and-at'em, if you want results. The world's finest drink demands the world's finest salesmen! If *you* don't have full confidence in your product, how do you expect your customers to have it? (*He takes a vial of fig juice out of his pocket.*) Take a glance at that fig juice— does that look like it's doing something or doesn't it? They tried to tell me nothing ferments in Long Home; they said it would take a miracle! (*He passes the fig juice to* KELLOG, *who regards it uncomfortably and passes it on to* MERWIN.) *You* think so, too. Let me remind you that miracles happen to be my specialty: I started on Earth with nothing but know-how and a little fruit juice, and parlayed that home-brewed beverage into the Number One fruit drink of a nation, coast to coast U.S.A.! (*with pride*) A man has his work cut out for him, no matter where he finds himself! And you can bet that, Up Above, work that's well done is going to be credited on the good side of the ledger!

(*Trumpets sound.*)

Old Viogen helped heal bodies. Our New Viogen will soothe souls. "Snap Up with Soul Sparkle!"

KELLOG
MERWIN } (*Together, overcome*): That'll do it! What a slogan! Wow!

KELLOG (*awed*): I take back all hesitations, Vern. Nobody but you could have come along and figured out how to get the business cycle going in Long Home. A place where nobody ever before tried to buy or sell, and where everything that's ordered is delivered free of charge!

MERWIN: Unnatural, to say the least! Vern, your trade-card idea is a stroke of genius!

KELLOG: And I'll bet it was no afterthought!

VERN: I picked myself an oversized coffin, long before I died, arranged with the undertaker to store away two bottles of Viogen and a supply of these cards inside the lining. Because I could see the whole thing beforehand — a virgin territory beyond all imagination!

KELLOG (*to* MERWIN): And those cards aren't all! What about the circulars he's ordered up, and the junior program he's started — premiums for twelve wing-feathers any Cherub turns in? How can we miss?

VERN: We can't miss! We can't, because we're filling a long-felt want, that's why! Thank you, gentlemen. (*shaking their hands in turn*) Now I know I can count on you! (*pouring Viogen into the punch*) Forty years in business, fifty-four years on Earth — I know my way around.

KELLOG
MERWIN } (*together*): A great mind! Everybody says so!

VERN: But I also know that none of us knows enough. Whether on that mortal Earth we left behind, or here on this Further Shore, there is a Power whose decision is all in all.

KELLOG: Luck, you mean.

VERN: No. I speak of One whose help made Viogen a household word. I speak of Him Above. With Him to sustain us, there is no such word as fail!

KELLOG ⎫
　　　 ⎬ (*together*): Amen!
MERWIN ⎭

VERN: Secure in him as our sponsor, I raise my glass to Viogen!

KELLOG ⎫
　　　 ⎬ (*together*): To Viogen! Down the hatch!
MERWIN ⎭

VERN (*reverently*): Thank you, God!

KELLOG: Whoo! This stuff is for real, Vern!

MERWIN: We ain't used to it no more!

VERN: Real Viogen! The genuine article from back on Earth!

(*Trumpets once more, then music—strange, throbbing and grief-stricken. There is a disquieting pause.*)

KELLOG: The end of Mr. Lumgarden.

MERWIN: He's getting dispersed in Generations Square, just two block away.

VERN (*putting down his glass abruptly*): That's disgusting! The only public activity they carry on here! If they have to do a thing like that, they ought to do it out of sight some place. They make a carnival of it to remind you of your sins — if you have any! (*with conviction*) Not that I accept what they're doing to Lumgarden. True, he was no national figure — just a small, mean man at bottom, with no interest in anything but a ringing cash register; still, he made his pile, as was his right and duty as a citizen, and that has to be respected!

KELLOG (*moved*): You're talking my language, now! We sure have needed a man of your caliber around here, Vern, to make them give us some appreciation!

VERN: We're carrying our lifework into the Great Beyond, because that's our nature! Stick with me, boys! If you've got it, you'll get there!

(BELLE *enters with a tray, goes straight to the table and starts removing all the glasses.*)

VERN: What are you doing?

BELLE: Breaking this up! Business projects beyond the grave! You know how dangerous it is, how it's resented —

VERN (*with dignity*): The Long Home Administration assigned me here, so they needn't be surprised if I find room for a healthy improvement in their setup! I'm doing a pioneer job, and I know that one day it will be gratefully appreciated!

BELLE: They won't let this scheme of yours go on! Here in the middle of the Afterlife! Surrounded by God's Angels! (*vehemently*) Do you hear that music? That's the end of T.S. Lumgarden, who thought he could do as he liked here! A big man in the hardware business — and soon he'll be dimmed out — vaporized! And you can sit here hatching up plans with these two louts —

VERN: Mrs. Falkimer, you're insulting my guests!

BELLE: I'll insult them with a flatiron if they ever come here again!

(*She stalks off to the kitchen, taking the tray with her.*)

KELLOG (*getting up, followed by* MERWIN): What are we, poison?

MERWIN: We can take a hint if we ain't wanted here.

VERN: You know how some women are — undignified. That little woman has all the tact and sensitivity of a steam shovel. . . . Sit down!

(*They sit again, reluctantly. The music has faded.*)

KELLOG: Still and all she's got something there about Mr. Lumgarden. Ever since he got indicted we've had a lot harder sell in this town. Everybody's suspicious.

MERWIN: You'd think we were trying to put something over!

KELLOG: And it all had to happen because he walked out on the Process after one lesson and sixteen other people followed him out! He shoulda thought of the risk to himself and his family.

MERWIN: And to everybody that was associated with him — don't forget that! They sent out the Guardians and rounded up everybody he knew or who ever knew him!

KELLOG (*earnestly*): Like I've been telling you from the start, Vernie—

VERN: Not Vernie. Vern.

KELLOG: Excuse me. (*making the correction*) Vern . . . Like I've been telling you from the start, Vern, the Process is the chief thing on their mind. They want everybody in Long Home to sit in class and think about their past life — what they shoulda done and didn't do and so forth. . . . But if you come along with your Viogen so they can feel good without any lessons —

147

VERN (*coldly*): Anything more?

KELLOG: They'll come down on your whole proposition and finish you off. And not just you. If you think they'll overlook me and Merwin —

VERN: Well! Now the truth's coming out! You're frightened stiff! (*scornfully*) I grant you this place is a desert — deliberately planned that way! There's nothing here — no business activity whatever, no shows, no night life — nothing but the Process! But do you see anybody breaking down the doors to get in there?

KELLOG: Not exactly, but still —

VERN: Did either of *you* ever go to that school?

KELLOG ⎫
⎬ (*together*): Me? No, sir! Not me!
MERWIN ⎭

VERN: Of course not! Most everybody here just can't stand it! (*emphatically*) Nobody's telling anyone in Long Home they have to take Viogen instead of going to that Process school. But if the ordinary man in the street wants some fast, practical help — a drink to soothe the soul — I'm making it available, that's all!

(DANNY *enters, lugging a package.*)

DANNY (*to* VERN): Here's your bundle! (*He slams it down behind* KELLOG.) Where's Mom?

VERN: Mom's in the kitchen. Sit down, Danny, relax.

DANNY (*picking up the bottle of Viogen, amazed*): How did this Viogen get into Long Home?

VERN: Danny, watch that tone of voice!

KELLOG: Wouldn't it be quieter downstairs?

(*He gets up.*)

VERN: Be right with you. (*He unlocks the cellar door.* KELLOG *and* MERWIN *exit to the cellar. To* DANNY.) Now — what's going on? What's all the agitation about?

DANNY: Will you take a suggestion in a nice way, Pop?

VERN: That depends.

DANNY: They've got this educational Process here — why don't you join up? You might catch on to a few Long Home rules — such as that alcohol is illegal here!

VERN: I know the rules and calculate the risks. Give me credit for my age and experience, son, okay?

148

DANNY: Okay — you've had your education. Anyway the school isn't what it used to be: arguments and fights. . . . Forget it.

(*He moves toward the kitchen.*)

VERN (*abruptly*). What were you doing yesterday on Deliverance Road?

DANNY: I was coming home from class. What were *you* doing there, with that gorgeous, hot babe on your arm? You think I didn't recognize her?

VERN: Of course you recognized her. You know her. She used to be my secretary— Lottie Aldrich. What's the excitement about?

DANNY: You know what it's about! You think I've forgotten *that*, too?

VERN: What was there to remember? You once hung around the plant for a few days and happened to see us working late on an inventory —

DANNY: An inventory of what, Pop?

VERN: Drop it, will you, Danny? You're being ridiculous. I was checking up on the company's accountants.

DANNY: Sure you were. Did you ever trust anyone in your life?

VERN: All right, Danny, that will do. Sarcasm, disrespect —

(BELLE *enters.*)

BELLE: What's the trouble?

VERN: Just getting together, father and son. Remembering the good old days . . .

KELLOG (*from the cellar*): Vern! Mr. Falkimer!

BELLE: I've got to talk to you, Vern! You're not going to trample over your family!

VERN: I'm fed up with both of you! You're both cutting away at me lately. I'll wait till you cool off.

(*He exits to the cellar, locking the door as* DANNY *starts to follow.*)

DANNY: He's gone down there to trade secrets with Kellog and Merwin. He's been acting like that for weeks — those two creeps can go in there, but we can't! (*exploding*) I'll get a look at that cellar one of these days if I have to break down the door!

BELLE: Must you add to my state of mind? I've been on pins and needles! What took you so long?

DANNY: I went straight to the Atonement Office like you asked me to — and I tell you, Mom, — I found out plenty. And I was rushing back, only I had to pick up that bundle from the printer's on the way. And when I got held up by the crowds in Generations Square —

149

BELLE: You stayed and watched the dispersion!

DANNY (*defensively*): The Process *wants* us to look at them, Mom — they're extracurricular credit! The Angels were assembled, the trumpets were blowing and the Guardians were moving the crowds along. . . . It's over now — time for ole Lumgarden to come out of the machine. (*with enthusiasm*) It was terrific this time, you know it? The Technicians were dragging him out of his house, his family weeping. . . . And when they threw him into the machine and locked the door — boy, the crowd went wild!

BELLE: Stop it — you're making me feel faint! (*Tormentedly.*) What did you find out at the Office?

DANNY (*taking out a circular*): Look at this, first. I got this proofsheet at the printer's, picked it off the floor. (*Reading*) "Are you bored, dispirited, listless? Does Long Home give you that dragged down feeling? Snap Up with Soul Sparkle! New Viogen, the Drink That's Here and Now!"

BELLE: Viogen! It's an obsession! What did you learn at the Office?

DANNY: He's put in for a transfer to Glory.

BELLE: Oh, my God!

DANNY: This Viogen project he's got here is only a step on his way. Glory Above — the Heavenly Regions — that's where he's *really* going to expand!

BELLE: The man must be mad! Why can't he stay here and rest up after the commotion of a lifetime? (*vehemently*) What's wrong with this garden suburb of Long Home? What's wrong with this lovely street, Rainbow Terrace? We're fortunate to be here! Fortunate! This place is for those not good and not bad; that means practically everybody — Vern, too!

DANNY: You'll never convince *him* he's everybody! He's special, all by himself — without even Norman to butter him up now.

BELLE (*frantically*): We've got to stop him, Danny!

DANNY: How?

BELLE: I'm going to the Atonement Office myself — right now! And you're coming with me! I've never been there. You've got to help me!

DANNY: Not me.

BELLE: I have no one but you to rely on, here. Don't say no to me, Danny!

(VERN *enters from the cellar followed by* KELLOG *and* MERWIN.)

VERN: Why do we always have to plead with him? Can't he do what he's asked without making it a Supreme Court case?

BELLE: Do you know what I'm asking him for?

VERN: What's the difference? No, I don't,

DANNY: Then why don't you find out, first?

VERN: Stop that, will you? Can't we have some civil conversation here? What's this about?

(FRED *comes to the door and rings the bell. He is a young technician in a black overall uniform.*)

BELLE: Making your plans for this family, that's what it's about — deciding for us, whether we like it or not —

VERN (*stung*): Do we have to go into personal matters now? There are other people here.

(FRED *opens the door and walks in.*)

FRED: Vernon Falkimer? Special delivery. (*He thrusts a blue envelope into* VERN'S *hand.*) Why don't you answer your blasted doorbell?

VERN: Why don't you mind your manners?

FRED: How much time do you think I've got?

VERN: You've got the rest of forever! And I don't like your tone of voice!

FRED: Just fill out those papers, mister. I'll be back for them before noon today.

(*Exits.*)

VERN: On Earth I wouldn't hire that kind to clean out toilets — here they order you around!

BELLE: That was a messenger from the Atonement Office. What's in that envelope he gave you?

VERN (*going to the desk to lock up the letter*): Just some forms to fill out.

BELLE: Forms requesting a transfer to Glory!

(KELLOG *and* MERWIN *start edging quietly toward the door.*)

If you think you can go hiding things from us forever —

VERN (*with restraint*): Let me make something clear to you, Belle. It's my duty, as head of this household, to rectify a mistake. A very serious mistake! Whoever sent me and my family to a place like Long Home, you can be sure of one thing: it wasn't the Good Lord Above! (*He catches sight of* KELLOG *and* MERWIN.) Where are you two going? (*They stop, irresolutely.*) I don't blame you. We'll

151

finish this conference on a park bench, some place. Wait for me.
(*To* BELLE) You've done it again, Belle. There's no place like
home for making a man want to be somewhere else!

KELLOG: Peace, ma'am.

(VERN *and the* SALESMEN *exit.*)

BELLE (*ruefully*): He's so offended, now, and I don't blame him. I just
can't control myself. Embarrassing him like that, in front of
others —

DANNY: Are you starting to excuse him?

BELLE: How can you be so insensitive? He's been so lost and humi-
liated once he came here! A man who is so forceful! A lion, a
tiger!

DANNY: A lion! A tiger! You're killing me, Mom! (a*ngrily*) Has he got
you on a leash or something? The things he used to do to you on
Earth! Always putting you down — complaining about your cooking, sneering at your clothes, going away on business trips and
always leaving you behind — I haven't mentioned the worst! And
you still hang on to him! What sort of life is that?

BELLE: It's all I ever had, and I'm used to it. I'll go, now, to the
Atonement Office and plead with the Angels for it. I'll get down
on my knees!

(*She starts for the door.*)

DANNY: Mom, you're twisting my arm! There's no sense going there —
I tell you the Atonement Office won't even listen!

BELLE: They'll listen to us. They'll have to!
(*There is an outburst of shouting and lamentation in the
street.*)
Oh! What now?

DANNY (*going to look out*): It's Lumgarden. He's let out of the
machine; he's going by.

BELLE (*now also at the window*): I see him . . . and his wife and
children, and the crowds — (*with a gasp*) I can look right
through him!

DANNY: He's vanishing, fading, right there in the sunlight in the street!

BELLE: Oh, my dear God — that mustn't happen to Vern! (*frantically*)
The Atonement Office! Hurry, Danny! Hurry!

(*She pushes him toward the door.*)

Scene 2

Long Home: The Atonement Office, Department of Adjudication, immed-

iately after Scene 1. An insistent sound of bells can be heard, as in an old-time department store, and the whirr of wings of arriving and departing Angels. BROTHER ANSTICE *and* SISTER GUTHRIE, *two of Long Home's lesser Angels, enter agitatedly, right, and go toward the conference table, center. They are the Blue Angels of Judgment, in sky-blue robes with the emblem of a gold balance on their sleeves.* ANSTICE, *dried-up and elderly, holds an enormous book;* GUTHRIE, *female and black, carries a briefcase.*

GUTHRIE (*as they enter*): Are you all right, Brother Anstice?

ANSTICE: Still shaken up. . . . I thought for a moment that mob was heading straight for us, running amuck! (*shuddering*) Yelling "Get down to the facts!" Those demonstrators are getting at least half of their encouragement from our own Brother Finch! "Never mind the Scriptures, look at the facts" — those are his very words!

GUTHRIE: I'm beginning to have some serious thoughts about Brother Finch. The line he's been taking about that man Falkimer — (*grimly*) This very morning he was telling me, "Falkimer used to make Viogen out of grapes, and grapes don't even grow here, so why worry?" I told him, "The man is using figs instead of grapes! He's got a cellar full of mash!" "What of it?" Finch says. "Nothing ferments in Long Home; it'll never happen, it'll never come to pass," he says —

(*A* CHERUB *enters from stage right with an interdepartmental envelope. He wears a sky-blue T-shirt and shorts. A large button with the name* PIP *is pinned to his shirt.*)

PIP: From Research. (*reading caption on envelope*) "Re Vernon J. Falk- imer Case." Sign here. (*taking receipt*) You guys got any old wing-feathers you don't want? Any that fell off?

ANSTICE: Any old wing-feathers? What for?

PIP: Collecting them, that's all.

GUTHRIE: We have no old wing-feathers, and we are not "guys" to you!

PIP: Don't bug me, Grandma. (*going*) Couple of glumps!

GUTHRIE: On Earth they take that kind and paddle their little bottoms.

ANSTICE: What insolence! That's a sample of Long Home today. They've picked it up from the humans. (*with a shrug*) Well, let's see what he's brought. . . . (*Looking over papers.*) Item: received too much change of a dollar bill and kept it. Item: washed uncanceled postage stamps off letters and used them again; more things of that sort —

GUTHRIE: What do they expect us to do with *that*?

(BROTHER MORIAS *enters. He is the Black Angel of Oblivion, in a black robe with the emblem of a gold circle on his sleeve. He is grave and preoccupied, with a face like ice. The* BLUE ANGELS *rise.*)

MORIAS: Peace, Brethen. Don't stand, please. . . . I'm sorry I'm late, but the trouble at the Lumgarden fading —

ANSTICE: Yes, sir. We were nearly overrun by the mob on the way here.

GUTHRIE: And we've just heard there's been more trouble at the Process.

MORIAS: Yes. Finch and Cheswick have also been delayed.
                      (FINCH *and* CHESWICK *enter.*)
        Here they are now.

(BROTHER FINCH *is a disarmingly mild, scholarly type in a white robe with the emblem of an open book on his sleeve.* SISTER CHESWICK, *who appears to be a typical bureaucrat, wears a robe and insignia like those of* ANSTICE *and* GUTHRIE.)

FINCH: Apologies. . . . We've had another outbreak at the Process.

CHESWICK: Second time this week. Throwing books, inkwells, and erasers, yelling, "Down with moral laws — "

GUTHRIE *(shrugs):* Is that surprising, when they see what some types think they can get away with? Maybe people like that should be *ordered* to register for the Process.

FINCH: Sister Guthrie, you can't teach anything to someone like Falkimer — that was clear enough in the Lumgarden case. As principal of the Process, I happen to know what we're up against. The old-time sinners at least knew enough to recognize their failings. What can we do with those we're getting now? Average citizens, toughened by a life of legal technicalities, sealed up in self-approval, unreachable and unteachable — at least not with the lessons I'm required to teach —

CHESWICK: Like "Honesty is the best policy," "Turn the other cheek," "If at first you don't succeed, try, try again — " You expect a grown person to go back to kindergarten?

ANSTICE: Kindergarten? I'm speechless! We're just a bunch of old fuddy-duddies, according to you and Finch — cut-and-dried specimens, pre-Freudian reactionaries —

FINCH: Not only pre-Freudian! No idea whatever of any modern science — satisfied to follow the code of a little sect of Israelites wandering in the desert —

ANSTICE: I've heard enough! Right is right and wrong is wrong — science or no science. That's Gospel, and it couldn't be plainer!

154

MORIAS: Sit down, all of you! We're setting a fine, angelic example to the inhabitants of Long Home! (*He taps the desk bell.*) I have asked for a briefing straight from the Higher Office Administration before we proceed to a vote.

(FRED *enters with a small black suitcase.*)

FRED: Technician Fred Stowell reporting.

MORIAS (*to* FRED): Show us what you have.

FRED: Yes, sir.

(*He takes receipts out of his suitcase.*)

MORIAS (*to the* ANGELS): Take a good look at those advance orders for Viogen, to be paid for on delivery.

ANSTICE (*astounded*): Paid for? How? With money?

MORIAS (*to* FRED): Show them.

FRED (*taking out cards*): Trade-cards like this one. Allotted to his distributors, who hand them out to their agents. These cards will be hard to get. The distributors receive only a certain number of them, and each customer gets only five dollars' worth.

MORIAS: A profitless capitalist system! Commercial canvassing in Long Home, and the prospect that our inmates will be walking around in a Viogen stupor instead of going to school. (*To* FRED.) Collect the cards. You may go, and thank you.

FRED: Yes, sir.

(*He puts away the cards and exits.*)

MORIAS: You now have a full-sized picture of what's been happening since Mr. Falkimer arrived here.

GUTHRIE (*rising*): May I respectfully inquire why all this has been allowed to go on so long, whereas we settled the Lumgarden case at once?

MORIAS: Mr. Lumgarden, let me remind you, had no background of intercessory prayers. The prayers for Mr. Falkimer, over the past six years — (*consulting a paper*) — stood, as of this morning, at 4,367,232. Meaning that, whether you like it or not, by Wednesday at the latest, there will be enough to guarantee his formal hearing for a transfer.

ANSTICE (*in great indignation*): He might be guaranteed it by genuine prayers, but these are bought and paid for! Prayers from a little religious group somewhere in the backwoods —

MORIAS (*sternly*): Our hands would not be tied, as they have been, if these prayers were invalid. Not Grade A prayers, of course, but

155

zealous prayers from a little congregation that doesn't see anything wrong with the bargain they've made.

ANSTICE: I move for an examination of Mr. Falkimer.

GUTHRIE: I second that.

MORIAS: Discussion?
> (*He looks toward* FINCH *and* CHESWICK, *but they are silent.*)
> Very well. On the motion: those in favor?
>> (ANSTICE *and* GUTHRIE *nod approval.*)
> Those opposed?
>> (CHESWICK *and* FINCH *raise their hands.*)
> Opposed . . . Finch and Cheswick.
>> (*He gives them a brief, searching glance.*)
> Since there is a tie, I cast the deciding vote. The motion is carried.

GUTHRIE: I move we adjourn.

ANSTICE: I second it.

MORIAS: Those in favor?
>> (*A show of hands.*)
> So ordered.

FINCH: Coming, Cheswick?

FINCH
CHESWICK } (*together*): Peace.

> (*They exit.*)

ANSTICE (*to* GUTHRIE, *as* MORIAS *gathers up his papers*): You're perfectly right about those two. Boring from within.

MORIAS (*picking up his briefcase*): The preliminary interview with Falkimer is Finch's department, as you know. I appoint you and Anstice herewith to conduct the examination.

GUTHRIE
ANSTICE } (*together, gratified*): We'll do our duty! Rely on us!

MORIAS (*emphasizing each word*): Brethren, I warn you both — on your guard!

CURTAIN

Scene 3

The Falkimer cottage, immediately following Scene 2. LOTTIE ALDRICH, a trim, luscious blonde of twenty-five, comes to the porch door and rings the bell. VERN, at the desk, examining the vials of fig juice, springs up to answer. They kiss. What follows is a scene of unabashed carnality under the dialog.

LOTTIE: Vern, dearest, I know we were supposed to meet at my place later today, but I couldn't wait till then to —

VERN: Get some loving.

LOTTIE: We shouldn't be doing this, dear — you know we shouldn't.

(They embrace again.)

VERN: Lottie, Babesie —

LOTTIE: I came to tell you I couldn't sleep all night, I was so worried after listening to your plans. Don't you understand why they assigned you to Long Home? Why they've given you this chance to enter the Process? It's to rededicate yourself! The way I have, Vern! *(Eagerly, taking a booklet from her bag.)* Here is the School prospectus; read it, do! It's about soul training; they teach you tolerance and patience, and after a while, self-discipline. The gross side of your nature drops away; you come out cleansed, purified —

VERN: You sound nervous, Babes. How about a drink?

LOTTIE: A drink?

VERN: We could both use one. Real Viogen tonic.

(He hands her a glass of punch.)

LOTTIE *(astonished)*: Real Viogen, in Long Home? How ever did you do it? *(putting down the glass)* But Vern, darling, I don't drink anymore. Things are different here.

VERN: Yes, indeed. You're purified. *(He holds her off, returning the prospectus.)* Prim as the day I took you into my private office — such a juicy little corn-fed, home-town babe, so prudish, virtuous, and sexy! They're revirginizing you here!

LOTTIE *(giggling)*: You shouldn't talk like that! It's so immodest—

VERN: What is that damn place you live in? Some sort of old maid's YWCA, where they teach you to say things like "Peace on this house?"

LOTTIE: "Peace *to* this house," silly. And I wasn't an old maid, ever; I was your woman — only twenty-five when I passed over.

VERN *(with an abrupt change in manner, carefully)*: Tell me something, Lottie —

LOTTIE *(tensing at his change in mood)*: What is it, dear?

(She pulls him toward the couch.)

157

VERN: When you came to Long Home and they gave you that examination —

LOTTIE: The regular examination, you mean, before the Haitus starts in?

VERN: Yes. What did you tell them about the way you died?

LOTTIE: The last time we were together? (*simply*) I shielded the purity of our love from any misunderstanding, just as you always taught me.

VERN: Tell me what you told them, exactly.

LOTTIE: Only that my heart failed, because I had a leaky heart valve; that's all I said — you can believe me, dear. And they didn't ask me any more about it. All they said was my heart would be fine from now on; I needn't think about it anymore. (*confidingly*) On Earth I used to think about it a lot, because I knew I couldn't last long. That was one big reason why I let myself go with you the way I did. (*quickly*) At first, I mean. It was all so different when I knew you loved me, darling! I was so proud and happy, then, that I'd given myself to you; I worried only because we'd have so little time together. But we can be together here for all time, now, can't we?

VERN: Together where? Here in Long Home?

LOTTIE: It's so good to be here! It's so restful, and there's no illness, there's no death in Long Home. I'm so grateful to be here —

VERN: No death, and the Process school for all the ages — that's what they ask you to settle for! And you're so grateful! (*with scorn*) Lottie, I don't live on margin! I don't settle for anything like Long Home! And you're not going to, either! I told you, Babes: I'm going to Glory — and you're coming with me!

LOTTIE (*alarmed*): Don't mention that again, Vern! You frighten me! That man they dispersed today — you see, I can't even remember his name, now; only the Angels still know it — he was just like you, demanding a transfer to Above. He's gone forever. Oh, Vern, take care, look out —

VERN: Look out for what? I have nothing to worry about! What will they find if I'm examined? That I never failed to revere the Lord Above and had an A-Number-One credit rating in Dun and Bradstreet?

LOTTIE: Vern, please listen to me! The Angels are so strict, so unbending! And this Viogen project you've started —

VERN: I know they don't like it. What do they expect? I'd have lost my mind just sitting around here! When it comes to the ear of the Good Lord Above how they've treated me, somebody's going to pay for it!

LOTTIE (*beginning to waver*): That's true. A man of your character and vision, your distinction —

VERN: Besides, the year before I died, I found that little church in Pichaville, Tennessee — the Gospel Brethren — left them a $5,000 annual bequest to shout their halleluiahs for me — (*happily*) And they've been shouting day in and day out, without a stop! Their prayers will guarantee my place in Glory! I put that little bunch of Bible-thumpers on their feet financially, and they're so all-fired genuinely grateful —

LOTTIE (*carried away*): Vern, honey, you're the most exciting man I ever met! You could always do things — anything you wanted! Not like me! You're going to Glory! They'll *have* to transfer you!

VERN: You, too, Babes! On our way to Glory!

LOTTIE (*dreamily*): On our way to Glory! (*then mournfully*) Oh, Vern, I'm such a nobody! Up There you'll have your choice of the loveliest girls, I'm sure. I'll be so jealous —

VERN: Jealous over me? I'm fifty-four, fat and balding —

LOTTIE: You're big and strong and handsome! You'll be the biggest catch in the Heavenly Kingdom!

VERN (*reaching for the zipper of her dress*): I don't need anyone but you! You're beautiful, Babesie! And what's more, you pay attention when a man has something to say! Do you know how rare that is?

LOTTIE (*clinging to him*): It's true, I try to listen and understand, don't I?

VERN: That's right, Babes. That's why I've got to have you with me, or it won't be Glory! (*vehemently*) The minute my memory came back I went looking for you everywhere, because I needed you so desperately!

LOTTIE: Did you, Vern? Did you really?

VERN: A man has to have love! I've always needed you, wanted you, ever since the day we met —

LOTTIE: The day we met! On Vernon Falkimer Day in McGrawtown! (*then, unhappily*) But finally everything was finished, wasn't it? Between us, I mean? You told me a divorce would be harmful to the family and hurt Belle — and damage the business, too — bad for the corporate image, is what you said —

VERN: What choice was there? That was my cross. And yours, too. We had to bear it together.

LOTTIE: It made me feel like just nothing!

159

VERN: Just nothing? A marvelous girl like you? You're so beautiful, Lottie! — Why are you crying?

LOTTIE: I haven't had a compliment in so long! All you have to say is "Lottie, you're beautiful" — and I'm lost! You're so dear —

VERN: Babes, Babesie — (*softly*) You're wearing the necklace I gave you —

LOTTIE: You know I've worn it ever since you gave it to me?

VERN: You really love me!

LOTTIE: Oh, Vern, I'm yours! Yours for all eternity!

(*She unhooks her bra. Blackout on her and* VERN. BELLE *and* DANNY *come up the path to the house.*)

BELLE: Why did that clerk at the front desk have to be so heartless? All he said was, "The man is over twenty-one. Who are you, his mother?" That whole crowd jeering at us when they found out who we were! That scrawny old man who said he took Viogen for more than thirteen years — that loudmouth who claimed she guzzled Viogen by the quart —

DANNY: Don't worry. Pop's always known how to weave his way out of things — he'll know how to get out of this. I'll see you later; I've got to think.

BELLE: Are you leaving me to handle him alone?

DANNY: Did he ever listen to either of us? Or to anybody else who didn't think he was perfect? (*wryly*) He used to get letters by the truckload from satisfied customers, telling him how he renewed their faltering courage and so forth. . . . That's what they wrote him while they were pepped up with the vino in his bottles. What did they write him when they sobered up? *Those* letters wound up in the wastebasket! Pop made money because people were out of luck. You know what Brother Finch says? "Don't profit by your neighbor's troubles; don't light your cigar on a burning house!"

BELLE: You don't understand your father. Or me either. Suppose he was a liar sometimes? Who isn't? (DANNY *moves off.*) All you ever did was brood about yourself! Roaming around, dawdling — Now you go roaming around the Hereafter!

DANNY: Maybe it's because I never had a home with you on Earth, Mom. I was the baby of the family, but you babied Pop, not me.

BELLE (*calling after him as he exits*): Don't be so disappointed in us, Danny! Please don't!

(*She follows him, torn; stops and turns back, then goes slowly up the steps to the porch. The light dims up on* LOTTIE *and* VERN. LOTTIE, *her shoes off, is lying stretched out on the sofa, a bed-pillow under her head.* VERN *is declaiming.*)

VERN: In your transparent robe of dazzling white, with a crown like Miss Universe, the Playmate of the Century! In the Radiant Land, that Land of Hope and Glory —

LOTTIE (*starry-eyed*): That Radiant Land! That Land of Hope and Glory! (*then sitting up*) And Belle! Is she going to be there, too?

VERN (*brought up short*): Belle and Danny, and Norman, too, when his time comes. We've been all through that, Babes.

LOTTIE (*helplessly*): Yes, we have, haven't we? It has to go on!

VERN (*brought up short*): I'm a family man, Lottie, Babesie, we've got to be reasonable. (*fixing his tie*) We took a terrible chance: Belle could have walked in on us any minute. Better let me zip up your dress. (*soothingly*) Don't look so hopeless; I'll make a deal for you. They'll understand true, genuine love Up There!
(BELLE *enters.*)
She's here! I told you! (*loudly, as* LOTTIE *hastily puts on her shoes*) Surprise, Belle! What do you think? We have a visitor!

BELLE (*with fake calm*): So I see.

VERN: Lottie Aldrich! You realize how long it's been since we've seen this girl? I ran into her in the street yesterday, made her promise to drop in. She's been telling me all about the Process.

BELLE: How educational!

LOTTIE: I didn't mean to intrude, Belle. I —

BELLE (*sits, wearily*): Oh, no, dear, it was thoughtful of Vern inviting you here. Very thoughtful indeed. I'm sure you've been having a real get-together with him; he's such a genial, entertaining host —

VERN: As a matter of fact we were on a very serious topic: I was just telling Lottie how we came to be here. (*To* LOTTIE.) We woke up in this cottage after the smashup. Griswold Pharmacies, Pittsburgh; you remember them. We bought out their whole chain. I was driving with Belle to a management conference when it happened.

BELLE: The only time in years he took me along on a trip. Said we might go on to New York from there, take in some Broadway shows. . . . Instead we came straight here.

LOTTIE: You poor dears! . . . But that's all behind you, now. *I* was telling Mr. Falkimer why Long Home is so nice to live in. You'll love it, Belle, when you get on to things. It's so nice: no rush about anything, nothing wears out —

161

BELLE: Except one's patience.

LOTTIE (*chattering on, embarrassed*): That's so. It takes time to get used to this place: no regular duties like marketing, and so little housework. . . . Of course you *would* like to see your loved ones again —

BELLE: Yes.

LOTTIE: Your two girls, and Norman and Danny. . . . It *was* Danny who was lost in the Korean War?

BELLE (*getting up*): It's kind of you to remember my family for me, Lottie. Yes, I *would* like to see them. . . . I'm tired and I'm going upstairs. Excuse me.

(*She goes to the stairs.*)

VERN: *I'd* like to see them, too. And my office. I have unfinished business to take care of.

BELLE (*turning back; to* LOTTIE): He can't remember what business; his memory keeps coming back in bits and pieces.

LOTTIE: It's the Haitus, of course. We all go through it for six years after we get here, remembering nothing from day to day. You and Mr. Falkimer are just coming out of it; you won't have your full memory back until it's over.

BELLE: You don't know Vern: he always did have a selective memory — convenient for forgetting all about his life with me. . . . You don't suppose he remembers our first date, for instance? He got mad when I told him not to paw me over. It was just his pride in his technique, of course . . .

VERN: Look, Belle —

BELLE: Vern, Vern, how many things you've forgotten that I still remember! . . . . The day we were married, when you stood there, tall and handsome, promising you'd look after me and be forever faithful. . . . And I can see again the hospital where I delivered our first baby, Norman. . . . How anxious you looked when the nurse brought him in — (*to* LOTTIE) Vern was scared he might be getting some sort of monster. We didn't get a monster. (*tenderly*) We got Norman — weighed eight and a quarter pounds.

VERN: Yes, we got Norman, thank God.

(*He moves off, annoyed.*)

BELLE: How is *your* memory, Lottie? Do you remember your last visit to our summer home in Rampagat, that night when you and Vern went through the woods to watch the moon rise over the lake? You were wearing the same neck-chain; I'm sure it means a lot to you!

(She exits upstairs.)

VERN: A fine knifing job *that* was!

LOTTIE: Poor woman!

VERN: "Poor woman"?

LOTTIE: I'm so ashamed!

VERN: She's the one who ought to be ashamed! You used to be so furious about her — ready to kill her on sight!

LOTTIE: I was bad, Vern. *(ruefully)* I can see now: how I never thought of anything but my own selfish desires, from the very first time we met — when I'd won the beauty contest and they made me Queen for the Day! . . . Riding with you in the open car while everyone applauded! Oh how I longed for you after that day's excitement! I saw your picture in the papers, I watched you on T.V. In my dreams you were my father, my brother, my secret lover! Why do you think I took a secretarial course? To be in Chicago, near you — in the Vernon J. Falkimer Building! Then came the morning when you picked me out of the stenographic pool! Then those heavenly days in your private office, the trips together, the hotels with adjoining rooms! How beautiful and wonderful that was! And how sinful! *(remorsefully)* We can never be together again, Vern. And Glory is not for me: I don't deserve it.

VERN: The big romance is over; you've decided that I'm too old for you —

LOTTIE: You're the most vital man I know or ever will know. No, dear, that's not it.

VERN: Then why are you running away and leaving me alone?

LOTTIE *(moved)*: Alone? You were always alone! Alone, inside yourself! That happy handshake and the glad voice on the telephone — that was you at the office. But it wasn't really you at all, was it? You're the lonesomest man I ever met, dear! *(Turning away to the door.)* I love you so! But I can't help you!

VERN: Don't leave me!

LOTTIE: *(opening the door)*: I couldn't help you on Earth, and I can't help you now, either. I'm not good enough, not smart enough, to know how. Don't expect anything from me — please forgive me — (BROTHER FINCH *appears at the door, carrying a heavy, portable machine. With a gasp of fear as she sees him.)* Brother Finch! The White Angel!

VERN: Don't leave me!

LOTTIE: Oh, Vern, please let me go!

(*She escapes, running blindly past* FINCH, *who puts down his machine and hurries after her.* VERN *turns back, shaken, to find that* BELLE *has been watching him from the stairs.*)

BELLE (*coming down*): Yes, I heard a lot of it, Vern. It was loud enough! Your playmate doesn't want to play.

VERN: Watch out, Belle. The bitch in you is showing.

(BROTHER FINCH *returns to the porch. He rings the doorbell.*)

BELLE (*seeing him*): There's Brother Finch back again. He probably talked to Lottie in the street.
(*She goes to the door.*)
They've scheduled this interview for a reason! Watch your step, Vern!
(*She admits* FINCH.)

FINCH: Mr. and Mrs. Falkimer? Peace to this house. I am Brother Finch — Adjudication Bureau, in charge of the Process.

BELLE: Are you here to start examining Vern?

FINCH: No; ma'am. Only to discuss that possibility, since he's interested in a transfer. (*To* VERN.) No doubt, sir, you've been wondering why you were sent to a place where nobody ever talked over a proposition or closed a deal. Mr. Lumgarden, who was dispersed today, felt the same way; he seemed to think he'd been assigned here by some miserable bureaucrat in our Office. (*opening his machine*) Until the last he was sure the Lord would take care of him. I've been given to understand that those are your sentiments as well, sir.

VERN: That's right. The Lord Almighty has been good to me; I'm as close to Him as I am to you this minute.

FINCH: Then perhaps you can tell me what He looks like?

VERN: What sort of question is that? He's God, that's all. Big. A big man with a long white beard, a nice, kind smile, cheerful disposition. . . What's so important what He looks like? I feel Him inside me, and that's enough.

FINCH (*with a sigh*): Yes. . . . We're going to have a look inside you. If you'll just sit here, sir —

VERN (*exchanging a dubious look with* BELLE): Are you a regular standard Angel, Brother Finch? This thing looks like medical equipment.

FINCH: Spiritual, not medical. An incisoscope. . . . Yes, I'm a regular standard Angel, as you put it, Mr. Falkimer, in the line of regular duty. Your right wrist, please . . .

(*He proceeds to fasten to* VERN'S *wrist an instrument that vaguely resembles the customary device for testing blood pressure. It has a disk attached.*)
Would you kindly snap on that switch, Mrs. Falkimer? The one on the machine? (*The disk is illuminated. To* VERN) Please look into the lens. What do you see?

VERN (*shrugging*): Looks something like pink wax, with holes in it and wires coming out of it.

FINCH: A square inch of your skin, pores, and hairs, enlarged.

VERN: Disgusting!

FINCH (*turning an indicator*): Let's come closer. What does that look like?

VERN: Like corn on the cob.

FINCH: That's right: your body cells. Made, in turn, of these particles — still smaller molecules — atoms —

VERN: What's all this getting at?

FINCH: We're not through yet, Mr. Falkimer; don't get up. Those vague shapes that rush past each other and sometimes collide — are the electrons that form the atoms. And now, vibrations. Those you can only feel, not see. That's as far as we go with this machine. (*He switches off the disk.*) The object of this demonstration is to restore your sense of mystery.

VERN (*increasingly resentful*): What mystery?

FINCH: The mystery of Almighty God, Mr. Falkimer. (*solemnly*) Are you sure it isn't Santa Claus you've been thinking of, rather than the Creator of all things?

VERN: Is that supposed to be a joke, Brother Finch?

FINCH: Heaven forbid! (*closing his machine*) Before you fully make up your mind about asking for a transfer, it's been necessary to give you a more ample notion of God — And that isn't easy. As you see, we finally get down to vibrations, and just what *they* are is still beyond us.

VERN: I can see it's beyond you. You don't have to give *me* "a more ample notion of God." I knew everything I had to know about Him by the time I was sixteen, when I was a reader in the local church — and *I* never found Him complicated! . . . Trying to tell me that I'm nothing but vibrations or corn on the cob! You admit you don't know what it's all about, but just the same you're running a Process here to teach people what you don't know!

BELLE (*distressed*): Please, Vern!

165

FINCH (*picking up the machine; to* VERN): You appear to know your own mind. I'll leave you to your decision about asking for a transfer.

BELLE (*hastily*): Brother Finch, Vern didn't mean that, about you're teaching something you don't know. He —

VERN: Stay out of it, Belle. He heard me say what I mean.

BELLE (*persisting*): He's been very upset, Brother Finch. . . . That young woman who was leaving here just as you arrived —

FINCH: Yes — Miss Aldrich; she attends the Process.

BELLE: Whatever *she* may have told you —

FINCH: Collecting evidence is not my function, Mrs. Falkimer. (*at the door*) You have a member of the family attending our courses, have you not? Your son, Daniel Falkimer. Headstrong, but Danny's a good boy; he may get there some day. (*To* VERN.) I congratulate you, sir, on your very definite opinions. If you ever *did* decide to enter the Process, you might learn to offer them with more caution.

(Exits.)

VERN: That egghead! And that Process of his — turning people against me and making a mystery out of God! (*seething*) The Good Lord Above is no mystery to me! When I was a little boy in McGrawtown my crazy Uncle Clem talked as if the Eternal God had blood in His eye and a strap in His hand, just like Clem himself! But I put my faith in a different kind of God — not full of wrath but kind and loving, like a father: the Helper and Protector of orphans, the One who has stood over me, loving me and supporting me all my life! So don't let anybody say it was He who sent me to this place!

(FRED *comes to the door and rings the bell.*)

BELLE (*imploringly*): Is your mind still on that, Vern? Give it up! You're not going ahead with your transfer after listening to that Angel? He had me shaking like a leaf.

VERN: That's enough of your trying to scare me!

BELLE: They see past technicalities here, Vern! The sort of tricky legal papers, for instance, that you used to make me sign for you —

VERN: Business! Ordinary business practice!

BELLE: And Lottie? What about Lottie?

(FRED *rings again, startling them both.*)

166

BELLE (*seeing him*): It's that messenger, back for your signature. I'll tell him you've changed your mind. (*She opens the door.*) If you're here for those papers, Mr. Falkimer is not applying.

VERN: Don't take charge of me, Belle. (*He goes to his desk.*) The papers are signed and ready. (*He takes them out of a drawer.*) Here they are.

BELLE: No, Vern! No!

(FRED *waits impatiently.*)

You'll be dead forever if you fail! Not like on Earth, where you died but are still remembered! This time everything will be forgotten: every word you ever spoke, every step you ever took — your face, your voice, your very name — (*anguished*) And what will that do to Danny and me? Don't we count?

VERN: Trust me. You're my family: you'll be part of the deal when the time comes. (*with utter confidence*) It's a calculated risk, but that's my specialty, making good on calculated risks! I'm ready! Let them examine me!

(*He hands the envelope to* FRED.)

Curtain

ACT II

Scene 1

The Falkimer cottage, late afternoon, a few days after Scene 3. ANSTICE and GUTHRIE are at the center table, their paraphernalia before them: for ANSTICE a stenographic notebook, for GUTHRIE a bulging briefcase and what looks like an old-fashioned pair of grocer's scales. The table also holds a pitcher of punch, and glasses. BELLE, her hands in her lap, sits on the couch, left. VERN has apparently been having a rough time: his clothes are rumpled and his tie askew. The ANGELS show evidence of having sampled the punch too liberally: GUTHRIE reclines in her chair, rubbing the back of her head; ANSTICE leans forward, scowling. The voices of a crowd are heard outside the house, increasing in volume as the scene progresses. At rise, ANSTICE is speaking.

ANSTICE: Yes, yes, you left every cent behind you. Very good of you, I'm sure! Mr. Falkimer, you created a family corporation, with your son Norman in charge, to escape inheritance taxes. That was the first time your family saw any of your money. (*curtly*) You baffle me, sir — all geniality and no generosity! Why didn't you distribute something while you were still on Earth? A cow is better than a pig, they say: a cow gives milk while it's alive, but a pig gives bacon only when it's dead!

167

GUTHRIE: Why must you shout at the poor man after everything he had to endure on Earth? (*to* VERN, *solicitously*) Please go on with your story, Vernon. As you told us, you were a poor little orphan, in McGrawtown, Missouri, forced on your Uncle Clem, a smalltown grocer who had no use for someone else's brat —

VERN: I was six years old when my mother left me in the church pew. It was a dull, rainy morning. She was going to the railroad station to buy tickets for us both; to California, she said, where the sun always shines and the kids eat mile-high ice cream cones. . . . She never came back. That was the day of my despair, when I put away childish things. From that day onward I thirsted for achievement as the hart panteth for the water-brooks.

GUTHRIE (*nodding*): "As the hart panteth" very well put — Psalms 42:1. (*To* VERN.) Yours was indeed a deplorable case, well documented in our records. You were shamefully exploited, underfed, and mistreated by your miserly Uncle Clem —

ANSTICE: Let me remind you that when he delivered groceries for that same Uncle Clem he stole three doughnuts out of the bag he was carrying! A straight transgression of "Thou shalt not steal" — at the age of nine, when he was old enough to know just what he was doing!

GUTHRIE: He was underfed and hungry. Besides, I'm sure the poor boy has been troubled by that incident ever since. Haven't you, Vernon?

VERN: Yes, indeed.

GUTHRIE: There you are! (*benevolently*) I believe we can afford to overlook that lapse, everything considered.

ANSTICE (*thoroughly annoyed*): Don't be so high-minded! Will you tell me why he's entitled to all that maudlin sympathy you've been bestowing on him? Other self-made men have also started as orphans — with monotonous regularity — and have been admitted straight to Glory! (*To* VERN.) Let's return to your bank statements. According to my figures —

VERN (*flaring*): All that seems to interest you is my money! Asking about nickels and dimes, like a government tax auditor!

GUTHRIE (*to* ANSTICE): There's something in what he says. After all, when it comes to business matters, on which we're not too expert—

VERN: That's right — you're not! What do you Angels know about life on Earth? I refuse to answer any more questions about my money— and I want that stated in the record!

(*He sits down with folded arms.*)

GUTHRIE: We have only been trying to do our duty, Vernon.

(There is a sudden rise in the volume of shouting outside.)

ANSTICE *(irritated)*: Mrs. Falkimer, would you mind shutting the windows for us? That noise is very distracting.

BELLE *(proceeding to shut the windows and draw the blinds, deadening the sounds)*: It's some of the neighbors: they're still arguing over that man's dispersion.

ANSTICE: They didn't like the ceremony, I imagine.

BELLE: No, sir. It made them very nervous.

ANSTICE: That is the intention. *(To VERN)* Very well, sir. We'll drop the financial aspects of the case and proceed with something else.
(He takes out of his briefcase the thin gold chain and little gold heart worn by LOTTIE in the previous scene.)
Will you examine that, please?
(BELLE freezes.)
Do you recognize it?

VERN: It looks like junk jewelry of some sort . . .

GUTHRIE *(indulgently)*: You never saw it before?

BELLE: Don't you remember, Vern, you bought it for me?

ANSTICE *(putting down the neck-chain)*: Sister Guthrie, if Mrs. Falkimer is going to give testimony, I want her to be sworn.

GUTHRIE: We must have correct procedure, Mrs. Falkimer. Come forward, please.
(She obeys, with a worried glance back at VERN.)
Do you solemnly swear to tell the truth, the whole truth and nothing but the truth?

BELLE: I do.

GUTHRIE: Please give us your testimony.

BELLE: When Vern and I were married, I was no bargain. I was not very pretty, and no one considered me popular. But I *did* have some money, and Vern asked if I'd be willing to put it into his bottling plant. *(adding, quickly, as she sees VERN frowning)* Of course it turned out to be a good investment.

ANSTICE: Louder, please.

BELLE *(raising her voice)*: It was a good investment. *(concluding, in a rush)* Vern and I had four children and a nice home with good plumbing and heating. He was a loving, considerate husband and never gave me a moment's care, so what woman could have asked for more?

ANSTICE: Well, well. *(He picks up a paper to show her.)* Is this your marriage certificate?

169

BELLE (*examining it*): Yes, sir.

GUTHRIE: You may return to your seat. (ANSTICE *hands the paper to* GUTHRIE.) That goes into the scales against him.

VERN (*outraged*): After everything my wife just told you about our marriage?

ANSTICE: You may call it a marriage. It sounds more like a plumbing and heating contract with a wife thrown in.

GUTHRIE: I'm bound to agree, Vernon. Your domestic arrangements —

VERN: I want to talk to your boss.

BELLE (*alarmed*): Vern!

VERN: This so-called proceeding is an outrageous farce! Judging sins with that out of date contraption —

GUTHRIE: We've tried to weigh every one of your statements with the greatest care. You think that's being unfair to you?

VERN: You're making a mockery of the man you're supposed to be examining! I thought Angels were supposed to be angelic!

(ANSTICE *is offended*.)

ANSTICE: Are you implying that we're not?

VERN: That's right! You're not!

ANSTICE: Then I have no more to say. We'll leave this to Brother Morias. We'll get our notes together and write up our report.

GUTHRIE (*to* VERN): I think we are not unfair!

ANSTICE: Suppose we both drop it now, Guthrie. . . . Let me have your papers.

(*They begin sorting out their notes.*)

VERN (*to* BELLE): And after lapping up all that punch! All wasted! Let them go on with their vaudeville act! With the Lord God on my side — and all those prayers rolling in for me —

BELLE: I wish I could feel as spotless as you! I committed a sin right here in Long Home lying under oath about you being a great husband and father!

VERN: Why do you call it a lie? You overdid the truth, that's all — and as a result they discounted everything you said. As for that necklace —

BELLE: It was one of the two presents you gave me during our entire married life. I wore it at our summer home at Rampagat, and when Lottie came out to visit, she was wearing the identical kind.

170

Where did you buy them, Vern? In a bargain basement, two for the price of one? I threw mine in the garbage can that same day — Is that where the Atonement Office dug it up do you suppose? Or did Lottie lend them hers?

(*She starts for the kitchen.*)

VERN (*following*): Belle! Will you listen just a minute?

(*They exit to the kitchen.* ANSTICE *and* GUTHRIE *are putting their notes in order.*)

ANSTICE: Brother Finch is right about one thing, I must admit: the sinners of Old Purgatory are a simple bunch of no-goods, satisfied to get what they deserve. But the devious denizens of *this* place —

GUTHRIE (*with a sigh, reaching for the pitcher*): Tell me, Brother Anstice, when they sent you here from Old Purgatory two months ago, did you think you were being promoted?

ANSTICE: I confess I did — in my vanity, but —

GUTHRIE: Hm. . . . Sure you won't have another drink? Falkimer prepared it to relax the proceedings, he said; a pleasing, tasty family beverage — makes you feel curiously afloat.

ANSTICE: It burns the tongue! I have a very strong suspicion that it's a distillation of the grape, and I can't imagine how it got here or how it relaxes the proceedings.

GUTHRIE (*drinking*): It has certainly relaxed me. Let's not overdo the solemnity, shall we? In Long Home we try to be less prissy.

ANSTICE: Prissy? In Old Purgatory I was considered quite advanced! (*emphatically*) *Reasonably* advanced, of course! There's some lesser Angels down there who secretly question everything in the Scriptures. They have no use for Job, I'm told — too meek for their taste. (*gathering up his notes*) And what's more, they claim God had no right to visit him with afflictions or to ask him afterwards, "Who are you to complain?" It seems they don't consider that very sporting.

GUTHRIE: Do you?

ANSTICE: I never discuss dogma, old girl. All I'm concerned with is my duty. And that's why I want to remind you: Brother Morias warned us to beware of Falkimer. The man's audacity stuns me! Does he intend to bring this sordid domestic triangle of his to Up Above? He's already brought it to Long Home!

GUTHRIE: Can you call it a triangle if nothing really sinful ever happened?

ANSTICE: Nothing sinful?

171

GUTHRIE: A spiritual passion — Vernon made that perfectly clear. If God hadn't willed it, it couldn't have happened, could it? Vernon pointed *that* out, too.

ANSTICE: Are you quite sure you know what you're saying, Sister Guthrie? I don't know if she seduced him, as he implied, or if he seduced her, or whatever — I can only refer you to Matthew 5:28: "Whoso looketh on a woman to lust after her hath already committed adultery with her in his heart!" He certainly entrapped her, no matter who started it: that obstinacy when she was asked to lend her necklace for this session! It took a court order to get it!

GUTHRIE: You're so intense, Brother Anstice!

ANSTICE: Enough. Let's get it written down.

(ANSTICE *and* GUTHRIE *exit. There is an outburst of loud voices in the street. At the same moment* BELLE *reenters angrily from the kitchen, with* VERN *at her heels.*)

BELLE: "A plumbing and heating contract with a wife thrown in!— "What a girl will do, just to get married! I deserved it, I guess: I knew what I was doing —

VERN: If you're thinking of taking back your testimony, let me remind you, Lady: you promised to be faithful. "Till death do you part," the preacher said.

BELLE: Death *did* us part. Remember? You got here fifteen minutes after I did.
　　　　(*The doorbell rings. She turns to answer it.*)
　　　It's Danny. (*admitting him*) Your shirt's torn! Catch your breath. What's happened to you?

DANNY: Where are the examiners?

BELLE: Reporting to Morias. They'll be coming back. Your father didn't like the questions they asked him.

DANNY: You mean to say they'll be back through that mob out there? (*To* VERN) How do you think I feel, having to fight my way through those former customers of yours from back on Earth? They're arguing and shouting, shaking their fists at this house — burned up because you're asking for a transfer!

VERN: That can't be! The people of Long Home are all for me!

DANNY: Not that bunch out there!

BELLE (*to* VERN): Stay away from that window. Go upstairs, get some rest while you can.

VERN: I'd better . . . (*He starts upstairs.*) Call me when Kellogg and Merwin get here. They're bringing a committee to speak up for me.

BELLE: I'll call you.

(*VERN exits.*)

(*To* DANNY.) Hand me your shirt. I have a needle and thread. (*ruefully*) Did you have to make your father feel worse, when he's so troubled?

DANNY: Rest easy, Mom — the Lord will save him.. . . The Lord didn't save me — He was somewhere else on that day when the guns were grinding us into dogmeat. But this is different: this is his old buddy, Vern Falkimer — He's got to roll out the red carpet for ole Vern —

BELLE: I forbid you to speak like that!

DANNY: I'm only talking Pop's language. (*harshly*) What sort of saint was he, to think he rates a transfer to Above? He was nothing but a businessman! Besides, everybody knew he had a mistress. They saw him a lot more with her than with you —

BELLE: He kept Lottie only to impress the other boys in the trade. When I found out about her I went away for a week but came right back. You don't live with a man thirty years without getting used to living with him.

DANNY: You call that a good reason?

BELLE: Yes. (*avoiding his glance*): He never walked out on his family— don't forget that.

DANNY: He walked out on us without ever leaving the house.

BELLE: All right, Danny! . . . I keep wondering what you've learned at the Process, if anything. Have some charity for us if you can't have understanding.

DANNY (*after a pause*): I guess you think I'm a disgrace to the Process.

BELLE: Here's your shirt; it's best I can do with it, for now.

DANNY: I'm supposed to be thinking over my life, in class. . . . I was sent to Long Home for killing people, Mom.

BELLE: That was the war. You couldn't even have known what it was about, at your age.

DANNY: They killed us and we killed them, that's what it was about.

BELLE (*embracing him*): Maybe; we try to think it isn't that simple when we get older.

(*A pause.*)

173

DANNY: I don't get it about Pop. A man who had a good income, a home and family, a wife and mistress — and he acts as if life never gave him anything!

BELLE: Are you trying to tell me a businessman has no right to ask why he lived?

DANNY: When I found out he was coming here, I ran all the way to school to boast about my father. I'd forgotten what he's like. (*wryly*) We're both stuck with him — that careful lion, that cautious tiger!

BELLE: He isn't that bad. He never was. A serious-minded young kid when I met him. A lot like you, as a matter of fact. Maybe what went wrong was my fault. Maybe I wasn't right for him. I bought him with my money.

(*Accompanied by menacing shouts from the crowd,* JOHN PERRY, MRS. BIANCO, TONY KELLOG, *and* JOE MERWIN *come to the porch, arguing.* PERRY *rings the doorbell — long and violently.* VERN *appears on the stair landing.*)

BELLE (*to* VERN): Is that the committee of your friends?

DANNY: They don't sound friendly.

BELLE: You'd better see them, Vern, whoever they are, and calm them down — before the examiners hear them.

(*She goes to the door and admits the group.*)

MRS. BIANCO (*pointing to* VERN): That's him — that's the big shot —

KELLOG: That's no way to talk!

MRS. BIANCO: Shut up!

PERRY (*to* VERN): My name is John Perry, and this is Mrs. Bianco — we're a delegation. Are you Vern Falkimer, the manufacturer of Viogen?

VERN: Yes, sir. This is my wife, my son, Danny. . . . Always glad to meet a customer —

PERRY (*violently*): You killed me, you ——! And now you want a transfer to Above?

BELLE (*frightened*): This must be some mistake —

PERRY (*to* VERN, *loudly*): I had a brain tumor — and I thought I could live on Viogen and hope! I died in a month — blind and paralyzed! And when my widow had the law on you, your three lawyers laughed her out of court!

MRS. BIANCO (*to* VERN): You're not gonna flap your way up to Glory 'so fast! Not after what you done to me! An infected liver and you gimme the idea I could cure it with Viogen! And that's only a sample of what you done to others!

VERN: Let's have straight talk, Mrs. Bianco! I gave you no medicine. All I sold you was Viogen, a tonic — plainly stated on the label!

(ANSTICE and GUTHRIE appear at the door.)

MRS. BIANCO: I'll label you, you two-faced —

ANSTICE (stepping between them): That's enough! Get out, all of you, before I loose my wrath upon you!

PERRY: Come on, Cordelia. I thought we'd get some satisfaction out of this faker in the Afterlife, but he's got pull here, too.

MERWIN (as the GROUP files out): They ain't on your committee, Mr. Falkimer, they only muscled in.

KELLOG: The right-thinking people of this community are with you, Vern!

MRS. BIANCO (lunging at KELLOG): "Right-thinking people!"
(KELLOG hastily retreats, falling over a chair.)
The support of two lousy Viogen distributors!

VERN (slamming the door after the VISITORS; to the ANGELS): You should have called out the Guardians! What do you mean by allowing the mob to threaten me like that!

ANSTICE: They were your customers. Their agony brought you a profit.

VERN: Why do you pick on me? Doctors make a profit out of people's agony. So do lawyers. So do undertakers. There's always plenty of agony to go around. I helped people to endure their agony!

ANSTICE: Don't listen anymore to that bilge, Guthrie. He'll steal away your mind!

(The crowd noise rises suddenly again.)

VOICES: Make way! The Black Angel!

DANNY (looking out; awed): The Angel of Oblivion! Brother Morias!

BELLE: He frightens me! I can't bear to look —

(MORIAS appears on the porch; faces the crowd.)

MORIAS: Where do you think you are? On Earth? There's a way to make complaints in Long Home; present them properly and they'll be considered in due course. . . . Leave this place — go to your homes!

(A few VOICES resume, meekly.)

VOICES: Yes, Brother Morias. Thank you, Brother Morias . . .

(*The* CROWD *begins to disperse.* MORIAS *turns to the door, and* VERN *opens it.*)

DANNY: Don't be scared, Mom . . .

MORIAS (*entering*): Peace to this house. (*To the* ANGELS) You let that rioting go on —

GUTHRIE: We deserve censure, I think.

MORIAS: I think so, too. And we'll all have it, myself included. (*To* VERN) You are Vernon Falkimer.

VERN: Yes, sir. I want to thank you, Brother Morias, for giving this your personal attention. I always say, if you have a complaint, take it to the top man.

MORIAS (*coldly*): I'm not the "top man," Mr. Falkimer, or anything like it. . . . What's your complaint?

VERN: I don't like your examiners. They weight sins like groceries. If they worked for me I'd fire the whole lot.

MORIAS: Only they don't work for you, do they? And you're not behind your office desk anymore. (*To* GUTHRIE.) See that the Falkimer family goes upstairs and stays there until we finish. Brother Anstice — the transcript.

(BELLE *and* DANNY *start obediently upstairs, followed after a recalcitrant pause, by* VERN. ANSTICE *is handing* MORIAS *the papers as the stage lights fade. When the lights return, the afternoon shadows have lengthened and the floor lamp illuminates the center table.* ANSTICE *and* GUTHRIE *are seated at the table;* MORIAS, *standing, is winding up his remarks.*)

MORIAS: . . . On the one hand, the Lumgardens and the Falkimers — people who have turned the God of the far-off galaxies into a good-luck image. On the other hand the know-it-alls for whom God has become an exercise in higher mathematics. . . · Simple atheism in either case! (*to the* EXAMINERS) You two were put on notice that this man Falkimer is an expert at technicalities; yet you let him cut short your examination. Why? (*witheringly*) Because you were drunk, Brother Anstice, when you took this testimony! So were you, Sister Guthrie! Both of you are drunk right now!

ANSTICE: Drunk?

MORIAS: We'll continue this session despite the fact that your brains are muddled. — Call down the family.

GUTHRIE (*going to the stairs to call*): Come down, please!

ANSTICE: We have sinned! *Peccavi!*

GUTHRIE: *Mea culpa!* That light-winged sensation has departed!

(*The* FAMILY *comes downstairs.* VERN *stands before* MORIAS *at the table. A pause.*)

MORIAS: Mr. Falkimer, I find no basis for your objections. You have had a remarkably indulgent pair of examiners here. (*As* VERN *is about to speak,*) Let me finish. Just the same they have recorded a long list of your transgressions. . . . I think you underestimate your problem, sir. The camel and the needle's eye.

VERN: Throw the whole quotation at me, why don't you? "It is easier for a camel to go through the eye of a needle than for a rich man to enter into the kingdom of God!" (*Indignantly.*) Communist propaganda! Perverting and slandering the normal and natural, God-given way of life! You're holding it against me because I was a businessman and prospered!

MORIAS: Not because you were a businessman, and not because you prospered.

VERN: Brother Morias, when you walked into this house I hoped for some realism here. I see that I'm mistaken, and I will therefore lay it on the line: you are not going to turn me off — because you can't turn off five million prayers, and you know it! When they reach that total by noon tomorrow —

MORIAS: They'll never reach that total. Your intercessors stopped for good at 4,864,103. Their store-front church is closed. They carried you along on credit for almost a year, living on hope, before they gave it up.

VERN: That's impossible!

MORIAS: No.

(*He turns to leave.*)

VERN (*shouting*): My son Norman's in charge of that arrangement! Let me see him! Let me talk to him!

MORIAS: If you insist on seeing Norman, you can do so. It's your right and privilege. (*less severely*) I'm frank to say we'd rather not dramatize your case any further; you'll be allowed to withdraw your application, if you do so at once. You'll be permitted to remain in Long Home — naturally under supervision from now on —

VERN: No.

BELLE (*fearfully*): Listen to him, Vern! You can be safe — you can stay here —

VERN: You heard him, Belle. He said I can have what I asked for!

(*A pause*)

MORIAS: Very well. My offer is withdrawn. You're going to see your son Norman. You'll be given full instructions before you leave.

177

BELLE: Brother Morias, we thank you for your mercy, your kindness —

MORIAS: You are entitled to justice — and justice is what you'll get. (*He turns to go.*) Come, Brethen. Peace to all here.

ANSTICE
GUTHRIE } (*together*): Peace.

(*They follow him out.*)

VERN: Peace, peace! They're full of peace! (*smoldering*) That's a great proposition Morias offered — letting me stay here!

DANNY: You had some nerve, arguing with him! What's all this about Norman looking after your obligations? You're not serious?

VERN: What do you mean, not serious? Norman lived for nobody but me! "You're the boss, Mr. F.," he used to say, "You're the boss —"

DANNY: Real sharp, Norman. Now *he's* the boss.

BELLE: Danny, leave your father alone!

VERN (*to* DANNY): You hate me! Why? I led a hard-working, decent life and gave you and the family all the comforts of living. That's enough for any man to do on Earth, and I did more than enough!

DANNY: I'm sorry. I'll go. (*ruefully*) I'm glad they're letting you go back for a visit — don't think I'm not. Remember me to Norman. (*hesitating*) You want to shake hands, Pop? Look, I'm offering to shake hands.
(VERN *shrugs and shakes hands.*)
Peace to you both.
(*He exits.*)

BELLE: A sweet child, Vern! He once went to work at the plant, just to please you.

VERN: And on his first day on the job he told the girls on the capping line they ought to join a union!

BELLE: You have no trouble remembering that.

VERN: When I turned him down he went straight to the recruiting office. Why couldn't he have waited for the draft like everybody else? Did he have to do it just to spite me? He came to his end far away, among the rocks, frozen, torn to little pieces. In Chongchon, Korea, someplace, on the very last day of the war! Eighteen years old, finished!

BELLE (*after a moment, unevenly*): You held him down all his life. All you cared about was Norman.

VERN: That's not true. Danny was on my mind a lot more than Norman.

BELLE (*tiredly*): I don't mean to say anything against Norman. I love Norman.

VERN. I'm not saying Norman has no faults. He had things all too easy — that always bothered me: he never earned a dollar by his own sweat and muscle. But he learned from me; he followed my example. Where I was concerned, he worshipped me, that boy!

BELLE (*soothingly*): Yes, he did. And now you'll be seeing him after six whole years. (*forcing a bright, cheerful tone*) Be sure and ask him about his family — Dolores and the grandchildren; and try to telephone our girls — Margaret and her husband, and find out if Sylvia is married. . . .

VERN: All right, all right, if I'm able to use the phone. (*eagerly, now*) I'm going to see the office with my old rolltop desk, that man-sized leather sofa. . . .

BELLE: Everything will turn out right, now, I know it will!
(*She kisses him. A letter flies out of the mail slot.* VERN *picks it up.*)
Is that for the family or for you?

VERN (*opening it*): Copy of my travel orders.

BELLE (*suddenly*): Forget the whole thing, Vern! Apologize to Morias! Tell him you want to stay on in Rainbow Terrace with Danny and me — that you want to go on with our family life —

VERN (*sharply*): I'm not staying in Long Home, Belle — forget it! Because there's something involved here that's a whole lot more important to me than whether we go on living a family life! I've got to know why I ever lived at all! (*passionately*) Is that damn Angel right? Is God nothing but some kind of mystery, way out there in the dark? When they laid me away, was I nothing more than two hundred-odd pounds of dead meat for the worms to feed on ? Try to understand me, Belle! I've got to know if my Lord God Eternal is still Up There watching over me! Because if He isn't, my whole life makes no sense!

Curtain

Scene 2

The Falkimer cottage, a week later, evening. The Technicians, STEVE *and* FRED, *are completing the installation of the stereoscreen. The machine, in the middle of the room, is invisible, and is represented only by its control board. When the "screen" images appear, they will be seen to be three-dimensional and life size. In charge of the occasion is*

179

SISTER GUTHRIE, *who has a notebook in which she occasionally makes notes. At rise, she is placing chairs for* BELLE *and* DANNY.

GUTHRIE: We have had trouble with excited onlookers. I must ask you not to interrupt once this starts.
 (*Doorbell rings.*)
 Company?

BELLE (*opening the door and admitting* LOTTIE): It's Miss Aldrich.

LOTTIE: I know you're surprised to see me, Mrs. Falkimer. (*Awkwardly.*) They told me at the Atonement Office that they're setting up the stereoscreen at your house. I was hoping you'd let me see how Mr. Falkimer gets along on his trip. I'm worried; if there's any way I can help —

BELLE: There isn't.

LOTTIE: I shouldn't have come here. If you want me to leave —

BELLE (*tight-lipped*): You can stay if Sister Guthrie doesn't object.

GUTHRIE: I have no objection.

LOTTIE: Thank you both. I'm truly grateful.

 (*She takes a seat at the opposite end of the room.*)

GUTHRIE: Are we ready, Steve?

STEVE: Yes, ma'm. Tuned in.

GUTHRIE: Attention, now — we're starting.

(*Blackout. The machine lights up, and in the fluorescent light* NORMAN'S *office becomes visible.* NORMAN *is at his desk under a dim spotlight, writing checks. In a foreground spot* VERN *stands looking around, bewildered. There is a rumble of traffic, subdued by distance.* MORIAS'S *voice is heard.*

MORIAS: Remember, Falkimer, you're not to touch your hand to anything material!

 (ANSTICE'S *voice is heard.*)

ANSTICE: We'll leave you now, but we'll hear everything.

(*The light rises on* NORMAN. *He is thirty-seven, handsome in Ivy League style. He throws a pill into his mouth and speaks into the intercom.*)

NORMAN: . . . Not now, I'm writing checks. . . . And phone that cruddy new analyst of mine, Dr. Noxley, Miss Barnes. Tell him those pills he ordered are doping me up, nothing more. I want results or I'll have to go crawling back to that last analyst who told me off! (*Preoccupied, as the whole office scene now lights up.*) When'd you get back, Pop? You're looking good. . . . How's the Southland Siesta?

VERN: The Southland Siesta?

NORMAN: Looks like you've got all your old zing back. I'm not a well man, but you're okay —

VERN (*quickly*): You're not well?

NORMAN: Still getting those dizzy spells . . . can't straighten up. Don't build on it, Pop; I'll be all right . . . (*He goes on writing.*) Where've you and Mom been staying?

VERN: A place called Long Home, on a street called Rainbow Terrace. Danny's there, too. Not at our house, but he visits us often.

NORMAN: Danny? (*He looks up.*) Danny's there, too? (*He rises slowly, still holding the checkbook. His voice is strained as he suddenly realizes.*) Is that you, Pop? (*terrified*) It can't be! We buried you — you've been dead for six years! Are you alive again?

(*The checkbook drops from his hands, the checks scattering over the desk.*)

VERN: You dropped your checkbook, Norman. (*He is about to pick it up for* NORMAN, *but stops himself.*) Don't be afraid; it's me, your father! I've got to talk to you and I haven't much time.

NORMAN: You're not alive?

VERN: No.

NORMAN: Ah! You're just a thought in my mind. I knew the strain was getting me —

(*He reaches for the intercom.*)

VERN: I'm not just a thought, Norman. Leave that thing alone.
(NORMAN *obeys.*)
Listen to me — I'm in trouble in the Other World, son. I'm in a sort of Purgatory called Long Home —

NORMAN (*his panic turning into amazement*): In Purgatory? You're not in Heaven? How can that be? (*Incredulously.*) I remember your preparations, three years before you died; you tried out coffins for size and style, went on a real splurge, for once — selected the best in the house, to carry you straight to your reward — and now you say you're not in Heaven?

VERN: I'll get there! I'll get there! That's why the One Above gave me this chance to see you! Only you'll have to cooperate, or I'm done for! (*in a choked voice*) Norman, they want to disperse me!

NORMAN: They what?

VERN: To disperse me. To put an end to me altogether, for all time! Unless I can prove that you've taken care of things properly!

NORMAN: Calm down, Pop. Everything's been attended to.

VERN: That's what I told them in Long Home! You had your old Dad in mind —

NORMAN: I took care of everything from the minute you left. Starting with the funeral services. (*with satisfaction.*) You should have been there! I mean you were, but you should have seen it! Everybody from the plant and the office came, even some of our competitors; some of the politicians, a couple of judges, some of the relatives. . . It was a big thing, Pop. I had old Reverend Cluett flown down from McGrawtown to preach over you. And every newspaper we advertised in remembered you: "Loss to the community, exemplary life," and so on, with your picture in the papers. You got the works, Pop.

VERN (*for the benefit of the* ANGELS): Ah! Can you speak a little louder?

NORMAN (*cordially*): And you're well buried, too: you and Mom in the family plot, side by side, with a solid marble headstone apiece. There's a simple, dignified inscription on yours: "Father."

VERN: First rate!

NORMAN: And on Mom's, "Mother."

VERN: Thank you, Norman. (*with relief*) I knew I'd find everything in order. Business as usual! Ah, that's a real satisfaction! To know your son is carrying on where you left off — (*looking around*) There's where the sofa used to be. . . . The deals that were made in this room! I'll never forget my life here! (*lovingly*) If only they would let me stay around here just for a while —

NORMAN (*quickly*): What for?

VERN: Just to keep a friendly eye on things. Norman, you say you're not well?

NORMAN (*hastily*): Did I say that? A bit overworked keeping up with the expansion —

VERN: Still expanding, eh?

NORMAN: We're moving 200,000 extra cases a week; getting into all the PX's and school cafeterias since we started our national TV hook-up. (*bringing out a sample case*) New packaging and a new formula. I added a teensy touch of strikosepsin: only on a permissive level, of course — a dirt-cheap chemical, costs less than one mill a bottle, but a real thirst-builder.

VERN (*admiringly*): Son of a gun! (*then, cautiously*) Sure it's all right, though?

NORMAN: Well, Pop, it's a sick world, sicker all the time, and I'm giving it a stronger tonic. Like you always said —

VERN: Yes, yes, Norman Not so loud (*with an effort*) Are our business partners backing you up? Otto Farber, Al Janice —

NORMAN: Forced them out long ago — bought them out for peanuts. I learned it all from you, Pop.

VERN: And the family? The girls?

NORMAN (*changing; grimly*): Ah, now you're on a sore subject! Bigger and better dividends is all they have on their minds! They get their returns regular as clockwork — $1,050 per year — but do you think they're grateful?

VERN (*opening his eyes*): $1,050? Is that what they're getting? With the sales running into millions? Dividends in line with earnings — that's what I specified.

NORMAN (*frowning*): You know those girls were ready to wring the firm dry? Even dragged me into court! I took them to the woodshed! (*severely*) A will is a sacred document, Pop! Don't forget that!

VERN: I won't forget it. I can't. Oh, my God . . . (*desperately*) Norman, you've got to change your ways, or I'm lost! And you'll be lost, too!

NORMAN (*indignantly*): "Change my ways?" I'm giving the firm my last ounce of strength — and you tell me I'm not behaving right? Is that why you came back? Sneaking into life, somehow, so you can be in charge again?

VERN: Stop it, Norman! You can't treat me like this! (*overwhelmed*) I loved you — I counted on you —

NORMAN (*harshly*): I loved you, too — before I found out it was all one way. Twenty years with your heavy fist on my neck! On the neck of everyone in the family! You should have seen your daughters at your memorial services, with your body lying right there! It was all they could do to keep from looking happy because they were free of you — they were getting some of your money at last!

VERN: That's enough!

NORMAN: And now you're in trouble — bad trouble. What did you expect? You, who never gave away as much as five dollars at a time —

VERN: You're lying! I gave away money freely, by the handful, wrote out the checks myself —

NORMAN: Yes — two months before your end! Money to hole-in-the-wall charities, to people I'd never heard of! You opened that hard fist of yours at last — because you were losing your grip: past your prime and with your kidneys acting up; scared at seeing the end of your road not too far ahead. . . What would you do next? If you could write out a check like that for the mother of that whore of yours, Lottie Aldrich —

VERN: Shut your mouth! How dare you talk like that about Lottie?

NORMAN: Don't try to tell me she was none of my business! Do you know what it cost me to hush up what happened the night she died? The last time you went to her apartment?

VERN: Quiet! Nobody knew about that! Nobody!

NORMAN: Nobody but two chiseling detectives who worked on her case! They said that girl friend of yours keeled over on the sofa with a heart attack — and the whole thing hit you over the head: what would happen if the reporters and detectives found you in her room? You were in such a hurry to get out of there —

VERN: That's a lie!

NORMAN: Was that check for Lottie's mother a lie, too? Four thousand dollars! Expiation money, four years later!

VERN: You're a liar and a cheat!

NORMAN: Is that what you're calling me? You, who taught me everything I know?

VERN (in a frenzy): Are you comparing yourself to me? I created a business! From the ground up — and handed it to you ready-made! What did you create, you grave-robber?

NORMAN (frightened): Keep away from me!

VERN: And I want to know what happened to those prayers you were supposed to take care of? Why did the Brethren stop praying? You were supposed to keep them at it — $5,000 a year —

NORMAN (bursting out, despite his fear): Five thousand a year for those blood-sucking bastards? I fought that crazy bequest of yours through the courts for six long years — got it knocked out of the will at last, just two days ago!

VERN (stricken): You've destroyed me! You've finished me!

NORMAN: Help! (backing away; screaming) Get back to your coffin, you carcass!

> (NORMAN slumps down on the couch in a faint.)

VERN (*wildly*): How will I save myself now?

(*He seizes the checkbook and slips it under his coat.* MORIAS *and* ANSTICE *are heard again.*)

MORIAS: Your time is up.

ANSTICE (*soberly*): Return flight, Mr. Falkimer.

(*The stereoscreen fades abruptly and the lights of the room go on. There is consternation in the Falkimer cottage.*)

LOTTIE: Oh! How dreadful!

DANNY: Mom! Help! My mother!

(LOTTIE *and* GUTHRIE *run to support* BELLE, *who is fainting.*)

LOTTIE: Let me take you upstairs, Belle.

GUTHRIE: Put her to bed.

(*As* DANNY *and* LOTTIE *assist* BELLE *up the stairs,* FRED *and* STEVE *put away their equipment.*)

STEVE: It happens every time I'm ordered to put up that screen: always somebody fainting or throwing fits. Anybody asks me, I don't know why they let the relatives watch them on the screen. What for?

GUTHRIE: It helps convince them they ought to register for the Process.

(*She takes out her notebook.*)

FRED (*in a low voice, to* STEVE): Are you going to need me after this, Steve?

STEVE: You've been having too much time off.

FRED (*exploding*): I've had it up to here! We're working our tails off with no overtime while the inmates sit around on their fat cans! The Book says the last shall be first, but we're still last!

STEVE: The last shall be first when they deserve it! Just because you got used to loafing on the job, hoisting up TV antennas in Greenwood, Ohio —

FRED (*dropping his voice*): I've got a Viogen card on me. Five dollars.

STEVE: Make it ten.

(FRED *hands over two cards.* GUTHRIE *looks up.*)

GUTHRIE (*sharply*): I'll take charge of those.
(STEVE *hands them over without a word.*)
Some more of those Viogen cards that are floating around — everybody doing favors for them, making deals and buying other people. This will add to my report. Are we finished?

185

STEVE: We were only —

GUTHRIE: Peace to this house.

STEVE ⎫
　　　　⎬ (*together, with a sigh*): Peace . . .
FRED ⎭

GUTHRIE (*as they leave*): It must be clear to you by now — our whole Department is due for a shakeup. The Administration won't let things go on like this.

(*They exit. After a moment* LOTTIE *comes downstairs and starts to leave. The porch door opens and* VERN *enters, looking the worse for wear. He slumps into a seat.*)

LOTTIE (*after a moment, pityingly*): We watched your trip, Vern. It wasn't good, was it?
　　　　　　　　(VERN *looks at her, dazed.*)
I'm very sorry. . . . It upset Belle; she's lying down in her room.

VERN: Did you see what Norman did to me?

LOTTIE: Vern, Vern —

VERN: Once there was a man, Vernon Falkimer, behind a big desk. His hand was against every man and every man's hand was against him . . .

LOTTIE (*quietly*): The Atonement Office outlawed Viogen this afternoon, Vern. They're digging up your past, working around the clock. What will you do when they find out how I ended, that night in my room?

VERN (*desperately*): I'm going to make it up to you, Lottie! Right now!

(*He takes* NORMAN'S *checkbook out from under his coat.*)

LOTTIE: What is that? (*frightened*) A checkbook! You brought that back from Earth? You took it?

VERN: Yes, I took it! I'm going to make it up to you, to everybody — I'll sign my signature over and over —

LOTTIE: You're mad, Vern! You're not on Earth anymore! Your signature's no good anymore; those checks are worthless here.

(*The light of reason returns to* VERN.)

VERN: You're right. I'm bankrupt!

(*He puts down the book, overwhelmed.*)

Curtain

186

Scene 3

Department of Adjudication. The ANGELS confer. FINCH *is speaking.*

FINCH: . . . As for the other counts in the indictment: when you consider that Danny Falkimer is one of those snot noses who condemn their elders and still wet their diapers; that Belle Falkimer is a housewife who can't bear to throw anything away — least of all a hopeless marriage: or that Miss Lottie Aldrich was lucky enough to have had a big-city romance brought into her small-town life —

ANSTICE (*livid*): Soon you'll tell us Mr. Falkimer was doing everyone a favor! *I* call his record a lifetime swindle, with God invoked on all occasions!

CHESWICK: As the man saw it, the Lord provided him with plenty of customers for Viogen, and in turn Falkimer gave them some temporary relief with his tonic. It was all he *could* give, wasn't it? He led the best life he knew how, considering his beginnings. The man was injured!

MORIAS: Did he have to injure other people because *he* was injured? He went into the world marauding and claimed that everyone else does the same!

CHESWICK: Don't they?

MORIAS: A vegetable has the right to say, "You planted me here and here I am." But a man is not a vegetable, Sister Cheswick. He could have found a better way! A better way than filling his social obligations and his pockets at the same time! (*Rising.*) I see no purpose in giving further time to the case of Vernon J. Falkimer. Especially in view of his coming here to break into our deliberations. I don't recall any presumption to match it in our entire history!

FINCH: He only asked if he could appear before us.

MORIAS: As a reward for bringing a checkbook here from Earth — to buy his redemption with it? (*with finality*) We will not see him. Peace.

(*He exits.* ANSTICE *and* GUTHRIE *get up to follow.*)

ANSTICE: I'm very surprised at *you*, Guthrie, sitting here all that time without a single word.

GUTHRIE: I was thinking that dispersion is so final.

(*They exit.* FINCH *and* CHESWICK *remain.*)

187

FINCH: It's not what Falkimer did on Earth that bothers them so much — it's what he's been doing right here. (*chagrined*) And we've encouraged him to do it.

CHESWICK: It was you who said, "Don't try to interest Falkimer in our cause; don't even go near him. Round up as many of his trade cards as you can find and spread them around where they'll set new forces in motion. Otherwise let him alone," you said, "and his energy will give the Administration the shaking up that's needed."

FINCH: You're right to reproach me. It's astonishing what he's caused here in so short a time! Those mobs in the street are drunk! Drunk without his Viogen — drunk with the mere possibility of *getting* drunk! Do you know what they're howling, now? "Admit to Glory every man, woman, and child who ever drew breath!" "No reward too great for those who bore the burden of bones and flesh!" He's inflamed everybody in Long Home. We wanted a program of reform. He's given us anarchy and revolution.

CHESWICK: And if the Administration makes a martyr of him —

FINCH: They're rigid enough to do it — we know them, Cheswick. . . . We must get him out of Long Home fast, without inciting the mob still further. I've explained that to you: he's got to go up, not down.

CHESWICK: And that will have to be authorized.

(*A pause.*)

FINCH: We can't drop him now without opening the way to chaos in Long Home. (*somberly*) Is the paper written out?

CHESWICK (*taking a document out of her briefcase; handing it over*): My signature's on it already. . . . You approved the wording.

FINCH (*reading*): "For the reason that all such offenses ensue from the natural disposition of mind and appetite as established by Almighty God." (*looking up*) Strong words! There will be consequences. Are we ready for them?
(CHESWICK *is silent.* FINCH *hesitates an instant, then signs. Returning the paper.*)
This paper has to go through channels . . .

(*Blackout. The stage lights return, discovering* BROTHER MORIAS *and* SISTER CHESWICK *at the desk.* MORIAS *is dictating.*)

MORIAS: ". . . I therefore desire to be relieved of the Long Home assignment as soon as the legal aspects of the case are disposed of, period." You have that?

CHESWICK: Yes, sir. (*looking up*) You're resigning under pressure. I don't see how it adds up, transferring you to Old Purgatory at a time like this. You've been so hard-working, so conscientious—

MORIAS (*dryly*): Thank you for your solicitude about me. It isn't necessary. I was never right for this job, and the Higher Officer knew it and I knew it. Trying to be fair to these misguided little animals who call themselves human — it's been too much for me. Let's go on: "In my opinion the Falkimer case can be concluded on schedule, although it is now complicated by other factors including an alleged official document . . ." (*a slight pause*) " . . . which is about to reach my desk."

(He stops reading.)

CHESWICK (*without expression*): "About to reach my desk, period." Anything more, sir?

MORIAS: Not for the present. . . . Addressed to the Higher Office Administration, Central Bureau, as usual, with the usual etceteras . . .

CHESWICK: I'll type this up at once. I suppose it's urgent —

MORIAS: Stay here, Cheswick. We have something to discuss.

CHESWICK (*after a slight pause*): Certainly, if you wish . . .

(PIP enters with an interdepartmental envelope.)

PIP: From Research. Personal for Morias.

MORIAS: Brother Morias. And don't lean on the desk.

PIP: Huh?

MORIAS: Head up, chest out, feet together. And let me have no further complaints about you and your little friends . . . You've been collecting wing-feathers for some reason or other — pulling out live feathers, lately, because you've run out of used ones. If I hear anymore about you —
(PIP backs away and off, with a series of salutes.)
Bratling! (*He takes a paper out of the envelope.* CHESWICK *rises.*) Where are you off to, Cheswick? (*in a new tone*) I asked you not to leave because I want you to look at this paper. (*showing it to her*) A Writ of Absolution for Vernon J. Falkimer, absolving him of all blame whatsoever. . . . Whose signatures are those?

CHESWICK (*levelly*): Finch's and mine.

MORIAS: On any authority but his and yours?
(No reply.)
A desperate measure, but you had to take it: Falkimer was your ready-made tool for disruption — too valuable to lose. . . . And

189

this has gone on all the time you've been working with me on his case. (*taking out superphone*) The Atonement Office is not as inept as you may have supposed: we've had you and Finch under surveillance for weeks. (*into phone*) Morias speaking. Give me the Guardians . . .

Curtain

Scene 4

The Falkimer cottage, late afternoon. The BLUE ANGELS *are making an inventory of the house,* ANSTICE *calling off the items and* GUTHRIE *checking them in her notebook.* VERN'S *desk is more littered than before with notes and calculations. A sound of trumpets in the near distance is barely heard above the echo of distant shouting.*

ANSTICE: One pedestal table, walnut finish. . . . One tablecloth, yellow velour. . . .

GUTHRIE: One pedestal table, walnut finish . . . . Check. One tablecloth, yellow velour — (*pausing*) Can you make out what they're shouting?

ANSTICE: "Smash the fading-machine!" (*nervously*) I don't like it, Guthrie. This is worse than the second time I visited Earth.

GUTHRIE: In the fifteenth century, I think you said?

ANSTICE: Sixteenth — my first visit after the Flood. . . . In 1557, it was, in England. They had two leading religious sects there, Catholic and Protestant, who were taking turns burning each other at the stake and chopping off each other's heads. But it was straightforward savagery, followed by remorse. I don't like to say it, but just between you and me, Finch isn't so far wrong when he claims things are different now. I tell you, there's no remorse left, down there — it's all psychic traumas: you kill somebody because your mother dropped cigarette ashes on you when you were an infant. All perfectly natural, according to Finch — so we needn't be surprised at the sort of characters we're getting here, these days. (*with a shrug*) Well, this isn't getting our work done. . . . One table lamp, brass base, parchment shade —

GUTHRIE: Brother Anstice, when you were there, did you ever actually see anybody die?

ANSTICE: No. Why don't you ask Brother Morias? That's his job. All I know about how those humans die is that their flesh turns cold and decays.

GUTHRIE: Isn't that very unpleasant?

ANSTICE: I'm sure they don't like it. Especially when it interrupts them in the middle of what they're doing.

(BELLE *appears from the kitchen. She is obviously worn and distressed.*)

BELLE: Are you finished with your inventory?

GUTHRIE: Almost. . . . How is your husband feeling? We haven't seen him since we came in.

BELLE: I've hardly seen him myself. He's been down in the cellar all day.

ANSTICE: Doing what?

(VERN *enters from the cellar.*)

VERN (*shortly, to* BELLE): What are they here for?

BELLE: We have to move, Vern — it isn't decided where, yet. . . . They're making an inventory of the house.

ANSTICE: Usual routine when people move. We've inspected everything but the cellar.

VERN: You can forget the cellar — there's nothing there but cobwebs and old chairs.

ANSTICE: What were you doing there? Sitting among the spiders? Or still trying to ferment something at this late date?

VERN: You never get tired of keeping after me, do you?

(*There is a muffled explosion downstairs, with the sound of breaking glass.*)

GUTHRIE (*solemnly*): There go the cobwebs!

(*The* ANGELS *go quickly into the cellar.* VERN *hurries to look down.*)

VERN (*coming back*): That's the end of that. The still blew up. Let them do all the inspecting they like, now. (*In vexation.*) Stop blubbering, Belle!

BELLE: They've brought that fading-machine over to Generations Square!

VERN: You haven't heard them setting it up, have you? And you're not going to!

BELLE (*firmly*): No. Because God's in His Heaven, that's why, and He'll never allow it.

VERN: Amen.

BELLE: Not even in a case like yours.

VERN (*astounded*): In a case like mine? What do you mean?

BELLE: Nothing, Vern.

VERN (*caustically*): He certainly shouldn't allow it in any case!

BELLE: Don't agitate yourself.

VERN: You know, I was just getting onto something when that thing blew up? But that's how it all has to be, at a time like this. . . . I left word for Kellog'at fourteen different places and still there's no sign of him.

BELLE: He'll get here. Everything will turn out all right, Vern — only you must have the kind of faith you used to have.

VERN: It had *better* turn out right, if I'm to go on having faith!

BELLE: I hope and pray that the One Above hasn't heard the way you've been talking about Him, lately! (*fervently*) Repent, Vern!

VERN (*bristling*): Repent? Repent for what?

BELLE: Even if you can't see for what! You were a reader in the church, once; you know how they love repentance, here: one lost sheep returned to the fold is worth ninety and nine that never strayed.

VERN: I'm not a sheep! You've gotten so sanctimonious this last week—

BELLE: Repent! Take yourself out of danger! How can you go on pretending you never sinned?

VERN (*angrily*): When did you ever hear me say I never sinned? You're exaggerating in your miserable way, as usual! Small indiscretions, I said; little human weaknesses — next thing you'll tell me my whole exemplary life was nothing but a crime!

(ANSTICE *and* GUTHRIE *return.*)

ANSTICE: Well! It's not hard to imagine what sort of experiments went on downstairs — but that's neither here nor there, now. The cellar will have to be cleaned out, Mrs. Falkimer, before you move; it's full of mashed figs and broken glass. We're leaving, but we'll be back with Brother Morias. (*hesitating*) Take courage, Falkimer.

GUTHRIE: Yes, do.

VERN: Thanks — I'm doing fine. *You* look a bit peaked to me, Sister Guthrie. I can see you're not used to catastrophes.

GUTHRIE (*uncomfortably*): We Angels exist, you know. We're not born, and we don't die. . . . Being born, fading — it's rather hard to grasp. Rather sobering.

VERN: Yes, well I'm not going to be faded! If you have any such notion you can forget it right now!

ANSTICE: *We* don't make those decisions. If you'll excuse us — peace to you both.

GUTHRIE: Peace.

(*The* ANGELS *exit.*)

VERN (*scornfully*): "Peace!" Did you notice Guthrie couldn't look me in the eye? After all the times she dropped in here to gab with me? She and Austice, mourning over me before they even know the verdict! I sent Danny to the Atonement Office to find out if the Writ's been served, and he's certainly taking his time, that boy!

BELLE: You're so unreasonable! When you know how terribly upset he's been about you all this week — so anxious to help you —

VERN: Yes, yes, yes. So you keep saying —

(DANNY *enters.*)

BELLE: Danny!

VERN: Well? Speak up! Why do you come here looking like the bottom's dropped out of the market?

DANNY: Brother Finch served the Writ yesterday afternoon. But the Atonement Office is blazing mad at you, Pop. Kellog's been up there, squealing his head off about you —

BELLE: And Lottie?

DANNY: Up there, too.

BELLE: Of course she'd be there — I expected nothing else!

VERN: Lottie won't speak a single word against me. I can count on her.

BELLE: That's what *you* think! As for that slimy little insect salesman of yours —
 (KELLOG *looks in at the door.*)
(*sweetly*) Oh, Mr. Kellog! Do come in, please —

KELLOG (*entering cautiously*): How *about* that! All of a sudden I've got the welcome mat set out! (*To* VERN.) I'd have got here sooner, only they had me up at the Atonement Office, asking about you. I didn't tell them anything worth mentioning.

DANNY: No?

KELLOG: They had me in a hot seat, Vern. And nobody else was there to talk up for you — none of your Long Home customers: the ones that aren't scared are tired of waiting. (*takes a bundle of forms out of his pocket*) Just one day's cancellation of Viogen orders; I've been getting them flung back at me for weeks. You shoulda come across with the bottled product instead of only promises on paper — it woulda made all the difference to people in backing you up.

VERN: They're too impatient! I've had to start from scratch here; no automation, no bottling plant, not even bottles — what did they expect? (*curtly*) I've been looking for you. We've got to talk to those so-called Angels; we've got to make them understand what their attitude ought to be —

KELLOG: They're not gonna listen to me.

VERN: They've listened to you plenty, up to now.

KELLOG: That's why. The more they heard, the madder they got. You know what they'll do to me for associating with you?

BELLE (*hopefully*): Fry you?

KELLOG: They'll put me to school in the Process. How *about* that! I even had to ask for it. You have to ask for it, or they don't put you in.

(DANNY *laughs*.)

What's funny? I come here, I level with you, and what do I get? A horse laugh! (*He starts for the door.*)

DANNY (*blocking his way*): You want me to take him apart, Pop?

VERN: How will that help? Let him go.

KELLOG: Peace.

(*He exits swiftly.*)

VERN: He ought to be ashamed! What he's done to me —

DANNY (*remorsefully*): I did something too, Pop. I found your cellar key and sabotaged your still last night.

VERN: You what?

BELLE (*quickly*): He meant it for your sake, Vern; to keep you here.

VERN: And you knew it and never told me! You let me tinker with that thing in the cellar all day long, trying to make it work —

BELLE: You were getting nowhere with those figs — you might as well admit it.

VERN: Do you know what you two have done? Just one bottle with my label on it would have made all the difference! Just one bottle! At a time like this, when I have to look for every way to save myself —

BELLE: Every way except your trust in Him Above! You've foresworn your God — oh, let Him not reply to you in His anger!

(*A rattling sound of hammering begins.*)

DANNY (*in a hushed voice*): They're putting up the machine.

BELLE (*speaking after a moment of stunned silence*): Danny, you've seen the dispersing-machine; you've seen how it works?

DANNY (*slowly*): It's a box standing on end . . . like an isolation booth, only all glass. . . . You go in and sit down, and they lock the door. . . . And everybody watches you until the box gets dark . . . very, very dark, for a few minutes. . . . Then it gets light again, and they let you out.

BELLE: Is that all?

DANNY: You start losing your identity after that. . . . All your memory begins to drain away; you don't know who or where you are, you don't even think about it. And in a little while after they let you out, you start to fade. Dad! Dad —

VERN: Don't you worry about me, Danny. Nobody's going to fade me, so get that out of your head!

(MORIAS *appears on the porch, accompanied by* ANSTICE. *He wears black gloves and carries a black briefcase.*)
BELLE (*seeing him*): Brother Morias is here.

(*A crowd of the* NEIGHBORS, *whispering and apprehensive, has been gathering outside. They now fall silent. The* ANGELS *come to the porch door as* VERN *hurries to open it.*)

MORIAS (*entering*): Peace to this house.

(MORIAS *opens his briefcase to take out a paper.*)

VERN: Welcome, Brother Morias! I've been expecting you to come —

MORIAS: Yes. I have here a Writ made out in your behalf. (*reading*) "Tamen reus criminis huius agitus est, aequum est iure. . . ." (*looking up*) This document dismisses all charges against you.

VERN (*jubilantly*): I knew it! I just knew it!

MORIAS (*putting down the document, icily*): Vernon Falkimer, this paper has no force or effect whatsoever. Its perpetrators were removed from office this morning, charged with insubordination and disloyalty.

VERN (*staggered*): I had nothing to do with them! They came to me, told me they were preparing some kind of Writ —

MORIAS (*turning to* ANSTICE): Is Miss Aldrich here?

ANSTICE: Yes, sir.

MORIAS: Have her come in.
(LOTTIE *is brought in, attended by* GUTHRIE *and guarded by* STEVE *and* FRED.)
(*To* LOTTIE) You asked to see him. Here he is.

LOTTIE: I want you to know it, Vern — I didn't tell them anything about us. They knew everything without my telling them; they had it all in their records. . . . What can I add that would be of any help to you?

MORIAS: Nothing. Try and compose yourself.

LOTTIE (*unheeding; to* VERN): The crowds are arriving to watch you disperse. . . . Oh, Vern, you're all I ever had — except my mother — and they're taking you away from me! Even the remembrance of you! And all because you were so careful! "We mustn't soil our spiritual love with material side effects," You said. You, who gave Belle four children!

ANSTICE: Brother Morias, will you let this shameful talk go on?

LOTTIE (*out of control; to* VERN): Belle had four children — I had none! An affair was all I had! I don't care what they say in the Process! I should have had your child — a remembrance of you they couldn't take away!

(FRED *and* STEVE *seize* LOTTIE.)

MORIAS: I asked you to compose yourself, Miss Aldrich. You'll answer for your behavior here. Now be silent!

(*She is conducted, sobbing, to the chair next to the desk.*)

BELLE: They bring her here — an immoral woman — just to make it look bad!

VERN: They frame people here! They must have done the same with Norman!

MORIAS: I knew I'd hear that from you again. And I made ready for it — with another chance for you to hear the truth.
(*At his signal* STEVE *snaps on a small machine resembling a transistor radio.*)
We recorded this an hour ago. Listen, Falkimer — your son confessing to his psychoanalyst.

(NORMAN'S *voice is heard*)

NORMAN: . . . . the cemetery manager called me this morning. Vandals broke in last night, knocked down and smashed Pop's gravestone, left beer cans on the grave — (*quavering*) Why *his* grave and nobody else's? Because I'm a sinner! I poisoned the public! Cheated my family! Called my dead father a carcass —

VERN: Aah! ————

(*A soothing voice is heard.*)

ANALYST: Try to be objective, Norman. You're letting your superego punish your id, dear boy, because you've had a sudden fright, that's all.

196

NORMAN: You're right, by God! The old son of a bitch was on my back so long that I'm bent over. . . . . Let the broken pieces of his tombstone lie there — let him rot in his goddam grave —

VERN: No more!

MORIAS (*signing to STEVE to break off, to VERN*): Your son Norman. A monster you created in your image.

VERN: No, no!

MORIAS: Your end approaches, Falkimer; look upward, let the scales fall from your eyes! Join me in prayer — thank Him who reigns Above for the earthly life He gave you!

(*He kneels. All but VERN follow his example.*)

BELLE: Repent! Repent, Vern!

MORIAS (*in a cadenced, ministerial tone*): Lord, give Thy compassionate farewell to this erring and obdurate soul, Vernon Falkimer, whose transgressions, unacknowledged, unconfessed —

(*Trumpets sound.*)

BELLE: Pray, Vern, pray!

(VERN *sways, then drops to his knees.*)

VERN: They tell me I'm a sinner, Lord. Help me!

BELLE: Amen!

MORIAS: At last! At last!

VERN: I did everything wrong, they say!

(*The* CROWD *joins in prayer.*)

MORIAS: Yes!

VERN (*violently*): But it's a lie! (*looking up*) They are your enemies, God!

(MORIAS *rises, followed by the others.*)
They mock religion! They persecute me, the true defender of your way of life!

MORIAS: Miscreant! What sort of prayer is that?

VERN: Smite them, Lord! Just two seconds to let your lightning strike them where they stand!

(*Thunder rolls overhead. There is a gasp from the CROWD. All draw back in fear. The thunder rumbles and crackles, then dies away.*)

MORIAS (*quietly*): We're still here, Falkimer. If that was a sign of His wrath it was you He condemned.

VERN (*rising; desperately*): He's abandoned me. He's taking back the gift of life He gave me! (*Fiercely, looking up.*) "The gift of life." To Hell with you and your gifts! It's a good thing for you that you hide in Heaven — if you lived on Earth, you'd get all that's coming to you!

MORIAS (*with deadly quiet*): We've heard enough. I now pronounce the Judgment issued this day by the Higher Office Administration: "The respondent Falkimer is consigned herewith to the fate of dispersion, annihilation, and eternal oblivion." *Fiat justitia!*

(*He signals to* STEVE *and* FRED, *who seize* VERN.)

VERN (*struggling*): Take your hands off me!

MORIAS: The prisoner will hold still.
(VERN'S *resistance ends abruptly, as though frozen.*)
(*to* STEVE *and* FRED) Take him.

DANNY (*as though coming out of a daze*): No, Dad! Don't leave us here alone! (*seizing his father's arm*) Mom! Lottie!

VERN: Don't — Don't —

(*The* WOMEN *and* DANNY *are torn loose.*)

BELLE: Don't look Up There in anger, Vern! Whatever happened, happened on Earth!

VERN (*in a whisper*): Yes, on Earth. I started out as an orphan; my mother left me in a church pew, in the house of the Heavenly Father — the only real home, the only father I ever knew . . .

(*The cries of the* CROWD *have become a dirge.*)

They're putting an end to me!

MORIAS: Think of it as a blessing, Falkimer. A sign of grace we Angels do not have. The right of nonexistence and the priceless gift of a conclusion. (*to* FRED *and* STEVE) We're ready.

(STEVE *and* FRED *take* VERN *out. The* NEIGHBORS *follow them off.*)

MORIAS (*to* BELLE): Be comforted. Say your goodbye to him and let him depart.

(DANNY *supports* BELLE *as they go out;* LOTTIE *goes with them. Shouts are heard.* GUTHRIE *comes forward and lays her briefcase on the table.*)

GUTHRIE: I can't go on with this, Brother Morias. The man has challenged his Creator. He deserves an answer or he won't be satisfied. Nor will I.

MORIAS: Blasphemy requires no answer. (*coldly*) Report to Personnel at once, Guthrie; you're under suspension. I was told I've had to keep an eye on you: you're unreliable — and a very likely member of the Finch and Cheswick conspiracy.

GUTHRIE (*without emphasis*): You've been misinformed, Brother Morias, I've never been a member of their sect — but I'm beginning to wonder if I should be.

> (*She marches out of the room and off.*)

ANSTICE (*wringing his hands*): I could see what was happening to Guthrie; I could see it a long way off. I kept begging her not to talk with Falkimer —

MORIAS: We're behind schedule; they must be nearly ready for us at the machine. Take my briefcase, Anstice; this is your job, now, until my replacement gets here. . . . I hope you'll remember me with forbearance. And Guthrie needn't worry — I'll see that she gets off with another reprimand. She gave me no alternative, but at bottom I don't know any more than she does.

ANSTICE: And Miss Aldrich?

MORIAS: Let's not be vindictive — after all, what can she do about her problem now? (He stops at the door; meditatively) Brother Anstice, have you ever by chance seen God?

ANSTICE: No.

MORIAS: Neither have I. . . . Do you really believe He sits Up There on His Throne of Judgment, condemning His creatures for their frailty? It was He Himself who made them out of jelly.

ANSTICE (*baffled*): I don't understand you, sir. He created the foundations of the Earth —

MORIAS: Exactly. That crowded little Earth, where everything lives by eating something else! Eat or be eaten! If you had created the foundations of a place like that, could *you* sit forever smelling incense while the Angels sing "Holy, holy holy?" Wouldn't you get sick of it? Wouldn't it come out of your ears? (*dryly*) Well, maybe not out of *your* ears, Anstice, but speaking for myself — and meaning no disrespect —
> (*Trumpets are heard.*)
God made those people in His image, then left them to their own devices — and what's the result? A lot of Vernon J. Falkimers! More of them all the time! I wonder if the Lord isn't going to get off His throne, one day, and take another look at that tenth-rate planet of theirs!

(ANSTICE *is staring at him.*)
Meaning no disrespect!
(*Music and violent shouts are heard.*)
We'd better hurry. That tumult! Trying to supress the mob, lately, is like throwing kerosene on the flames!

(*They exit. The shouting rises to a crescendo.*)

CURTAIN

CASTING

The meaning of RAINBOW TERRACE can be almost entirely lost if, in spite of its tragic end it is produced without a sense of the ridiculous. Its casting ought to have the following traits in mind:

VERN. Fifty-six. Big, very impressive; great masculine charm and monstrous masculine ego. Glib, shrewd, commanding, self-righteous. Always relaxed, even in his most vehement moments.

BELLE. Fifty-two. Plain and sarcastic.

DANNY. Eighteen. Idealistic, morose. A war veteran.

LOTTIE. Twenty-three to twenty-eight. A very pretty small-town girl with a father complex.

NORMAN. Thirty-two. The complete junior executive. Handsome, nervous, and razor-sharp.

MORIAS. Indeterminate age. Big, quiet-voiced, and stern. His complexion is very pale, almost white; but he can also be played by a majestic-appearing black.

ANSTICE. Sixty-five. A fragile, dried-up oldster.

GUTHRIE. Forty to fifty. Female, black, and considerate of Vern.

FINCH. Forty-seven. Scholarly.

CHESWICK. Thirty to sixty. Female. A clerk.

KELLOG. Forty-two. Crude, fast-talking, and sporty.

MERWIN. Any age. Second-rate, and admires Vern.

PERRY. Any age over thirty. A middle-class citizen with a grievance.

MRS. BIANCO. Fifty. A loud-mouth.

FRED. Twenty-five. Fast and snappish.

STEVE: Forty-five. A senior workman.

PIP. A tough little kid. Any pre-adolescent age, up to ten or twelve.

EMBLEMS OF THE LONG HOME
ADMINISTRATION, DESIGNED BY
MORDECAI GORELIK, FULL SIZE,
TO BE USED FOR BADGES OR
SHOULDER PATCHES

1

2

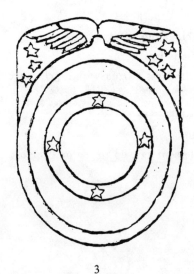

3

Following are instructions for all
emblems: wings, oval frames, and all
stars, gold. Upper sections (outside
frames), gold stars on a white field

*1. Anstice, Cheswick, and Gurthrie
all have the same design: a gold
balance on a field of light blue.*

*2. Finch: on a white field, an
open book in white, edged with gold;
above the book a gold chalk-eraser
over a pen and pencil, crossed; below
the book, an ink-pot, gold.*

*3. Morias: on a black field, a gold
cricle with a star at each of the
cardinal points of the compass.*

THOUGHTS ON *RAINBOW TERRACE*

I thought it was a fine script, an exceptionally fine script. I thought this is one of those cases you read about where the damn commercial theatre is going to keep a good script from getting produced. In other words, its chances of being a success in Broadway terms are not great enough to cause someone to spend $150,000 trying to find out. It seems to me that you will have to settle for some off-Broadway production. Of course, ideally this would be in one of the fine repertory theatres, not just what we call off-Broadway.[15]

Such a good piece of writing deserves to have something happen to it, and I hope it does. But I haven't the courage.

— George Abbott, Broadway producer

I think you have written an extraordinarily absorbing play . . . it has a wonderfully fresh idea, bitter and tender through clenched teeth. The people seem finely individualized in their persistent human stupidities, and the 'immortals' sharp in their functions, Morias especially.

Do you remember what Claudius says in HAMLET? 'But 'tis not so above. *There* is no shuffling, there the offense lies in his true nature. And we ourselves compelled, even to the teeth and forehead of our faults, to give in evidence.' The play made me think of that. Also that in spite of the quote you supply from Isaiah, the vessel will demand of its maker the reason for its being.

You can see that TERRACE has started me thinking. About its ability to play there's no question.

— Morris Carnovsky, actor and director

Rainbow Terrace is one of the *finest* plays I've read in recent years — the theme has tremendous import and it has been handled with such skill, sparkle and dramatic imagination that there is little I can say except to reiterate: I was fascinated by it. If I have any criticism at all it is simply the deplorable fact that the play hasn't been done on the New York stage or at least somewhere near the metropolitan area so that theatregoers could share this experience.

— Stanley Richards, drama editor, The Best Short Plays

203

Mordecai Gorelik presents a unique situation with dramatic interest and fine dialog. The characters have dimension.
— David Emmes, South Coast Repertory Theatre (California)

I very much enjoyed reading *Rainbow Terrace*. You have a fine sense of comedy, as well as satire, and I want to compliment you on your wonderful gift of dialog.
— Dr. Samuel Selden, University of California (Los Angeles) (California)

It seems to me that you have written a contemporary play in the manner of the medieval or miracle play. . . . While God seems to be dead on some college campuses, theatre fare that makes its audience think and react in response to universal truth is popular. . . . You have written a message play yet given dialog to your characters so that this message comes across without preaching. You give us an *actors'* play — rare in so many scripts.
— Sister Mary Xavier Coens, Clarke College (Dubuque, Iowa)

You have written a forthright and perceptive contemporary play.
— Gordon Davidson, The Theatre Group (Los Angeles) (California)

Rainbow Terrace is more than a fine play; it's a disturbing one.
— George Dessart, Documentary Unit, WCBS-TV

The strong point of the play, and the reason I think it should be presented, is the derisive exposure of hypocrisy, self-deception and inability to see any evil in one's self, using a distorted form of religious belief to support this big lie.
— Dr. Henry W. Wieman, theologian, S.I.U.

Thank you for sending me your most imaginative play *Rainbow Terrace*. Your years of theatre knowledge are most apparent

in your having chosen to write such an unusual play thematic-
ally as well as the crisp dialog and structural excellence.
— Nina Vance, Alley Theatre, Houston, Texas

My husband and I read *Rainbow Terrace* and enjoyed it
tremendously — if one can "enjoy" such a savage indictment of
our social vices. I say "our" for we have just the same in a
smaller way. We found it intensely amusing, too.

We both felt that your use of fantasy was a particularly
brilliant way of forcing home your comment upon our society.
The actuality of Long Home is completely convincing. We
found the dialog penetrating and sparkling. Through it the
characters come out clearly in the round. Too clearly perhaps
for your declared intention that it must not be taken
tragically. I think the force of the characters you have
written — particularly Falkimer, Mrs. F. and their son, obliges
us . . . . to become involved to the point where I felt the
final solution as tragic. Falkimer is so perfect a product of
our world that his passion to carry it into the Hereafter is
pitiable as well as ridiculous. We hope you will come back
and produce it at the Ensemble (Ensemble Theatre, Sydney).
I'm sure it would be a production of great importance — more
than dramatically.
— Dame Dymphna Cusak, Australian dramatist

And a letter from Sir Tyrone Guthrie, stage director:

I have read *Rainbow Terrace* with very much enjoyment. It's
splendid and delightfully unpretentious: I'm sure the humor
plays splendidly, it arises so naturally and spontaneously — and
is genuinely humorous," not the usual frantic, smart-alecky
attempt to be "witty." The play's a sort of *Everyman,* isn't
it? *The Summons of Everyman* is one of the archetypal
dramatic plots.

There are many felicities. I love poor dreary little Miss
Aldrich and her sincere desire to be "helpful" — it's so nice
(and so unusual) to present her as something so dim and *res-
pectable,* instead of the stock floosie. I think the angels
would be very funny. *Of course,* Pip must go — he's right in
the bull's eye of the Cute Dept. I was happy to find an
angel called Guthrie — first time I've ever met a character of
that name in all the thousands of scripts I've plodded through
down the years.

I couldn't help wondering whether the angels mightn't be
funnier sans wings. Do the wings look like reaching for the

Long Home ain't just one more garden suburb of that hell-upon-earth L.A.!

The one thing which, to me, doesn't quite "do" is Norman. I should have thought the whole situation could be treated obliquely, without a confrontation. But if we have to have their scene together, why shouldn't Norman arrive at Long Home? If, as I think you intend (an intention with which I don't think I agree), the confrontation between father and favorite son is the *scene à faire* then I think it's too short, too trivial.

Another small carp: I wonder if the fading-machine isn't a rather too prosaic idea — sort of in the gadget department. When one thinks of Enoch or of Oedipus at Colonus . . . but perhaps a poetic disappearance isn't appropriate in the environment of Long Home. You can see I've been very interested. Thank you.

Dear Guthrie: I would have no objection to a newer type of vestment for the angels, although there is at least as much to be said for the Biblical variety. I would not be heartbroken without Pip in the cast. And the *scene à faire*, for me, comes later, when Vern denounces the angels. But how much I value Guthrie's appraisal, accompanied by his suggestions!

THE FEAST OF UNREASON

1970-1976

Out of Ireland have we come
Great hatred, little room
Maimed us from the start.
I carry from my mother's womb
A fanatic heart.

— William Butler Yeats:
Remorse for Intemperate Speech

TOWARD A LARGER THEATRE

The Feast of Unreason has been a finalist in three play contests: the National Playwrights Conference, the Sergel Drama Prize and the Towngate Theater Contest. Its title refers to the madness of the religious war in Northern Ireland — a phenomenon by no means unknown to other areas of our dangerously fragmented world.

My choice of Ireland as the scene of a play, and still more, my knowledge of Irish dialect, has surprised some of my friends. As a denizen of the New York slums I grew up with Irish youngsters who fascinated me with their turns of phrase and the lilt of their speech, as well as their religious zeal, which was excessive.

If Jesus ever needed vengeance, he received it at my expense from the gang of Irish kids. I would come home beaten and bloodied, to face a scolding by my mother who demanded, "Why do you play with those bums?" It did not matter that I had no wish to play with them. There was an open season on Jews whether on East 70th Street or anywhere else in the Catholic sections of New York.

My mother was a little woman, sarcastic and dramatically superstitious, worn down by a family of five children whom, with no help whatever, she had to feed, clothe, and bathe, in addition to her other household duties that included a war on bedbugs and cockroaches — all this while "spelling" my father at our newsstand. She had little tenderness left for wailing over me until one day, on coming back from school, I was caught and held by the gang while one of them squirted down my throat the kind of scalding oil used for hunting bedbugs. I reached home with my mouth and throat on fire. Mom, this time thoroughly alarmed, took me by the hand and led me to the Irish lady whose offspring had doused me with "bedbug juice." Mrs O'Grady, or whatever her name was, leaning on a cushion in her open window, merely told her, "Gowan home, you Kike," and that was the end of the episode. Fortunately I recovered.

It remains to be noted that I loved the annual St. Patrick's Day Parade on Fifth Avenue so much that in 1951 I timed my visit to Dublin in order to see the parade on its home grounds. (It proved to be a great disappointment.) At the age of sixteen I knew enough Irish history to share the grief of the New York Irish at the tragedy of the Dublin Easter Rebellion. Later on, the plays of Sean O'Casey were a revelation to me when they were performed by a visiting Abbey troupe. And in the fifties in New York and Hollywood, I twice directed Irish plays.

OUTLINE

Northern Ireland, before the British intervention. Connie Flannery, whose father and brother are members of the Royal Ulster Constabulary, works as secretary to a leading member of the Town Council of Craigie. An unmarried Protestant, she is unjustly awarded possession of one of the new municipal cottages. The award is challenged by a Catholic seminarian, Dennis O'Connell, who is joined by Eileen Torrance, a secret member of the terrorist Provisionals. It is Eileen who brings a slum family of Catholics, the Hallinans, to occupy the cottage even after Connie has moved in. Hoodlums attack the house, and the family replies with homemade petrol bombs. When the police, led by Connie's father, order the cottage cleared out, Eileen uses Connie as a hostage. The family leaves the cottage safely, under police protection, but Eileen, overpowered, is shot down by the mob. Connie's remorse over the "poisoned gift" of the house turns to anguish as her father is also shot down before her eyes.

Setting: a cottage and part of the roof above it. (Properly designed, the roof can be a separate setting.)

Cast: 3 women, 6 men, boy 14, boy 10, little girl 6.

CHARACTERS

Connie Flannery
Jack Flannery, her father
Tom Flannery, her brother
Dennis O'Connell
Eileen Torrance
Liam Hallinan
Gwen Hallinan, his wife
Kevin, their son, fourteen
Paddy, their son, ten
Moira, their daughter, six
Grady
Malone

Recorded Voices:

Chairman
Everett Doyle
Clem Sheels
Harold Norton
Nigel Yardley
Danny Timothy
Inspector
Sergeant

Place: Craigie, a town in the west of Ulster.
Time: 1971*

---

* For a brief summary of the political conditions in Ulster forming the
background of this play, see the Author's Postcript, p. 248.

ACT I

Scene I

As the house lights begin to dim, we hear a distant singing, to the accompaniment of an accordion:

> *It may be for years and it may be forever,*
> *Oh, why art thou silent, thou voice of my heart?*
> *It may be for years and it may be forever;*
> *Then why art thou silent, Kathleen Mavourneen?*

The house lights continue their slow dimout, to the sound of VOICES, *recorded:*

First Recording

CHAIRMAN: The Chair recognizes Councilman Harold Norton.

NORTON: I yield to Councilman Nigel Yardley.

CHAIRMAN: Councilman Yardley.

YARDLEY: We meet, this day, at a time when our town is menaced by the miasma of hatred that is spreading throughout all the six counties of Ulster, spread by criminals across the border, determined to subvert by violence the lawful government of Northern Ireland — with the help of their sympathizers who hide their faces from the law.
(*Applause and cries of "Hear, hear!"*)
Our people by a majority of two to one have voted repeatedly to retain our union with the United Kingdom and the British realm. And what, indeed, have we or our Catholic fellow-citizens to gain if we are absorbed by our neighbor to the south, the Republic of Ireland? What has that republic to show for its "independence" except blasted hopes and the misrule of those who receive their secret orders from Rome?
(*Cries of "Shame!" and a commotion in the hall.* CHAIRMAN *raps for order.* YARDLEY *continues):*
Has anyone seen a mass migration of Ulster Catholics to that republic? Instead, its people come knocking at our doors, knowing that our wages are higher, our medical care is free to all, and religious liberty is denied to no one — in fact, the Catholic parochial schools are more generously supported by our government than even in the affluent United States of America! (*Raising his voice.*) Nevertheless in these parochial schools too many adolescents learn to hate their fellow-citizens of a different faith, joining the gunmen who come here to terrorize and slay from ambush! They, and they alone, claim the right to decide our destiny and to take human lives in consequence!

211

(*The latter part of this speech has been greeted by a few cries of protest and some catcalls and jeers. Now follows a deafening applause.*)

Scene 2

After a brief silence the curtain rises on a newly-built cottage in Craigie, a town in the west of Ulster. It is a bright, early afternoon in August 1971. The cottage is a one-story structure, with its roof and chimney-pots visible. Above its roof, across the street, there is a line of two-story brick buildings. Below the roof we see the living room of the cottage, which has a large window and a door leading, presumably, to the bedrooms and kitchen. A few pieces of furniture are scattered around the living room, together with some paper cartons, partly opened, containing dishes, towels and other properties, evidently those of CONNIE FLANNERY, *who has just moved in and is putting the place to rights.* CONNIE *is a thirty-four-year-old Protestant spinster, prim but by no means docile. At rise, she is sitting on a stool, stitching the hem of a window curtain and singing to herself.*

CONNIE:

> *Would you like to swing on a star,*
> *Carry moonbeams home in a jar —*

(*Her singing is interrupted as she sees her father approaching the door. She goes to let him in.* JACK FLANNERY *is a compact, ruddy-faced man in the uniform of the Royal Ulster Constabulary, a man whose gruffness is lightened at times by an engaging smile. He looks around the room.*)

FLANNERY: Almost moved in, are ye?

CONNIE: Almost everything's here; not all opened yet. Give me two more days.

FLANNERY: Tom an' me are goin' to miss ye sore, girl.

CONNIE: I know, Dad, and it hurts me. You'll get along, though. You'll have Sheila to come in and help with the suppers, anyhow, and I'll be over anytime I can make it, and that'll be almost every evening.

FLANNERY (*returning after looking into next room*): I hope not. Time fer ye to be trappin' some young man in this nice layout, snugglin' with ye evenin' on that sofa —

CONNIE: Ah, go on with you, Dad! "Trapping!"

FLANNERY: Don't I know how the girlies go about it? Sidlin' up so carefully to a man they hardly know at all, givin' him a shot out o' their big blue eyes an' flappin' their eyelids with frantic embarrassment? Only you never learned how it's done!

CONNIE: You know I wouldn't stoop to those tricks, Dad.

212

FLANNERY: Oh, aye! Still ye don't want a couple o' policemen always with ye? Sittin' aroun' in their braces an' stockin' feet every time a young fella comes to call? It's been goin' on too long. Now you're in yer own digs in yer own home, what's more, an' that's a good bait for any sensible lad. All he's got to do after the weddin' is to move to right in, with everythin' all prepared an' a roast waitin' in the oven.

CONNIE: Well, I know I'll be happy here.

FLANNERY: A girl like you is one to be appreciated. That's why this place is yours. Eight whole years with the town's leadin' barrister an' member o' the Town Council —

CONNIE: Six years only, with Mr. Yardley.

FLANNERY: Long enough to show yer mettle, anyhow. A legal secretary — now is that any small thing?

CONNIE: I'll match anyone in the county for the speed of my shorthand and typing or for the clear, spaced pages and clean erasures. And I don't turn to the *Handy Desk Dictionary* every second and a half, looking for the words like "receive", "exaggerate", or "parallel."

FLANNERY: Aye. An' that's why Mr. Yardley wanted to show you his appreciation when it come to the new town dwellin's. The Council's not in the habit o' givin' them out to some single unmarried young woman.

CONNIE: I'm very grateful I'm sure, Dad.

FLANNERY: Tom an' me'll be along shortly, soon as we sign ourselves in; we'll give ye a hand with the unpackin', so don't ye do all the liftin' an' haulin'. An' when the Apprentice Boys parade lets out, we'll be here again.

CONNIE (*suddenly*): Daddy, take care! Last time —

FLANNERY: A criminal with a gun on him, crazed with drink. It was him or me.

CONNIE: Seeing somebody lose his life, even now I'm shaky all over and ready to scream when I think of it.

FLANNERY: Then don't think of it, girl. Ferget it!

CONNIE: You're right, Dad. I'll try.

FLANNERY (*grimly*): That half-crocked element's a headache fer all decent Orangemen an' the police force every year, with their own way o' celebratin' the Apprentice Boys, King Billy, the Battle o' the Boyne, an' whatever else. They're already at it in some o' the Protestant pubs hereabouts. But they've had their lesson. (*Dismissing it, cheerfully*) Soon as the parade's over we'll be aroun' fer a housewarmin' with a pint or two the by.

CONNIE: Not for me, though.

FLANNERY: I'm not sayin' it's fer you. You're yer mother's own image — all that passionate primness. Tha's what done her in, in the end — takin' everthin' too hard.

CONNIE: It had nothing to do with it. You shouldn't say so.

FLANNERY: Right, I shouldn't. It would have made her heart glad to see ye set up in this house. So no more lip, now, an' set the table.

(*He turns to go.*)

CONNIE: Dad! You're glad, too, you said.

FLANNERY: Of course, daughter.

CONNIE: Thirty-four years old and I'm disgracing you by still being a lone woman.

FLANNERY: Ah, now —

CONNIE: It's true I don't know the tricks. They run circles around me, those young women; they scoop up the men they want. I'm left with my typewriter. (*With feeling*) It's just what you say, Dad. I've got this house, and it's my chance for the last time, maybe. A house for me, for a man, and for the kids to grow up in . . .

FLANNERY (*with a pat on the shoulder and a hug*): New start, child!

(CONNIE *watches him leave, then shuts the door and starts removing dishes from a carton; continues her singing.*)

CONNIE:
>   *And be better off than you are?*
>   *Or would you rather be a mule?*
>   (*There is a knock at the door.*)

CONNIE: Who is it?

(*She gets up.* DENNIS *enters. He is a young and breezy seminarian. Wears glasses.*)

DENNIS: You're not moved in already, Miss Flannery?

CONNIE: I am. And how does that concern you, Mr. Dennis O'Connell?

DENNIS: You're not forgetting I'm secretary of the Housing Action Committee?

CONNIE: A committee with no legal standing whatever! You're here to make trouble, are you?

DENNIS: Well, now —

CONNIE: Where's the rest of your army, pickets, and placards? Sure you're not carrying on all by yourself, this time?

DENNIS: Not entirely.

CONNIE: Ah, right! You've the help of the Lord, as always __

DENNIS (*as* EILEEN *enters*): And of a new member of my staff. Eileen Torrance. (*To* EILEEN) This is Miss Flannery. She's moved right in.

EILEEN: Quick work.

(EILEEN *is stunningly beautiful, but her face is pale. She carries an armful of circulars.*)

DENNIS: Miss Torrance is a university student from Derry. She's visiting in town.

CONNIE: And helping you make an uproar with those circulars. (*To* EILEEN) You're doing the Lord's work too, are you?

DENNIS: She in her way. I in His.
(EILEEN *hands* CONNIE *one of the circulars.*)
All about the new public housing. We were at the Town Council this morning — threw a lot of these down from the balcony.

CONNIE (*to* EILEEN): You'll have a most interesting time, dear, working with Mr. O'Connell. Dandy Dennis, they call him. He's on the same team with the Deity against heathens like me — it's what gives him all that robust belief in whatever it is the Catholics believe in. (*To* DENNIS) You don't know how it impressed me, your leading that wild charge of the pickets outside my boss's office! Superb! You had to be removed by constable. (*She tosses away the circular.*) The same old junk about anti-Catholic discrimination! There's very little of that in Craigie, Miss Torrance.

EILEEN: Like only a little pregnant.

CONNIE: I don't know what that means. (*Coldly*) If you're both supposed to be students, why aren't you in school, studying, instead of going around making heroes of yourselves?

DENNIS: We're not attending classes at the moment. The provost at my seminary doesn't like uproars, as you call them, so I'm suspended. And Eileen for the same reason, at her university.

CONNIE: Very interesting, I'm sure, and I'd love to hear more; but if you don't mind, I'm still putting things to rights here and can't invite you to tea.
(*They don't move.*)
So a good afternoon to you both, and I wish you a nicer type of visit to this town, Miss Torrance.

DENNIS: One moment —

EILEEN (*abruptly*): Are you married, Miss Flannery? I ask because it says, in this Housing Bulletin, "Miss Constance Flannery is awarded Council House Number 24."

CONNIE: I'm in my house by legal right, Miss Torrance. And I'm not answering insolent questions, especially from outsiders, so good day to you both.

EILEEN: We are not leaving.

DENNIS: I have to notify you, Miss Flannery, that I'm here in my formal capacity — appointed, anyhow, by the Catholic community of this city. We are trying to learn why almost all of the new Council houses are going to Protestants — least of all to an unmarried single woman who works for a leading councilman.

EILEEN: Simple. By sexing her boss.

CONNIE (*furiously*): How dare you? Mr. Yardley is sixty-five years old, a gentleman of the highest reputation. He would no more think of —

DENNIS: He's pretty far gone, I agree. Still he has a lot of clout in this town. He paralyzes the other bureaucrats by being literate. He even scares them by quoting Latin and Greek.

CONNIE: Mr. O'Connell, we need no dirty-minded hussy coming here to make accusations!

EILEEN: Against any mildewed old maid the likes of you!

DENNIS: Och, now! Spare my ears, ladies! I'm modestly unaccustomed to such lovely springtime flowers having a go at each other!

CONNIE: Let her know she's talking to a lady!

EILEEN: We'll try not to give you away!

(EILEEN *goes to the door.*)

CONNIE: Go and address yourself to the Council, Mr. O'Connell. You, too, Miss Torrance, although you don't even belong in this bailiwick. In the meantime I'll thank you both to leave these premises immediately — in other words, get out!

EILEEN (*opening the door and calling*): You can come in now.

(*The* HALLINAN *family enter.* LIAM, *the father, is raw-boned and unshaven, an unemployed navvy. His wife,* GWEN, *is a toilworn woman. Their children are* KEVIN, *fourteen,* PADDY, *ten, and* MOIRA, *six.* KEVIN *has an accordion.*)

LIAM (*in a nasal drawl*): What's all the blather? We been out there coolin' our bloody heels while yous is havin' a convention!

CONNIE (*startled*): Who is this gang?

EILEEN: They're the Hallinan family, moving in.

CONNIE: They're *what*?

GWEN: We need a home, missus. We've no right place to live in.

CONNIE (*staggered; to* DENNIS): Did you bring them here?

EILEEN: Dennis never thought of it, I'm the one who invited them

CONNIE: Then you can invite them right out again! I'm sorry they don't like where they're living, but this happens to be my legal residence.

GWEN: Legal yer arse!

CONNIE (*faintly*): What did she say?

EILEEN: She said, "Legal yer arse."

CONNIE: I'll have the lot of you up for trespassing, forcible entry, obscenity, and insolence! A bunch of five-in-a-bed Fenians barging in here —

LIAM: Five-in-a-bed Fenians, is it? Somebody take houl' o' me before I strike a woman!

DENNIS: Wait, now —

GWEN (*furiously*): Listen to Missus Upperosity — a single, sour oul' maid takin' over this whole place for herself alone, while we have to do with half a rotten oul' floor for two families an' one cruddy oul' toilet!

KEVIN: You can say that again, Ma!

LIAM: I seen her kind at the Baroo, where they like to put down the proletariat — pattin' their hair an' shovin' yous aroun' from one windy to th'other, like yous is thryin' to rob the guvmint be comin' in for yer dole!

GWEN: Right y' are, Liam, dear!

LIAM: "Sorry, me man," says they, "this is the wrong windy, thry Number Four, an' who paid for that tobaccy you're smokin?"

(MOIRA *comes out of a closet dragging a framed sampler.*)

PADDY: Look what our Moira's got, Ma! "Nearer My God to Thee"!

(*He wrests the picture from her.*)

CONNIE: My mother's needlework! — Let her alone, you hellion, or I'll —

GWEN: Don't you be threatenin' me childer, missus!

(PADDY *runs off into the next room with the picture, pursued by the weeping* MOIRA.)

217

CONNIE: I'll do more than threaten, in a minute! (*To* KEVIN, *who is fingering the window curtain.*) Come away from that with your filthy hands before I hit you a clout!

KEVIN: You an' what army?

DENNIS: Let's have a little order! Mrs. Hallinan —

CONNIE: I said get out! Now go!

KEVIN: Up yours!

GWEN: Mind yer language, ye cheeky lump! You're not back in yer oul' dump of a home!

KEVIN (*singing*):

> Oh, I wish I was a fascinatin' bitch,
> I'd never be poor an' I'd always be rich —

(PADDY, *still followed by* MOIRA, runs in, clapping hands to the rhythm.)

CONNIE: I'm raging at the lot of you!

KEVIN: (*swinging to a new rhythm on the accordion*):
With a too-ra-nanty na!

PADDY AND MOIRA (*skipping and singing*): Sing too-ra-nan nanty na!

GWEN AND LIAM (*joining in a jig*):

> While the echoes prolong
> The sweet notes of his song,
> An' his too-ra-nan naty na!

ALL (*ending in a cheer*): Hooroo!

CONNIE (*wildly*): Scarecrows! Get out! Get out!

(FLANNERY *and* TOM, *both in helmets and battle dress, have burst into the scene on* CONNIE'S *last line.*)

FLANNERY: What's going on here?

CONNIE: Dad, I'm so glad you've come!

FLANNERY: What's the row, girl?

CONNIE: They want to take away my house!

TOM: Who are they?

FLANNERY: I know this one, O'Connell. (*To* DENNIS) Another of your provocations?

EILEEN: A protest. Why was this place handed over to your daughter — if that's who she is?

FLANNERY: That's who she is. An' you're takin' the law into yer own hands, are ye?

EILEEN: Just so.

DENNIS (*quickly*): Sergeant, the Hallinan family's had their names on the Housing Application three years or more, getting nowhere. It's well known the Council is loaded against the Catholics —

TOM: We need no cheap Taigs here!

FLANNERY: Easy, Tom! (*To DENNIS*) You been doin' too much oratin' about it all, Sonny. Let's say it's true — that still don't give you, nor nobody else, the license to go floutin' law an' order! There's a grievance procedure —

DENNIS: Also loaded.

TOM: Willya cut this gab?

LIAM: We're talkin' peaceful, mister.

FLANNERY: You're not peaceful at all. Clear out or face a criminal arrest.
    (KEVIN *plays a sour note on his accordion.*)
An' take that brat with you.

GWEN: He's no brat, an' don't you say it!

FLANNERY: Righto, he's not — only take him away just the same.

EILEEN: The family is not leaving.

TOM: Says who?
    (*His hand goes to his holster.*)

FLANNERY: Stow it, Tom. (*To DENNIS*) You've got two minutes to obey a lawful order. Will you be leavin' quietly, or waitin' to be shoved?

VOICE (*calling loudly from outside*): Sergeant Flannery, are you there?

FLANNERY: What is it, then?

VOICE: You and Tom both wanted at H.Q. At the double!

FLANNERY: Comin'! Tom, get crackin' — I'll follow.
    (TOM *exits. To the* OTHERS.)
Don't let me find you here when I get back! (*To CONNIE*) Rest yer mind, daughter — these tramps will get the hell of a bounce out if they don't go by themselves.

(*The music of a distant flute and drum band becomes audible.*)

Lock up this place soon as they're gone, and get back to our digs in a hurry — there's trouble not far off.

CONNIE: Yes, Dad.

FLANNERY (*to* EILEEN, *taking out his notebook*): Now then, what's *your* name?

EILEEN: That's for me to know and for you to find out.

(*A shrill whistle is heard from outside.*)

FLANNERY (*shutting his notebook*): I'll find out.

(*He hastens to the door as the light blacks out; then a slow dim up to* VOICES, *recorded*):

Second Recording

CHAIRMAN: The chair recognizes Councilman Everett Doyle.

DOYLE: Mr. Chairman, our learned colleague, Mr. Nigel Yardley, informs us of the violence committed by a few individuals dedicated to uniting the people of Ireland. Meanwhile he chooses to overlook the three hundred years of massacres perpetrated by Elizabeth, Cromwell, William of Orange, Lloyd George — (*Loud cries of "Bringing up the bloody past again!"* CHAIRMAN *raps for order.*) As for the famous two-thirds majority — meaning the privileged Protestant majority alone —

(*Tumult: boos, hisses, and shouts of "Sit down!"*)

CHAIRMAN (*rapping*): Mr. Doyle, you are called to order and warned.

DOYLE: Unlike the many speakers, today, who have favored us with a high moral tone and nothing more, I have a few resolutions to offer:
1. No more proprietor-based voting. One man, one vote.
2. No more of the gerrymandering that explains why the one-third Catholic minority of Craigie is represented in this Chamber by four Catholics as against twenty-seven Protestants.
3. No more religious discrimination in employment.
4. A points system for allocating the new city housing —

A LOUD VOICE: Good lad, Everett!

DOYLE: I could say more, but I'll stop here, for the favoritism practiced by certain members of this Council is so open and outrageous —

(*The noise mounting all through* DOYLE'S *speech breaks into storm of protest.*)

CHAIRMAN (*banging his gavel*): Order! Order, I say!

(*His voice is drowned in a blackout as the music previously heard rises and is accompanied by singing*):

> *We'll fight and not surrender*
> *We'll guard old Derry's walls*

With heart and hand and sword and shield
We'll fight for victory!

On the green grassy slopes of the Boyne
Where King William his Orangemen did join
Where they fought for our glorious deliverance
On the green grassy slopes of the Boyne . . .

(*Blackout*)

Scene 3

The living room. The action of the scene continues.

DENNIS: The sergeant has to enforce the law.

EILEEN: The law as laid down by the Protestants in Stormont assembled.

CONNIE: The law applies equally to all — Protestants or Catholics, rich or poor! Like God's commandments!

EILEEN: You don't say!

DENNIS: The law's all right, I guess, only it's the Ulster Protestants who interpret it. . . . I wonder, sometimes, if God isn't a mite too willing to leave that to the Protestants. Maybe he feels they're doing Him a favor by believing in Him.

EILEEN: Come to the point: what's to be done now?

DENNIS: I make bold to offer a suggestion: let them share the house.

CONNIE: I, with them?

DENNIS: And them with you.

CONNIE: You're making fun!

GWEN: Us, livin' in the same house with that policeman's daughter?

LIAM: Are ye daft, man?

DENNIS: Then let's agree we have called attention to a soft spot in the body politic, and having made that point, let us now quietly depart and return to picketing.

EILEEN: I don't wonder they call you Dandy Dennis, if picketing is all you know! The family must stay and dispute possession! Who'll give them a new home if they leave this one — God Above? You just told us: He's too busy obliging the Protestants!

DENNIS: Sure you can't be asking them to remain here, to be dragged out by the police? And not only by the police — they may have this whole neighborhood on top of them! With a solid block of Protestants across the street —

221

(KEVIN *and* PADDY *sneak off into the next room.*)

EILEEN: Let the family decide.

(*Blackout, with a spot on* GWEN *and* LIAM; *the* OTHERS *freeze.*)

LIAM: I'm after thinkin' the same thing, BeGod. We could be sittin' on a powder keg in this place if the word gets out there's Catholics occupyin' it.

GWEN: What then? There's always somethin' — Prodestans or no! Do we wait to our dyin' day for a perfect dwellin' an' watch some other policeman's daughter snaggin' it first?

LIAM: No, yer right. This place could be made to order fer us, barrin' it had a right-size parlor fer entertainin' guests.

GWEN: Guests, is it? Liam, dear, yer mind is wanderin'. You're not wantin' yer oul' auntie in County Wicklow to come an' plunk herself down in our midst?

LIAM: I was only debatin' with meself wouldn' it be a grand thing havin' a proper room to be sociable.

GWEN: I can see it — three or four of yer butties that's idle like yerself makin' theirselves aisy in it all day, with me to be servin' them a la card! Ferget it, Liam! Long as we'll still be havin' a room fer the two boys to be sharin' it together —

LIAM: An' a foldaway bed fer Moira in the kitchen, like before —

GWEN: That's another thing — there's not room enough to swing a cat in the kitchen in here. Compacted like all the rest o' this layout — "modren," they call it.

LIAM: Residential! I'd be out maybe half o' me pay an' half o' me sleep when I'm assed to work again, ridin' at lease two diff'rent buses to get there! An' even with the both of us out workin', how could we hole on to this kind o' premises? You don't think the Town Council's goin' to pay the rent an' the rates?

GWEN: We'd be down a bog hole for sure! (*Seething*) Will ye tell me, now, how we let that woman give us a royal rookin' to be follyin' her to this place? I misliked her looks the minute I seen her!

(*Light returns and* the OTHERS *unfreeze.*)

EILEEN: Well?

GWEN (*succinctly*): We're leavin'!

DENNIS: Believe me, Mrs. Hallinan, that's a wise decision.

EILEEN: You call that wise? Giving up their one chance for a decent home?

222

LIAM: There's no more cause fer natterin'. We are removin' ourselves from this place.

EILEEN: What's become of the fighting Irish?

GWEN: Don't ye be givin' us no lectures, missus — we don't need no outsiders comin' here to start what they can't finish!

LIAM: Stay an' fight the polis if you like, but don't be shovin' us into it!

GWEN (to Eileen): Go peddle them circulars, you Commyunist! An' anyway, Torrance — What kind o' name is that, now? It's no Catholic name I ever heard on!

EILEEN: I'm no Catholic and no Communist, either.

CONNIE: Only a brazen troublemaker!

EILEEN (to Dennis): You were right: you can't expect anything of these people. Not yet.

DENNIS: You had a bash at it — let that console you. Now back to the circulars. (To CONNIE) We'll have a look-in on you later to see is everything quiet. Coming, Eileen?

(As he and EILEEN turn to go, little MOIRA takes EILEEN'S hand.)

EILLEN (startled; tossing off the child's hand): No, no! Stay away from me!

(She follows DENNIS out the door.)

GWEN: Didja see that? Just because the poor chile's hand was dirty!

LIAM: That's them intellekchools fer ye! Makin' poor folk into catpaws fer their radicalism, then dodgin' out when the cops start clubbin' heads!

(MOIRA darts into next room.)

CONNIE: Let me congratulate you, Mr. and Mrs. Hallinan, on realizing you've been used.

GWEN: We'd never a' thought of housebreakin' if we wasn't so propagandered by that woman. Comes here havin' a go at bein' Lady Bountiful stickin' up for the Taigs!

LIAM: You know who she is? Dennis told us: Torrance Gold Label Whiskey. The Torrance one an' only child!

CONNIE: No!

GWEN: Spoiled rotten at home! No wonder she don't know her place. Comes from High Episcopal an' mucks aroun' with the likes of us!

CONNIE: A traitor to her class! Even if she thinks she means it for the best, that's no way to go about it, stirring people up to no good!

LIAM: Right y're, missus, Like I says to them boyos that hang aroun' outside the Baroo, enticin' the workin' class, handin' out circulars an' leaflets: "You're goin' about it the wrong way entirely." I says, "'Stead o' handin' out circulars you got to slam right into them exploiters or they pay ye no heed whatever!"

GWEN: Exactly. Fetch the childer, Liam, dear. We have got to go, an' not be embarrassin' Missus Flannery any more than we done already.

CONNIE (as LIAM goes to the next room): You know, Mrs. Hallinan, I really think your coming here has made its point, as Mr. O'Connell remarked. When it gets around how people like yourselves are so needful, there'll be more care taken about the housing.

GWEN: I do hope so, truly, for it's a blessed shame, so it is, the way we live.

(LIAM returns, herding the kids.)

LIAM: Will yous have a look? Soaked to the naked skin, all three of 'em!

PADDY: We had showers, Ma!

KEVIN: Hot an' cold wather springin' outa the wall!

PADDY: An' we're all smelled up, too!

CONNIE (alarmed): With my perfume!

GWEN (to the kids, angrily): Don't yous know betther than to be misbehavin' like eejits in other folks' houses? Wait till I get yous home!

KEVIN: Home? Ain't we livin' here, now?

LIAM: We are not.

KEVIN (relieved): Sure we was wonderin' how me an' Paddy was goin' to pass the time aroun' here.

PADDY: With nobody to be playin' with.

KEVIN: No shops, no markets an' a whole block full o' Prods right across the way —

GWEN: That'll be enough from yous both! (To CONNIE) Missus Flannery, me an' Liam want to apologise for all the disthurbin' we done here. We know the meanin' of a proper home.

LIAM: We are sorry for the pother, Missus Flannery.

CONNIE: A good day to you all, and I don't mind about the children, they're so high-spirited.

GWEN: A good day to you, too, dear.

(The FAMILY *troop out,* KEVIN *bringing up the rear with a note or two on his accordion. The door closes and* CONNIE *leans against it in vast relief. Suddenly it opens again, and all the* HALLINANS *pour in once more.)*

CONNIE: What did you forget?

GWEN: Nothin', Missus. We had a change o' mind, that's all!

> *(Blackout, and a song by* KEVIN *recorded)*:
>
> *Oh, Saint Patrick was a gentleman,*
> *Who come from honest people —*
> *He built a church in Dublin town*
> *An' on it put a steeple.*
> *His oul' man was a Gallagher,*
> *His mother was a Brady . . .*

(As the light returns to the living room, we hear the first faint thudding of the great Lambeg drum accompanying GWEN'S *speech and the ensuing dialog.)*

GWEN: We can't face it, Missus Flannery, goin' back to that oul' tenimint. There's not even the gas an' electric turned on. It's unhuman! Just because we can't pay —

LIAM: There's not enough of the dole to go round, d'ye see? Most I can do, come Michaelmas I put all the year's bills into me cap an' stirs them aroun', pickin' out one or two, blindfold, fer payin' off.

CONNIE (*coldly*): And what about the rest?

LIAM: Them that get huffy with me I don't even put 'em in me cap.

GWEN: Then they cut us off — fastest service we ever got.

CONNIE (*reaching for her purse*): Here's some pound notes for the utilities — pay them right now, on your way home.

GWEN (*waving her away, half-weeping with frustration*): That's only the start of it. You don't know the neglectment — the roaches an' rats, the cold, the damp an' the smell, forbye the WC in the hall, where you wait outside for the neighbors to have their turn —

KEVIN: You can say that again, Ma!

CONNIE: I wouldn't like that, I'm sure. Nevertheless —

GWEN: An' don't think that's all! The kids, with never enough to eat, roamin' aroun' the streets gettin' into mischief the while I'm doin' other people's housecleanin' an' Liam is trampin' the streets lookin' fer work —

PADDY: We don't do nothin', Ma.

LIAM (*to* PADDY): Don't tell *me*! You and Kevin both, snatchin' an' maraudin' —

225

CONNIE: You needn't go on. I can see how it is, but you can't expect me to personally right the wrongs of the world. Besides, the more you do for people, the more they think you owe it to them. So make up your minds you're going for good. You heard the officer —

GWEN: *You* heard him. He said go back to your own digs, is what he said!

CONNIE (*firing up*): And what do you think you're doing? Settling in here and throwing me out?

GWEN: That'll be up to you, won't it? If you won't go peaceful —

CONNIE: I won't go at all! Just try and make me!

KEVIN: You want me to chuck her out? She's only a Prod, anyhow —

GWEN (*turning to* LIAM): Liam, show madam out!

LIAM: Who, me? Och, now Gwen, think what you're doin'. The polis —

GWEN: Polis or no, we have to hole on to this place! Where's the choice?

PADDY (*pushing* CONNIE): Out with you!

CONNIE: Hands off me, you imp! (*To the* OTHERS) You dare try pushing me —

(*Blackout. The Lambeg drum is heard more distinctly, then fades. Spotlights reveal a small table and two chairs on the forestage.* GRADY *enters followed by* MALONE.)

Flashback

GRADY: You may be a wee bit prejudiced, Malone, You sleep with her.

MALONE: Is that a crime on our books?

GRADY (*sitting at the table*): Sit down, man, sit down. You tell *me*: what'll we be up against with her now? Ratting on us?

MALONE: She's not that kind! Commander Grady, you're a menace. Distrusting everybody in the group, disciplining and threatening. . . . You fairly ask people to turn themselves in to the cops. There's nobody not liable to make mistakes — you included.

GRADY: Take it easy! I was never near the supermarket — only handed down the order for it. It wasn't even my idea.

MALONE: It was the damnedest luck, all around. The thing went off five minutes too late in the morning, when the first customers were already showing up.

GRADY: And why was it planted in the morning?

226

MALONE: We had only that interval. The street was close guarded except for when the police detail was changed. A matter of minutes, no more.

GRADY (*with a sigh*): There's always some hitch or other, with never enough precautions thought of. Inept is the least you can call it. Even our best friends can't excuse it; and as for its effect on the public — (*shrugging*) Call her in.

MALONE (*calling*): Come in, dear.

(EILEEN *enters.* MALONE *offers her his chair.*)

GRADY: Let her stand.

MALONE: What for?

GRADY: Because I say so. (MALONE *is silent.*) Volunteer Torrance, you know why we've called you in.

EILEEN: Yes, Commandant.

GRADY: We want to hear you out before your case is taken up by the Disciplinary Committee. You are charged with leaving your post in front of the market when you were placed there as a lookout. Immediately the device went off, you disappeared.

EILEEN: I didn't go anywhere except home.

MALONE: And she reported to us next day.

GRADY: The arrangement was for you to meet Malone and Timothy afterward, not to drop out of sight. The charge against you is cowardice and desertion.

MALONE: She only —

GRADY: Let her answer.

MALONE: Can't you see she's trembling?

EILEEN (*slowly*): After it went off I started toward Coleraine Street to find the boys.

GRADY: Then?

EILEEN: Then I was sick.

GRADY: Sick? What way?

MALONE: You were wrong to put her on that detail, Grady — a first assignment for somebody like her! There's a streak of sadism in you. Or class hatred, if you'd rather put it that way.

GRADY: Leftenent Malone, if you can't be civil, you may soon be up before the Committee yourself. (*To* EILEEN) Go on.

EILEEN: I had to stop because I began to vomit.

MALONE (*to* GRADY): What could you expect? Five passersby torn to rags, guts and blood smeared over the pavement, people still alive and shrieking —

GRADY: Shut up!

EILEEN: I saw them coming toward the store. A woman with a baby in a pram and a little girl skipping along with them, and people coming from the other direction, too. . . . Then everything flew up in the air. The baby carriage, and the little girl with her head ripped off . . .

GRADY: We have no heart for killing children. Least of all for Catholic children, as it happened.

> (EILEEN *looks away.*)

A bad mess, and the worst kind of public relations, but we have our duty. (*Hard*) Then you went home to mama, did you? Laid down on the big bed with fresh linen, took a warm perfumed bath —

MALONE: Will you quit it?

GRADY: Take her back for a minute. I want a talk with you. (MALONE *takes* EILEEN *off, as* GRADY *shuffles through papers.* MALONE *returns.*) I have her original application here. What made anybody like her want to join up? Born in a cushy family, had everything she ever wanted . . . expensive private school, brought to school every day in a limousine, attended a select young ladies' academy . . .

MALONE: Hard for you to understand, isn't it? A bright intelligence trying to *escape* from it all! Lost! An only child, given no love or attention — only toys to play with . . . Practically cut off, in school, from anybody but the smarmies sucking around her, learning to detest her stupid parents, envying kids with a normal family life and the freedom of the streets, even if their homes were no more than a hole in the wall. . . . (*feelingly*) You know what that's like? No purpose, no adventure in your life — rattling around, half crazed, in your own boredom? No, you don't know what it's like — you *couldn't* know.

GRADY: Then she discovered you.

MALONE: Discovered us, Grady. And a cause to put her life into focus.

GRADY (*after a moment, shrugging*): Bring her back.

> (MALONE *goes and returns with* EILEEN.)

GRADY (*to* EILEEN): What'll you do now? Write a book, go on the telly, saying how you broke off with murderers like us?

EILEEN: I'm not like that, Commandant Grady.

GRADY: Better not be. There'd be consequences. (*He puts down his papers.*) Leftenant Malone offers in your defense that you had too

228

tough a job on your first time out. I will recommend that you be given a chance to redeem yourself.

EILEEN (*eagerly*): Thank you, Commandant.

GRADY: We've had an executive session this week, on the state of things in County Eoghan. You know about that.

EILEEN: Yes, sir.

GRADY: You'll be on your own. Show what you can do.

MALONE: She'll be all right.

GRADY: Dare to struggle, dare to win, Volunteer Torrance!

(*Blackout as they get up. The Lambeg drum resumes, then fades as the curtain closes.*)

ACT II

Scene I

The curtain rises to the throbbing of the Lambeg drum, which provides a steady undertone to the flute and drum band, the scraping of marching feet, and the increasingly audible muttering and scattered shouts of the parade. The sun is going down. Across the street, over the roof of the cottage, Union Jack flags have appeared at the windows, accompanied by a banner proclaiming "Up the Unionists." The living room is empty at the moment. On the roof, KEVIN and PADDY are lounging against the chimneys, looking off. The words of a hymn float up to them:

> O God our help in ages past,
> Our hope for years to come,
> Our shelter from the stormy blast,
> And our eternal home . . .

KEVIN: Looka all them bowler hats!

PADDY: An' the sashes!

KEVIN: An' they singin' church hymns! What's reelijus about it? The Prods have two Walks ev'ry year just to be provokin'!

PADDY: Provokin'!

KEVIN: Celebratin' the Battle o' the Boyne. The "glorious" battle, they call it, in the year of 1690.

PADDY: 1690!

KEVIN: The year of Irish sorrow an' despair!
(PADDY *groans.*)
An' celebratin' the Apprentice Boys in the siege of Derry in the year before, when the Prods were holed up in the city, all ready to

be wiped out, because the city gates were open — only that the thirteen apprentice boys, riskin' their life an' limb, went an' slammed shut the gates.

PADDY: Because they were brave boys!

KEVIN (*disgusted*): Ah, houl' yer whist, willya? Them were Prods, not Catholics!

PADDY: Ya, Prods!

KEVIN: I coulda licked any four o' them boys with one hand tied behind me back! (*Sings*):

> *It was there I learned readin' an' writin',*
> *At Dick Croly's, where I went to school,*
> *An' 'twas there I learned howlin' an' fightin',*
> *With me schoolmaster, Misther O'Toole . . .*

(*Below*, CONNIE *enters the living room from the bedroom, speaking to* GWEN.)

CONNIE: Flooding the whole bedroom with the showers, flushing the toilet to see the water run, spilling and breaking my bottles of perfume —

GWEN: Arrah an' what do ye expect of boys o' their age?

CONNIE: Vandals who've never been disciplined!
(*Little* MOIRA *shuffles in, with her feet in* CONNIE'S *white satin slippers.*) There's the other one, ruining my shoes! Take those off!

(*She removes the shoes.* MOIRA *grabs her mother's skirt.*)

MOIRA: I'm hungry.

GWEN (*to* CONNIE): You seen the boys have a hearty appetite, bless them, but this wan that arrived when we were haven' it bad enough without her — she eats nothin' only bread an' jam, an' always whinin', with a cold an' a runnin' nose. You dunno when yer well off, with no kids to pester ye all day an' half the night, shoutin' "Gimme this" an' Gimme that" until they fair drive ye outa yer mind!

CONNIE (*stiffly*): I think children grow up in the way their parents love and care for them. At least you appreciate your boys —

GWEN: It's plain ye can't wait to have some o' yer own, like all them that want a baby at the breast. . . . I wouldn't take a million pounds for neither o' them boys, but I wouldn't give a haypenny for another — an' I coulda had another three, at the least, only for pushin' Liam offa me at night. (*Tenderly*) It's a pity of him, so it is. He keeps at me because he's that downhearted an' bored he needs the bit o' comfort. Hasn't worked in the shipyards nor nowhere else in more than half a year, hardly feels he's human anymore. He's ashamed to see his oul' workmates now — can't look them in the face; all he does is read the paper if he finds one somewheres, or listens to the telly if he gets the chance.

CONNIE: And drinks?

GWEN: Thanks be to God, no. A glass o' **malt** only, if he's ever treated. (*As* LIAM *enters, filling his pipe.*) Or a smoke now an' again. (*To* LIAM) Have a lie-down now, dear, on the sofa.

LIAM: I will that.
(*He goes to the sofa near the window.* MOIRA *whines.*)
Only if you'll remove the female pest.

CONNIE (*to* MOIRA): Come on, I've strawberry jam in the pantry.

(*She takes the little* GIRL *to the next room as* GWEN *brings* LIAM *a cushion.*)

GWEN: There, me darlint, that'll be more comfy, won't it?

(*She exits to the bedroom.* LIAM *picks up one of the crumpled newspapers in which* CONNIE *has wrapped her dishes.*)

LIAM: The Belfast *Trumpet*, less'n one week old!

(*He lies down, smokes, and reads. On the roof the* BOYS *are alarmed.*)

PADDY: Ay, Kevin, some people comin' this way with rocks an' clubs!

KEVIN: Right up this street! An' some of ours comin' to meet 'em! Whisht, Paddy, behine the chimleys!

(*They take refuge between two adjacent chimneys. In the living room* LIAM *reads his newspaper.*)

LIAM: "Statement by His Eminence Cardinal Cogan: 'The man who kills others, no matter which side he is on, sins against God. You cannot say 'A life for a life' without denyin' the teaching o' Jazus.'" (*feelingly*) God's own truth, BeGod! (*Reading again.*) "Statement by the Western Executive o' the Sinn Fein: 'The kind o' veenomous attack on the ideals o' the Republican Movement issuin' from the sanctity o' the Church to a captive audience is a lamentable thing.' " (*emphatically*) Couldn't be said better, beJazus!

(MOIRA *enters, eating bread and jam. She stands looking solemnly at* LIAM, *who continues reading*):
"The silent majority o' the middle class still remains silent, thryin' to mind their own affairs while their lives are endangered amid the furious flames o' their burnin' homes."

MOIRA: I'd rather be a boy!

LIAM: (*turning the page*): "Polis seek perpitraiters of supermarket outrage, hold IRA suspect — " (*To* MOIRA) Couldn't a been an IRA. "Irish Republican Army" they call theirselves. "I Ran Away," *I* call 'em! Not half the direct action they're always blatherin' about! The

231

Provisionals, now, d'ye see — them's the boys make a splash, though they do it with bombs —

(*There is an eruption of a sullen roar from the crowd outside. MOIRA, frightened by the sound, scampers off into the next room.*)

KEVIN (*on the roof*): Whisha! They're whuppin' the Catholics in the street! We better get down inside!

(*They scramble off the roof. At the same moment there is a crash of broken glass, below, evidently in the bedroom or kitchen, followed at once by a brick shattering the window next to the couch on which LIAM has been resting, and flinging shards of glass over him. He jumps up shaking off the fragments of glass.*)

LIAM: Now what kind of a thing is that, at all?

(*The BOYS rush in excitedly.*)

KEVIN: Hand over that brick, Paddy!

(*PADDY brings it to him. KEVIN hefts its weight, then pitches it out of the hole in the window.*)

PADDY: Bloody Prods!

KEVIN (*looking around for something more to throw*): We'll smash their bloody kneecaps!

PADDY: Smash their bloody noses for 'em!

KEVIN: Slice off their bloody balls! (*He finds CONNIE'S dishes and flings one out of the window.*) Ay, how's that?!

LIAM: What are yous doin'? Them's dishes!
            (*Neither BOY pays any attention.*)
Give over, yous hear me?

PADDY: Ah, leave us alone, willya!

            (*LIAM grabs PADDY by the collar and shakes him.*)

LIAM: BeGod I'll teach the both o' yous a mite o' dacency!

KEVIN: Ay, take yer mitts offa him, oul' man!

PADDY: Leggo me! I'll tell Ma on you!

            (*GWEN enters, shoving both BOYS away.*)

GWEN: That'll do! Where's the respect fer yer father?

PADDY: He ain't our father, not him!

KEVIN: If he is, we'd like a diff'rent father!

GWEN: Ain't yous ashamed, fightin' like Kilkenny cats while payin' no mind to our bran' new home gettin' knocked apart? Both the front windies smashed, yer Da all in splinters — (*To* LIAM) Lemme see, dear, turn aroun'. (*Relieved*) No cuts — must've all bounced off.

LIAM: It's only be desperate good luck I wasn't fractured altogether!

CONNIE (*entering with broom and dust pan, followed by* MOIRA *carrying a paper bag*): I did all I could with the glass in the bedroom. It's your turn in here.

GWEN: Right enough. (*To the* BOYS) Take them things an' start in.

KEVIN: Ah, no, Ma, we're no parlor maids!

(*He and* PADDY *go reluctantly to work.*)

CONNIE: That howling mob out there! Protestant or not — where's the sense in breaking the windows because they don't want you in my house?

GWEN: *My* house. But what can you expect from a Prodestan pig only a grunt?

(*There is a prolonged cheer outside.* GWEN *and* LIAM *rush to the window.*)

LIAM: The Prods are gettin' pasted!

GWEN: They're fallin' back to the corner!

LIAM: *Erin go bragh*! For God an' Saint Pathrick!

(*The* BOYS *abandon their task and rush out, to be presently visible on the roof again.*)

CONNIE: Is it better if the mob is Catholic?

GWEN: Is it simpleminded ye are, dear? They're only good Catholics defendin' their homes!

LIAM (*at the window*): The street is clear. And Dennis an' Eileen are comin'!

(*He unlocks the door quickly for* EILEEN, *who hurries in, followed by* DENNIS. *Both are out of breath, and* DENNIS'S *jaw is cut and bleeding.*)

DENNIS (*to* EILEEN): The family's still here!

CONNIE: What's happened to you?

EILEEN: We were caught in the middle of the brawl, and he stopped to pray and make a speech of conciliation.

CONNIE: After telling off the Protestants, I'm sure.

EILEEN: Right. Why stir things up? *You're* satisfied.

(CONNIE *goes angrily into the next room.*)

DENNIS: How do you know she's satisfied?

(*Outside, the bellowing voice of* CLEM SHEELS, *known as* "the Vindicator," *rises above the banging of the Lambeg drum.*)

SHEELS (*recorded*): I hear the tormented cries of "Peace, peace!" But there is no peace, there can be no peace while His Sacred Eminence, the Pope, leads on his priestly pack to undo the Protestant Reformation and return us all to the Middle Ages. . .

LIAM: Clem Sheels!

GWEN: The bloody bounce with the lashin' tongue!

DENNIS: The Vindicator! Self-appointed!

(CONNIE *returns with a basin, bandages, and antiseptic.*)

SHEELS: I serve notice here and now that the Papists and priests, and their champions, the gunmen from the South who come here to terrorize and slay, will meet with the avenging spirit of Luther and Calvin! I warn the emissaries of evil that they will be repaid many times over, blow for blow!

CONNIE: I wish that rabble-rousing crawthumper would give over! He's a shame and a disgrace and a menace to us all! (*as she proceeds to bandage* DENNIS'S *jaw*) Hold still!

(*A song rises from the street*) :

I was born under the Union Jack,
I was born under the Union Jack.
Do you know where Hell is?
Hell is up the Falls.
Kick all the Popeheads and we'll guard Derry's Walls . . .

(*A distant shot interrupts the song.*)

EILEEN (*quietly*): The guns are coming out.

LIAM: The guns?! Ah, no!

CONNIE: Never! That's insane!

DENNIS: Not here in Craigie! In Belfast, maybe! In Derry! Not here! Why would anyone take to shooting?

EILEEN: Because there's a score to be settled after three hundred years.

CONNIE (*desperately*): No shooting! The police will never allow it!

GWEN (*at the window*): Sure you're not puttin' it past them Prodestan hoodlums? I see the polis right from here, on the street corner, passin' the time o' day with the Prods, lovely as you please!

CONNIE (*wildly*): What does that prove?

EILEEN: It proves the police know what side they're on.

234

CONNIE: Bitch!

(Across the street a new banner goes up. It reads "Fuck the Pope.")

GWEN *(after a shocked silence)*: They'll be roasted alive for that when they're dead!

LIAM: It's an insult to God, that is!

DENNIS: Don't worry about God — He can take care of Himself. It's those poor creatures out there, stalking each other in His name, who call for our compassion.

EILEEN: Protestant and Catholic, middle class and working class, whipped up to murder each other!

DENNIS: Maddened by Satan, the enemy of both!

EILEEN: You mean religion, the enemy of both!

DENNIS *(with a sigh)*: Satan, in the hearts of men. Put the blame where it belongs, dear: true religion has never yet been tried.

(KEVIN *and* PADDY *rush in, shouting.*)

KEVIN: The Prods are comin' back!

PADDY: Behine a cement-mixer lorry!

KEVIN: Pushin' it up the street!

PADDY: An' walkin' behine it!

KEVIN: With guns!

(*The* BOYS *run out again as the street song continues*:)

I was born under the Union Jack,
I was born under the Union Jack.
If Taigs were made for killing,
Then blood is made to flow.
You've never seen a place like little Sandy Row . . .

(Shooting starts outside.)

GWEN: Gentle Jazus! Mary, dear Mother o' God! Abide with us in the comin' dark o' this day!

(Blackout. The pounding of the drum fades to a complete silence. VOICES, recorded, as the light slowly rises.)

Third Recording

POLICE INSPECTOR: Ready to talk, is he?

POLICE SERGEANT: Yes, sir — come down a bit off his high horse. The spell in solitary has done him good.

235

INSPECTOR: Where do they recruit these young scuts burning with the flame of Holy Ireland?

SERGEANT: From the back of the bog. Here he is, sir: Dan Timothy.

INSPECTOR: Take a seat, Danny. Sit down. . . . Cigarette?

TIMOTHY: Don't want none.

INSPECTOR: Give over, Danny. We've proved it on you. You're the one who was delegated to sneak the gelignite into the refuse can outside the market. That was a right neat job you brought off there, boyo — tearing apart five innocent people, three of them Catholics like yourself. You call that holy?

TIMOTHY: No, sor. 'Twas desperate bad luck an' I'll be answerin' for it in the Hereafter.

INSPECTOR: You'll be answering for it right here, and you might as well start clearing your conscience now as then. . . . Who were the two with you that morning?

TIMOTHY: Don't you be forcin' me to break me sacred oath!

INSPECTOR: Sacred? A killer's oath! Speak out, think of the families you've ruined, the mangled bodies of little children. . . . You'll be up for murder, and God spare your soul!

TIMOTHY: Breakin' me sacred oath . . .

(*His voice falters.*)

INSPECTOR: Come on. . . . Who was the man?

TIMOTHY (*finally*): Malone.

INSPECTOR: Malone who?

TIMOTHY: Ronny Malone.

INSPECTOR: And the woman?

TIMOTHY: Eileen Torrance.

INSPECTOR: Torrance? Like Torrance Gold Label Distillers, is it?

(*Blackout. The drum resumes.*)

Scene 2

Night. Compared with the end of the previous scene, the stage seems almost quiet, although there is desultory shooting, and the Lambeg drum, gradually fading out, can still be heard. No one is on the roof of the house. The living room is lit only by the reflected glow of the street lamps. The front door has been barricaded with furniture. From outside comes a radio broadcast, to which DENNIS and CONNIE are listening, CONNIE with little MOIRA, half asleep on the floor beside her.

RADIO VOICE: We appeal to the people of Ulster to practice Christian charity, mercy, and forgiveness. Renounce violent measures: they can only defeat themselves and bring tragedy to both sides! When in any society the love of one's neighbor is denied, when the sacredness of human life is devalued, that society is sick with a sickness unto death. . . .

(The voice fades.)

CONNIE: Isn't that a grand, marvelous speech?

DENNIS: Idle talk! I'd be more impressed if he got down to some issues. What's the use of his talk about about Christian charity and loving your neighbor if his own party members call him soft on Catholics and walk out on him at Stormont any time there's a proposal for reform?

CONNIE: How can you call it idle talk when it's so inspiring? When I stop and realize how selfish I've been all my life, how little I've cared how the other half lives — I can even see why people like you and Eileen can get so wrought up over their troubles.

DENNIS: You feel, now, that the Hallinans should have this house, because they need it more?

CONNIE *(stung)*: Don't I have needs of my own? You're the sly one, Dandy Dennis! Is it a Catholic you are, or a Communist?

(There is a rattle of scattered shots outside. MOIRA *who is holding* CONNIE's *leg, whimpers at the sound.)*

CONNIE: There, there, dear.
    (She picks her up.)
You've got your sticky hands all over my stocking.

MOIRA *(dreamily)*: You're so pretty an' you smell so good . . .

DENNIS: If she gave herself a chance, little girl, she could be just as nice inside.

CONNIE: I'm not sure that's even a halfway compliment, Dandy Dennis. *(She deposits the child on the sofa.)* She's asleep, poor thing. An unwanted little kid. Her mother is proud of those two snots, but hardly tolerates her. And Eileen even hates her, have you noticed?

DENNIS: How could she hate a little child?

CONNIE: Because there's something about that woman that's really dreadful.

DENNIS *(puzzled)*: What way? She has a distant manner — comes from an elite family, if that's any explanation. But she's one of the dedicated. In earlier times she could have been a nun.

CONNIE *(shortly)*: Could she, indeed?

237

DENNIS: She came to Craigie especially to be useful — sent me by one of my old classmates.

CONNIE: Also "dedicated"?

DENNIS: Yes, dedicated. Ronny Malone — dropped out of school and went underground with the IRA — maybe even with the Provisionals, for all I know. An idealist, heart and soul.

CONNIE: "An idealist," is it? And it was the likes of him that sent her to you? How a believing Catholic can credit anyone like her is past my understanding!

EILEEN (upon entering): What's past your understanding, Miss Flannery?

CONNIE: Your telling the family to stay on in this house, so they can be slaughtered!

EILEEN: There's no prospect of their being slaughtered, madam, however that idea may interest you. They're at the back door, now, conferring with their Catholic neighbors from across the yards, because the hooligans in the street are regrouping for another assault. Only this time they'll be met with more than bricks and bottles. There's not only armed Protestants on the roofs, now, but Catholics, too.

DENNIS: Both sides ready to kill!

EILEEN: Shooting's the only exchange that's left between them. You still expect the Catholic working class to go on trusting the police?

CONNIE (heatedly): Will you put an end to your maligning the police and justifying violence? And don't you talk to me about the working class — I'm working class myself!

EILEEN: Sweating at a typewriter.

CONNIE: Forty or fifty hours a week, taking the boss's orders: shorthand, typing, filing, phoning, receptioning — besides humoring his moods, lying to his clients, listening to his nasty-old-man's jokes — and at the day's end, rushing home to do the housework! What do you do, besides living on your family's income and posing as a warrior for Holy Ireland?

(There is a new outburst of shooting, waking MOIRA, who begins to cry.)

CONNIE (with restraint): If you'll excuse me, now, I'm taking this unloved child to her family. They don't seem to care whether she exists.

(She takes MOIRA into the next room.)

EILEEN (soberly): She's right about the kid. And about me, too, you know: I'm no Irish warrior, just a newcomer finding my way. . . .

238

But neither is she a proletarian — only a middle-class virgin in a stupid office job, dreaming of marriage. (*harshly*) Meanwhile she sees the wrinkles coming on, the bosom dropping, the arse starting to sag, her childbearing days soon over —

DENNIS: It's a hard wallop you're giving her Eileen

EILEEN: Let her go on sighing — as I did, once — for wedding bells and bridal veils and a rosy honeymoon. She'll wake to a dutiful son of an Irish mother snoring in her bed, and kitchen drudgery for the rest of her lifetime! (*violently*) Let her be cured of her snug little dream forever!

DENNIS: Is that a guilt so damning that you must hate her for it? Hate, rancor, and brawling, the Irish disease come over a land that's divided!

(*Shots echo from the street.*)

Listen to that, now! Does that bloodstained quarrel make a tither of sense?

EILEEN: It's not only sense that's wanted, Mr. O'Connell — it's organization. The troubles will end when there's a green Ireland from Derry to Cork.

DENNIS: Then God speed the day, for it's only Himself who can do it! (*in despair*) How do our Ulster Catholics know they're even wanted in the South? Hasn't the Republic enough problems without importing half a million Catholics on the dole? And without adding five times that number of unwilling Protestants — spreading the religious war over all the rest of Ireland?

(*A single shot, smashing a street lamp, leaves the room even darker than before. And the song returns*):

> *I was born under the Union Jack,*
> *I was born under the Union Jack.*
> *If guns are made for shooting,*
> *Then skulls are made to crack.*
> *You've never seen a better Taig*
> *Than with a bullet in his back.*

EILEEN (*after a silence*): Rosaleen will reign on her golden throne, Reverend O'Connell. When the idols are thrown down, Catholic and Protestant workers, together, will take over Northern Ireland before the next day's breakfast. (*She takes an automatic pistol out of her handbag.*) Meanwhile, let's be prepared.

DENNIS (*startled*): You'll not be wanting to use that gun?

EILEEN: Just getting ready. (*She inserts a cartridge clip into the gun, snaps it shut and drops it back into her bag.*) Sure my way is not yours, Reverend O'Connell. Will you stop mad dogs with an appeal to reason and a prayer? You've tried it!

239

CONNIE (*running in breathless with fear*): They're bringing in cans of petrol from the neighbors!

DENNIS: Who?

CONNIE: The family!

EILEEN (*calmly*): Why shouldn't they?

CONNIE: Petrol! They're making bombs!

(*The HALLINANS enter, LIAM lugging a milk crate full of bottles, GWEN and KEVIN each with a can of petrol, PADDY with an armful of rags, and MOIRA trailing after them.*)

DENNIS (*to LIAM*): Are you gone out of your wits?

CONNIE (*as the family seat themselves on the floor with their materials*): Stop it, all of you! You'll not be endangering this house!

EILEEN (*to CONNIE*): It was you who endangered it first.

(*EILEEN settles back to watch the operation.*)

LIAM (*commanding, to the family*): Stand ready for instruction, for it's no good the way yous are operatin', everywan for hisself! Paddy, take wan bottle at a time an' hole it steady whilst Kevin dashes in the petrol, only haltin' three inches from the top, like so. . . . Now, Kevin, you pass the bottle onto yer Ma, who is tearin' up them rags pre*pare*atory to shovin' them in the bottles. . . .

MOIRA: Me, too!

LIAM (*to GWEN*): The pest can hole the strips of rags yer tearin' up. I meself will be applyin' the match to the product, as needed!

KEVIN: Up on the roof!

LIAM: With the cooperation of yous all!

GWEN (*in admiration*): Ain't he the whole man, though, when he gets goin'!

DENNIS: This can't go on!

CONNIE (*desperately*): They'll set the house afire!

(*CONNIE snatches at one of the bottles. The petrol spills on the floor.*)

EILEEN: It's out of your hands. Keep away!

LIAM (*with dignity*): I'm notifyin' all present not to be interferin', vexin' or twartin' this family in the pursoot of its preparations!

GWEN: An' to that I add the proclamation to all an' sundries not to be layin' theirselves in the way o' the last stand against the horde o' the heathens! Up with the barricades!

KEVIN: Up with the barricades!

PADDY: Up with the barricades!

EILEEN (*calmly*): And down with the idols!
(*Guns rattle outside and a lurid reflection of fire rises over the rooftops. Blackout, and a new song, close at hand*).

> My dark Rosaleen!
> My own Rosaleen!
> 'Tis you shall have the golden throne,
> 'Tis you shall reign, and reign alone,
> My dark Rosaleen ...

Scene 3

On the dark stage a spotlight picks out DENNIS, *kneeling, reading from a pocket Bible.*

DENNIS: "Why standest thou afar off, O Lord? Why hidest Thou thyself in times of trouble? Lord, Thou hast heard the desire of the humble. Thou wilt cause thine ear to hear, to judge the fatherless and oppressed ..."

(DENNIS *gets up, continuing to read to himself. As the spotlight blacks out, light rises on the roof of the house and on the buildings opposite. At the trapdoor of the roof,* GWEN, *head and shoulders visible, is handing up the petrol bombs to* LIAM, *who lights them before passing them on to* KEVIN *and* PADDY. *The* BOYS *are wearing kitchen pots improvised as helmets. Lying flat on the nearer side of the roof and protected by the chimneys, they rise only to send the bombs, crashing, to the street below.*)

PADDY (*with an Indian war whoop*): Aya! You got that fella good, Kevin!

KEVIN: Hand us the next! Aisy, now, don't spill!

(*A bullet whistles past them, smashing into the neighboring roof tiles; another chips fragments of brick from the nearest chimney.*)

GWEN (*shocked*): Mind them snipers! Me heart lepped!

LIAM: Lurk this side o' the roof, lads — don't be showin' a hair o' yous to be seen!

PADDY (*throwing a bomb and whooping*): There she goes!

KEVIN: An' another! (*throwing, with a whoop*) The terror kiddies, that's us!
(*There is a great roar from the crowd below.*)

PADDY (*watching over the edge of the roof*): Ay, looka all them people!

KEVIN (*abruptly sobered*): I never seen so many! An' more of 'em more nastier ev'ry second!

       (*Sirens are heard.*)

The polis loudhailer comin'!

LIAM: Down offa there — in a hurry!

PADDY (*throwing*): There's the last!

(PADDY *and* KEVIN *scramble off the roof and into the kitchen, following* LIAM, GWEN *and* MOIRA. *Light rises on the living room, where* DENNIS *has looked up from his book at the sound of the police sirens.* CONNIE, *behind the curtains of the broken window, is also listening intently, and so is* EILEEN, *in the middle of the room.*)

CONNIE: The street's so jammed with people, the police can hardly cut through.

DENNIS: The whole neighborhood's here.

EILEEN: At the heels of the hunt!

(KEVIN *and* PADDY *run into the room, hastily removing their* "helmets," *as* LIAM *and* GWEN *follow,* GWEN *pushing* MOIRA *in front of her.* MOIRA, *who wears a saucepan* "helmet" *is trying to get it off.*)

GWEN (*to the* BOYS): Whillya be good enough to remove this pot offa her head? I can't budge it, an' she's howling'.

KEVIN: She wanted it on, didn't she?

LIAM (*to* MOIRA): Give over that screechin'! The lads tried to oblige ye, tryin' all them pots on ye — all were too big an' this wan too small. (*He joins* PADDY *in trying to yank it off.*) I give up — it's goin' to need a tinsmith for sure!

(KEVIN *and* PADDY, *dropping the* problem forthwith, run into the next room, pursued by MOIRA, *still tearful.* At the same moment the voice of the police bullhorn rises above the ominous hubbub of the crowd, giving pause to everyone in the room.)

POLICE: Attention! Attention! This is Police Captain Clarence Murphy, speaking to the occupants of Council House 24. Leave at once, by the front door, or we'll use tear gas. Repeat: Leave at once!

DENNIS: That's the end of housebreaking.

EILEEN: Don't panic. They won't use tear gas while Connie is in the house.

    (CONNIE *goes quickly into the bedroom.*)

DENNIS: You're surely not interested to see if they'll use it?

EILEEN: I'm more interested in whether they have control of that mob.

GWEN (*glancing into the next room*): She's picked up a suitcase. Starting to pack up.

LIAM: That settles that. We go out the back way — and fast!

KEVIN (*returning*): It's no good, Da. There' a mob in the back, now, just waitin' for us to come out. An' not a son no polls!

GWEN: Move away that furniture!

(*As she and the* BOYS *rush toward the barricaded door, a fusillade of gunfire outside is followed by a tremendous roar of the mob.* GWEN *staggers back.*)

GWEN: They're lyin' in wait for us, surely! Will yous listen to the sound of it? They'll have our blood when we go out that door! (*To* EILEEN, *fiercely*) "Stay here an' fight it out," you says! Fight it out with the mob that's come to have the enjoyment of our finish!

KEVIN: They'll do us in with crowbars!

PADDY: Hack us with axes!

LIAM: An' tear off our balls, beGod!

EILEEN: A family of frightened mice!

LIAM (*stung*): Mice is it, now? Who are ye callin' a mouse?

EILEEN: Yourself, and those like you — swaggering until you meet a test, then squeaking in terror! Brainwashed, you are, by the priests and politicians, till your backbone is dissolved!

GWEN: Don't ye be criticizin' the people like us that have nothin' an' know what they're up against! We're not wrapped aroun' in pound notes like yerself!

DENNIS: Enough, now! Is this a time to be scrapping, with the violent mob out there and the police giving orders?

(CONNIE *enters with a suitcase, ready to leave.*)

POLICE: You'll not keep us waiting on you! You've been told — get moving!

CONNIE (*to the others*): The door has to be opened, so take away that furniture!

GWEN: Take it away yerself, missus — we're not yer servants!

CONNIE: Don't tell me to do it. I didn't put it there!

(*A different voice comes over the bullhorn.*)

FLANNERY: Connie! Are ye there, Connie Flannery?

CONNIE (*calling back*): I'm here, Dad, ready to leave! (*To* GWEN) I want that door opened — immediately!

DENNIS: The family's scared of the lynch mob out there, Connie. They must have police protection if the door is opened.

FLANNEY: Connie! are ye comin' out?

CONNIE (*answering*): The door is barricaded!

DENNIS (*loudly*): Sergeant Flannery, the family must have safe-conduct to their home. We ask police protection.

FLANNERY: We'll not strike bargains with lawbreakers! Open the door before we knock it down!

EILEEN: Policemen have limited minds, you see. (*Calling out*) Mr. Flannery, the Hallinans want safe-conduct out of that raging mob outside. Cooperate, Mr. Flannery! We have a hostage here!

FLANNERY (*after a pause*): You're Eileen Torrance. We know you.

EILEEN: Good you do!
         (*She points her gun at* CONNIE.)
Now speak up!

CONNIE (*in a choked voiced, calls*): I've a gun pointed at me!

DENNIS (*to* EILEEN): Don't aim at her, for God's sake!

EILEEN: Stand out of the way or I'll blast you both! And I mean it!

CONNIE (*calling out, desperately*): Dad, what will I do?

FLANNERY: Hold on, girl, till I consult with the captain. (*Anxiety thickens his voice.*) Make no mistake about the Torrance woman: we've tracked her down — one of the gang at the supermarket murders.

DENNIS (*stunned*): It can't be!

EILEEN: It can! (*In a voice of command*) I'm taking charge here. You'll obey my orders!

(*There is a gasp of horror from those in the room. They stand motionless, waiting.*)

FLANNERY (*after a moment*): We agree to a safe-conduct for the Hallinans.

CONNIE (*to* EILEEN): It's my father speaking. You can rely on my father!

EILEEN: I can rely on this automatic! (*To the* HALLINANS) Clear away that furniture!

        (*They set to work frantically removing the barricade.*)

LIAM: It's clear.

EILEEN: Very well. The family can go.

GWEN: Come, childer. (*She tearfully gathers the frightened* KIDS *around her. To the wailing* MOIRA) You too, with the saucepan on yer head!

EILEEN (*almost wildly*): Stop that child's crying! Stop it and get out!

KEVIN: We're going!

(*Shakily he starts to play an American hymn on his accordion. The family join in, their terror lessening with the words*):

> *We shall overcome,*
> *We shall overcome,*
> *We shall overcome some day.*
> *Oh, deep in my heart*
> *I do believe*
> *We shall overcome some day . . .**

(*The* FAMILY *goes to the door.*)

GWEN (*turning to* CONNIE): Please to excuse us, Missus Flannery, for whatever we done that we shouldn't. An' the blessed Virgin reward ye.

DENNIS (*as the* FAMILY *exit, shutting the door*): The song helped put heart into their leaving, only I hope it wasn't heard out there, for it would be doubly asking for trouble.

(DENNIS *and* CONNIE *rush to the window. Outside there is a silence, broken only by a few muted outcries.*)

CONNIE: Thank God! They're getting through, unharmed!

FLANNERY: Attention, Torrance and O'Connell! You have safe-conduct, Come out, holding up your hands!

EILEEN (*to* DENNIS *and* CONNIE): You can go.

CONNIE: Are you not coming with us?

EILEEN: No.

CONNIE (*startled*): You can't be staying on here? You're mad, for certain!

EILEEN: You heard the man: why don't you leave?

DENNIS: Why do you stay? To destroy yourself? You know they'll not spare you if you challenge them!

EILEEN: I have not asked your advice.

(*She moves away.*)

---

* Ludlow Music, Inc., New York, copyright 1960 and 1963. Used by permission.

DENNIS (*vehemently*): Eileen, whatever your sin may be, do not compound it with an added guilt! It's not for you but God and the law to judge you — and you may find them more merciful than you think!

EILEEN (*almost whimsically*): Ah, but you have it all wrong again, Reverend O'Connell, with your catalog of sins and forgiveness! It isn't sin that concerns me — it's my duty. I've failed it twice now, and it mustn't happen again.

DENNIS (*in desperation*): Is this what you've come to, at last? Congealed in anger, lost to all meaning of a normal life?

EILEEN: (*with increasing contempt as she speaks*): What was normal about my life? Unwanted — a child abandoned to the care of servants! A cheating businessman for a father, a dressed-up doll for a mother — mean-minded churchgoers, both! On my seventeenth birthday, being then ignorant and stupid, I slashed both my wrists. (*changing; calmly*) Your life is your religion, Dennis; mine is something else, and it's no more open to discussion than your own. (*She lifts her gun.*) There's no more time for talk. Leave, now! That's an order!

CONNIE (*suddenly, with a cry of fear*): Look out!

(TOM FLANNERY *has entered swiftly and silently from the next room.* EILEEN *swings around, shoots at him — and misses. She is expertly overpowered, disarmed, and flung violently to the floor.*)

CONNIE (*as* EILEEN *is handcuffed*): Don't hurt her!

TOM: Shut up, you! You almost cost me my life! (*He calls*) Sergeant!

(*The door is thrown open by* FLANNERY, *who steps into the room.*)

CONNIE: Dad, look after her, I'm so frightened —

FLANNERY (*roughly*): We'll be back for you and O'Connell, to take you out of the mob. Don't try it without us.

(EILEEN *struggles as the two men drag her out. There is a blood-freezing roar from the crowd as she appears outside.*)

CONNIE: Pray for her, Dennis! She has nothing at all, now! Not even the death she wanted!

(*There are two shots in immediate succession.*)

CONNIE: The snipers! (*agonized*) Oh, the mad brutes! She's down! They've killed her! (*hysterically*) By what right? By what right? If she was guilty, I am, too! I caused her death! I should have refused this house! The poisoned gift of this house!

DENNIS (*sharply*): Let's have no more accusations! No more charges and countercharges, with reason or no reason — and threats of punishment, deserved or not! You did not take the life of Eileen

Torrance! She died because she played with terror as children play with matches! (*ruefully*) Matches! How long ago that sounds, now, when little children play with bombs — "And smile to see men quartered by the hand of war"!

(FLANNERY *and* TOM *come to the door with guns leveled.*)

FLANNERY: We can leave now — it's letting up a little. (*tiredly*) We couldn't help it — about her. No one could — not after the killings at the Derry Supermarket. . . . We had no real control over this huge crowd.

TOM: Too big, and not enough police.

FLANNERY: So much senseless hate let loose — it's not to be believed! The new houses are burning, Connie, the new Council houses —

(*He is shot down. With a scream,* CONNIE, *falls to her knees beside him.*)

TOM (*shaking his fist at the rooftops*): You'll get yours! Butchers! Dogs!

(*He strides off.*)

CONNIE (*sobbing unrestrainedly*): Dad! Daddy! Oh, God, forgive us all!

DENNIS (*as* CONNIE *keens over her* FATHER): That bullet may well have been meant for me, not for him, you know — everything's so distracted and confusing in the dark. . . . (*unevenly*) We stumble, all of us, toward the arms of our heavenly Father through the night of our Hell on earth. (*Kneeling beside the body of* SERGEANT FLANNERY, *he intones*):

> *Almighty everlasting God,*
> *From envy, hatred and malice defend us —*
> *Lighten our darkness,*
> *Take not vengeance of our sins!*

(*The house wavers in the shadows of flames. The shouts of the crowd continue.*)

CURTAIN

AUTHOR'S POSTSCRIPT

I have attempted, in this play, to reflect the beginning of the current troubles in Northern Ireland — troubles whose origins go back hundreds of years in Irish history, during which the English invaders established their hold over the warlike Irish. The English conquest was finally consummated at the Battle of the Boyne, in 1690, by which time the economic basis of the Anglo-Irish wars was overshadowed by the bitter religious dispute between the Catholic population and their Protestant adversaries.

Not until after the Easter Rising of 1916 was England obliged to relax its grip on its neighboring island. In 1921, the Irish Republic was established, with jurisdiction over twenty-six of Ireland's counties. The remaining six counties, comprising the Province of Ulster with its two-third majority of Protestants, remained loyal to Britain. As a solution to the Irish question, this division was bound to prove unsatisfactory, leading to an increasingly savage religious confrontation as Catholic "extremists" sought to re-unite the whole of Ireland. In 1969, British troops were deployed in Belfast and Derry to "keep the peace" in Northern Ireland — a measure which has yet to accomplish its purpose.

The action of this play was suggested by a struggle that broke out in 1968 in the village of Caledon, in western Ulster, but this incident has served as nothing more than a point of departure for a fictional account of *personae* and events. All the characters, on or off stage, have been invented, and any public speeches have been paraphrased; only the two banners described in the text are documentary.* Furthermore I have not limited myself to 1968-69 in making use of any material which may help to illuminate the dramatic issues involved in the travail of the Six Counties.

While I believe most of the allusions in the dialog are self-explanatory, it may still be helpful to define some of them. The Stormont is the seat of Parliament of Northern Ireland; it remains dominated by the Unionists, the political party favorable to Britain. The IRA is the Irish Republican Army, dedicated to militant action in uniting Ireland, and outlawed in both the north and south of Ireland. The Provisionals is a group that has split off from the IRA and which is generally considered even more terrorist than its parent. The Sinn Fein is an extremist Irish party, nationalist but opposed to the less headlong policies of the Irish Republic. "Taigs" is a contemptuous name for the Catholics and "Prods," likewise for the Protestants. Both "Cathleen Mavourneen" and "Dark Rosaleen" are personifications, in song, of Ireland herself. The hymn of the civil rights movement of the American blacks, "We Shall Overcome," has also been used by the Ulster Catholics.

---

* Onstage the banner about the Pope is not intended to appear.

The huge Lambeg drum is favored by Protestant demonstrators; its thudding falls ominously on the ears of the Catholics. The "Baroo" is the local Welfare Bureau. Britain's Union Jack flag is also the flag of the Province of Ulster. An Orangeman is a member of the Orange Order, a Protestant fraternal society memorializing the English king, William of Orange, who decisively defeated the Catholics at Derry and Limerick in 1690.

The play's title derives from Alexander Pope's "the feast of reason [and the flow of soul]." — *Imitations of Horace.*

CASTING

Recordings 1, 2, or 3 may be staged as flashbacks if desired. In that case, 1 and 2 (the Town Council meetings) can be given "live" at a lectern downstage center, with the stage dark and the speakers pinpointed. The remarks by the CHAIRMAN and reactions from the floor should remain on the sound track: I would not agree to have those comments come from actors planted in the audience.

In Recording 1, YARDLEY is deliberate and elderly, but a practiced speaker. His address rises to a crescendo of accusations. DOYLE is much younger and his speech has a touch of blarney in spite of its grimness, but it is clear and distinct as he makes his points.

Recording 3 may instead be played as a flashback. The POLICE INSPECTOR is quietly ironic, the SERGEANT is playful. Their prisoner, DAN TIMOTHY, remains stubborn and glum until remorse breaks him down.

In the Flashback, it is MALONE who is on the offensive — a passionate, sensitive man, very concerned for EILEEN, to the point that he tells GRADY, "There's a streak of sadism in you." GRADY, his superior, is a disciplinarian, a soldier who gives and takes orders and must shrug off the mistakes and misfortunes of war. Someone like EILEEN is new to him as a volunteer; he is baffled and suspicious, but her respect for him as her commandant is so obviously sincere that he will let her try again: "You'll be on your own. Show us what you can do."

JACK FLANNERY, as a father, is gruff in speech and manner, but his love for his daughter is clearly evident. As a police sergeant, he is thoroughly professional and even-tempered, with a rare smile and glints of humor.

TOM FLANNERY has inherited none of his father's patience. Tense police jobs are too much for him: he is bigoted, raging, and quick to reach for his gun.

CONNIE FLANNERY is noted in the text as "a thirty-four-year-old Protestant spinster, prim but by no means docile." It would be a great mistake to play her as tough: she is a self-possessed, hardworking secretary with a caustic wit under stress. Essentially middle class, she is no match for the HALLINANS. The mob-attack on the house breaks down her poise, revealing a compassionate nature and a self-reproach that finally turns into agony. She is the central figure of the play.

EILEEN TORRANCE, next in importance to CONNIE, is far more sophisticated and disillusioned, with a curtness acquired in her training as a terrorist. Under that hardness is the endowment of a quick, sensitive woman, as when she is sickened by the bombing of the supermarket. DENNIS is right when he says, "In earlier times she could have been a nun." Her dedication to her cause is like that of a nun to her God, with the same honesty and readiness for self-sacrifice.

DENNIS is youthful, brisk, and eager. His religion is as real to him as his task of leading a demonstration against the Town Council. This seriousness co-exists with a lively mind and a dry wit. He is the "norm" character of the play.

The slum family, the HALLINANS, have come to Ulster from the South a few years previously. They came in quest of a better life only to find, after an encouraging start, that they are no better off than before. They are not to be played as clowns, or as "scarecrows," as CONNIE sees them; nor are they "mice," as EILEEN describes them. Independence is their most salient quality.

LIAM, the father, is unemployed — a humiliation he bitterly resents. He has heard of the "class war," and has been told that he is a "proletarian" but he is not too sure what those terms mean: what he wants is work, not "propagander." Idle for months, and dependent on the dole, he wanders, depressed, around the streets or hangs around the house. He has thereby lost the respect of his two impudent boys, but GWEN, his wife, loves him tenderly and understands him. In her eyes, when LIAM takes charge of the manufacture of petrol bombs, he proves himself "a whole man."

GWEN is the unmistakable head of the family, whose problems she meets with the unfailing support of her religion. She is proud of her two sons, with very little affection left for her daughter, a snivelling little girl who arrived, unwanted when the family had already fallen on hard times.

KEVIN, the older son, is a street-wise kid.

PADDY, the younger son, adores his older brother.

MOIRA, the unwanted child, has a total of four one-sentence speeches. She can be played by an older child not over nine years in appearance.

Consistency of thought, it should be noted, means nothing to the HALLINANS, as when LIAM reads with great moral fervor the precepts of Cardinal Cogan against killing people, but this is followed immediately by his admiration for the Provisionals, "the boyos who make a splash with bombs."

The family's exit becomes more motivated as DENNIS reminds them that the police will be coming to drag them out of the house. We now take note of the suspiciousness that is also part of the HALLINANS' makeup. They can reverse their opinions about anybody or anything without a moment's notice. GWEN has had second thoughts about the house; it is just across the street from a tough "Prod" neighborhood. LIAM realizes that he would be much too far away from his job at the shipyards — if he should ever get a job there again. CONNIE joins the discussion, asking how they expect to pay off the mortgage on the house while living on the dole.

The BOYS return, exhilarated by their showers (with their clothes on) but protesting against being taken away from their old haunts. That tears it, and GWEN announces "We're leavin'."

She and LIAM now agree with CONNIE that they've been used by EILEEN — which, of course, is true. And since GWEN and CONNIE are now in accord, CONNIE is gracious and GWEN even apologises for the family's intrusion. With that, the group exits, to CONNIE's enormous relief as she leans against the door. But the HALLINANS are no sooner out than they all pour in again. (This anticlimax is, or should be, funny.) GWEN explains they have changed their minds: the instant the door closed behind them they knew they had no alternative but to remain and "dispute possession"; come what may, they are *not* going back to their "cruddy 'oul' home" in the dirty slums.

THOUGHTS ON *THE FEAST OF UNREASON*

From Lloyd Richards, *artistic director, National Playwrights Conference,* New York:

We think that you should know that *The Feast of Unreason* was one of the very few out of almost one thousand scripts that was seriously considered for production.

From *a leading New York* play agent:

Certainly you have selected dramatic material, using the quarrel between the Catholics and the Protestants in the north of Ireland. However, this is not really new material . . . The entire play is only 48 pages long, which is not enough if this is meant to be a full-length play. Also, I found the ending needlessly melodramatic. For all these reasons, I am afraid I can't help you, much as I would like to.

Both my *personae* and my plays themselves have now been dismissed so often that it should be enough to dispose of the whole Gorelik opus. There is still room, however, for more original contributions such as the following:

Suhrkamp Theater Verlag, *publishers, Frankfurt, West Germany:*

The most striking thing about *The Feast of Unreason* is undoubtedly the extremely realistic setting, the atmosphere of anxiety, terror, and the hopelessness of the presented actions. From the authentic setting and the ring of dialog I got the feeling that you must have lived in Ireland for a long time. [Not true.] But what is missing is a new understanding of the Irish problem. An average German theater audience that knows almost nothing about the real background of some terror actions of the Provisionals and the Protestant organizations will find itself reassured, by the play, that the Irish are a very strange kind of people who are not to be understood.

My reply:

I had imagined that the play makes crystal clear the fact that in Northern Ireland the Catholics are discriminated against by the Protestant majority. The situation is examined not only in the dialog but in the political speeches and newspaper comments of both sides. If anything, I could be criticized for including such material: Sean O'Casey, for instance, took it for granted that the audience knew the background of the English-Irish conflict of his period, and even his foreign audiences did not ask for that information.

The theme of *The Feast of Unreason* is that the political antagonisms of Ulster, like those of the Near East, the Far East, Africa, South

America, and in fact, everywhere in the world today are almost never solved rationally but explode into an armed test of strength and irrational hatred. In that respect, the Irish behavior is no stranger than that of any other race of people — certainly no stranger than that of the Germans under Hitler. As a dramatist I have made that statement in mourning, and as an appeal for a saner approach to human affairs.

> From Tomas Mac Anna, *the Abbey Theater, Dublin*:
>
> It is with regret that I am returning *The Feast of Unreason* to you as we feel that such a play at this time is not suitable for our audience here. I have no doubt the work will find ready audiences in America. I wish the playscript every success.

> From Winifred Bell, *the Lyric Players Theatre, Belfast*:
>
> Unfortunately we were not able to find a place for *The Feast of Unreason*, though our panel of readers was impressed with your work.

No theatre is going to sponsor a play that could offend a section of its public at a time of national stress. The Abbey has not forgotten the riots that greeted Synge and O'Casey. Putting on *The Feast of Unreason* in present-day Belfast could invite trouble.

In cases like these the dramatist can be grateful for the praise that sometimes comes with rejection. The friendly comment of the Irish theatres is especially welcome. I would have been well clobbered in their replies if I had not known what I was talking about when I wrote *The Feast of Unreason*.

I, to Anta West: Your reader's report that "O'Casey and Behan have pretty well covered the ground" [of the tragedy of Ulster] is news to me. In which plays did O'Casey or Behan deal with Ulster?

> From William Talbot, *editor, Samuel French, Inc., New York*:
>
> Ethnic plays, particularly Irish and Jewish, do not sell well in our markets at all. But yours is such an uncommonly good piece of writing . . .

> From Robert E. Lee, *dramatist*:
>
> *The Feast of Unreason* surely deserves production . . . From the authentic ring of the dialog, I suspect you may have been born O'Gorelik!*

---

* To Bob Lee: Not born Irish — only brought up with Irish kids in New York.

From Prof. Dennis Carrol, *University of Hawaii at Manoa*:

I was very impressed with the vigor and spryness of *The Feast of Unreason* and was intrigued with the unexpectedness of the surprising but plausible reversals of the play — particularly the one in which Connie thinks she has got rid of the family and then is confronted with them once again at the door. The flashbacks are also well integrated with the forward flow of the play, as are the "flashouts" — for want of a better term — to the larger social environment represented by the public speeches. My one reservation could be tested only in production — the fact that a lot of the final action involving the crowd takes place off stage. This, in a way, makes the crowd itself seem more irrational and frightening; but at the simpler more realistic level I wonder whether the audience might not feel deprived at not seeing it function directly.

THE SHORT PLAYS

MRS. DISASTER

1950-1976

OUTLINE

In this dramatic snapshot Marvin Santley, the burdened young owner of a struggling new ad agency, comes home from a futile business trip in a raging mood that his pretty wife, Tess, tries vainly to soften. Steve, 9, gets the edge of his father's helpless anger. His sister, Peachie, 7, also suffers, even though not under attack. It is Tess who finally brings Marvin up short, but not before we catch a glimpse of what "Getting there" can do to some families.

Although this play was written in 1950, the language of the children is like that of the cartoon characters in *Peanuts* — an incredible mixture of the naive and the sophisticated — often self-contradictory, unexpected and desultory. And if you think kids of 9 and even 7 have never heard of sex, you're mistaken.

CHARACTERS

Marvin

Tess, his wife

Steve, age 9

Peachie, age 7

SETTING

The parents' room, night. Right, door to hall. Left, door to PEACHIE'S room. Center, rear, a window with curtains drawn. A bed; lamps; a table with a doll's house on it; a mirror; a telephone. On the wall, left, a small bracket-shelf.

At rise, PEACHIE, *who has been working on her doll house, drops her task to tiptoe over to the window. She peeks out through the curtains. A flute, outside, is playing "Sentimental Journey" or something equally nostalgic. The music sounds closer.* PEACHIE *hurriedly drops the curtains and goes back to the doll house just as* STEVE *enters, right, with his toy flute.* STEVE *casts an inquiring glance around the room.*

PEACHIE: Marvin hasn't come yet.

STEVE: Fruit! You think I care?

PEACHIE: I am *not* a fruit! Whatever that is — you just made that up.

STEVE: Tooty-Frooty!

(He wanders up center.)

PEACHIE (*after a moment*): Marvin hasn't called, either.

STEVE: Did any telegrams come for him at his office?

(PEACHIE *shakes her head.*)

He's not going to like that. He'll be sore.

(Pause)

PEACHIE: You'd better tell him about that golf cup, Steve, when he gets home.

STEVE: Are you going to keep bringing that up? Do I know who took it? A burglar took it, I guess, by the light of the silvery moon.

PEACHIE: Yeah?

STEVE: Yeah! (*Plays a few insulting notes on the flute.*) Fruit! I'll punch you!

(Phone rings.)

My turn to answer the phone!

PEACHIE: No — mine!

(*Door opens, left, and* TESS *runs in from* PEACHIE'S *room. She is a beautiful, spirited woman. Right now she is in dishabille.*)

TESS: Gangway, Peachie. It's my turn, kids! (*Grabs the phone.*) Hello, dear! (*dismayed*) Oh, it's you again! (*icily*) No, Marvin isn't here — do you mind! And I don't know when!

(PEACHIE *and* STEVE *watch her solemnly.*)

I'm sorry too! (*Hangs up; gaily*) That wasn't Marvin.

STEVE: His plane was supposed to come in an hour ago.

TESS: Don't worry. Your Pop will be here any minute — probably stopping at the office for his mail.

STEVE: Sometimes planes don't come in at all. Every day they have crashes.

TESS: Sometimes they're a little delayed, that's all. "Every day they have crashes"! (*Rumpling his hair.*) Your name is Stephen Santley — not George Q. Disaster! Don't try to compete with Marvin, you prophet of doom! Marvin's been carrying on that kind of talk for years — he's an expert. . . . You'd think I was Mrs. Disaster! (*Eying herself in the mirror.*) Do I look like that? No! Tess Santley — you're very, very pretty!

(*Exits, left.*)

PEACHIE: She is, too! Mom is beautiful! Even when she gets up in the morning. (*Sorrowfully.*) Now she won't be sleeping with me anymore in my room. She'll be sleeping with Pop.

STEVE: How you talk!

PEACHIE: I wish I could be like Mom. Always chirpy —

STEVE: She is *not* chirpy. (*tooting his flute*) She's hectic! She's been dolling herself up all afternoon — with perfumery! Marvin's been away so long that she's sex-starved. She ought to go yowling with the cats on the back fence.

PEACHIE: You're nasty. (*Sighs.*) Tess has to keep ahead of all those bewitching young girls, and she is old, almost thirty-two.

STEVE: More than that.

(*He resumes his wandering around the room.*)

PEACHIE: Pop always picks up women on his travels, but Tess is true to him. That's real love. So many husbands are bachelors at heart. (*Darkly*) You know who that phone call was from? We saw her once.

STEVE: It was that redheaded tart, Dorothy.

(*He pokes into the doll house.*)

PEACHIE: Third time she called today to ask if Marvin was back. Isn't that a nerve?

STEVE: What does she want?

PEACHIE (*taking a piece of doll furniture away from him*): What does any woman want? Love, of course.

STEVE (*disgusted*): Love! That's so fruity! Love — love — lurve! Women like to talk about love, but they're only out to get somewhere. Bunch of liars —

PEACHIE: What are you talking about?! You're a liar yourself. You took Marvin's champion silver-plated cup and squashed it. And don't think I won't tell.

263

STEVE: You'd better not gab if you know what's good for your health, you gyppie.

PEACHIE: Oh!

STEVE: All women are gyps; it's a part of their nature. First they call you dear, darling, and honey-boy, then you're nothing at all. Don't you talk to me, understand? (*yearningly*) Wait till Marvin gets here! Pop is a man, like me; we get along. I can't wait for him to get here. I'll show him my new school marks — he's going to be proud of me. Two A's and two B's.

PEACHIE: And three C's.

STEVE: I got a gold star in geography and a silver star in history. And I made the track team and the orchestra.

PEACHIE: Wait till I tell Marvin the swear words you are using, and the ideas you are starting to go around with —

STEVE: Shut up!

PEACHIE (*in a gloating mood*): You know what the silver cup meant to Marvin.

STEVE: Silver-plated!

PEACHIE: He won it in the county amateur open golf, and he had that stand made for it. That cup was the first thing he showed to anybody that came to visit. And now where is it? Ha, ha! You remember how he almost went wild when you dropped his pipe, last time, and it broke in pieces —

STEVE (*furiously*): Listen, sport —

(*Seeing the fire in his eye*, PEACHIE *races desperately for the door, right, slams it in his face. Phone rings again and* STEVE *turns to answer it, but* TESS *has entered again, this time fully dressed; she swiftly answers it.*)

TESS: Hello! Oh, Marvin dear! Oh, darling! We're just fine. Pining away for you, after a whole month, Peachie, Stevie and I . . . I knew you'd stop for your mail. . . . Don't waste another minute coming home. Bye-bye, dear. . . .

(*She kisses the phone deliriously. Hangs up.* STEVE *starts to exit, right.*)
Stevie, dear, your father is back!

STEVE: Okay, I know it.

TESS: Don't act so coldly, Stevie. It's your own father.

STEVE: I know you love him.

TESS (*pressing him to her*): We all love each other in this house, don't we? I'll tell Marvin how good you've been all the time he was

264

away. You've been so good! You were the man of the house all this time. What could I have done without a man in the house? You've been my helper and protector, haven't you, darling?

STEVE: Have I?

TESS: Yes, you have. You've been a real handy man, too. You fixed the front-door lock and changed half the washers in the faucets —

STEVE: And I painted the back fence and mowed the lawn every week. I did it all better than Marvin.

TESS: Yes, you did. (*Looking at him*) Why is my big boy crying?

STEVE: I'm not crying. What a whopper! (*In spite of himself*) I'm afraid of Marvin, Mom.

TESS: Why should you be afraid of him, honey-boy?

STEVE: Mom . . . you're not going to tell him about . . .

TESS: About what?

STEVE: About me.

TESS (*puzzled*): No, no. Of course not.

STEVE: Mom . . . if Pop had been born when I was, and I'd have been born when he was, then you could have married me instead of Pop, couldn't you? And then we could have had Pop instead of you and Pop having me. That would have been great.

TESS (*doesn't get it*): Darling . . . you'll be good and considerate with Pop here, won't you? Marvin's our breadwinner. It's not easy to be a breadwinner; you don't just raise your hand and catch dollars . . . Marvin has a lot on his mind; he's nervous — and where can he relax if not with his own family? You want us to be a happy family, don't you? Don't you, Stevie?

(PEACHIE *bursts in, right.*)

PEACHIE: Mommie! Pop is here! He's here in a taxi! Oh, my!

(*She rushes out again,* TESS *following, leaving the door open.* STEVE *goes to the window to look out.* MARVIN *enters, right, carrying a suitcase. He is flanked by* PEACHIE, *with a heavy briefcase, and by* TESS, *who has his overnight bag and topcoat.*)

MARVIN (*entering*): I told you — I had my dinner on the way; forget it, Tess. All I want is a bicarb.

TESS: Right away. Let me hang up your coat, dearest. . . . Sit down. Let me look at my handsome husband.

MARVIN: This airline has a record for good trips. But when I'm on a plane it has to all but comes in half. It almost had a fire in Tucson, shook itself almost apart in Wichita —

TESS: Almost, but you're here. (*To the* CHILDREN) Put that down right there, Peachie. Steve, help me move the chair over for Daddy. Where are his slippers?

(PEACHIE *and* STEVE *carry out various duties.*)

MARVIN: No telegram from Dunn . . .

TESS: No.

MARVIN: I knew there's nothing to expect there.

TESS: Don't aggravate yourself over it, will you, dear? Let me get you your bicarb.

(*Exits, right.*)

STEVE: Pop, I got two A's in my school report.

MARVIN: The old kid. (*affectionately*) Bet you've added two inches since I saw you. First thing we know we'll have a man on our hands. (*teasing him*) How have things been going here? You and Peachie massacring each other, Tess screeching, tub full of dirty laundry — everything as usual —

STEVE: You haven't changed either, Pop. (*appraisingly*) You're getting more of a bald spot —

PEACHIE (*to* MARVIN): And your belly is sticking out some more —

MARVIN: Okay, as long as you two are improving.

(*He digs into his briefcase.*)

PEACHIE: What did you bring, Marvin? Chocolates for Mom?

MARVIN: How did you know?

PEACHIE: I guessed.

MARVIN: You're smart, Peachie. (*Bringing out a large box tied with a ribbon*) American Beauty Creams. . . . I have a few little things for you two kids; I'll dig them up later. . . . Where's the bicarb?

PEACHIE: You want your pipe, Marvin?

MARVIN: That pipe that Steve busted. . . . That was a good pipe; saved it from my days in college. My old pipe.
                    (*TESS enters with bicarb.*)
I'm tired. Very tired. (*Drinks the bicarb.*) I got you something, Tessie.

TESS: You didn't have to. What did you get, darling?

MARVIN: This box of the best. American Beauties.

TESS: Oh. (*evenly*) I'll keep it for later.

MARVIN: It's the best.

STEVE: Pop, they put me on the track team. And I'm in the orchestra.

MARVIN: That's fine, Steve.

(*His glance follows* TESS *uneasily. She has put down the chocolates.*)

STEVE: Pop, is Duluth in Minnesota? Is that where they have the Mesaba Range? No, I guess it's Yellowstone Park.

MARVIN: Maybe.

STEVE: I wish I could have been there, too. I want to see it all, every state in the Union.

MARVIN: What's this big doll house doing right here, Peachie?

PEACHIE: I'll move it.

MARVIN(*to* STEVE): Help her take it out of here.

TESS: Go help her, Stevie.

(PEACHIE *and* STEVE *pick up the doll house and carry it off, left.*)

MARVIN: You two stay in there and play.

(*He shuts the door on them.*)

TESS: The kids are on their best behavior for you; really they are.

MARVIN: I know. They're good kids. I work my head off for them, giving then everything they want. Doll houses — (*Knocks his pipe against the table.*) It takes years to break in a good pipe, and that kid put an end to the best one I had. I had a dozen pipes here in this rack, but he picked out the best.

TESS: He just happened to pick that one.

MARVIN: Everything just happens that way. Why doesn't it happen the other way? (*mordantly*) I told you before I left — this trip to Duluth would be a waste of time. . . . The deal fell through. It just happened that way.

TESS (*dismayed*): Oh, Marvin, I thought it was in the bag, that deal!

MARVIN: In the bag and me with it. . . . After all that happy correspondence, Skip asked me out to lunch and talked about everything but the job. "Always a joy to see you, Marvin," he says. I saw the handwriting on the wall. "You've got a good little contracting firm there, Marvin," he says, "a crackerjack little firm; I checked into it. This is a big job, though," he says. "I can swing it," I told him, "I can get the financing." "I don't know, Marvin," he says, "There isn't time." Then it comes out: he'd already set the deal with Bryan & Crosswaith.

TESS: Not that bunch?

267

MARVIN: What was there for me to say? They're a firm that knows how to advertise; they put up eyesores from coast to coast; cheap construction, big maintenance. . . . You can't talk your competitor down — you're an interested party; nobody believes you. Besides it doesn't say much for the judgment of the man who picks them; he won't love you for pointing out his mistake.

TESS: No.

MARVIN: I'll always be a crackerjack little contractor! Look at the men who started out when I did: Markheim, Dunn —

TESS: Why do we have to look at them?

MARVIN: Because they got there! They had the right kind of start! (*burning*) Just a few thousand dollars more in the bank and I'd have had that contract in my pocket. . . .But my old man —

TESS: Leave your father out of this, Marvin.

MARVIN: I won't leave him out of it! That's how he's always been: the s.o.b. is bursting with money, but he can't lend his own son a few dollars to make things easier! He'd rather lose it on one of his own smart-aleck real estate deals. (*He strides up and down.*) That's what you can expect of relatives. And friends! No telegram from Dunn — my old classmate, Dunn. Another contract lost — just when we're idle, when I need it most. It just happens that way —

TESS: You don't know. Maybe he's been ill.

MARVIN: He *has* been ill. He wrote me: he got sick just when he was ready to sign. Then his partners got to work on him, and he listened. . . . It's maddening. Always some damn thing like that — always! I tear myself apart trying to keep our little outfit together — trying to keep this home going —

TESS (*alarmed; embracing him*): Don't carry on that way.

MARVIN: I've been living on bicarbs, you know that. . . . It's got me, finally: in the stomach. . . . They wouldn't sell me life insurance.

TESS: It's a nervous stomach, that's all.

MARVIN: The insurance companies know — they have the statistics. They wouldn't insure me. They give limited insurance to guys with bad heart trouble; but not to me —

TESS: For the hundredth time, Marvin — didn't Dr. Meyers tell you there's nothing organically wrong? You told the company doctor you'd lost weight — you were trying out a diet; and that stupid company doctor was suspicious. They don't bother to go into a case like yours; they have more trade than they can handle. (*angrily*) There ought to be a law about them — leaving a man like you with the idea he's ready to die. You'll live to be a hundred and fifty. (*Pause*) Oh, Marvin, Marvin! (*Holding him tightly.*)

MARVIN: What would I do if I didn't have you? My beautiful, sensible Tessie! Why does everything have to go the hard way? I wake up nights, and feel the world turning around me — a cosmic plot against Marvin Santley.

TESS: You frighten me, talking like that.

MARVIN: I know it can't be true ...

TESS: Don't even think like that, it frightens me. That's not healthy talk. Why don't you see the thing rightly? All the friends you have; the people you've worked for — they know you do good work. You have the respect of honest people, Marvin.

MARVIN: Count your blessings.

TESS: Yes, yes, count them. How many people are as lucky as we are? A lovely little home all our own; a car; even a few extra dollars in the bank. We're a regular *Ladies' Home Journal* family! You have a wife and children who love you. Think of the kids, Marvin, so sweet —

(*A squabble breaks out in* PEACHIE'S *room.*)

MARVIN: That goddam fighting — it's a curse!

TESS: They're normal kids.

MARVIN: Something's the matter with Steve, I tell you.

TESS: He's nine years old, Marvin. They go through a lot at that age — things you've forgotten about.

MARVIN: What's he got against me? What did I ever do to him? He starts tearing me down the minute I get home.

TESS: It's the growing-up age. He has some peculiar phases.

MARVIN: Breaking my pipe. For what goddam reason?

TESS (*worried*): Suppose he breaks a thing or two? I meant to talk to you later —

MARVIN (*with sudden suspicion*): What did he break now? He's broken something else of mine — what is it? (*Getting up*) I knew there was something missing in this room. My golf trophy!

TESS: (*clinging to him*): It's mislaid.

MARVIN: Mislaid nothing! He's got hold of it. He's done something with it. Deliberately.

TESS: Not deliberately!

(*Outcries from the next room. A crash, and a loud shriek from* PEACHIE.)

TESS: The doll house!

(MARVIN *strides to the door, left, opens it.*)

MARVIN (*wildly*): Steve! Come in here!

TESS: Marvin!

(STEVE *enters, dropping his flute.*)

MARVIN: Pick that up! (*as* STEVE *does so*) Why are you cringing like that? Nobody's laid a hand to you — yet! (*to* TESS) Is there anything I haven't done to please him? When I was his age I didn't have a proper pair of pants. . . . He has a bike, skates, a closet full of clothes, candy in his pockets. . . . Why must he be so lousy?

TESS: He only —

MARVIN: What did you do with my silver cup? Where is it? (*shaking him*) Where is it?

STEVE (*rattled*): I don't know . . . the cup . . .

MARVIN: I'll make you talk! (*to* TESS *shoving her aside*) Don't stay here! (*He flints open the door, left. To* PEACHIE) Clear out!

PEACHIE (*enters, frightened*): He didn't mean it, Daddy!

(*She runs to* TESS, MARVIN *gives* STEVE *a push through the open door and follows, locking the door.*)

TESS: (*bangs on the door*): Oh my God!

(*The door remains shut. There is a short-lived silence, then the sound of a beating.* PEACHIE *breaks away from* TESS *and runs out of the house.* TESS *remains crumpled in an armchair. The door opens again and* MARVIN *enters. He is pale.*)

MARVIN: He makes me sick . . . obstinate little bastard . . . obstinate. Not a sound out of him. . . . Father and son. . . . I've been kind to him. Done everything to make him a pal. . . . I'm ashamed of myself. Beating up a kid. It's sickening. (*tormented*) Why does he hate me? I hated my father, but I had a reason. I always said I'd know how to raise a son of my own — not the way I was raised!

TESS: Yes.

MARVIN: Is that all you have to say?

TESS (*getting up slowly*): What do you want me to say? That I think you're perfect?

MARVIN (*violently*): Okay, I'm not perfect. I can leave here if you need a perfect husband, and let you find one. I've left many times before, on my trips — you've had your chances —

270

TESS: For God's sake, Marvin, don't you see you come here like a four-alarm fire, and you expect us to behave normally? You come home after you've had setbacks —

MARVIN: Setbacks!

TESS: Put it your own way. You don't get the breaks, outside, you don't get a square deal, and you come back raging, ready to take it out on your family.

MARVIN: That's not true!

TESS: Yes, it is true. You're frantic and punitive, because you've been punished outside. . . . Then you wonder why Peachie's so skinny — why she's in a state of hysterics —

MARVIN: Who says so? She's a little underweight —

TESS: She's underweight, poor little thing, because she's in a constant state of hysterics. And Steve drinks —

MARVIN (*startled*): Drinks?

TESS: He drinks water . . . quarts at a time, when he thinks nobody's looking —

MARVIN: What for?

TESS: I don't know. It must make him feel more solid, or something. He doesn't feel solid anymore. . . . You know what a daredevil he always was: he used to go off the high diving board in his gym — now he's afraid to swim across the pool. He won't take his bicycle out anymore — hangs around the house —

MARVIN: Why didn't you tell me?

TESS: You weren't around to be told. (*She pauses.*) I'm worried about myself, Marvin. I think I've lost my taste for chocolates. Even for American Beauty chocolates — Watch out, Marvin. Our family may not always be a family.

MARVIN: What's got into you?

(*He moves toward her; she holds him off.*)

TESS: I've been almost as bad as you about the kids — screaming at them for their noise, worrying about what the neighbors think of them —

MARVIN: What's wrong with that? That's important.

TESS: The kids are important, not the neighbors! What are we holding the family together for, if not for the kids? We strain every nerve for the family, and meanwhile the family goes to hell! And when it gets unendurable, you threaten to walk out.

MARVIN: You're blaming it all on me.

TESS: No, that's not true!
(*Phone rings.*)
Answer it.

MARVIN (*picking up phone*): Hello! (*Taken aback for an instant.*) I just came home. . . . I'm staying in tonight. I'll call you. . . . Let me call you. (*seething*) That suits me! (*Hangs up.*) Business call . . .

TESS: I didn't ask you what kind of call it was. (*Turns.*) I'm bringing Steve in here. I want you to talk to him, alone. Differently from the way you talked to him before. I don't want it to be too late, Marvin.

(*She goes out, left. MARVIN goes to his chair, picks up his briefcase indecisively, puts it down. TESS comes back with STEVE. STEVE'S clothes are messed, and he seems to have grown suddenly smaller.*)

TESS: I'm going out to find Peachie, now.

(*Exits, right.*)

MARVIN (*quietly*): Steve, sit down here.
(STEVE *sits, obediently.*)
Don't act so scared of me. I'm not going to punish you anymore. I only want to know something. Steve — where is the golf cup?

STEVE: You hit me.

MARVIN: I'll never do it again.

STEVE: You kicked me.

MARVIN: That's a lie. Why do you lie all the time?
(*No answer.*)
What did you do with the cup, Steve?

STEVE (*after a pause*): I took it off that little shelf and dug dirt in the garden with it. Then I threw it around and hit rocks with it. Then I jumped on it until it all caved in. . . . It's in the back of the clothes closet, now. It's no good anymore.

MARVIN: Why did you do that?

STEVE: I don't know why. (*struggling with tears*) I don't feel the same as I used to. . . . Something gets hold of me. . . . I feel like I'm all empty in the inside. (*suddenly crying out*) Daddy!

MARVIN (*holding him*): Don't let it worry you.

STEVE (*convulsively*): Dad!

MARVIN: People who are lots older than you get that empty feeling inside — when they can't control their lives — when things start running away with them —

STEVE: Let's not stay in this town. Let's go back to Cookstown. I liked it there. Let's go back.

MARVIN: You've forgotten, Steve. You didn't like it. You always wanted to leave there.

(STEVE *slowly disengages himself,*)

There's no going back for any of us. We have to take it the way it is, boy. I have to; you have to; we all have to . . .

STEVE: Not you.

MARVIN (*surprised*): Not me? You mean, especially me!

(TESS *returns with* PEACHIE.)

We've had our talk.

TESS (*kissing* STEVE. *To* MARVIN): I'm glad. Let him alone now. Come with me, Marvin.

(*She and* MARVIN *exit, right.*)

PEACHIE: Marvin didn't want to hit you, Stevie. I know he didn't.

STEVE: He's worried about his contracts. Pop is a frightened man; he's afraid he won't make the grade. I hope he never gets another contract. Never, never!

PEACHIE: Oh!

STEVE: I hate him! Some day I'll grow up and be as big as he is, and I'll beat the daylights out of him. He's a dirty, scared coward —

PEACHIE (*stopping her ears*): I don't want to hear you. Marvin is good. You know he's good.

STEVE (*subsiding*): I guess I don't mean that. I guess I do love Pop. . . . I don't know how much, but some. Only it doesn't matter a bit. I don't feel about him the way I used to. He's just another man, that's all . . . (*with cold violence*) I'm glad I broke that cup, because that's what I wanted to do, and I did it. . . . I'm going away.

PEACHIE: You mean, for good?

STEVE: I'm never coming back. I don't care how old Marvin and Tess and you ever become, I'll never see you again. I'm going to wander all over . . . all over the earth. (*dreamily.*) I'll go every place, like Marvin. I'll have women everywhere I go, just like Marvin, and I'll treat them all like dirt.

PEACHIE (*impressed*): Why will you do that, Steve?

STEVE: Because women are all double-crossers. They're all dogs, that's why.

PEACHIE: No they're not.

STEVE: I wouldn't trust them with one of my old shoelaces! Bitches — that's what they are!

PEACHIE: Tess is not a bitch!

STEVE: She's the worst of them all! Sweet double-talk, but all she can think of is Marvin. Even *he* is all right, but she isn't. I'm never going to see her again.

PEACHIE: When are you going away?

STEVE: Right now, of course. . . .And if you tell them — if you breathe one single word that I'm gone — I'll come back and cut you up into little pieces . . . and I'll fry the pieces in oil!

PEACHIE (*in a strangled voice*): Goodbye, Steve.

(STEVE *exits, right.* PEACHIE *goes to the window and peeks through the* curtains. STEVE'S *flute is heard.* TESS *and* MARVIN *come back.*)

TESS (*as she enters*): Don't worry, I'm taking the box. I still like chocolates. Only it's always chocolates — isn't it? And every time you come home from a trip, it's a bigger box than before!

MARVIN: What's the matter with that?

(PEACHIE *bursts out crying.*)

TESS: What's the matter, honey-girl?

PEACHIE: Steve's gone! He's running away from home, Mommie!

TESS (*alarmed*): But I can still hear his flute —

PEACHIE: He's going for good. He means it. And he said you're a — a — I can't tell you.

MARVIN: Another gesture! Full of phony gestures, that kid _

TESS: Don't say any more, Marvin! You don't know anything about him. (*distressed.*) He's going through a crisis — you don't see that. And we're the ones who made the crisis. We've been so busy "getting there" that we've left him behind. We've thrown him to the wolves. You have me when things get bad for you. What has Steve got? I've deserted him!

MARVIN: If you're going to compare —

TESS (*with deep feeling*): You're going out to the street before the sound of that flute fades away, and you're going to beg Steve to come home. You're going to beg him on your knees if you have to!

MARVIN: Are you crazy? . On my knees to that little. . . . He'll come back; he's just faking —

TESS: Maybe he will come back by himself. But I want him to come back different from the way he is now. I don't want him the way you are. That pattern of self-torture is not going to be repeated in this family.

MARVIN: What are you talking about? Self-torture! We're as normal as anybody else on this block!

TESS: That's true. We're a typical family, aren't we? We have a mother who sees things happening to her kids. A father who lives on bicarbonate of soda, who wakes up in the middle of every night and stares for hours at the walls and ceiling, waiting for some new disaster to come and find him.

MARVIN: Is that how you see me?

TESS: A father who runs around the country womanizing because he can't bear to stay in the home he made! And that's what you call "getting there"! If that's what "getting there" means, then to hell with it! And if that's the way it is for everybody, then it had better be changed for everybody! (*stamping her foot*) Go out there and bring Steve back, you hear me?

CURTAIN

THE BIG DAY

1942-1977

The Big Day appeared in *The Best Short Plays of 1977*, edited by Stanley Richards. (Radnor, PA: Chilton Book Co.), 1977.

OUTLINE

When Doris Nesbit begs Les Palmer to give her husband, Joe, steady employment, Les, the supervisor of a machine shop, Ajax Pumps, agrees to keep him on, although Joe is considered a notorious "troublemaker." But Ajax has become a subsidiary of a giant conglommerate, Superior Acrylic Industries, whose representative, the plant manager, Ramsey, fears Joe's influence at a time of industrial crisis. When Ramsey orders Joe fired, Les disobeys, knowing that his authority is being undermined; besides, his conscience is troubled because he earned his own position at Ajax by selling out Joe many years ago, when Joe was foreman of the shop. Ramsey is ready to replace Les with Les's assistant, Harry, but backs off when he finds that Harry is not prepared to take charge at once. Les is exhilarated at having defied Ramsey, until Joe reminds him sardonically that Les's rebellion will have to be paid for with the loss of his "gravy train" job. Rudely shaken out of his momentary independence, Les is grateful for the reconciliation offered by Ramsey at Joe's expense.

The play offers a comparison of two men — one who has occupied a "safe" job for two decades, and another who has been battered from pillar to post in the same years. Les Palmer has no one dependent on him and has settled long ago into a feeling of security, usefulness, the respect of his subordinates and the approval of his employers. The other, Joe Nesbit, is a labor organizer and "troublemaker" who maintains his independence at bitter cost to his family and himself. The test of both men comes when Les's firm is taken over by a giant conglomerate.

I have heard that *The Big Day* had a favorable tryout in a provincial theatre in England in the fifties. In the U.S. it has yet to be staged or even given a cast reading. Apparently, to the mind of our contemporary American theatre, a drama that takes place in a machine shop is more alien than any piece imported from abroad.

The Big Day was published in the 1977 edition of *The Best Short Plays*, edited by Stanley Richards. (Chilton Book Co., Radnor, PA).

CHARACTERS

Fern, Lee's secretary

Doris, Joe's wife

Chet, a machinist

Prout, personnel manager

Ramsey, plant manager

Dylan, Union business agent*

Les, shop supervisor

Harry, Les's assistant

Joe, a machinist

Photographer*

*Dylan and Photographer can be played by women.

LES PALMER'S *work-office at Ajax Pumps, a branch of Superior Acrylic Industries Corporation. Right of center, a small vestibule next to the hall door. A low railing separates the vestibule from the office proper. Door to Superior offices in the center of the right wall. Door to the machine shop in the left wall.*

Filing cabinets, lockers and a blueprint-table against the rear wall. Left stage, LES'S *desk and telephone. Right stage,* FERN'S *desk and typewriter. Three or four chairs. An office bench in the vestibule. Jobsheets and clip boards hang on the walls. In the rear wall, a narrow, horizontal window above head height, with fluorescent lighting visible behind it.*

There is a clatter of machines and the grind of metal on metal; but the noise is muted except when the shop door is open.

At rise, FERN *is carrying a sheaf of papers from the files to* LES'S *desk. On the way she glances at* DORIS, *who sits motionless on the bench in the vestibule.*

FERN *(putting down papers, to* DORIS): Really, it's like I told you: there's no use waiting. You've been here half the morning —

DORIS: I have time.

FERN: Mr. Palmer's the supervisor here, and he has a lot on his mind. Especially today. He can't have strangers barging in on him. If you wanted to see him you should have made an appointment.

DORIS: He'll talk to me.

FERN: He's a considerate man. *Over*-considerate. I wouldn't presume on that.

DORIS: Don't tell me I'm presuming! Who do you think you are? Mrs. Ajax Pumps? *(She starts for the shop door.)*

FERN *(blocking her way)*: I have my orders, if that's what you mean, and I carry them out. Write Mr. Palmer a note, if you like. (DORIS *hesitates.)* How will it help if you lose your cool?

(CHET enters, left, with a small flat carton.)

DORIS: No notes. I'll come back.

(Exits.)

CHET: Who was that?

FERN: Somebody with no respect. She wouldn't even say what she wants or who she is. They all try to walk in here — salesmen, busybodies, soreheads — If I let them all get at the company —

CHET: What company?

FERN: What do you mean, "What company"?

CHET: Ajax Pumps or Superior Industries? Since we got taken over, I don't know who's in charge here — Palmer, in this machine shop, or Ramsey, and Prout, in the new front office. I get my paycheck from Superior, my orders from Ajax —

FERN: All too confusing for your young, weak mind? I'll unravel it for you, Chet. We're not a little independent outfit anymore. Ajax is part of something a whole lot bigger; and speaking for myself, I'm proud to be with a great concern like Superior which pays my salary and is entitled to the best I have to give.

CHET: And the best is none too good.

FERN: Chet, dear, you're not always funny.

CHET: I guess not.

FERN: Let's see that package.

CHET: For Lester W. Palmer, from "Superior Acrylic Industries, Michigan." What you've been expecting?

FERN: That's it. Take it upstairs and open it where he won't see you. It's a surprise.

CHET: You call that a surprise? It must be one of those framed testimonials they always send, and a gold-plated watch always comes with it.

FERN (*frostily*): Not this time.

CHET: No?

FERN: Mr. Prout sounded me out a month ago for the Home Office — what would Mr. Palmer like better?

CHET: And that makes you think they care.

(*He goes to the file drawer.*)

RAMSEY (entering; to FERN): Will you ask Dylan to step in here, Miss Carmine? The Union business agent. You'll find him out there; Mr. Palmer is talking to him.

(PROUT *enters.*)

FERN: Yes, Mr. Ramsey.

RAMSEY: Mr. Prout and I will be using this office for the next half hour or so. If there's anything you have to do —

FERN: Oh. Yes, sir.

(*She exits, left.*)

RAMSEY (*with a glance through the shop door*): Still talking to Dylan. About "Let's everybody be reasonable," you can bet on it. As if there were two sides to this — Superior's and Union's. How long has Palmer had that list?

PROUT: Almost four days.

RAMSEY: What in hell did he wait for? If we had put it through at once, we'd have had an accomplished fact by now. Instead of that —

PROUT: Don't think I didn't make it clear. I told him. "It's a bad mistake to do it by degrees — you'll get the Union on top of us."

RAMSEY: And he has. "That couldn't happen," he told me. "I know the Union," he said. "It's nothing but a dues-paying club; it won't lift a finger." "Then what are you trying to appease it for?" I asked him. And while he talked, Nesbit got busy.

PROUT: Exactly.

RAMSEY: I know the Union doesn't investigate unless it gets a complaint from a member. But *are* we sure it was Nesbit who made the complaint, George? He's been employed in this shop only three days; the Union wouldn't act that fast.

PROUT: He was in the shipping area last month.

RAMSEY: Only a few days there, too.

PROUT: I can't be entirely sure, Ed. Even Harry isn't absolutely sure why the Union started to act up. Dylan is probably the only one who could tell us, but he's a politician — he's not talking. But one thing Harry made perfectly clear to me; it's a different Local since Nesbit transferred into it last month.

RAMSEY (*as* DYLAN *enters, left*): Well, Mr. Dylan. Seen all you wanted to see? Quite a while since you were here last. You remember Mr. Prout: Personnel?

PROUT: Please have a seat, Mr. Dylan.

RAMSEY: Please do. Give him that chair, George.
(DYLAN *sits.*)
Always a pleasant visit with you, Mr. Dylan.

DYLAN: Same here, and I'm sorry about this. Always enjoyed doing business with Ajax: wages and working conditions right, nothing more than minor complaints — we hoped it would be the same with Superior coming in here.

PROUT: And isn't it?

DYLAN: It was — up to six weeks ago.

RAMSEY: A partial layoff when the economic crisis finally hit us. Something entirely out of our control.

PROUT: The men understood that.

RAMSEY: And we've been grateful for their loyalty.

DYLAN: They tried to help you out, sir. But now you're separating some of them for good.

RAMSEY: Let's have the figures, George. Mr. Dylan, nobody feels worse about that than we do, here at Superior Industries. But Ajax is only a subsidiary, and the home plant in Michigan is taking a beating. (*Takes sheets from* PROUT.) Look at these figures. We have a moral obligation to our shareholders, Mr. Dylan. (*Hands over the sheets.*) You can see how we're hurting. And we're not the only ones: the whole U.S. economy is in reverse gear. We need a breathing spell to see us through.

DYLAN: Same with our members, Mr. Ramsey. With a sky-high inflation going on —

PROUT: Is Superior Industries responsible for the inflation?

RAMSEY: All right, George.
(DYLAN *hands back the papers.*)
Mr. Dylan, give us credit for going about this in a good way. We can't offer more work when there isn't enough to go round. It may be painful, but it's more humane to let some of these fellows go. The sooner they leave us, the sooner they'll find well-paying jobs elsewhere.

DYLAN: Well, now, I have to tell you, Mr. Ramsey; the men don't see it. I wouldn't have thought it possible as late as a month ago, but now they not only won't stand for being cut off — they want a cost-of-living increase. At least thirty percent, and they'll go to the Labor Board for it.

PROUT: How will it help if they wipe us out? They'll be out in the street or on Welfare.

DYLAN: And not on "well-paying jobs elsewhere"? (*dryly*) Mr. Prout, you can't ask us to support you. If you can't make a go of it, that's your hang-up, isn't it? Not ours. As long as you keep going, it has to be on Union terms.

RAMSEY: And what about loyalty? The Union members' wage scale these days is unbelievable: some of them own two cars apiece and send their sons to college. We've given your men continuous work for years, but they owe nothing in return — is that how you see it?

DYLAN: I'm here to talk business, not moral questions. And if I were, it would cut both ways: the men don't want to lose what they've gained. Whatever they have, they've earned. (*with a change of tone*) I wasn't sent to be tough on Ajax or Superior, you know that, sir. We wish you well and always have, you know that, too. And speaking personally, Mr. Ramsey, I don't make the policy of the Local. There's been a big change there, lately . . . . Phone me if you want to negotiate.

(*Exits.*)

RAMSEY: The honeymoon is over.

PROUT: The s.o.b.! He never talked like that before.

RAMSEY: He's under pressure himself. We've got to act, or else and last, too.

PROUT: I'm ready for them, Ed. I can hand out the pink slips myself, this very afternoon if I have to, and cut off all the temporary help The steadies will back off if they think their own jobs remain safe. Harry's got a good, compact following of the right-minded element in the Local; with his help we've swung the membership before, and we can do it again. At least long enough to quiet things down while we get this complaint taken out and lost some place.

RAMSEY: Provided we impress the men.

PROUT: Right. Throw Nesbit the hell out of this shop — out of the Local, if possible — nail him to the barn door, and there'll be no more loudmouthing.

RAMSEY: I'm leaving him to you.

PROUT: Right, sir. I'll give him a going-over in front of Palmer.

RAMSEY: There comes Palmer himself. Two birds with one stone. You're positive about your information on Palmer?

PROUT: Absolutely. I've had Harry check and double-check, here, and Michigan sent me its records.

RAMSEY: Then my mind's made up. Even the Union business will be worth it if we can knock Palmer on the head once and for all. He'll have his showdown today.

PROUT: Today, right when he's getting his testimonial from the head office?

RAMSEY: It's a routine matter with the Corporation, but that's not how he'll see it — he'll have a rush of importance to the head. No, it's got to be done today; it'll be harder tomorrow. Only go easy — give him all the rope he needs.

LES (*entering with HARRY, left*): That's all well and good, Harry, but there's no substitute for experience. When I was starting in here — (*Seeing RAMSEY and PROUT at the door, right*) Coming to see me, Ed?

RAMSEY: Later on, Les.

(RAMSEY *and* PROUT *exit.*)

LES: Desk men — their company sends them down here to administrate. Conglomerate machinists: they wouldn't know a cam from a bushing. (*Picks up a swipe; cleaning his hands*) They can't fire my mechanics; even my best men won't stay here if they let out any more people — and I can't run a machine shop with chemists. (*Goes to his desk; takes out a box of cigars.*) It's my day — hand these out to the boys for me. Best on the market for the price — have some yourself.

HARRY: Yes, sir. (*Turns to go.*)

LES (*somewhat too casually*): If you see Joe Nesbit out there, Harry, send him in.

HARRY: Yes, sir. He gets cut off tomorrow. He came in on the Union hiring list, a month ago, for three days; and he has three days, now, in the shop, but that's all he's entitled to.

LES: I've been thinking about him. He's a blue-chip machinist and we're short of the more experienced people; I don't see why he can't go on steady.

HARRY: You don't mean that, Mr. Palmer?

LES: He's been out of work a long time, you know that. It explains a lot. He's minded his own business around the shop, so far. A couple of months' steady employment and you'll see him change his whole nature.

HARRY: You believe that, after the way he's carried on around the Local? The Union Executive Board hates his guts, and so do all the regulars.

LES: He called you a company stooge in open meeting — you told me that. Nobody is perfect, Harry. You're running for secretary of the Local; when a man runs for office, he's bound to be sized up and called names.

HARRY: It doesn't matter what he calls me personally. It's what he's done to this company — a firm with a great national reputation. Ever since he checked into the Local he's been on the floor at every meeting, making speeches, agitating —

LES: Let's get this straight, Harry. I'm in charge of hire and fire in this shop. Let Ramsey look out for Superior Industries — I'm looking out for Ajax. What has acrylics got to do with building pumps? Next thing you know we'll be owned by a dairy products company or a fried chicken syndicate! (*With finality*) Either I mean something here or I don't. I'll take the responsibility for Nesbit. And for the rest of the boys, too. I know them all — I've weeded them out for years, getting rid of the ones that wouldn't play ball. Unless they're given no way out — like seeing they're next on the chopping block — they'll never raise a peep.

(FERN *enters, right, with flowers.*)

HARRY: I've given you my opinion.

286

LES: I appreciate that. It's my big day; let's have good feelings here. Look in at eleven o'clock, Harry, that's when the ceremony comes off. The publicity man will be here and they're taking pictures.

HARRY: I'm looking forward to it of course, Mr. Palmer. (*Exits, left.*)

FERN (*as the door closes*): He'll be around to the front office in a minute, talking to Mr. Ramsey. Nothing but a shop steward, but he has conferences with the plant manager when your back is turned! He's learned how to butter up Ramsey and Prout; he spreads it on with a trowel, Chet says.
(LES *opens a second box of cigars.*)
Doesn't it bother you?

LES: What for? He looks out for himself, and so do I — we all do. This place is like a merry-go-round, Fern; you jump on and try any way you can to keep your seat. I've seen lots of others get bounced off but I'm still here. . . . You think I don't know what they're saying? They say this testimonial is nothing but a put-on; that Ramsey is grooming Harry to take my place —

FERN: And you don't believe it.

LES: I'm Ajax Pumps and Ajax Pumps is me. I was here when Ajax was nothing but the back of a junkyard. There isn't a machine in the catalog that didn't go through my hands. (*with pride*) I build pumps. What does Ramsey know — how to sign checks? Let him try and budge me — he'll get further trying to shove that stamping press out there with his bare hands.

FERN: It all depends who your friends are, don't you think? Mr. Ramsey's friends are all in Michigan.

LES: Sure — he's been sending them reports ever since he's been here: how everything is fine, everything is under control — except me. He wasn't here three weeks before he ran to Nat Webster — Nat was the original owner here — with complaints about me. That was two years ago, after Nat sold Ajax and was made a vice-president of Superior Industries. "I put my bet on Palmer." The old man told him; and Ramsey backed down the way he always does in a pinch. Let him talk, let him make reports . . . (*Waves job-record sheets.*) You've been getting these out of the files for me, and they talk louder than anything he can say. There's my record: clean jobs, everything planned, no waste, no stoppages. This whole year Ramsey's been running the plant at a loss, but my department shows a profit.

FERN: You know what I think? I think if a person gets too sure of himself it's just too bad.

LES (*lighting a cigar; tolerantly*): All right, I'm a dead duck, and you're bringing me flowers.

FERN: I borrowed these from Publicity just for the occasion. (*Goes to the door, right.*) Don't say you don't like them. They smell better than your cigars.

LES: I like them, Fern, I like them. Don't take my head off.

FERN (*calling*): You can come in now, Chet.

(CHET *enters, carrying a package and blueprints.*)

LES: What's he doing in here? I told him to take those prints upstairs.

CHET: I brought them back again. It's cozier here.

FERN (*to* LES): He was on his way, but I had him uncrate this picture for you. (CHET *removes the wrapping.*) It came by express today from the head office.

CHET: Congratulations, Mr. Palmer.

LES: Well, well.

FERN: Look what it says: "Faithful employee. . . . devoted service." Hand engraved. You should be proud.

LES: You bet I am. See those signatures? All the vice-presidents except Mr. Webster; he passed away this year. (*Moved)* Nathan T. Webster — one of the old school; carried a micrometer in his pocket to his dying day. Kept his eye on me from the day I started as a learner, saw me doing my job, day in, day out, cheerful and willing; he recognized me as the kind of man they needed. Twenty years with the company — twenty years today. Do you know how it makes me feel?

CHET: Like you're wondering about your next twenty years.

LES: Stand that picture up there, on the locker. I know how you kid about Ajax Pumps; you think it's something to kid about.

FERN: Quote, by Chet Mayfield: You don't have to be crazy to work here, but it helps; unquote.

LES (*to* CHET): Get going — take those drawings up to Engineering and give them an argument.

CHET: I don't know what they drew. Whatever it is, it won't pump.

LES: Make up a query sheet first.
(CHET *exits, right, with blueprints.*)
I know who takes him seriously.

FERN: Chet's a machinist, Mr. Palmer. He may be tall, dark and handsome for all I care.

LES: Don't tell me. He's got brains and some backbone, not like the rest of them. What's more I swear he's kissed you a couple of times. Or you him. Right in this office.

288

FERN: I've crossed off marriage. I was engaged once, to someone, but men are so disappointing, even when you don't ask for much.

LES: What did you ask for?

FERN: Just to be happy. Is that too much to ask?

LES. Not if you don't overdo it.

FERN: You're laughing at me. (*going to the files*) You might as well know it, Mr. Palmer. Chet is leaving.

LES (*startled*): Chet? Why would he leave? That's nonsense — he's been getting on fine here. (*suddenly*) That's what's bothering you —

FERN: I'm free, white and going on thirty. Nothing bothers me, Mr. Palmer, nothing in the wide world!

LES: I'll talk to Chet. This place is steady for somebody like him, and he knows it. Safe and steady; he could have a job here the rest of his life if he wants it.

FERN: He doesn't want it. (*controlling herself*) I have to take down the time sheets.

(She exits, left. LES closes the files; turns, finds DORIS standing at the partition.)

LES: It's you, Doris! I'd been wondering when you'd look me up —

DORIS: And hoping it wouldn't happen. . . . Never mind, don't answer me. You don't seem to believe it's me, the way I look, now —

LES: Is that what the years have done to you?

DORIS: We're going under.

LES: As bad as that?

DORIS: You can't imagine it. The last of our unemployment insurance money used up, and nothing left for rent. We have two kids; they never fill their stomachs. We came back to this town last month because we didn't know where else to turn to anymore. Joe's had six days' work here since we came back — it's the first time he's worked in half a year. He doesn't know I'm here talking to you; he wouldn't allow it.

LES: He's a damned crazy fool. Got himself boxed in for fair, and you with him. Just what I knew would happen! (*Going to his desk*) He never even asked me about work: he came here off the Union hiring list. He saw me in the shop and turned his head away.

DORIS: I haven't room for pride anymore, but he'll be that way to the last. Hellish pride! But you're not going to abuse him in front of me!

LES: All right, all right —

DORIS: You've got to help us, Les.

LES: How?

DORIS: Give him his chance to work. Whatever else he is, he's a good workman. Put him on steady, give us a chance.

LES: He's been working here.

DORIS: Three days each month?

LES: It so happens that it's not a good time to ask that, Doris.

DORIS: It's never a good time to ask a favor.

LES: You don't know the ins and outs of things here. It's a bad time. It isn't that I don't want to help —

DORIS: Only it's not convenient.

LES: If you'll take some money to tide you over —

DORIS: I'm down so far I wouldn't even refuse that. Only how long do you think we can live on handouts? Let him work. I know he's no concern of yours.

LES: I didn't say that, either. You know I'd never say that, after what you've both meant to me. . . . Did you think I'd forget about you through all those years of my marriage to the wrong woman?

DORIS: Les —

LES: Don't worry — I'm not going into it. (*Changing, forcefully*) Doris, believe me, I've wanted to keep Joe on. But it's not easy. He worked in another section of the plant last month; he kept his mouth shut, but they knew about him and didn't keep him on. They don't want him here.

DORIS: It's for you to decide in this shop. You're the boss here.

LES: They're crowding me. You don't understand — Ajax Pumps is not the same since it was taken over.

DORIS: Is that how far you've got in all this time — you can't give Joe a job when we're so desperate?

LES (*dismayed*): Don't let go like that, Doris. You can't think what it means to me to see you this way. I'll do my best for you — and him. I promise you. I'll do it right away. Only it'll be a fight. They have a plant manager on my neck, sent down from Superior Industries, and everything is departmentalized: I can't scratch my nose without getting approval in triplicate —
(FERN *enters.*)
Pull yourself together —

290

FERN (*to* DORIS): So you're here again! (*To* LES) she had no appointment, but she hung around for hours. I told her you were not to be bothered —

LES: That's all tight, Fern. It's Mrs. Nesbit. She came in to talk to me about her husband.

DORIS: I'm sorry; I'll go now.

LES (*going with* DORIS *to the hall door*): Don't worry — you'll hear from me. (DORIS *exits.*)

LES (*turns to* FERN) You're taking a lot on yourself, Fern. Why wouldn't I talk to her? She's up against it; she came to plead for help —

FERN: She walks in here and you fall for her line! That husband of hers —

LES: I can use him steady.

FERN: Him? A known troublemaker, everywhere he goes?

LES: That's Harry's opinion.

FERN: Everybody in the office says so. Everybody can't be wrong.

LES: Yes, they can! The man is a crackerjack machinist, born right in this town —

FERN: You know all about him?

LES: His wife just told me. (*sharply*) You've got the fever too, now! Every lunch hour Ramsey and the other big shots sit around their table at Belardi's Restaurant talking about how the bleeding hearts are letting troublemakers destroy this country; they get so they yell anarchism if they can't find their socks in the morning. A bunch of corporation minds — they don't half believe that junk themselves but they've got you barking up a tree!

FERN: I'm of age. I know what I believe in. (*Sits.*) Let me tell you something, Mr. Palmer. You ought to stop smoking. If you didn't smoke so much you'd have a clearer mind.

(PROUT *enters, right.*)

PROUT: How's the big day going, Les?

LES: Hardly had time to notice. Have a couple of these on me, George. (*lighting* PROUT'S *cigar*) What about Dylan? What was the upshot?

PROUT (*sitting*): Not good, Les. They'll drag us before the Labor Board, or throw a picket line around the plant. An old, established firm like Ajax —

LES: It'll blow over if we're half-way reasonable. The only labor trouble we've ever had here was way back when they first began union-

291

izing this shop. The Union's been satisfied ever since; and as old Webster used to say —

PROUT: Let's forget old Webster — he's dead, now. (LES *turns away.*) *You* said the Union would never go as far as it has.

LES: Maybe I did, George; we're all entitled to our margin of mistakes. Your office has made mistakes, too, ordering part-time layoffs while a runaway inflation is going on. Now you want to drop people altogether.

PROUT: Only the newer hands.

LES: We've got orders on our books, George. Who's going to do the apprentice work? Our best machinists? They'll laugh at you; or worse yet, they'll see the handwriting on the wall and you'll have the Union on your back for fair. You can sit at your desk and scribble on a piece of paper; but I have to turn out pumps.

PROUT: You're crossing bridges before we get to them. (*Leans back; evenly*) Something I'd like to know, Les. This Joe Nesbit who's working with you —

LES: What about him?

PROUT: Is he one of those you have to keep here? He's just a substitute. And I believe I told you — we dropped him out of Shipping.

LES: I need a good man on the radial drill. He's an expert.

PROUT: Is that your main reason?

LES: What other reason do I need?

PROUT: You're not touchy about this, are you, Les? I only want to make it clear to Ed. (*Getting up.*)

LES: When do we have a conference about the Union situation?

PROUT: Who?

LES: You, me, and Ed Ramsey.

PROUT: There's none scheduled between you, me, and — Ramsey.

LES: He doesn't need my advice anymore, is that it?

PROUT: I don't know what's on his mind. (*Pause*) About Nesbit — there are still plenty of good machinists walking the streets; if you need a man for the radial drill you can get one. As long as there's no special reason to keep him —

LES: He fills the bill, as far as I'm concerned.

PROUT: Right. Well, I'll tell Ed your point of view about Nesbit. This isn't a bad cigar, Les.

292

(Exits.)

FERN: The merry-go-round is going round, Mr. Palmer.

LES: Let it go round.

FERN (*getting up*): I guess I just don't understand you anymore, do I? (JOE enters, left.) Here's your friend, Mr. Palmer.

(Exits, right.)

JOE: Is that a permanent cramp — her nose in the air? Or just whenever she sees me?

LES: She's all right; a little teed off today, that's all.

JOE (*casually*): To hell with her. (*surveying the room*) Flowers — testimonials —

LES: Have a cigar.

JOE: I'm not used to cigars. What do you want of me, Les? The congratulations of a mere mechanic?

LES: I seem to be the punching bag today. Step up, everybody; you, too. (*curtly*) I sent for you because I want to help you.

JOE: I didn't ask for your help.

LES: That's right, you didn't. (*without rancor*) You don't like me, Joe — that's your privilege. But I'm going to tell you just the same, I've struck my neck out on account of you. Personnel doesn't want you here. That bastard of a Harry has gone around raising an alarm; Ramsey's all steamed up —

JOE: What's all the uproar? They don't have to keep me.

LES: No. And you don't have to work, either. You can go beat your brains out.

JOE: I get along.

LES: Okay, you get along. Sit down at the other desk and fill this out. (*Hands him a blank form.*) It's the employment questionnaire for Personnel. You're starting in the tool room tomorrow morning; there's no seniority problem there. It's a good job; you'll punch the time clock steady from now on. How does that suit you?

JOE (*with a faint grin*): They want to throw me out, and you're putting me on steady? You know I'm on the blacklist.

LES: Nobody's blacklisted. It's illegal. (JOE *chuckles.*) Fill out that form, that's all I'm asking you to do; I'll see that it gets by the front office. I'll tell them the truth about you; you're not organizing anymore, you've learned better. I'll even tell them you'll keep quiet around the Union —

JOE: So that's it!

LES (*stung*): What do you care what *I* tell them? You can go on keeping your jaws clamped while you're on the job; you *can* do that much? That's all I ask. You're in. Go back to your machine, now. Tell Doris the good news when you get home tonight.

JOE (*not moving*): Would you mind telling me why you're doing this, Les?

LES: Why shouldn't I do it for you?

JOE: Don't tell me I dreamed everything that's happened. You couldn't hide your hatred of me — not even from the beginning, no matter how you tried. When Doris —

LES: Don't drive nails into me, Joe!

JOE: You couldn't stand me, for a whole list of reasons: because I had more life than you — because I always led, while you followed —

LES: I'm not listening!

(*Door, left, opens and HARRY enters.*)

HARRY: I'm sorry, Mr. Palmer — the detail sheets on the Tri-County job —

LES: They're on Charlie Conroy's bench.

HARRY: Yes, sir. I'll look there again.

LES: Did you want to see me?

HARRY: No, sir, not right now.

(*Exits.*)

LES: He spies on me; I sit in this office spying on the men. You don't remember what my job is like: the bootlicking and conniving. All you know is that I've been riding the gravy train while you've been knocking around every hole and corner. That's all you want to know —

JOE: I've got what's coming to me. Is that what you're working around to, Les? There's no law says I have to listen.

LES (*with feeling*): You think I'm doing myself a favor looking out for you? I know how you see it — I don't even rate a thank you. (*changing*) Since you bring it up, let me remind you: it was your own fault to start with — and you know it. When I first came here as a learner you'd already been foreman two years; but everybody knew you couldn't last. You couldn't or wouldn't keep the men on line. Your head was full of idealistic notions that had nothing to do with your job. Then came the walkout —

JOE: And my finish.

294

LES: The day before the walkout you and I stood outside this shop, talking. You'd never go through a picket line, you said. I pleaded with you. I said, "You're the foreman here, Joe. Where's your common sense?" And what was your answer?

JOE: My answer was to stay home two days running And on the third day you quit the Union and went up to Webster's office, begging for my job.

LES: They wouldn't have taken you back for a present. Someone was bound to replace you — if not me, then somebody else. I went in and made good — is that something to be ashamed of?

JOE: Of course not. You're in the great tradition, Les. Walk over people till you get there, then do them favors out of the kindness of your heart.

LES: Joe, I believe in lending a hand when I can — "We pass this way but once," as the book says. You say I've always hated you, but you're wrong. I could have been a little jealous once, and it was understandable; but it was never my real feeling. Sit there; there's something in this locker I want to show you. (*Takes dusty clothes out of the locker.*) You know what these are? My old overalls and work shoes; I put them in there the day I became foreman. That was before I got harnessed up here like a goddamn mule — when I was still a raw kid, learning from you. Life was juicy in those days — the sky was bluer and the grass was greener. There were places like Raymond's Joint on the turnpike, where we used to go; the girls, Doris and Emma — we laughed a lot and learned a lot. (*Putting clothes back*) You may not consider it a debt I owe you; but I do.

JOE: What do you owe me?

LES: A thought of something more than this machine shop — industrial democracy, you called it, a better world, not dog-eat-dog. . . . Go on hating me if you have to; but you need this job and I want to see you keep it. I have my hands full in this place, and I may be a fool for taking this on, in addition. But what have you got to lose? Nothing — not even your opinion of me! (*quietly*) You baffle me, Joe. It can't be that you're just ornery — I know better. When I replaced you on this job, I was sure you'd boil over. All you said was "That's how things are," and then you simply went away — you and Doris — out of my life . . . .

JOE: Yes.

LES: I try not to keep grudges, but I don't think *I* could have been so tolerant. It's gone on bothering me. Especially after all those years of silence, when you learned that Emma had died and you sent me a message. I wanted to tell you how grateful I was, but you'd written from some place unknown. (*Almost pleadingly*) What's made

295

you so frozen, unforgiving, and unreasoning except for that one time? What's turned you into an outlaw — and why must Doris and your children have to pay for it?

(*A pause, as* JOE *remains silent.* CHET *enters with blueprints.*)

CHET: If you're busy, Mr. Palmer —

(JOE *goes slowly to* FERN'S *desk with the questionnaire; picks up a pen.*)

LES (*with relief*): It's all right, Chet.

CHET: There's the list, boss. Those Engineering boys with their little pencils —

LES: You're up in the air, too. What for?

CHET: I got blown up by a land mine in Vietnam. Maybe I'll never come down.

LES: Fern says you want to leave here; is that true?

CHET: Why should I hang around when the company is getting ready for a mass layoff? They'll get away with it, too: the Union will let them.

JOE (*looking up*): Maybe not this time.

CHET: Sure it'll let them. That's the kind of Local we have. (*without heat*) I know how you talk, Nesbit: "Stick together and it won't happen." But we've got no Union; all we have is a debating society — you and Harry tearing each other apart at the meetings. And you call that sticking together! I don't know what it's all about and I don't give a damn — I've got a good offer somewhere else.

LES: Look before you leap, Chet.

CHET: Yes, sir, I'm looking. Meanwhile I'll go see those white-collar boys upstairs. When they draw something we have to build it. I wonder if they know that?

(*Exits.*)

LES: That's youth for you. Spit and vinegar. He'll find out what machine shops are: they're all alike.

JOE: Some day he'll learn to be a part of the Union — that's even more important.

(*Puts down pen; gets up.*)

LES: Where are you going?

JOE: Back to my machine. I can't answer this. You'd think they were passing me through the pearly gates instead of the employees' entrance. What'll I write down? That I was a union organizer once, out west? That I've been kicked around from here to hell and gone? That I often changed my name to try and hold a job?

296

LES: Not even a good organizer, were you? Too headstrong — too outspoken —

JOE: I'm not accountable to you.

LES: You're accountable to your wife and kids. Doesn't that trouble you?

JOE (after a moment): It does.

LES: Fill out that form. Leave the rest to me.

JOE: It's no good, Les. The Union's toughening up; that means your front office will cut my throat if they can do it. I've been on my feet at the Local, talking up for a wage hike, fighting the layoffs. Your office knows it; they know everything that goes on — or almost everything.

LES: You're impossible! I fought the layoffs too, didn't I? Anybody can tell you. And I'm still doing it. Answer that thing any way you can, and I'll accept it — Remember that little place around the corner — the Giotto? We'll go in there later and hoist a couple of beers to celebrate your job.

JOE: No, Les. You've been warming that chair of yours too long; you can't see that things don't come as easy as sitting down. How much can you do with the front office fighting you? It's all over the shop that they're ready to take you apart. Forget this gesture of yours — it doesn't suit you.

(*He starts to exit.* PROUT *enters, right.*)

PROUT: Just a minute, Nesbit — I want to talk to you.

LES (*at once*): What for?

PROUT: We have something to ask him, Les.

LES: He doesn't have to answer.

PROUT: I think he does, if he wants to work here. We want to know who complained to the Union about this place.

JOE: I'll answer that. It's none of your business. The charge against the firm is made by the Union, not by any one member.

PROUT: Are you ashamed to admit *you* made it? I thought you pride yourselves on your principles — you and your kind?

(RAMSEY *enters, right.*)

JOE (*ominously*): What do you mean by "my kind"?

RAMSEY: The hate-America kind.

JOE: Who are you?

LES: Mr. Ramsey, the plant manager. Take it easy, Joe.

JOE (*calmly*): So you're Ramsey! Suppose we talk about *your* kind — star-spangled jokers who pad their expense accounts, leeches who live off the work of others, fixers who buy off the people's representatives, "patriots" who don't even pay their income taxes if they can help it —

LES: That's enough!

JOE: The kind who tell me to get off the earth —

LES (*losing patience*): What sort of talk is that? You had a chance to clear yourself —

RAMSEY: Let him go. He's said enough to hang him.

JOE: Try and hang me, Mr. Ramsey — I have a hard neck. (*Exits, left.*)

RAMSEY: Are you satisfied? I couldn't believe my eyes when George showed me his record. A professional agitator! You know he started his career here, in this very shop? He even got to be foreman before they threw him out —

PROUT: He's knocked around the country — a man with a string of aliases. Last year he worked at the plant in Michigan until they caught up with him.

LES: He makes a bad impression if you jump on him that way. He's his own worst enemy — one of those bad-tempered idealists. But he didn't sign that complaint, Ed — I'm sure of it. It's immaterial, anyhow, if the Union backs it up —

RAMSEY: We'll not discuss it any further. I want him fired, and at once, whether he signed a complaint or not. (*Pause*) Do you refuse?

LES: I do.

RAMSEY (*quietly*): I had an idea it would come to this, Palmer. This isn't the first time you've set yourself up as absolute in this shop. You've resisted every attempt to make Ajax a part of Superior — because the Corporation means nothing to you, and I, as its representative, mean still less. You've entrenched yourself here; you've built up a little empire with everybody taught to ignore any authority but your own. (*To* PROUT) Give him that paper, George.
(PROUT *puts a legal paper on the desk.*)
This is a formal statement of Corporation policy on Ajax Pumps. So that there will be no further misunderstanding on employment or wage policies, I want your signature on that paper.

LES: Before I sign anything of the kind I expect to be consulted on it, Mr. Ramsey. I'm a shop supervisor here, not a foreman. (*He crumples up the paper, throws it into the waste basket.*) Go ahead and take this up with Michigan. I'll match my department against the rest of this plant any day. I show a profit. What do *you* show?

RAMSEY: You may show a profit here, because you haven't deducted your share of the gross overhead. You show no percentage profit, which is all that matters. I don't expect you to understand that. But I'll tell you something you *can* understand: I've had enough of your obstruction — from now on I'm running this whole plant, and that includes Ajax Pumps. (*To* PROUT) Find Harry. Tell him to give Nesbit his walking papers.

PROUT: Right, sir.

(*Exits, left.*)

RAMSEY: That takes it off your hands.

LES: I don't recognize this firing. Nesbit is on our payroll until I say he's off.

RAMSEY: He's off as of this moment.

LES (*after a pause*): I quit.

RAMSEY: That's ridiculous. The man's notorious, and you're making an issue of him —

LES: Nobody can take the hire and fire out of my hands. I'm leaving when the whistle blows. (*Goes to the locker, starts getting his things together.*)

RAMSEY: You can't walk out just like that. You have obligations to this firm.

LES: I have no contract with this firm.

RAMSEY: Nobody's telling you to leave. We're only asking you to recognize that Ajax Pumps is part of something greater.

LES: It's still Ajax Pumps to me — you can explain that to Michigan when they ask you why I left.

RAMSEY: You seem very sure Michigan will be interested.

(LES *doesn't answer.* PROUT *comes back with* HARRY.)

PROUT (*to* RAMSEY): Nesbit's getting out of his overalls. If you want Harry for anything else —

RAMSEY: I have some news for you. Palmer has taken it into his head that he wants to terminate here.

PROUT: Well!

RAMSEY: He seems to mean it. He says he's walking out at noon.

(RAMSEY *and* PROUT *exchange glances. They both turn to look at* HARRY.)

RAMSEY: What do you say, Harry? Can you take over — beginning this afternoon?

HARRY: This afternoon, Mr. Ramsey?

RAMSEY: I know it's very short notice. We're running at top speed, just now.

HARRY: Yes, sir, it's pretty sudden. (*sweating*) I could get into the swing of things in another week or two —

LES: Not today, Harry? It ought to be easy for a bright boy like you, stepping into another man's shoes. All you need is a little nerve. What of it if you *do* make a mistake or two? Like the time you forgot to drill the oil holes in the Fairmount job and we had to tear out the whole job and bring it back —

HARRY: Give me a chance at it, Mr. Ramsey. I can do it.

RAMSEY: We'll talk to you later, Harry.

(HARRY *exits, left.*)

RAMSEY (*to* LES): You've taken good care he didn't learn the ropes. It's up to you to break him in before you leave. We're entitled to that much loyalty, at least — we've paid for it all these years.

LES: I've given my life for this firm — cracking the whip for you, cutting corners off the payroll, gouging your customers — I couldn't sleep nights; and now you call me disloyal!

RAMSEY: It's my belief that this whole Union trouble started with you — that you put yourself against the layoffs to show we can't run this place without you.

LES (*staggered*): That's a contemptible lie!

(FERN *enters.*)

RAMSEY: Michigan will want to know why you want to keep this man Nesbit here; why you've handled him with kid gloves; why you refused point-blank to fire him —

PROUT: And why he wanted to put Nesbit on steady just this morning — even after the Union came down on us —

LES: I told you why!

RAMSEY: Isn't there something you forgot to mention? Hasn't Nesbit been a bosom friend of yours for almost twenty years?

(*Pause*)

LES: He married a girl I was engaged to. What does that prove?

RAMSEY: Come on, George. (*He and* PROUT *turn to go.*)

LES: You think I owe him anything — someone my girl friend married just for spite? (*They stop.*) To spite me! It's true Joe Nesbit once was foreman here — that's how we met him, Doris and me. She didn't care anything about him until he was thrown out of here,

300

then she turned around and blamed me — and that's the last I saw of either of them until he came here looking for work.

RAMSEY: You can tell that story to Superior Industries for what it may be worth; only this time there'll be no Nat Webster to validate it for you. George and I have a different testimony about the way you've been apologizing for management, telling the men it's not *your* fault they're laid off. . . . And it doesn't end there; all that talk about industrial democracy, anarchistic claptrap — You and Nesbit, two sides of the same coin!

PROUT: Only Nesbit is aboveboard.

LES: Get out of this office! I've had enough from you both!

RAMSEY: You've been aching for a showdown, Palmer, and you can have it. Leave here whenever you like — now or later. Ready or not, Harry will take charge. And let me warn you: if there are any Union repercussions over Nesbit, it will all be in your lap — Miss Carmine!

FERN: Yes, sir.

RAMSEY: That paper Mr. Palmer threw into the waste basket a minute ago — if he stays here, I want it signed by him and delivered to me before noon today.

FERN: Yes, sir.

(RAMSEY *and* PROUT *exit, right.* FERN *picks the crumpled sheet out of the basket, lays it on* LES'S *desk.*)

FERN: Is this the paper he means?

LES: They saved up their maneuver for today!

FERN (*calmly*): What are you going to do about it?

LES (*shutting the locker*): I'll give Ramsey a run for his money — that's what I'll do! That's how they work, the Ramseys and the Prouts. While people like me build machines, they sit behind their desks writing notes, juggling figures; they spin webs just like spiders! Acrylics is showing a loss — that's why they have to frame me.

FERN: That's a reckless statement, Mr. Palmer. Mr. Ramsey and Mr. Prout are gentlemen, both of them.

LES: Maybe to their mothers! These administrators are all the same from Maine to California, yammering about loyalty and looking out for Number One. And anybody who interferes with their racket is "notorious"!

FERN: Nesbit is a buddy of yours — I heard you admit that yourself.

LES: Is that a crime I committed?

FERN: You ought to be more careful about the sort of accusations you make, Mr. Palmer. You'd do a lot better to show you're against Joe Nesbit and everything he stands for.

LES: How about the accusations you and they make? I didn't know you could be like that, Fern. You give me goose pimples with that talk.

FERN: I can't take it as calmly as you can, Mr. Palmer. I believe in loyalty and gratitude. My brother Clive died fighting for his country while you sat here making a good salary all through the war. (*Exits, right.*)

LES: Goose pimples!
(JOE *enters, left.*)
Come on in. You're just the man I want to see.

JOE: Just give me my time slip, will you, Les?

LES: I suppose you think you gave them a high-minded answer!

JOE: The way I answer is nobody's business but my own.

LES: You're wrong! It's my business, too. Ramsey jumped on me after you left. I threatened to quit, and he called me on it.

JOE: You threatened to quit? (*sobered.*) He can't let you do that. He'd have to explain it to the home office.

LES: He thinks all he needs to say is that you're a friend of mine.

JOE: Is that another thing he knows?

LES: He knows it, and he'll use it. . . . Just because I wanted to help you.

JOE: I told you I don't want your help.

LES: Doris wanted it. She asked me for it.

JOE: Doris was here? (*angered*) She had no right to come here!

LES: She had a right to ask for help. (*bitterly*) Forget it. Ramsey's been looking for any excuse to get me, and the fat was in the fire when I didn't carry out his order. Now that Webster's gone, he thinks he has a clear field. . . . But he'll learn different. This is only the beginning: when Michigan hears the truth, like you said —

JOE: It won't do, Les.

LES: What won't do?

JOE: Forget about Michigan. You're not acrylic. You won't get a hearing when they know you've been friendly with someone like me.

LES: That's insane! I'm the opposite of you in every conceivable way —

JOE: Will you listen to me? I worked at Superior Industries in Michigan last fall — you'll find that in my record. That's where all this panic is coming from in the first place — they've got over two thousand employees, and they're leaking in their pants for fear those people will go militant on them. Why should they believe you instead of Ramsey? Superior sent Ramsey down here because they have confidence in him, because he's their kind of administrator. You think he hasn't been writing to them all this time, poisoning their minds against you? And now he'll tell them you've been encouraging the Union, with my help —

LES: And they'll swallow that?

JOE: Did you ever try talking sense to anybody who's afraid of losing his shirt? It's either you or Ramsey, and Ramsey knows them all at the head office. Who do *you* know, now that Webster is dead? If Ramsey can't prove you encouraged this Union action, he'll have no trouble showing you condoned it, at least. One thing is sure: you're not with them, and that's an unforgivable sin. . . . I'm not the only one who sticks in their throats; you do, too! You said so! They want you out, and you've given them the excuse they needed. Any stick to beat a dog! (*grimly*) Better go back and make your peace with Ramsey; ask him to forgive you. I'd ask him for you, only I doubt if he'll listen to me.

(*Pause*)

LES: You think I'll go beg Ramsey to forgive me? So I can be a straw boss from now on, passing orders for him? After all my work here?

JOE: You have no choice.

LES (*fiercely*): Yes, I have. There are other jobs, by God!

JOE: Other jobs like this one? At the same wages? The idea appeals to you, I can see that: walking out of here, saying "To hell with them." That feels good — that's a little taste of freedom; you'll kick up your heels for a week or two or three. Then you'll start looking for the kind of job you had, and you won't find it. You'll never have it again. Twenty years in one place, a shop supervisor used to giving orders, not to taking them. You're well into your forties now — that's a good age for bankers. And you walk out of here with a bad report card. Who's going to sponsor you? The men who kicked you out of here? You'll start looking for work —

LES (*frightened*): That's your own picture you're painting, not mine!

JOE: Are you sure? You're breaking into a cold sweat, just listening to me talk. What will you do when you're really up against it? When you pound the sidewalks looking for a job, and everywhere you go they whisper, "That's Les Palmer, the dog who bites the hand that feeds him"? If you're lucky you'll be back where you were twenty years ago. If not, you'll get into your overalls and cry with relief if somebody lets you go to work by the day, by the hour —

LES (*shouting*): I can do it if I have to!

JOE: *I* can do it. I'm tough, because I've had to do it all my life. But you — you bag of mush! . . . There's only one way to square yourself now — and that's to join the manhunt!
(*Phone rings.*)
That's for you. Why don't you answer it?

LES (*picking up the phone shakily*): Hello! Oh, Mr. Ramsey. I — That's all right. . . . (*more relaxed*) We both did, Ed. I have a way of shooting my big mouth off sometimes. . . . Naturally. . . . I see what you mean about Harry. . . . more experience. . . . Nesbit? No, he's through. Even told me he doesn't want to stay. (*Pause*) Yes, sir, I have the paper you left. Thank you, Edward.
(JOE *laughs.* LES *hangs up.*)
I knew he'd weaken. The whole thing was just a flareup. He wants to go on like before —

(*He reaches for the crumpled sheet, signs it hastily.*)

JOE: Not like before. You think they'll forget what happened here today? You'll stay on just to show Harry how to take your place. You know that, but you're shutting your eyes tight, thinking only how much longer you can hang on. Another hour, another minute — (*Hard*) You thought you were building security here, brick by brick. You worried more about this place than your boss did. And somebody like Ramsey raises his voice and you're through for good.

LES: Laugh if you feel like it — but you're the one who makes the big mistakes — not me. You had your chance and you chose the hard way. I don't make mistakes like that — not big ones. Sometimes, like today, I begin to get excited — but I always get cold feet, and that's what keeps me safe. I've spent my whole life playing safe, and I know the game backwards. It's a game you'll never learn.

JOE: Sign my time slip.

LES (*signing it*): I tried to help you — don't forget that.

JOE: I'll remember it. Among my souvenirs. (*getting up*)

LES: You can't go before you promise me something. You're not going to complain to the Local about being fired?

JOE: Why not?

LES: You can't do that, Joe. Ramsey'll hold that against me — he said he would.

JOE: You think I ought to lie to the Local for your sake? Ramsey knew I'd be through here tomorrow night, but he couldn't wait for that.

"At once!", he said — and you let him do it. It's a real issue for the Local to fight on.

LES: You're going to drag this whole business into your Union meeting?

JOE: Certainly. That's where it belongs.

(HARRY *enters with a clip board, left. Seeing* JOE *and* LES *together, he starts to back out.*)

LES (*deliberately*): Come on in, Harry — I want to talk to you. Nesbit, here, is making threats: he claims he was wrongfully dismissed. What will the Union do? Take *his* word?

HARRY (*looking from* LES *to* JOE, *sensing a trap*): You two slugging it out — it's not what I expected. It'll be up to the Local. If he makes out a case he'll be supported. If not —

(FERN *and* CHET *have entered quietly, left.*)

LES: What sort of case can he make out, after practically assaulting the plant manager? A gadfly, a subversive and dangerous malcontent — all the years I've known him!

HARRY: At last we're getting the truth.

JOE: A smidgen of truth in a full load of horseshit. You expect to sell that to the Local? Who's going to buy it?

HARRY: The Ex-Board, to start with. They'll call a special meeting to take care of you — and the Union will tear up your working card and throw it in your face.

JOE: We'll see about that when the time comes, Harry. It's a backward Local, that's true: fallen asleep in a dream of prosperity forever; and some of the members haven't liked the way I talk at meetings. But the times are jolting them awake. Nobody wants to be separated from his job in the middle of a raging inflation, and the Union knows I fought this company while you were making excuses for it. . . . And the Union's Ex-Board has long been used to pulling the Red scare — but they're out of date: that steady diet of red herring has finally turned everyone's stomach.

HARRY (*ignoring him; To* LES): Have you decided if you're leaving this afternoon, Mr. Palmer? Because if you are, I'd better start on the work sheets.

LES: Rest easy, Harry. I'm not leaving this afternoon — or tomorrow — or the day after. I'm not leaving, period. I'm staying in charge here.

HARRY: You took that up with Mr. Ramsey?

LES: Mr. Ramsey took that up with me.

HARRY: Yes, sir. I was only asking.

(He exits, left.)

LES: That two-faced little bastard! He's not eating me. Not yet.

(He becomes aware of FERN *and* CHET.)

FERN: You fairly took my breath away, Mr. Palmer. I want to congratulate you —

LES: Who asked you two to come in here, in the middle of this?

FERN: I ran into Chet upstairs. I've been trying to make him reconsider staying here. His future —

CHET: What's my future in this place? What I just saw? What'll I turn out to be — a foreman like Les Palmer, brown-nosing all my life? Or a hustler like Harry Fulton? If that's my future, you can have it.

LES: Where do you get the insolence to talk like that? You're not dry behind the ears yet; learn your place!

CHET (*to* JOE): It hit me all of a sudden, Nesbit — when a pair like Harry and Les put their heads together, none of us is safe.

(Exits, left.)

FERN (*running after him*): Chet!

LES: There's no respect anymore. Every punk thinks he has the right to wipe his feet on you.

JOE: He doesn't go for your kind of world, that's all.

LES: He'd better learn to live in it. It's his world, too.

JOE: What if he's not sure it's going to last forever? Lately it's been looking very sick.

LES (*savagely*): It'll last! You had me scared for a while with that hard-luck picture of yours; you have imagination, I'll say that for you. . . . Maybe you're right about this is my end as a supervisor. Well, I'll be a foreman, if they'll have me; when a man is older he takes what he can get. And even if I never work again, I still have a small balance in the bank and my home almost all paid for — besides social security and retirement. It may not add up to much, in your opinion, but I have no one to support, and it'll be enough. I was never in a fix like yours, and never will be. (*changing*) I'm sorry at the way things turned out, Joe. I had to act the way I did, you know that. You'd do the same if you were in my place.

JOE: You're throwing your garbage into my yard.
(RAMSEY *enters, right, with* PROUT *and a* PHOTOGRAPHER.)
Here comes your owner.

(JOE *withdraws upstage.*)

RAMSEY (*to* PHOTOGRAPHER): Ready? Let's go! (*Extends his hand to* LES, *reads from a mimeographed sheet*) "On this auspicious occasion it is indeed gratifying to honor one who has served Superior Industries and its subsidiary, Ajax Pumps, so faithfully and so well"

(*They shake hands formally.*)

LES: Thank you, sir.

(HARRY *enters, left, joins the group at a nod from* PROUT.)

RAMSEY (*continues*): "On behalf of the Superior organization — its officers and shareholders, its supervisors and employees — it is my great privilege to present to you, Lester Woodrow Palmer, in commemoration of your twentieth year with the company, and as a small token of our affection and regard, this gold cigar lighter."

(*Presents the lighter.*)

PHOTOGRAPHER: Hold it that way, please. Let's see the cigar lighter. Move in closer together, folks. (*Flash*) Just once more. A little more animation — (*Flash*) That will do nicely. Thank you one and all.

RAMSEY: I'll take that signed paper now, Les. . . . I'll see you and Harry in the afternoon: we have a lot of work ahead of us on the termination schedule of this department.

(RAMSEY *and* entourage *exit, right*; HARRY *exits, left.* JOE *starts to leave.*)

LES: Joe! Wait a minute! (*Counts out bills.*) I want you to take this money; it's for Doris and the kids, not you. I'll see that they get more if they need it. Only don't keep them and their grief in this small town, where I and others have to see them.

JOE: We're staying right here to fight this out, Les. Shove that money up you-know-where! (*He turns to go.*)

LES: You're telling yourself it's your turn at last, is that it? Evening up the score with me — with this place.

JOE: No. Not really.

LES: Rubbing it in that nobody owns you. . . . That's true: you're ownerless as a stray dog in the street. I hang on here because I've got something to hang on to. What have *you* got? The love of a family you've made miserable? The respect of your enemies, who step on your head? The conscience of a pauper? What's brought you to this pass?

JOE: I can't hope to make you understand it, Les. It's the sound of a different drummer.

307

(*He exits, right. Pause.* LES *starts to light a cigar with his new lighter,* as FERN *enters, left.*)

FERN (*exclaiming*): You have your present! Don't tell me the ceremony is all over!

LES: One, two, just like that.

FERN: Couldn't they have waited? Goodness, how annoying! Now I have to take these flowers back. (*Picks them up.*) I tried to talk things out with Chet, but it's useless. It's all for the birds, he says. You know what I'm beginning to think? He's just another one of those soreheads! And he seemed like such a serious type at bottom! I'm so relieved you spoke out! The way you stood up to Nesbit! It took moral courage!

(LES *tosses down the lighter, his cigar unlit.*)

FERN: Is something wrong, Mr. Palmer?

LES: A little let down, that's all, Fern, after a big day.

FERN: You smoke too much, Mr. Palmer. You ought to give up smoking. It isn't too hard to stop, if you make your mind up. It only takes a little moral courage. (*She dabs her eyes.*)

CURTAIN

THOUGHTS ON *THE BIG DAY*

From Prof. Robert Hethmon, University of California, Los Angeles:

> *The Big Day* is a good play. The atmosphere is well exe-
> cuted. I thought the sense of a working machine-shop is
> quite authentic. The dialog is entirely stageworthy. The
> conflicts strike me as very exciting. I mean to imply that it
> is truthful, but what it says is pretty familiar to any adult
> who has knocked around America. The picture of
> maneuvering and conniving is applicable to almost any work
> situation in an organization. There is, thus, universality, but
> it's a fairly commonplace reality. What Joe and Chet are
> fighting remains very generalized. If the situation could
> symbolize a whole social system in microcosm, that would
> give it an interest that for me it does not now have. The
> irony of giving Les congratulations and twisting his arm on
> the same day does not quite work for me: I simply take it
> for granted that any large organization or institution will
> have an ambivalent relationship to individuals within it; thus
> the irony seems a little made up for stage purposes. I would
> be interested to see the play onstage — provided you could
> cast it with people who could be believed as working stiffs.

How much did my good friend Bob Hethmon expect of a one-act
play? If *The Big Day* isn't a "microcosm of a whole social system," it at
least touches on what can happen to some of the people in that system.
Long-time security has weakened Les, while the idealism of Joe has been
purchased at the expense of his family and made him headstrong. I can't
say I admire either of my "heroes." *The Big Day* is not for people who
would rather not hear about them.

That Les gets congratulated and has his arm twisted on the same
day does not seem to surprise this particular reader because he knows
that any large organization is ambivalent. If that is so, the occasion is
all the more ironic as a stage metaphor. That the story is "pretty
familiar to any adult who has knocked around America" may be an
excellent reason for showing it to playgoers, whether or not they have
knocked around America. But I agree that the play may not be easy to
cast at a university. Not many blue-collar people are inclined to take
theatre courses.

TOWARD A LARGER THEATRE

From an ANTA WEST reader's report on *The Big Day*:

> I don't think it's a bad play: it has a certain amount of
> crude power — but I do find it hopelessly outdated. A play
> *about* the Thirties might be interesting, but this play is
> written in the *style* of the Thirties, the John Howard Lawson
> era. (And it lacks the poetic overlay of Lawson's and Odets'
> plays.) We have been over this ground so many times before it
> all seems cliche: the villainous corporation men, the malev-
> olent shop steward, the shop supervisor who caves in to
> economic pressure, etc. The "personal" story of Les and Doris
> (and Joe) is sketchily drawn and unconvincing. It has none of
> the fire that other "proletarian" writers used to summon. The
> irony of Les's job being in jeopardy on the day he is to
> receive a gift and citation for twenty years' service is too
> heavy to be effective. It simply comes off contrived.

To ANTA WEST:

It may be a coincidence, but is your reader the same one who was
so displeased by *Andrus, or the Vision*? In any case I want the names of
any plays from which I allegedly borrowed or plagiarized my cliché plot
or out-of-date characters.

I am no proletarian, and neither was Odets or Lawson. If your
reader is unhappy about not finding fire and poetry in *The Big Day*, I
can only point out that I had a different purpose in writing it — namely,
to try showing what our industrial system can do to people's minds. The
fact that this play is soberly written does not mean that it lacks its
own kind of drama — what your reader calls "a certain kind of crude
power."

As for Les risking his job on the very day he receives his gold
cigar-lighter: this is par for the course of a one-act play. I have chosen
it for the end of *The Big Day*, and am not going to change it.

PAUL THOMPSON FOREVER

1947-1950

OUTLINE

Paul Thompson, a foreman, who has just died and been laid to rest, suddenly reappears, to the consternation of his wife, Jeanie, his daughter, Carol, and his dog, Tippy. He explains bitterly that he has not yet been admitted to the Afterlife "Because they don't believe I'm me."

Enter Calkins, an investigator from the Beyond, who has the task of certifying the identity of Paul Thompson. Paul was created in the image of his Maker, but that image is no longer recognizable, and the sardonic Investigator is not easy to convince. But with the aid of a few lies by Jeanie, and her recollection of a day's joyous picnic when Paul was *least* like himself, she finally impresses Calkins. Paul will be admitted to an Afterlife as futile as himself, and he'll have to enter it through a rat-hole, but he'll enter. This sounds like doubletalk to Carol, but her father reassures her. "I know the place he means — you sit around in your stocking feet and read the funnypapers morning, noon, and night." He exits happily after Calkins.

With the visitor gone, Jeanie, relieved, tells Carol, "You think I had to wait for Calkins to tell me what to do, now that I'm a widow? The day they carried your father out of the house I had my first thought in thirty years: your Pop had made me over in the image of Paul Thompson. I'm going to make myself right back to my own image. When my time comes, I don't intend to crawl through any rathole!"

CHARACTERS

Paul Thompson
Jeanie, *his wife*
Carol, *his daughter*
Tippy, *his dog*
Mr. Calkins

The Thompson living room-dining room-kitchen. JEANIE *and* CAROL *in night dress.* JEANIE *at the table,* CAROL *at the sink.* TIPPY, *a mongrel dog, asleep.*

CAROL: How about supper, mom? I'm cooking some. You've hardly had a mouthful since the ceremonies. *(washes dishes.)*

JEANIE: This root beer will do me. (*weeping*) I'm almost cried out.

CAROL: Pop isn't the first person who ever died. Why carry on like that, Mom? Why torture yourself?

JEANIE: Your father was a good man, Carol, and don't you forget it. He worked all his life and paid every installment we owed, right on the dot.

CAROL: All right, Mom. I heard you.

(TIPPY *whines.*)

The dog is fretty. It's late. I hope Arthur put the kids to bed on time. (*Leads* TIPPY *behind dresser.*) Arthur's so useless around the house.

JEANIE: Your father was a peaceable man. He always wanted to die in his own bed, and he did, too, after the stroke, I'll never forget how he looked: he was lying there in his best suit, so peacefully, sure of the reward to come. The neighbors all came and said goodbye to him. (*Bitterly.*) The neighbors had more feeling than you.

CAROL: Quit needling me! I knew Pop better than the neighbors! You and he had fights all the time, but now that he's passed away he's full of all the virtues.

JEANIE: We never had a fight in our lives. A difference of opinion now and then —

CAROL (*calmly*): You had a fight with him on Tuesday— the very day he passed away. What was that about?

JEANIE: I didn't know you were listening. Your father was only talking loud; it was nervousness, that's all. Dying makes a man nervous.

CAROL: I never met anybody more intolerant than Pop. All his life he never thought of anybody but himself. He wasn't interested in anything. He never looked in a magazine or a book. He used to go to the movies and fall asleep — (*with genuine curiosity*) Tell me something, Mom — did you really love him?

Jeanie: That's a funny thing to ask.

Carol: I mean really? Was that real love that went on between you two?

JEANIE (*angrily*): I was his wife, wasn't I? The day we were married he and I became one, for better for worse. Of course I loved him.

315

CAROL (*unconvinced*): All right, I guess it must be so if you say so.
(*Water faucet bangs.*)
That loose washer again! Everything in this place is full of leaks and holes, everything has to be fixed, and the bugs come out of the walls and look around. I'm telling you again, Mom —

JEANIE: I don't want charity. That's the one thing I don't want.

CAROL: That's ridiculous! Staying with Arthur and me, you call that charity? You and Pop could have lived at our house, eating off our table; but no, Pop has to go and live in this dump and drag you with him. That's puffed-up pride. He hadn't had a job in years; he was living off his savings, but he still thought he was a foreman giving orders —

JEANIE: Being a foreman isn't so much. You take more orders than you give. You have to work that off some way.

CAROL: Not on your own family, you don't.

JEANIE: Where else if not on your own family? Your pop talked so loud around the house because he was timid at bottom — that's the way most people are. Sure, he was a hypocrite sometimes — who isn't? It's easy for you to talk. You can have all the ideals you want, because you don't have to pay for them like he did. (*agitated.*) I guess you think it's honest, the way you talk, but you haven't an ounce of feeling in you, and you never did have. Talking ill of the dead!

CAROL (*suddenly*): Was that a noise at the door?

(TIPPY *growls.*)

JEANIE: Talking like that about your own father, who brought you into this world! Your father who left us and is never coming back; who is gone from us forever!

(TIPPY *growls again. The door opens slowly as though by itself.* PAUL *looks in. He has on a good suit but no hat.* CAROL *sees him.*)

CAROL (*frozen*): Mom. Pop's here!

(JEANIE *looks toward the door.* TIPPY *howls.*)

PAUL (*coming in*): Tippy, quiet!

JEANIE: Oh my God, Paul — is that you? Tippy, lie down!

PAUL: Damn fool dog don't listen to me no more. (*His manner is elaborately casual.*) The sideboard — the table and the sofa — everything looks the same, but it don't feel the same. I thought I'd find you here alone, Jeanie.

CAROL: You think I was going to leave Mom alone in her sorrow?

PAUL (*curtly*): All right, Carol, (*with pretended indifference*) Eating and drinking as usual, just like nothing happened. Go ahead and don't bother about me; I ain't hungry. I won't be staying long. The Afterlife is waiting for me and I got no time to waste, so don't give me a big welcome, I don't expect it —

JEANIE: We're struck dumb with surprise, Paul, that's what it is —

CAROL: We thought you went away for good when they carried you out, Pop. All the neighbors thought so, too.

PAUL: Yeah, and that's what I thought, too. I'm not alive no more and not immortal, neither. (*with restraint*) I come back for a little while because I'm in a certain kind of a spot, that's why.

JEANIE: What kind of a spot, Paul?

PAUL (*to* CAROL): This is gonna make you happy, I know that. They're investigating.

JEANIE: Investigating?

PAUL: They don't believe it's me.

CAROL: Who don't?

PAUL: *They* don't. (*his poise beginning to go*) They stopped me at a place called the Ultimate. "You don't pass," they said. "We got to know who you are, first."

JEANIE: Oh. (*hiccups.*) It's the root beer.

CAROL: What does that mean — "Who you *are*"?

PAUL: I thought I was all set for the next world. Well, I had what they call a rude awakening. All the chosen were going on to Immortal Life, but *I* got stopped at the door. All my life every thing was against me. Now, even in the Ultimate — (*bitterly*) I got the Investigator with me.

(CAROL *and* JEANIE *exchange glances.*)

CAROL: What Investigator?

PAUL: For God's sake answer him the right way. I'm telling the both of you: if he gets the wrong idea I'm done for, understand?

JEANIE (*soothingly*): We understand, Paul.

PAUL (*goes to the door, calls*): You can come in now, Mr. Calkins — I explained it.
(*Exits.*)

CAROL (*low, to* JEANIE): Wouldn't you know it? After everything we went through — all that grief and mourning! Other people have it over with once and for all, but we —

317

JEANIE: I'm frightened, Carol, This Investigator — Pop's going to need our help. Watch out what you say!

CAROL: You expect me to lie to an Investigator from Up Above?

(TIPPY *is growling again. They break off abruptly as* PAUL *comes back.*)

PAUL: Don't mind Tippy, Mr. Calkins — he's harmless.
(CALKINS *enters. He wears a derby hat, a Chesterfield coat, and carries a neat tan briefcase.*) Jeanie and Carol, I'd like you to meet Mr. Calkins. He's the Investigator.

CALKINS: How do you do?

CAROL (*awed*): Likewise.

PAUL: Make yourself at home, Mr. Calkins. — Give Mr. Calkins a chair.

CAROL: Here you are, Mr. Calkins. — Tippy, you be quiet!

(TIPPY *complies.*)

PAUL: Have something to eat, Mr. Calkins. Give him something to eat.

CALKINS: Thank you, never mind. I'm very pressed for time.

(*They sit.*)

CAROL: We didn't expect company; please excuse the appearance.

PAUL: Carol's my daughter, Mr. Calkins. She's married to a salesman, Arthur Grable. A very fine man, let me tell you. They have two wonderful kids — (*But* CALKINS *is staring fixedly at the floor.*) It's only a bug, Mr. Calkins.

JEANIE: Just a cockroach. (*Steps on it.*)

CALKINS (*with as shudder*): Let's get down to business, shall we? My report is overdue. And I don't enjoy standing around musty hallways, as it happens. (*Takes papers out of briefcase; glumly*) Always like this: these grimy buildings, like rabbit-warrens; hordes of people standing on each other's heads; noise and dirt — (*Shakes off his mood.*) You'll all oblige me by answering questions directly, briefly and to the point. (*To* JEANIE) You believe yourself to be the wife of this man?

JEANIE (*wonderingly*): Yes sir, I am. Or was.

CALKINS: Are you sure? You've always known him to be Paul Thompson?

JEANIE: Of course it's him. It's even the way his collar climbs up around his neck.

(PAUL *instinctively straightens his collar.*)

318

CALKINS: I assume you're aware how important this interview is, madam? Your supposed husband returns from the Ultimate across the vast depths of space, and you show as much emotion as that coffee cup.

JEANIE: (with dignity) It's Paul, all right, and I'll speak for him all I can. Only don't expect me to get too emotional. I can see you're not human like us, or you'd know that after four solid days of mourning you get pretty numb for a while.

CALKINS: Hm. We'll see. (To CAROL) And you claim to be his daughter?

CAROL: Yes sir.

PAUL: There you are, Mr Calkins! And you thought I was a plain liar —

CALKINS: I don't know if you're plain or fancy. This examination is just beginning.

PAUL: But —

CALKINS (to the WOMEN): Perhaps I'd better explain this situation a little more, ladies. I am a special representative of the Ultimate.

JEANIE: You mean the Hereafter, Mr. Calkins?

CALKINS: No, the Ultimate. That's still this side of the Hereafter; it's where we do our bookkeeping, pass on credentials and so on. I'm part of the accounting department.

CAROL: That sounds awfully complicated. I thought souls were just weighed —

CALKINS: Yes, we used to weigh them in the balance. That's how we judged the Judases and Caligulas, in the old days. But that's all changed; now we have the percentage system, with all the trimmings: charts, statistics — (wryly) I still think the old way was better, but then, I'm considered an old fuddy-duddy. At any rate, four days ago this gentleman — (indicating PAUL) — appeared before us and announced himself as one Paul Thompson, lately on earth. We gave him the usual checkup — without too much cooperation from him, I regret to say. We found his memory unreliable, even refractory. We can cope with that, of course — short memories are nothing new in our experience. What troubles us about this case is something else: something that's been happening far, far too often lately — (impressively) We found Mr. Thompson unrecognizable.

(PAUL mops his face with his handkerchief, sulkily.)

CAROL: Why do you keep saying that, Mr. Calkins? Are you kidding?

CALKINS: Madam, I am not kidding, as you put it. (*Takes out paper, reads*) Here is the list of what he was endowed with: ordinary intelligence — fundamental decency — simple curiosity — native good will. That was the Paul Thompson we sent into the world. What's become of him? There isn't a single point of resemblance!

PAUL (*to the* WOMEN): That's what I'm up against with them people! I told them I had a birth certificate. "That don't prove a thing from our point of view," they say. "We've got to check up. Looks like you may be scrapped — erased forever!" (JEANIE *gasps*.) Erased! What could I do? I give them an argument. I hollered and yelled. I busted out crying. The most they could do was to let me come back here and prove it. So here I am, back across all that black and lonesome space, just a shadow of myself —

CALKINS: Let's have no more of these scenes, please — They don't impress me. (*to the* WOMEN.) I've been making a note of your testimony. As usual in such cases, it fails to settle the matter. We're concerned with a certain Paul Thompson, listed in our General Register as Index Number 41G657F330T92. Is that person and the Thompson whom you both know, one and the same? That still remains to be shown.

CAROL: I don't get it. If Paul Thompson isn't Paul Thompson, who is he?

CALKINS: That's what we should very much like to know.

CAROL: You mean to say the Ultimate doesn't know that much?

CALKINS (*nettled*.): Would I be here to search out facts if I were all-knowing? I tell you *there is no resemblance*!

CAROL: No resemblance to what, Mr. Calkins?

CALKINS: To the image, naturally.

JEANIE: The image?

CALKINS: The image of God. (*He rises*.) "And God created man in His own image, in the image of God created He him". (*He recites to music:*)

> You were made in the image of God.
> Where is that resemblance now?
> Have you damaged it, thrown it away,
> Deliberately destroyed it?

> You say you don't know?
> Ignorance is no excuse.
> Be sure you'll be held to account for it.

Don't think you can take advantage of us.
Too many people want all the credit
When they expect a reward for good works,
But blame it all on fate,
Or anything else that's handy,

When they're caught trying to get away with something.
Don't fool yourself.
Bad intentions, ignorance, apathy or stupidity —
You'll pay for them all in the end!

(*A faint sound of rolling thunder crosses overhead.* JEANIE *and* CAROL *retreat a little, while* PAUL *turns pale.*)

CALKINS: Now do you realize the gravity of the situation?

PAUL: I bet you don't make none of them bankers and brokers or stuffed shirts go through nothing like this! I bet you take *their* word for it!

CALKINS: I bet I don't.

PAUL: I want to know why I'm getting picked on. All my life I kept out of trouble and minded my own business. I was loyal to my employers and I never deserted my wife. I didn't drink or smoke too much. I kept my pants pressed and I took a bath every Saturday night. I was kind to animals and I liked baseball. I even had civic spirit: I wrote two letters to the editor of the daily paper —"How any American can lick six foreigners" and "I didn't approve of Hollywood divorces." What's wrong with that record? (*bitterly*) Just because I was a workingman, a nobody, a plain and ordinary —

CALKINS (*sharply*): You were one of the millions like you, neither more nor less important! Don't think you can weasel out of this, Mr. Thompson — You're by no means as dopey as you tried to make out all your life. I know you were loyal to your employers, you never bit the hand that fed you — but you snapped at everything else. Always looking for people you could safely kick around: the workmen in your shop, your wife and daughter —

CAROL: And he knew how to mind his own business, all right — like the time he closed his ears when Arthur was out of work and needed a loan —

JEANIE: Carol!

CAROL: Don't stop me, Mom. You can excuse him if you like — you always did; but this is the time to tell the truth. (*To* PAUL) It took Arthur and me five years to get on our feet again; we lost our car and our furniture, but you only patted Arthur on the back and said we had your good wishes. If you think *that* proves you're my father —

PAUL: You little flannel-mouth! You're my flesh and blood, sorry as I am to say it! (*To* CALKINS *shouting*) I told you who I am. I'm Paul Thompson! That's my story and I stick to it!

CALKINS: We're getting exactly nowhere! (*Takes superphone out of his inside pocket. It crackles with flame. Into phone*) Hello! Give me Long Home 4400, extention 339. Ambrose? This is Calkins. I'm delayed on the Thompson case. Yes, still; he's obstinate as a Missouri mule. How do I know how much longer it will take? (*Pause*) Don't pass the buck, Ambrose. I used to know where I was before you boys got this percentage bee in your bonnet. I took care of some of the headliners in my time, and don't you forget it — Pontius Pilate, Titus Oates — all without indexing or tabulating! (*Pause*) All right, call back. (*Puts phone back wrathfully. To* JEANIE) Mrs. Thompson, bring me the family bankbook.

PAUL (startled): The bankbook? What for?

CALKINS: To examine, of course. When other things fail, I consult the family bankbook.

JEANIE: I — everything's upset, Mr. Calkins — I don't know where I put it.

CALKINS: In the top right-handed drawer of the sideboard; that's where everybody keeps it.

(JEANIE *goes slowly to sideboard, brings the book.*)

What's the matter, Thompson? You look a little green. (*Consulting bankbook*) This little volume makes interesting reading. I find that deducting your expenses from your weekly earnings, you banked far more than the remainder. Almost one-third more. Where did the rest of it come from? (*checking his papers*) Since you won't talk I'll have to answer from my own records. That sum of money belonged to the men whom you bossed. They turned back part of their wages to you. I believe that's called a kickback, in your parlance.

PAUL: It's an old custom, Mr. Calkins, When a foreman hires you, it's a way of showing your appreciation. I used to pay kickbacks too, before I became a foreman; it's a custom, everybody knows that — (*exploding, agonized*) Money, money! All it does is make trouble — I always said that! (*To* JEANIE) I don't want my money no more — none of it! Give it away! Give it all away, you hear me?

JEANIE: I hear you — you don't have to shout. (*To* CALKINS.) He's upset, Mr. Calkins, because it was all my fault about those kickbacks. I made him collect the money.

CAROL: *You* did?

JEANIE: You shut up, Carol — you don't know a thing about it. Paul couldn't stand wringing that money out of poor workingmen and their families; it broke his heart. I forced him to it. I talked him black and blue. "Your wages don't go far enough," I said. "We have to have good furniture, a car, everything that's in the stores," I said.

CALKINS: Hm . . . you admit that?

JEANIE: I guess I'm just a poor, weak woman without moral fiber, as they say. (*Wipes her eyes.*) I'll tell you how it was. Paul was getting on in years. He'd had a stroke once before. He kept talking about how he'd have to face his Maker very soon. The kickback money was sinful, he said. He was going to give it away.

CALKINS (*dryly*): To whom?

JEANIE: To a man named Handley, that used to work in his shop.

CAROL (*astonished*): Not Joe Handley? Pop always hated him!

CALKINS: No more interruptions, please!

JEANIE: Joe was one of the people that Paul collected kickbacks from. He and Paul used to be buddies once but Joe lost his job at the shop; he was down and out and his family was suffering. Paul wanted to help him —

(PAUL *is staring at her open-mouthed. She turns her head away.*)

I just couldn't see it, that's all; we needed every cent. I told Paul, "You know you'll never have a job again, don't you, at your age? Suppose we live another thirty years, who's going to support us? Suppose one of us gets sick? And what about Carol and the grandchildren — don't they come first? They're your own flesh and blood," I said. "All in all the idea is ridiculous," I said. "All that money —

CALKINS: An idea like that is not ridiculous; it comes of a generous impulse.

CAROL: I don't agree. Why should he give his money away to strangers?

CALKINS (*glares at her; to* JEANIE): Proceed, Mrs. Thompson.

JEANIE (*blows her nose.*): There isn't much more to it. Friday morning he insisted he was going to the bank to draw out the money. We had another fight, the worst we had, and he flung out of the house in a rage. He got his last stroke on the street two blocks from here. (*tearfully*) He made me promise on his deathbed that I'd carry out his wishes.

(Pause)

CALKINS: I see. It's as you say — the whole sum of the kickback is deducted in the bankbook.

JEANIE: I guess that's all, Mr. Calkins. Except that he got two lines in the newspaper when he died — if you want to see that.

CALKINS: I never read the papers; they're full of stories that never happened in heaven or on earth, and I'm after facts, not fantasies. (*sternly*) I'm not satisfied with your testimony, madam. I won't say I consider it a tissue of lies —

JEANIE: Oh!

CALKINS: There may be a few facts in it here and there; but it's a remarkable concoction just the same. There isn't a word about this good deed in our records.

CAROL: There Mom — I told you.

CALKINS: Besides, even if this good action really happened, it came too late to be recorded. There was a time when people could afford to be nasty all their lives; they needed only to be sorry when the jig was up. We've changed all that; and may I add, *that's* the kind of reform I approve of. (*To* PAUL) You swindled your way through life, Thompson. A last-minute polishing won't remove the soot.

PAUL: Even repentance don't count no more for me! You call that fair? I may not have been no angel, but I wasn't worse than the average —

CALKINS (*losing his temper*): You've made that statement before! Don't rub it in! (*bitterly*) Time was when my job had caliber: I used to weigh heinous villainies, grand larceny, mayhem and murder. Now I'm reduced to collecting Paul Thompsons — broken-down rubbish, nonentities, hundreds of thousands of them. Up There they go on turning out a thousand souls a minute, bright as new dollars — and what for? Most of them sheer waste. Junk for the junk pile! My patience is wearing very thin!
(*He speaks, accompanied by drums and trumpets.*)
For one moment, Paul Thompson,
Life plucked you out of the dark.
What did you do with your moment?

You breathed.
You stood and you sat.
You slept and you woke and you slept again.
You ate and were hungry again.
You took sick and got well.

And so the moment passed —
The moment more precious
Than all the wealth of the world.

Here is your score in my report,
By items:
Birth, an accident.
Youth, a mistake.
Manhood, an apology
Old age, a regret.
Sum total:
In life, ridiculous,
In death, forgotten.
Humiliation without end, amen.

(*To* PAUL, *shouting*) What ticket did you vote — Republican or Democrat?

PAUL: I didn't vote in years and years. Why should I? It was all politics, anyway.

CALKINS: (*furiously*): I vote! You might call me a sort of Do-Gooder. Goodness knows, that's milk-and-watery enough — But you? Nothing! Nothing at all!

JEANIE (*to* CALKINS): What do you want him to be — a Communist?

CALKINS: No Red-baiting, please madam! His time is growing short. Better urge him to remember something — anything — that will make him recognizable. According to your story, he got into this trouble with your help, but don't think you can help him sneak out of it! (*To* PAUL) I want to know what you did with the image of your Maker. Speak up — you could bellow loudly enough when you wanted to!

JEANIE: You'll have a fit or something, Mr. Calkins, if you go on like that; you'll burst a blood vessel.

CALKINS: Don't worry about my system: I have none. It's my mind that feels the strain! (*To* PAUL) Paul Thompson — or whoever that you are — I tell you solemnly, do not harden your heart. Be not as the ass for stubbornness. Think! Try to remember!

(*A strange light grows in the room.*)

CAROL (*to* PAUl): He means it for your own good, Pop. Remember!

CALKINS: (*advancing on* PAUl): Rack your brains! It's your last hour!

JEANIE: Think, Paul!

PAUL: I can't remember! (*He struggles fearfully with himself.*) I used to be something else, a dumb kid — a pushover —

JEANIE: Oh, Paul. Paul!

PAUL: I can't remember myself no more — too far away. I'm dead now! (*The rumbling overhead comes back. The* WOMEN *spring up in terror.* TIPPY *starts to howl.*) Oh! Oh my God — I'm lost forever!

325

(*A prolonged peal of thunder. Lightning.*)

JEANIE (*screaming*): I can't stand it! Mr. Calkins! Mr. Calkins! (*Drops on her knees.*) I lied; I wanted to help Paul. Don't hold it against him. He's suffering, Mr. Calkins. Give him another chance!

CALKINS: Another chance? Another chance, Mrs. Thompson? You miss the whole point — he's had all the chances there are! It would be simple enough if there were another chance left. We could talk it over in a nice, reasonable way. We could say, "All right, Brother Thompson, that wasn't such a good try. We'll set up the pins in the next alley. Try it again — " (*He shows signs of exhaustion.*)

JEANIE: Paul didn't make the world; it was there before he was born. And no matter what you may think, his intentions —

CALKINS (*pacing the floor*): Negatives! All negatives! It's only the positive things that count now! (*Thunder dies away.*) I'm all in. I want him to get by, do you understand, my dear Mrs. Thompson? So far I've got nothing out of him — nothing! It's extraordinary — it doesn't seem possible. He *must* have done something — said something —

JEANIE (*desperately*): Something more personal, you mean?

CALKINS (*stopping*): Was he ever personal? Was there anything inside? Deep down? Was there anything besides the wise guy and the tough guy? (*earnestly*) I'm going to ask you a question, madam; you don't have to answer it if you don't want to. Take a good look at your alleged late husband.

JEANIE (*firmly*): Yes, sir. I'm looking.

CALKINS: Did you love him? The truth, this time.

JEANIE (*after a pause*): I've always said, "Of course," when I was asked that. A good wife loves her husband, and I was a good wife. But I think it was true just the same; I must have loved him.

CALKINS: Think carefully, now. Can you remember some of the occasions when you really thought that?

JEANIE: Yes, Mr. Calkins. (*slowly*) I can remember several times he said to me, "You know, you're not such a bad looker, Jeanie." He said it just like that, for no special reason.

CALKINS: Good. Go on.

JEANIE: He used to moan in his sleep, sometimes. I'd shake him and wake him up, and ask him what he dreamt. He didn't remember. But once he said to me, with the sweat pouring down him, "Jeanie I was born a man — I'm going to die a foreman."

CALKINS: (*scribbling hurriedly*): What did he mean by that?

JEANIE: I'm not sure. But I know I loved him at the moment.

CALKINS: Anything else?

JEANIE: On the day Carol was married he said to me, "Carol takes after my side of the family. I might as well admit it — "

CAROL: (*astonished; stiffly*): What was the point of that crack, Mom?

JEANIE (*not hearing her*): Then there was the day they fired him from his job; the place he worked for was closing up for good. He'd been there almost as long as we were married — knew no other place to go. He came home and piled us all into our car — Carol and the kids and me, and Tippy, the dog. We drove out to the lakeside and had ourselves a picnic. Carol took the kids in swimming and we all ate hamburgers, even Tippy. And we laughed; and on the way home we sang songs. (*Her mind is far off.*) What a happy afternoon that was!

CAROL (*angrily*): Mom, Mom — if you think you can save him with that silly gossip —

CALKINS: Hm. I suppose the next day was bad; he must have yelled at you and Carol and kicked Tippy.
    (PAUL, *his face in his hands, begins to sob quietly.*)
Just the same, Mrs. Thompson, there's something there. The last feeble traces of the image of his Maker; you've pointed them out. They're not much, but they're something. — So that was your life together! You shouldn't have nagged him all the time.

JEANIE (*in a low voice*): I didn't nag him enough. I should have nagged him into being a man, but I didn't. That was my biggest fault.

CALKINS (*looking at her*): Yes (*sighs.*) I think that will do me, Mrs. Thompson. A dreary recital, but there's something there. (*He takes a rubber stamp and stamp-pad out of his briefcase. Stamps the papers.*) He passes.

JEANIE: Oh — thank God!

PAUL: (*dazed; to* CALKINS): You — you're letting me pass?

CALKINS: Yes (*sternly*) Frankly, you wouldn't have stood a chance in the old days. But the new regime Up There — they're impressed by every tiny impulse. You didn't do too much good, but you didn't do too much harm, either: you didn't start a war, for example, or burn people in gas ovens, or misinform the public. They've fixed up a special place for people like you; you'll find it suited to your modest requirements — it's as dull as you are. And you'll enter it through a rat-hole, but you'll enter.

PAUL (*eagerly*): You hear that, Jeanie and Carol? I'm saved!

CALKINS: Yes. Saved by the percentage system! (*dourly*) There was a time when you could weigh a man right off and make up your mind about him; but today you're faced with extenuating circumstance — environmental influences — psychic traumas — factor this and factor that. All very right and proper and important. Only it's getting so you wonder if anybody is responsible anymore for anything. Passing the buck — on the biggest scale since Pontius Pilate washed his hands! (*Starts packing his briefcase angrily.*)

CAROL (*low to* Jeanie): Well, Mom — you may think it's all settled. I don't.

JEANIE: It's settled enough for me. (*Puts coffee pot on table.*)

CAROL: Sometimes I don't understand you. (*She goes to* CALKINS *determinedly.*) Where are taking him to, Mr. Calkins? Where is Pop going? Up *there* or down *there*?

CALKINS: Neither.

CAROL: Neither. What place is that?

CALKINS (*calmly*): Unless I'm much mistaken it's a place you may see for yourself some day. It's hardly worth describing. (*Superphone rings.* CALKINS *takes it out of his inside pocket.*) Hello! Yes, this is Calkins. Yes, yes, Ambrose, we're starting back right now. I'm pooped. He passed, all right. Another one of those dime-a-dozen cases. I haven't had a juicy item since Benedict Arnold! I'm fed up. Just wait till next election time, my friend. We'll bounce you out of office, the whole kit and kaboodle of you — *(Pause)* He hung up on me. (*Puts superphone back.*) Ignoramuses! Ought to give them a taste of human affairs — ought to rub their noses in it! (*To* PAUL) Time to go.

JEANIE: Won't you have some coffee first?

CALKINS: We've stayed far too long already, Mrs. Thompson. Thank you just the same, and until we meet again — if we have to —

JEANIE: You think we'll have to, Mr. Calkins?

CALKINS: That's going to depend on you, isn't it, Mrs. Thompson? You have a lot to live down, I'm afraid. (*not unkindly*) But you still have years left, madam, so take this warning in time: Life is a loan, not a gift. (*Recites to music:*)

> Your life is a loan, not a gift,
> One day you must return it,
> So use it while you can.
> Do things!
> Good things!
> Plant trees and gardens.
> Builds houses; keep them in repair —
>   (CAROL *absently turns the faucet. It bangs.*)

Fix things like that.
Have children and be kind to them.
Be kind to dogs and cats,
But not to bugs and rats.
Earn good money
Wear good clothes,
And punch bad people on the nose!

How's that for a program? Are we all agreed?
(TIPPY *barks joyously.*)
That makes it unanimous! (*Pause.*) Good-bye! Ready, Thompson?

(PAUL *follows* CALKINS *to the door. The* INVESTIGATOR *exits.*)

JEANIE: You're going away for good this time, Paul?

PAUL: Can't just be coming back on visits, you know. I got the Afterlife waiting for me. And remember, the both of you — I passed my test, so be sure and honor my memory.

CAROL: We're worried, Pop. I asked him whether you were going to be punished or rewarded, and he gave me doubletalk.

PAUL: You can quit worrying right now. I know all about the place he means — I picked up that information while I was hanging around outside them doors up there. It'll be an easy life — you sit around in your stocking feet and read the funny papers, morning, noon and night. Yessir, it's gonna be perfect. (*To* JEANIE.) I got by fine, but it's just as well you spoke up, Jeanie; you were helpful.

JEANIE: That's good.

PAUL: All you got to do from now on is lead a good, careful life, the way I did, and you'll get by, too.

JEANIE: I keep thinking about that rat-hole.

PAUL: Don't worry about it. I'll crawl through, all right. Everything's turned out fine — I'm saved, I'm gonna continue! (*happily*) So long, Jeanie, Carol, and Tippy. I feel like a million. Like that day — the day of the picnic!

JEANIE ⎱
⎰ (*together*): Good-bye, Pop.
CAROL ⎰

(TIPPY *barks furiously.* PAUL *exits. The door closes behind him.* TIPPY *subsides into a faint growl. Music lingers like an echo.*)

CAROL: Well, they're gone. Whew! That awful Calkins —

JEANIE: He had me shaking like a leaf. But he had a soft heart after all.

329

CAROL: He's like all those reformers — it's his head that's soft, not his heart. Why should somebody like Pop go on forever? (*marveling*) The lies you told for his sake! Saying Pop ordered you to return that kickback. You lied to Calkins — You put your immortal soul in danger for the love of somebody like Pop!

JEANIE: I stuck up for your father, because I loved him; even if I didn't love him the way they do in the movies, in technicolor, with music. I never thought he was perfect. Even when he was dying he was stubborn: I begged him to even up the score by giving Joe the kickback money, but he wouldn't hear of it. That's why he was cussing so before he died. (*quietly*) Joe is going to have that money. I took it out of the bank today to give him.

CAROL (*alarmed*): What now? Are you going to carry Pop's order to give away his money? He was only showing off in front of Calkins. "Throw it all away!" he says. What does *he* care about money — now that he's dead?

JEANIE: I'm not going to give it *all* away — don't worry; I'm not headed for a charity home. Paul's gone and provided for, but I still have a life to lead. You can't lead a decent life and be dependent. I ought to know. (*Feelingly*) You think I had to wait for Calkins to come and tell me what to do, now that I'm a widow? The day they carried your father out of this house I had my first thought by myself in over thirty years; that's when I saw it clear as day — your Pop had made me over in the image of Paul Thompson. I'm going to make myself right back to my own image — the image I was born with. When my time comes I don't intend to crawl through rat-holes! (*Tranquilly*) Pass the cream and sugar, Carol.

CURTAIN

CASTING

Carol is in her thirties, a young matron who tries to live down her parents, Jeanie and Paul, in public. She is a little in awe of her mother. She never liked Paul, but her hostility is tempered by the fact that he was her father and that he has just died. She is self-assertive and capable. Wears a good house dress.

Jeanie is between fifty and sixty, a hard-working woman capable of lying with a straight face. Loyalty to her husband, Paul, is the keynote of her character, but by no means a blind loyalty. There is a dry humor about her. She wears an old wrapper.

Paul, Jeanie's husband, a foreman, is heavy and heavy-handed, self-centered, self-pitying and incorrigible. His complexion is ruddy. He wears his best store clothes, rather old-fashioned. A stiff collar, heavy shoes.

Calkins is a prim social-worker type — at least that is the first impression he makes. His clothes are old-fashioned: a derby hat and an old-time Prince Albert under an overcoat with velvet lapels, a wing-collar shirt with cuffs, and a black four-in-hand tie. He has a judicial mind but with it an irascibility that at times rises to Old Testament wrath. He comes down to the footlights for his recitations, which he delivers straight to the audience. His superphone is the speaking-and-receiving end of an ordinary phone, painted silver or otherwise tricked up; it hangs on a hook under his left armpit, between his vest and his jacket.

Tippy is any dog, not too big, the more mongrel the better. He is tied on a leash upstage of the dresser, and Carol quietly leads him behind the dresser and hands him, unseen, to the prop man, after her line, "Arthur's so useless around the house." The audience thinks Tippy has retired to his box; but he continous to be heard on cue. His "lines" are recited for him by someone with the requisite talent.

331

THOUGHTS ON *PAUL THOMPSON FOREVER*

To a play publisher who liked, but rejected, this play because "Plays on the theme of death, like *The Shadow Box*, are losing their popularity," I wrote "I hope you are right that plays on the theme of death are losing their popularity. Only I am startled to hear that *Paul Thompson Forever* is in that category. I wrote it as a farce-comedy, even though it takes place immediately after a funeral. Death is not its theme, and no one in our audiences thought of it that way".

Paul Thompson Forever, published by Walter Baker, Inc. in 1950, had a preface that related, "This is the first work by the internationally distinguished scenic designer. In this delightful social fantasy the newly found playwright brings a fresh fund of human understanding and wit to a grateful stage." I was more than gratified about *Thompson* until some time in the seventies, when I wrote to Baker ordering a few copies of the play and was told that it has long been out of print. However, the publishers were happy to learn of my whereabouts because they owed me a few royalties. I have no idea who had ordered any copies of the play, let alone who produced it. Whoever they were, I salute them for their open minds.

TOWARD A LARGER THEATRE

The fish is in the water and
the water is in the fish.

— Arthur Miller

A Southern university reader's report on *Rainbow Terrace* was tabulated in questionnaire form:

	Poor	Fair	Good	Strong
Originality of basic idea				✓
Basic theatrical value of script				✓
Believability of characters				✓
How interesting is the plot?				✓
How effective is the dialogue?				✓
Quality of the playwright's style				✓
Reader's level of willingness to work with this script to help produce it				✓
Relative degree of audience interest			✓	
Your opinion of the overall worth of this script				✓

This was followed by:

"Recommended for others to read? Yes.

Recommended to keep in the running? Yes.

Other remarks, comments, problems, question? Excellent play — have some reservations about doing it under our auspices."

*   *   *

The *envoie* about "our auspices" is refreshing compared with the large number of favorable readers' comments followed by "Unfortunately it won't do for our next season" — meaning that the play won't do for next season or any other season.

From Stanley Young, Executive Director, ANTA (American National Theatre and Academy, New York):

> You should be aware that of over 350 scripts your play *Rainbow Terrace* was within the top contenders for final consideration.

From John B. Welch, Baker's Plays (Boston, Mass.):

> We have met with our staff of readers for a discussion of Gorelik's plays and we are led to believe that he is a writer of great passion and with a strong ability for play structure.

335

TOWARD A LARGER THEATRE

From William Shorr, Pilgrim Theatre Co. (Aspen, Colorado):

> Re *Yes and No*, *The Big Day*, and *The Feast of Unreason*: in each case the readers found the plays fast paced, with well-defined characters, and most importantly concerned with issues of importance.

From Dr. Marta Feuchtwanger, University of Southern California:

> I think every one of your plays could bear the title *Yes and No*. There is much of the social critic one found in Odets' plays, but not their violent injustice, and one can find much of the humane understanding which makes the plays of Chekhov so endearing. I am truly grateful that you let me read them. I repeat I found all three plays gripping and suspenseful.

In the light of these and of similar compliments that I have quoted, I was naive enough in the 60's to think *Rainbow Terrace*, at least, would be sought out immediately by any leading professional or academic theatre that hears about it. I was mistaken. I can testify that the adventures of a "budding" dramatist like myself are as hectic as a ride on a roller-coaster.

The reward for virtue in a playscript can consist of a prompt rejection. Nothing can match a script, or even a whole stage production, for evoking differences of opinion, from high praise to harsh reproof — and for an utmost variety of reasons, some justified, and some because of prejudices that may have nothing at all to do with the merits of the case.

From a New York play agent:

> I'm sorry to say that I just don't think we would have luck finding a producer for your plays.

From a Hollywood play agent:

> None of this material is of any interest to me.

From a Broadway producer:

> Your play is written with an extremely heavy hand, and the characters are terribly uninteresting.

It is evident that my scripts are of a kind whose right to be seen onstage has to be defended — even when their merit is appreciated.

From Robert Snook, Cleveland Playhouse (Cleveland, Ohio):

> *Andrus, or the Vision* is a most intriguing script, but we do not feel it is right for this theatre.

From Lynn Holst, Literary Manager, Play Department, New York Shakespeare Festival:

> Mr. Papp has asked me to return your play, *Rainbow Terrace*, to you. I'm sorry to say he didn't feel it's for him, but appreciated the chance to consider it. It's a very interesting piece. Thanks for sending it in.

From Dr. Horace Robinson, University of Oregon (Eugene, Ore.):

> I hope you will pardon the length of time we held the copy of your play, *Rainbow Terrace*. I wanted my entire directorial staff to have a chance to read it. I found it a deeply moving play, but I think it presents a problem in casting for the average college theatre. There is a maturity and perception in the characters which it would be difficult for undergraduates to handle. My other directors made such comments as "The dialog is clean and pointed," "The character is fully developed. Ideal for a civic theatre." I am sure that this will be a play to be reckoned with and we will watch its progress with great interest.

The need for great acting has never prevented any university theatre from doing Shakespeare credibly. Nor does *Rainbow Terrace*, whose style is that of ironic farce comedy, require all that much acting in depth. More important for *RT* is a director with a live sense of humor, provided it isn't "college" humor.

From Prof. Marston Balch, Tufts University (Medford, Mass.):

> In reporting that *Rainbow Terrace* did not impress my colleagues, who are younger by 15 or 20 years, I must add that I personally am drawn to this kind of play but I confess that it dates me. I agree that it is thought-provoking; my difference happens to be that the thoughts it provokes have already gone through the mill and are no longer provocative — to me.

There is no doubt that this play dates both Prof. Balch and me. I think, however, that it dates me ahead as well as in the past. I have lived through nine-days-wonders on the stage. They have come and gone, but the ancient art of drama remains — and lends its support to those who seek to know more about the forces that shape our lives. And having witnessed the enthusiasm of our students for *RT* at Southern Illinois I do not accept the opinion that it is of no interest to younger people. What comedy, before now, has pictured the sort of man who creates a God in his own image? This is part of the issue presented by the God Is Dead movement that is agitating some of the modern clergy and their congregations.

TOWARD A LARGER THEATRE

From Dr. Samuel Selden, chairman, Department of Theatre Arts, University of California, Los Angeles, June 1966:

> At last I am glad to write you about *Rainbow Terrace* and assure you that it has had a good reading by the staff of our department.
>
> I am not so happy to have to tell you about the decision by the staff. The play aroused plenty of interest, but the department has decided not to produce it — at least at the present time. The response to it was somewhat mixed. The negative comments were summed up in two phrases: "too bitter" and "rather bald." I shall have to confess that in this part of the country which tends toward a rather cynical view of present American life there is this kind of response to your comment on middleclass materialism. However, there it is . . . Personally I am very much interested in *Rainbow Terrace* and I hope strongly that I will be able to see it on the stage one of these days . . . I am returning the script to you with thanks from all of us for giving us an opportunity to get acquainted with it.

Press review, November 19, 1966, by Ben Gelman, drama critic of *The Daily Southern Illinoisan,* describing the premiere of *Rainbow Terrace* at Southern Illinois University:

> Whether or not you have serious thoughts about God and religion — and that includes just about everyone — you cannot fail to be highly entertained by Mordecai Gorelik's new play, *Rainbow Terrace.*
>
> The tragi-comedy about an American businessman's trials and tribulations in a modern version of Purgatory was enthusiastically applauded Nov. 18 by a world-premiere audience of 500 at Southern Illinois University's new $1 million playhouse.
>
> Although the plot of the drama is obviously fantasy, it falls within Gorelik's own definition of "realism" in theater because it deals with a subject — "How is man to be judged for his actions?" — which is of concern to most people in the real world outside the theater.
>
> The play opens with Vern Falkimer — played by Paul Mann — a former manufacturer of a souped-up fruit juice tonic called "Viogen," awakening in "Long Home" with his wife Belle after a car accident took their lives.
>
> A dynamic figure on Earth, Falkimer carries his aggressive business methods right with him into the After-life.
>
> He finds both his younger son, Danny — killed in the Korean War, and his former mistress, Lottie Aldrich, in "Long Home."

His plan is to take them and his wife along with him to "Glory" — Heaven — where he believes he should have been sent in the first place.

He attempts to set up a "Viogen" distributorship in "Long Home," although no money is allowed there and despite the fact that experiments in his basement are beginning to show that fruit juice will not ferment in the After-life.

A prudent man, he had thoughtfully set in motion a series of intercessory prayers before his death which he hopes will help pave his way to "Glory."

What happens to Falkimer as he pursues this course, while straining at the too-quiet existence in the cottage on the quiet residential street of "Rainbow Terrace," is both hilarious and curiously disquieting.

Do you think of God as a big, kind hearted man with a long beard? Or are you confusing him with Santa Claus, as one of the angels in the play suggests Falkimer is doing?

You may want to re-examine your feelings and beliefs after seeing how Falkimer fared.

While Gorelik gets triple credit for writing, designing and directing the play, the success of the production also is due to the outstanding performance of Paul Mann in the leading role, with excellent support by a cast of SIU students and faculty.

It is the contention of "epic theater" supporters like the late Bertolt Brecht — who was a close friend of Gorelik — that a theater audience can be entertained at least as well by a play which examines an important religious, social or political issue as by a light farce or musical which has "nothing to say."

Rainbow Terrace, as presented at SIU, bears out this contention all the way.

While tickling the fancy of its viewers and often shocking them into laughter about concepts usually taken up only in church sermons, the play brings out into the open many of the inconsistencies of our religious thinking. Not only does the former businessman protagonist of the play question traditional moral concepts, but the very angels who are assigned to judge him find themselves in dissension in "Long Home," Gorelik's aptly titled version of new Purgatory.

TOWARD A LARGER THEATRE

From Dr. William Longman, First Christian Church, (Carbondale, Ill.), in a pastoral letter, November 1966:

> Vern Falkimer is certain that God will stick by him and get him promoted to "Glory." After all, hadn't he dedicated himself to the One Above in his business ventures while on Earth? "With Him as your backer there can be no such word as fail!" "Are you sure it isn't Santa Claus you're thinking of, rather than the Creator of all things?" an angel asks Vern. How often do we think of God according to what He can do for us instead of what we can do for Him? One of our deceptions is a God created in our own image.

From Dr. Harry T. Moore, Professor Emeritus, Southern Illinois University:

> *Rainbow Terrace* is a beautiful and effective play, and we must thank you for a wonderful evening in the theatre. At times the play has a Shavian quality; it is good and witty, and you had a good part of the audience chuckling or laughing outright most of the way through. The production was brilliant; Paul Mann gave it a fine pace, and the rest of the cast seemed as good to me as I have ever seen in a college production; they have been magnificently directed . . . The play is full of living people and vital problems, and the portrait of Falkimer is a notable one.

I offer, now, the comments of two of the people invited by my university to see the stage production. Their reservations, it seems to me, bring up some of the most disputed issues in the art and practice of theatre. They were William Krasner, of *Transaction* Magazine and Henry Hewes, of *The Saturday Review*. First, Krasner:

> Vernon Falkimer is the hero — in fact the nucleus — of Mordecai Gorelik's new, spectacular and absorbing play, *Rainbow Terrace*.
>
> Is God a kind of Santa Claus — or some sort of chairman of the board of a heavenly chamber of commerce? Or is He still the Old Testament God who judges and will not be mocked? How responsible is a man for his actions? And will he be punished if he transgresses?
>
> It is a very serious and laudable thing when a play — especially with many theatrical virtues — not only tackles great moral problems but throws itself into them. This play vibrates with excellence like an overfull corn-popper. The design and staging are very impressive. The dialog is sharp, pungent, and revealing — a remarkable achievement for an author's first full-length play. Bits of vivid theatre, speech and character are thrown about as though from a bottomless

340

source. But viewed as a whole, the play's flaw becomes apparent. It is the basic pitfall facing any message play that the characters will develop not into human beings but into an illustration for an argument.

Although he seems about to do it several times, Vern Falkimer never really acquires three dimensions. His defenses, rationalizations and justifications are one by one torn away; he faces a series of revelations about himself that would have broken Oedipus down early; but his behavior does not seem to change — except that he gets more harassed.

We don't know his underlying motivations; we don't sense much, if any, internal struggle or doubt. We get glimpses; he tells his mistress how he needs her in tones beyond those of an older man lusting for a younger woman; in a peculiar halting fashion he answers questions about his childhood — and it is possible that there is an abandoned, intensely lonely and driven boy back there, striking back, reaching for an all-powerful and all-accepting father to fill the vacuum.

But this is treated as an alibi; the playwright is pursuing his demon, the man who confuses God with Santa Claus. There are angelic arguments on both sides; but Brother Morias, the black angel who presides at the tribunal, shuts it off by pointing out that other men had bad childhoods without doing bad deeds, and he purges all dissenting angels like a Stalin of the Afterlife. At the climax Falkimer calls on God to strike down his "persecutors" — the angels who have condemned him — in accents more desperate, but otherwise not much different, from those he used earlier.

Like Jacob, Mordecai Gorelik wrestled with the angel and was lamed. But this was only after he had won a partial victory. And it is perhaps the kind of laming that only comes from wrestling with the divine, and is the mark of it.[16]

From Hewes:

Since Mr. Gorelik means his play to be a satire, he has drawn Falkimer as a ridiculously deluded man. Unfortunately, the audience tends not to regard him so. Rather he emerges as a near tragic figure, a powerful representative of his society, unfairly treated by a callous God. This may be partly because the university has augmented its student company with a professional, Paul Mann. Although his appearance as Falkimer is droll, his performance seems deeply motivated and powerful. However, one suspects that some of the fault is with a script in which the crass, repulsive hypocrite we meet at the beginning of the action becomes the only character strong enough to rebuke God for having placed him in the position He did.

The play is also weakened by a contrived subplot involving insurrection within the administration of angels, and one suspects that *Rainbow Terrace* might have been more effective as a drama focussing solely on the social forces that created such a protagonist. In attempting to be all-inclusive, it has become somewhat inconclusive. As it stands, the play is still a substantial creation. The religious attitude of Falkimer is indeed interesting. One angel argues that since most of Falkimer's life was hardworking and joyless, and since he never attempted anything seriously illegal, he hardly deserves severe punishment. Isn't that a point of view that gives comfort to many moderns?

Finally, Mr. Gorelik has the head angel affirm human responsibility for not finding a better way of life. But the same angel also criticizes God for condemning human beings He has failed to make intelligent enough to deal with the world He created. "Eat or be eaten!" — If you had created the foundations of a place like that, could you sit forever smelling incense while the angels sing "Holy, holy, holy,"? These qualities are valuable. And as other directors elsewhere mount different productions of the play it may well acquire a fuller theatricality to go with its challenging but as yet too ambiguous and diffused content.[17]

It is evident that both Krasner and Hewes took *Rainbow Terrace* seriously. It is also clear, however, that neither reviewer was able to fit it into an accustomed pigeonhole. A dramatist who has anything of real substance in his play, these days, must expect to run risks with critics whose way of thinking has hardened. (Our audiences at Southern Illinois University had no such problem.)

Krasner thinks of *Rainbow Terrace* in terms of tragedy as defined in the classroom: he asks for more depth psychology and an "inner" change in Vern Falkimer — "harassment" is not enough. To my mind Vern's tragic disillusionment at losing the support of his private God is change enough. If Vern remains incorrigible to the bitter end, that is basic to his nature and basic to the genre of the play, which is that of a satiric tragi-comedy. Nor is there any need for a burden of depth psychology in this style. You won't find it in any comedy from Moliere to Brecht.

It would be interesting to know who "tipped off" Hewes that I set out to write a cheap farce about a funny character, and that Mr. Mann turned the play into something more important and persuaded the audience to accept his version. Nothing in the script supports such a notion. I wrote Falkimer not as "droll" or as a "crass, repulsive hypocrite" but as a man of impressive human dignity in spite of his lies, his hypocrisy, his headlong self-righteousness and his infantile religious notions. Perhaps Hewes does not believe such a combination exists, but I consider it a very real American phenomenon. And it is precisely someone who is not a good man who would revile God for refusing to come up to expectations.

Why the dissension among the angels should be labeled a "contrived subplot" that weakens the play is past my understanding. A basic disagreement Up There has been known, before now, to acquire a political dimension, as when Lucifer was ousted from Heaven. When someone like Vern must be judged, the basis of that judgment becomes a major issue. The play could become "conclusive" only by becoming completely arbitrary. I do not find it "ambiguous" that Morias, who orders Vern to be "dispersed," at the same time wonders about God's responsibility for part, at least, of Vern's guilt. It is Morias's problem that he is a liberal judge who must pass sentence according to the statutes, but who does so with a sense of futility and uneasiness. Some such qualms overcome even earthly judges.

Part of Hewes' review relies on evidence unsupported by the playscript, by its production, or by its reception by our university people and townspeople. His conclusion — that I ought to have written a different kind of play — is immaterial and irrelevant.

From John Howard Lawson, dramatist:

Rainbow Terrace is an exciting theatre experience. I saw the play twice, once at the world premiere and again a few nights later: on both occasions it moved the audience to ready laughter, and at the same time it *moved* and troubled the spectators in a way that both deepened and contradicted the laughter. The double quality of the play — the comic surface and the darkness beneath the surface — is ironic and tragic, and is understood in both aspects by the audience. This is rare in contemporary "serious" drama, which all too often substitutes pretentious "problems" for theatrical vigor.

Rainbow Terrace asks questions about moral values, business practice, God and Purgatory — questions that cannot be answered — even the angels are caught in a mystery they cannot solve. But even in Purgatory there is sex and drunkenness and foolish dreams, and a desperate search for dignity and love. The enigma centers on the character of Vernon Falkimer, ridiculous in his illusions, his faith in a God who resembles Santa Claus, his moral blindness — yet the final judgment which condemns Vern to destruction is tragic and terrible, because it concerns us all, our world, our values.

343

TOWARD A LARGER THEATRE

From R. Buckminster Fuller, scientist:

> In Mordecai Gorelik's play *Rainbow Terrace*, Paul Mann stars in a superbly convincing manner as Vern Falkimer, archetype of the business breed. Gorelik succeeds convincingly in presenting the successful self-deceit of "enlightened selfishness" and its credo of an ever benevolent, accommodating, wheeling and dealing, rationalizing and exclusively personal God. None have succeeded as has Gorelik in portraying the ultimately almost contagious fervor of the selfishly enlightened entrepreneur as has Gorelik — even as shown in the final grief of Mrs. Falkimer which manifests Gorelik's doubt regarding his own justice, wisdom and magnanimity in exercising his playwright's privilege to sentence the entrepreneur's soul to absolute extermination during the wait list period in the suburbs of heaven, as Falkimer's private God forsakes him.[18]

I have said that a playreader should know how to read playscripts— but his responsibility does not end there. He should learn to recognize dramatic talent even when it accompanies a theme excluded by Broadway or by our present *avant garde*. He can then find that the script is obviously "not right for us" or will not do "under our auspices."

From the Henschel Verlag, publishers, East Germany:

> Unfortunately we see no chance for *Rainbow Terrace* on our stages. We are in accord with our play readers that, in its theatrical form, this piece is certainly very attractive and stageworthy, but because of its basic concept it can scarcely mean anything to an audience in the D.D.R.

From the Habimah Theatre, Israel:

> We have read your play *Rainbow Terrace* with great interest and are deeply impressed by this theatrical creation. We found that you approached this most interesting subject with great art and skill. Taking into consideration that we are the *National Theatre of Israel* and to touch such subjects is still very problematic in Israel — we came to the conclusion that it would not be wise to produce a play which deals with such a topic.

Understandably neither Israel nor East Germany, however their official rules on theatre may differ, can afford to arouse the passions of the orthodox, who may view a work like *Rainbow Terrace* (very unjustly) as "approaching religion with levity." Less excusable is the self-censorship of the theatre of the U.S., which has decreed that only domestic drama or psychopathology — both in a vacuum — are permissible onstage.

From the literary manager of a New Jersey foundation for the encouragement of new playwrights, to whom I submitted outlines of *Yes and No* and *RT*:

> Quite frankly neither of the pieces interest us enough to ask you to send completed scripts. Since ours seems to be a very non-political and disengaged age, we are currently looking for pieces that stress the debilitating ennui that most Americans suffer from. Plays about radical idealism really don't seem to shed the light that's needed.[19]

Dear Literary Manager:

You write that you are looking for "pieces that stress the debilitating ennui that most Americans suffer from." I find it pathetic that this sorry picture of a spiritless America is the best that our theatre has to offer. What must one think of a theatre that finds no room for any insight into the forces that shape the lives of its audience? If it has nothing more revealing to show, if it cannot even shake off its lethargy, you can truly assert that our conventional theatre, along with its advance guard, has "lost the name of action."

When I entered the theatre, in 1920, it could boast that it specialized in themes the movie dared not touch. The opposite is now true. I don't have to name the hundreds of outstanding films and TV plays, documentaries, educational films and other kinds of productions dealing with events and issues of public importance — even very controversial ones — at a time when our theatre fare is restricted to family troubles, weird characters and kinky adaptations of Shakespeare and the Greeks.

We live in the most dramatic era in all history, but you'll find almost no awareness of it whatever in our present-day theatre. To turn from the front page of any newspaper to the nearest playhouse is to enter a Never-Never Land. Here there are no echoes of economics, politics, religion or industry, no reference to war, world famine, new diseases, inflation, rampant crime, including rape, murder and incest, no thought of unemployment, poverty, vandalism, drug addition, world-wide terrorism, financial fraud or default, political corruption, racism (including the Nazi abomination), ecological poisoning, the energy crisis, the population explosion, insect plagues, urban decay, or the immanent possibility of the destruction of the planet Earth with everything living on it.

If the contemporary theatre is in flight from the onrush of all these perils, it is even more curious that it also ignores the astonishing achievements of this century — the revolution in physics, the almost miraculous advance in medicine (especially in surgery), of technology (especially in microelectronics), the exploration of the ocean depths (along with the recovery of riches from ships submerged for centuries), the thrilling voyages of our astronauts, the new astronomical instruments probing far beyond all past limitations.

Today's playgoers are put off and even alarmed at the suggestion that people are imprisoned by the social, political and economic regions in which we all exist. A young professor at a Hawaiian college writes, about two of my plays:

> *The Big Day* and *The Feast of Unreason*, although technically well-wrought, lack something. Human behavior (free action) is too strictly limited by economic and socio-political "realities." I am too much the poet and rebel to accept the worlds these characters find themselves in.

My reply: I agree that "human behavior is too strictly limited by economic and socio-political realities." I question only the quotation-marks around the word "realities." These realities, alas, are only too real for the everyday people who interest me and about whom I write.

Early in his career Harold Clurman made an observation that surely merits a place in Bartlett's *Quotations:* "There is no enemy in the middleclass world except an intangible 'fate': there is no fight except with one's own contradictions — and real life enters upon the scene like a fierce and unexplained intruder.[20]

A true pathos inheres in this poetic statement, made in the depths of the American Depression. The "intruder" is the unrelenting pressure of political economy (*a.k.a.* socio-economics), which can tie up people before they even know what's happening to them. If that "fierce and unexplained" horror is allowed to intrude onstage, let it at least be draped in a classical Greek toga, disguised as "fate."

From Dr. Marjorie Smith, California State University, Los Angeles:

> I am very impressed, first of all, with the quality of the dialog in both *The Big Day* and *Yes and No:* the language, the build and flow of thought between characters, appears natural and very convincing as individual patterns of speech. I also think there is great merit and potentiality in the personal conflicts and intimate human interrelations reflected in both plays.
>
> The conflicts and confrontations of Les and Joe in *The Big Day* are excellent when they are *personally* revealed or centered, but now and then they do sound like "agents" with a message. For example, I think Fern is really believable, but I am unprepared for her "My brother Clive died fighting for his country while you sat there making a good salary all through the War." To me your truly great strength of conflict in human relationship (Ibsenesque) is in conflict with the larger social canvas (Brechtian).

In *Yes and No* the characters of Don, Ruth, Larry, Murchison, Dale, the Commune and Scorpions appear, by contrast, to be a more melodramatic and villainous set of "agents" — and therefore unconvincing. The basic conflicts between Don and Larry are promising and meaningful but there is never any real confrontation between them — of any length onstage — and I'm caught between the *personal* inner-workings of Don and Larry (two darned good characters) and a thesis expose of Corby-America.

Although this is a sympathetic review is warns repeatedly that my characters must not lapse into becoming "agents with a message." "Your truly great strength of conflict," writes Dr. Smith, "is in *human* relationship. Ibsenesque." But Ibsen was a target for abuse in his lifetime because he drew no line between personal conflicts and their origin in public issues. The middleclass audience, as much today as ever, is sensitive to the acrid smell of the fierce intruder, and will detect his presence even in plays about the social problems of the American past, as in Miller's *The Crucible* during the Joe McCarthy era.

From a theatre professor at the State University of New York (Albany):

I liked your play, *Rainbow Terrace* although I found some of it a little too sit-com. The central issue, though, held me, and I even wish you had developed the agon-dialectic more fully than you did. I can't help thinking more might be added to Vern's "case" in terms of his representing something rather like the life force (albeit of a crass, de-spiritualized society, if not the world).

I: Only I wonder if Vern isn't "a crass life force" already, without the label.

From an associate producer of a Broadway musical, I received an urgent advice not to tell any of my readers how to think:

It is dangerous, I think, to *tell* the reader how he should accept the play, The undersigned, for example, hasn't found *Rainbow Terrace* satirical or a single funny line in it. As a producer, what I'm always looking for in a play is a character I care for, care about — the one I'm either rooting for or find loathsome on a grand scale (*Richard III*). Sadly what I found lacking in *Rainbow Terrace* is even one person I cared for. They are all such singularly unattractive people — all lower-middle class stock characters — the abrasively bombastic husband, the sniveling, "hurt-Pekinese-eyed" wife, the morose son, the vacuous mistress, a covey of cretinic pedants (dressed up as angels) and served up with a gravy made up of an assortment of delivery boys, appliance repairmen — all seen a hundredfold on our stages and more attractively so. What I'm

> trying to say, dear Mr. Gorelik, is that your stage characters
> must be larger than life. Venom or shouting does not make
> stage characters large.

From Harold Clurman, drama critic and director:

> I read your play, *Rainbow Terrace* with interest. I agree with
> Abbott that its chances on Broadway are very slim. This is a
> play for an adventurous repertory company.
>
> I had some little difficulty in accepting the premise even as
> fantasy or theatrical metaphor, but given such acceptance,
> which an audience is likely to grant you, the play is amusing
> and well written. Thanks for letting me read it.

Translated: Maybe o.k. for an unsophisticated audience.

As taught in our schools, drama deals only with individuals.
Shakespeare is revered for his insight into human behavior; but the fact
that his *personae* emerge from a historic context is of no interest.
"Denmark's a prison," says Hamlet, and the problem in class is to learn
how to speak that line. That "Something is rotten in the state of
Denmark" is taken to mean nothing more than that the King, Queen and
Polonius are no-good people. The students don't even wonder why
Fortinbras and his army belong in this story.[21]

Another of our most favored dramatists is Anton Chekhov, the
kindly biographer of the pre-Soviet Russian middleclass. His plays are
limited entirely to the private anguish of his provincial characters, with
no mention of the events that were shaking the very foundations of the
Russian *vlast* (government): inflation, food shortages, strikes, peasant
unrest, Tsarist censorship and arbitrary jailings, student agitation, and
anti-Tsarist riots and terrorism, the massacres of Russian Jews, the
oncoming humiliation of the war with Japan, the outbreak of world war
and of the Bolshevik revolution. Weighed down by personal anxieties,
Chekhov's people talk of some sort of indefinite "work" as their
salvation:

> Vershinin, in *The Three Sisters*: The only thing we must
> do is to work and keep on working.
> Irina: The time will come when everyone shall know the
> reason why people must suffer . . . We must work, we
> must only work.
> Tuzenback: This longing for work, oh, dear God in
> Heaven, how dear that is to me![22]

The soul-searching of Chekhov's *Three Sisters* may differ from the
sad vaudeville of Beckett's *Waiting for Godot*, but both are safe from
being dismissed as "problem plays" that look to the influence of social
problems on individuals or groups instead of viewing "man as a private
entity." To this argument Arthur Miller has replied succinctly:

I hope that I have made one thing clear, and it is that society is inside of man and man is inside society, and you cannot even create a truthfully drawn psychological entity on the stage until you understand his social relations and their power to make him what he is and to prevent him from being what he is not. The fish is in the water and the water is in the fish.[23]

*   *   *

A correspondence more than forty years ago between Robert Edmond Jones and myself concerning my book, *New Theatres for Old* (then about to be published) soon turned into a discussion on the future of the American theatre. Bobby had no sympathy with my contention that the theatre should reflect the age of science — that in fact it had already started to do so. He retorted, "The theatre of the age of science is drawing to a close and a new theatre is about to begin that has no relation to scientific laws. You will live long enough to see this new theatre rise up."[24]

Bobby was enthusiastic about Wilfrid's "color organ," which projected abstract patterns of color, as an example of what was coming; and he confused the theatre of the scientific age with the bygone theatre of naturalism. But he was certainly accurate in his prophecy: what "rose up" was an irrational theatre of absurdism and ritual.

Vital, peppery, and boyishly romantic, Jones called for "ecstasy" in the theatre; he maintained that "poets are the best reporters" and he cherished dreams, which he said were realer than working life. I am not sure, though, that he would have cherished the absurdists, with their sad vaudeville of "the human condition"; and, New Englander that he was, he might not have recognized orgiastic frenzy as a proper substitute for ecstasy.[25]

Nor would he ever have agreed with Antonin Artaud, patron saint of absurdism, that dramatists do not belong in the theatre. "Those human snakes," as Artaud described them, offend the purity of theatre and the stage. (And he did not mean only the hack playwrights of the Paris boulevards, but the greatest masters of the dramatic medium in all history.)

When Artaud called for "a theatre in which the verbally oriented actor would be retrained as an "athlete of the heart" [not of the brains]. Tom O'Horgan obliged as an "athlete of the heart" by creating a hugely successful spectacular, *Jesus Christ Superstar*, that not only outraged conservative Christians but brought forward once more the notion of Jewish collective guilt for the bloodcurdling crucifixion of Jesus. It evidently did not count that the Catholic Church had finally disowned this atrocious libel after two thousand years. "I just like to stir people up," explained this director.[26]

TOWARD A LARGER THEATRE

In 1969, *Masque*, an Australian magazine to which I had contributed, sent me for comment a published debate between one of Australia's best-known dramatists and myself. Alan Seymour (author of *The One Day of the Year*) had been "carried away" by sensuous, ritualist staging, to the point where he called it "one of the most exciting and profoundly innovative movements we have ever seen in the history of theatre." His essay closed with a plea on behalf of dramatic writing: "I ask only that we be allowed to include some words with the music of the anti-verbal theatre, for the words may help a little in the turbulent times ahead, when we may need all the help we can get."[27]

What a picture! The dramatist, hat in hand, begging to add a few words! Hoping for some little place in the triumphal advance of irrational theatre!

Why did a gifted writer like Seymour allow himself to be trampled on? The work of the playwright consists, not of adding words to a theatrical event, but of creating and channeling a dramatic *action*, using all the elements of staging in order to make a meaningful statement to an audience. The dramatic writer is scarcely needed in the circus or in similar entertainments. But he *is* needed, very badly, in the higher forms of theatre. I am left cold by experiments that have no use for Shakespeare except as a springboard for stage gymnastics. I am not convinced that unconscious meanderings are a substitute for dramatic conflict onstage or that a "non-matrixed" program of sheer sensations is the noblest accomplishment of theatre.

In the first half of this century, world theatre had found renewal in the vanguard productions of independent, sometimes entirely amateur companies whose influence shook the established theatres out of their torpor. Antoine's Théâtre Libre, in Paris; the Freie Volksbühne, in Berlin, the Moscow Art Theatre; the Independent Theatre, in London; the Abbey Theatre, in Dublin. Later, the workers' theatres in the U.S., were also products of a theatrical vanguard that accompanied political change — not to mention the contributions, after World War I, of the German theatre, and of the Soviet theatre before its crackdown by Party ideologists.

Since then a new phenomenon has appeared in vanguard theatre — namely two divergent movements: the theatre of Piscator and Brecht, continuing the line of political challenge, versus the theatre of the mad and suffering Artaud proclaiming its descent from the frenzied ritual of Dionysos. (The task of theatre, he announced, is "to create a metaphysics of speech, gesture and expression in order to rescue it from its servitude to psychology and human interest.")[28]

The line drawn between these two philosophies did not leave me in doubt about my own preference. I consider that as an *avant garde*, the theatre of Artaud-Beckett-Genet *et al.* is a feeble descendant of its forebears. If the primal form of theatre was an irrational, god-intoxicated ritual, ancient theatre, as it developed, arrived at a

350

hard-won thoughtfulness. I was not ready to throw away this precious achievement in favor of a renewed emotional orgy.[29]

In contrast to the chilly reception of Brecht's Epic theatre, Artaud's absurdism was greeted as a liberating force that by meeting people's emotional needs could even take the place of organized religion.[30] If I remained less enthusiastic, it was not because I am a relic of the *ancient regime*. The Firebugs, by Max Frisch, which I translated, adapted and designed, had been certified as absurdist by no less an authority than Martin Esslin, author of *The Theatre of the Absurd*. I appreciated the stupid innocence of *Waiting for Godot*; I found *Rhinoceros* a sardonic parable on conformism; I thought *Oh, Dad, Poor Dad* a fantastic lampoon on "momism" and the "international set"; I relished Peter Brook's elegant staging of *Marat/Sade*, Tom O'Horgan's acrobatic direction of *Hair*, John Dexter's *Equus* and *Amadeus*. Richard Foreman's treatment of *The Threepenny Opera* was perhaps the only original staging of it since Brecht's own version in 1928. These productions had a basis, however minimal, in playscripts of social import, but a show like Trevor Nunn's *Cats* did not even need that much of a theme — any more than if it were an ice ballet or a flea circus.

I have always welcomed anything that adds to the resources of theatre. The anti-dramatic experiments of "metatheatre," "happenings," and other improvisations could be contributing grotesque metaphors never seen onstage before, and were undoubtedly opening the way for a new school of directors. But when I was presented with callow, pseudo-philosophic scripts like Albee's *Tiny Alice* or Genêt's *The Maids* and heard them praised for their "awesome depths," and was told they are "a shaft driven down into the core of being" — and further, that Goldberg and McCann, the two mysterious gents in Pinter's *The Birthday Party*, are an embodiment of the Judaeo-Christian ethic, I began to feel that enough was enough. The importance of these sophomoric charades was being tremendously overrated.[31]

Obviously the demand for an end to dramatic theatre was not taken seriously, even by our leading improvisational groups. But on Broadway, and off, dramatists and directors, freed from having to make a responsible statement onstage, showed that mysticism could pay off. Harold Pinter, whose dramatic writing was technically expert, raised Grand Guignol melodramas like *The Birthday Party* and *The Homecoming* to cosmic heights by the simple device of leaving out all motivations. Other mystical dramatists depicted anything, the weirder the better, that entered their heads, secure in their belief that, whatever it might mean, it could "carry away" an audience.

The absurdist authors told us that inertia and stagnation are a true picture of life, which Beckett illustrated by putting his characters inside rubbish cans or vases, or by burying them up to the neck in a sand-pile. The two tramps in *Godot* stand asininely waiting while exchanging lines from vaudeville, and Krapp, in *Krapp's Last Tape*, is a decayed old man who keeps mumbling to himself or munches toothlessly on a banana. Senile or moronic types abounded in these anti-dramas — supposed human beings with arms and legs as inoperative as their minds. The argument was, of course, that the Estragons and Vladimirs of *Godot* are *not* people but abstract tokens of the human race. Writes Esslin:

> Because the theatre of the absurd projects its author's personal world, it lacks objectively valid characters. It cannot show the clash of opposing temperaments or study human passions locked in conflict, and is therefore not dramatic in the accepted sense of the term. Things happen in *Waiting for Godot*, but these happenings do not constitute a plot or story; they are an image of Beckett's intuition that *nothing really ever happens in man's existence.* [Emphasis Esslin's.][32]

But it may still be questioned whether these cardboard figures involved in no problem except that of "existence" in general, and with no hope of any resolution except idiotic vacancy, are a true picture of the human race. The action, if any, of the absurdist figurines resembles the spasms of a dead laboratory frog under an electric charge. That sort of "action" is far removed from anything like the developing struggle of protagonists who have the breath of life. (And among these protagonists I include even the troubled Hamlet, Prince of Denmark.)

Action may seem useless to philosophers like Ionesco, Beckett, Arrabal or Genet. The rest of the human race believes in action, as anyone can tell who reads the daily papers. And we might wish that some of the monsters of history had felt as powerless as the adherents of absurdism: a certain Corporal Adolf Hitler, for instance, who took action to turn the world into a permanent hell, and who might have done it, too, if some other people, unaware of the uselessness of action, had not stopped him in his tracks.[33]

Invited to reply to my view on absurdism, Esslin maintained that it represents "the nobility of facing the world with gay defiance." He seemed particularly disturbed over my reference to remedial action, which is an aspect of the human condition that the absurdists ignore. "*Romeo and Juliet*," he retorted, "is no worse a play for not providing a recipe for the avoidance of unhappy love." And "If Beckett or Ionesco express a sense of the inevitability of death, for example, what action would Professor Gorelik recommend to remedy that state of affairs?"[34]

I offer no quack remedy for the avoidance of unhappy love, but I find in *Romeo and Juliet* the theme of "a plague on both your houses" the root cause of that tragedy. I have no remedy for death, either, but the work of medical science has lengthened the life-span of people astonishingly within a few generations. Nor would I expect any writer of plays to offer solutions to the problems on which experts in various fields are still at work. But it is certainly a dramatist's business to be aware of what is happening to his fellow mortals and himself instead of pondering vacantly on "the ancient, familiar themes of death, art and time."

Bypassing language is more than a technical innovation: it is an admission of defeat. It is much easier to go in for colorful stage effects than to deal with specific issues that require verbal definition. Brecht's motto, "Truth is concrete," rebukes the notion that truth is something that sweeps you passionately away. A comment by a leading American exponent of the new form revealed, at the time, "The hidden fear I have about the new expression is that its forms come perilously close to ecstatic fascism."[35] — thereby echoing an observation made almost thirty years earlier in *New Theatres for Old*: "Uniforms, martial music, cheering and heiling, flags and searchlights, substitute for rational thought." Seymour, too, had some misgivings:

> There is a seductive looseness about ceremonies made up of physical and sensuous excitement, lacking words, lacking focus, lacking precision. Something of the kind was tried with great success in Hitler's Germany. Visceral theatre will be one of authority's ways to distract from genuine problems.

Unlike Esslin, I could not find "gay defiance" or the joyousness of life in the products of the absurdists. "Gay defiance" is not exactly the mood of the masterpieces of tragic drama, either, but these manifest a moral triumph over disaster and death. I see no evidence of anything like that victory in the absurdist doctrine. Esslin himself has described history as "a process whose sole meaning is its meaninglessness"; or, as Jan Kott would have it, "There is no escape from nightmare, which is the human fate and condition."[36] The difference between *Romeo and Juliet* and any absurdist play you can name, is that Shakespearean tragedy is not about abstract tokens of the human race but about living, struggling people caught in a real dilemma.

Not observable life but the mystic "inner space" of the mind was the habitat of "gut" theatre, "ritual" theatre, "non-linear" theatre, "happenings," "metatheatre," "anti-drama" and the "me" theatre or "theatre of the self." We have met with this "inner space" phenomenon before: Europe, in the 1940s, knew it as "the inner migration" — the retreat of art and artists before the advancing legions of barbarism.

*   *   *

The hegemony of the playscript had been challenged because it implies an obligation to make sense onstage. This requirement, it is argued, is a "literary" one that has nothing to do with theatre. Indeed, not only the script, but the idea that the theatre should "intend" anything was flatly contradicted: a stage production should simply be a phenomenon with "its own reason for being," and that is all.

Suddenly the writing of plays became delightfully simple. College students discovered that anything coming from the unconscious mind is automatically gifted and needs only to be jotted down in dialog form untroubled by the cruel laws of drama.

In 1967, as a Fulbright scholar in Australia, I visited a number of schools including the University of Melbourne, where I drew on a blackboard a diagram of dramatic form:

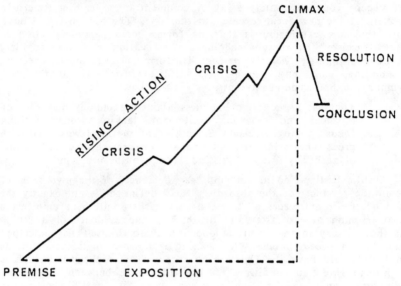

My talk was received with a brief silence, after which I was told, "Mr. Gorelik, all that suspense and climax and so forth is nothing but a tired stage convention."

I asked, "Do you mean that it is an arbitrary exercise invented by dramatists or directors for stage use?"

"Exactly. We are beyond all that."

I replied, "We are *not* beyond all that and never will be. The structure of drama was not born on the stage; it was brought to the stage from the world outside. And let me add that dramatic structure does not refer only to conflicts and wars. It governs human biology from birth to death, as well as every conceivable kind of activity, human or otherwise, on this planet".[37]

(I must add that no hard feelings followed the day's lesson. That evening the students invited me to a party at which our discussion was animatedly renewed over some good Australian wine.)

*   *   *

In a 1977 article in *The New York Times*, "Drama in the Age of Einstein," Robert Brustein, at that time dean of the Yale School of Drama, wrote:

> The experimental theatre is now pressing past the prosaic world of surface reality into a poetic realm of metaphor and myth. This movement is characterized by a radical questioning of the basic premises of the naturalistic universe — namely that case A precedes consequence B, which in turn is responsible for catastrophe C . . . The post-modernists, in short, have been attempting to repeal the fundamental law of cause-and-effect . . . that rules the linear, logical, rationalistic world of literature and, in particular, the Western literature of guilt.[38]

If Brustein was dissatisfied with isolated family drama in this age of advanced social, political and economic illnesses, he could have been justified in criticizing playwrights for not looking beyond the family circle to the pressures that make the American family what it is. But that was not at all what he had in mind. He seemed to dislike the suggestion that there are human agencies whose guilt can be demonstrated by the "fundamental law of cause-and-effect." This law, he evidently agreed, should be repealed, along with the "facile guilt-mongering of our accusatory playwrights." Instead, our future "metaphorical" dramatists would fly off into Einsteinian space, returning with plays of such high conceptual thought that they would presumably be inhaled rather that understood by their audiences.

It is curious that Brustein quoted Edmund, in *King Lear*, in support of his thesis, for Edmund very clearly is not impressed by the "excellent foppery" of those who "make guilty of our disasters the sun, the moon, and the stars." Edmund well knows that tragedies, as distinct from natural catastrophes, are caused by people, not by heavenly bodies, and that scoundrels and fools are accountable for their actions, which can be documented by means of the law of cause-and-effect. That law can no more be repealed than the law of gravity.

The Brustein essay is about as far as one can go in glamorizing the principle of escape from anything of substance in the theatre. But maybe its author was just being fanciful. His American Repertory Theatre, in Boston, went on to stage a mother vs. daughter drama, *'Night, Mother,* that was as "accusatory" as a family play can be.

It is just *because* theatre is a public art that it is subject not only to profound historic changes but also to fads that for a time occupy center stage, creating great excitement before they are consigned to the theatre's museum of mild curiosities. By the end of 1982 it was evident that irrational theatre was vanishing from the headlines of the entertainment columns, along with the names of its practitioners.

It cannot be said that it had met with no opposition. In June 1971 the drama critic of the Sunday *New York Times*, Walter Kerr, had lent his column to the charge by Roger Copeland that

> American plays, by and large, are concerned with personal problems, private neuroses, identity crises, marital discord, sibling rivalries, Oedipal struggles — almost everything except issues of social or public consequences.[39]

Three years later Margaret Croyden followed up with "The current state of the American theatre raises the question whether the serious playwright can ever be an artistic force again."[40] And Kerr himself summed up the weakening of American drama: "More and more, we are making theatrical mountains out of less and less solid rock."[41] It was by no means the first time he had shown uneasiness at the spread of anti-drama. Incidentally my own defense of rational drama, *The Absurd Absurdists*, had appeared in the same column (August 8, 1965).

In the past, world theatre has shown that it can live up to its responsibilities. I believe it will do so again. The escapist mood of our theatre will change — and not just because it will be fashionable to do so. It will change because theatre has the task of clarifying, not dulling or mystifying, the minds of its audience. It will change because, as our period's long and terrifying series of world crises mount to a climax, our theatre's playwrights and playgoers will no longer be able to close their eyes and ears to the extreme peril into which we are drifting.

Nor will the renewed theatre prove to be superfluous compared with cinema and television. Nothing can match the flesh-and-blood immediacy of the stage or the ceremonial of its relation to its audiences. What it needs at present is the willingness to recognize the mundane pressures that dominate the lives of its playgoers. It is in this sense that I speak for "a larger theatre."

"You will not have an easy time of it," Bobby Jones warned me in 1920, "The quality of your work is not soft and comforting." Then, in an afterthought, "It's like the art of the cellist Pablo Casals."

*   *   *

Here ends the apologia for my long years in the American theatre and for the defense of my plays, which belong, together with those of many far younger dramatists, in a theatre more receptive than the one that exists at this moment.

ABOUT THE AUTHOR *

By Marie J. Kilker

"When Doris Aronson died last year, there passed from the scene the next to the last great American stage designers of the past half-century. The procession included Robert Edmond Jones, Lee Simonson, Norman Bel Geddes, Donald Oenslager, Jo Mielziner and others." Thus did Norris Houghton introduce and "honor the last artist of that great company"[42] in welcoming Mordecai Gorelik to the College of Fellows of the American Theatre Association at its August, 1982 Annual Convention in New York City. Fittingly, Houghton did not stop with his praise of Gorelik as designer. Though his work as a scenic artist, most notably for the Group Theatre, in New York, made Gorelik famous, his "development of an aesthetic that was underpinned by and responsive to the social and political forces in society"[43] brought him far beyond the point where his accomplishments can be tagged with a single label. "Stage designer-director-playwright-scholar-educator" was the only accurate epithet applicable in "A Tribute to Mordecai Gorelik," a panel climaxing the 1982 ATA national meeting. As one of the panelists, I made the point that Gorelik had entered the scholastic world at Pratt Institute over six decades ago as a student, with the ambition of becoming an illustrator, but he has spent most of his life in the real world as an illuminator.

In Mordecai Gorelik's opinion, the real world and the theatrical one should be partners, combining all their assets to their mutual profit. He has practiced his own preachings. Known as the first champion in this country of the Epic theatre created by Brecht and Piscator, Gorelik looks "beyond personal comedy or tragedy to the relationships which are bigger than people," relationships that are "the fundamental cause of comic or tragic events."[44] In his classic *New Theatres for Old*, first published in 1940, he asked over and over that new theatre make logical inquiries, seek facts, and teach, for "What experience is greater than a heightened awareness of life around us? What sensation is more thrilling than a wider and keener understanding of the outer world which surrounds us?"[45] Further, he insisted:

> The vital and truthful theatre of the future will not betray its audiences. It will not trick its audiences into a sense of false security in the midst of catastrophic events by giving them "Olympian," art-for-art's sake productions when a useful and practical knowledge of the world is absolutely necessary.

---

* Adapted from "Mordecai Gorelik: 'Altogether' Theatre Man" by Marie J. Kilker, Southern Illinois University (Carbondale). *Cue Magazine*, Spring-Summer 1983.

MORDECAI GORELIK   1984

Theatre is entering on a long struggle to maintain its integrity and freedom of thought, to hold on to its sacred duty of clarifying life. In the effort to remain clear in judgment, it will reach its greatest moral sensitivity, its most scientific accuracy, its most stirring imagination.[46]

In the ensuing years, Mordecai Gorelik joined the struggle for the truthful theatre by using his own judgment, moral sensitivity, logic, and imagination in a variety of roles, not least as scholar and teacher, adding to his knowledge of stage production in a study of the new Soviet theatre in 1932, followed in later years by research in nine different European countries, culminating, in 1967, in his acquaintance with theatre in Japan and Australia. In France in 1945-46, immediately after World War II, he served as scene designer, instructor and director at the Army's GI school at Biarritz, and in 1949 he was expert consultant in theatre for the U.S. Occupation Forces in Germany.

It was during his work at the Biarritz American University that he conceived his now famous approach to educating, not merely training, designers — an inductive process relating the setting metaphorically to every other element of a play, its production, and its relation to both theatrical and actual reality. An outgrowth of his own procedures to stimulate creativity, the course was based on and developed as Gorelik's theory of *The Scenic Imagination,* which he later imparted in seminars to theatre professionals in New York and to students in several universities, but mainly during his twelve years as research professor in theatre at Southern Illinois University at Carbondale, where he completed an accompanying (but still unpublished) text.[47]

Upon his retirement from SIU in 1972, Mordecai Gorelik could list himself as designer of over 50 professional stage and screen productions, director of collegiate and semi-professional presentations, visiting professor at the Cornish School (Seattle), and at the Universities of Toledo, Hawaii, California State (L.A.), Brigham Young University (Utah), Bard College (New York), University of Kansas, U.C.L.A., University of Puerto Rico, and University of Massachusetts. Not to mention at least half a dozen universities in Australia. He is a holder of Guggenheim, Rockefeller Foundation and Fulbright awards, translator of *The Firebugs,* by Max Frisch, former advisor to the Illinois Arts Council, recipient of the 1971 Theta Alpha Phi Medallion of Honor, the 1982 American Theatre Association Fellowship, and the U.S. Institute for Theatre Technology award in 1981. As editors of over a dozen biographical directories can attest, Gorelik has not allowed his emeritus status to keep him from continuing his work, as visiting professor at the University of Southern California, Long Island University, and Kansas State University. He is still adding to the stream of articles he has turned out since the very beginning of the Twenties. These reflect his many concerns, but especially that theatre not betray its audiences by rejecting true drama for sheer theatricalism. His principal cause became the need for new playwriting:

> Are we at a point of exhaustion in dramatic writing? Unable to deal with an onrush of national and world problems complex and ominous beyond anything previously known, contemporary drama limits itself to a repertory consisting mainly of domestic problems, detective stories and melodramas, leaving center-stage to theatricalism of an anti-rational variety, mind-blowing stage effects, verbal acrobatics, pornographic "exploitations," sexual deviations, ritual, celebrations, "guerilla raids", and "conceptual" dramas on the hopelessness of being human.
>
> It is impossible, however, to believe that the future belongs to theatrical technique alone with "words" excluded or reduced to grunts, screams and gibberish.[48]

As a major personal investment in the future of theatre, Gorelik had begun to write plays as early as 1921, at first a group of one-acts called *Saturday Stories* (not registered until 1967). These were mostly boy-and-girl comedies. From then on, not a decade passed without a draft or collaboration, the most celebrated of the latter being an aborted co-authorship with Brecht in 1945 of *Nothing But the Best*, "about the desire of every American worker for the best in material comfort at the cost of dog-eat-dog strivings to get ahead." In 1947 Brecht was in the audience for a showing at the Actors Laboratory Theatre, Los Angeles, of Gorelik's own one-act, *Paul Thompson Forever*.[49] Published by Walter H. Baker Company, 1950, it hinted at such later preoccupations of the author as the trial/judgment motif and indictment of business/labor malpractice.

What was clear then and in the following years, and what stands out in Gorelik's "retirement" dedication to revising earlier playscripts, and writing new ones, is his insistence on the engagement of his characters with society at large. These presentations, like his designs and productions, are always logical, vivid, and related to the real social and moral problems to which audiences not only can but must relate. In *Rainbow Terrace*, there is the liberal vs. fundamentalist clash of views on what should be the fate, in the Afterlife, of an unscrupulous but dynamic businessman. *Yes and No* explores a generations gap in the context of a civil rights issue. *The Feast of Unreason* mirrors the ongoing struggle in Northern Ireland through a deadly dispute over housing. *Andrus, or the Vision* describes an Inquisition against a medieval man of simple faith and his heretical projections of a miraculous future in which people can fly. All, like Gorelik's other contributions to the theatre, "illuminate."

Obviously Gorelik, unlike the contemporary theatre he questions, is not "at a point of exhaustion in dramatic writing." As he has done with his scholarly, scenic, directorial, and educator's talents, he is eager to share the results of his playwriting efforts with the theatre of the future and its students today.

END NOTES

1. (p.3) Mordecai Gorelik, *"Life With Bobby,"* *Theatre Arts Magazine*, April and June 1955.

2. (p.4) Gorelik, *New Theatres for Old* (New York: *Samuel French*, 1940).

3. (p.9) Gorelik, "Soviet Scene Design," *(New Theatre and Film Magazine*, New York, Jan. 1936).

4. (p.9) Taylor, *People's Theatre in Amerika* (New York: Drama Book Specialists, Publishers, N.Y. 1972).

5. (p.10) It cannot be said that Brecht was the only playwright who ever objected to the way in which one of his plays was being staged. In the well-known case of *Anton Chekhov vs. the Moscow Art Theatre*, the dramatist complained that his *Cherry Orchard* was being misinterpreted. He had "frequent outbursts of anger" during the rehearsals of *The Sea Gull*. (See David Magarshak in *Anton Chekhov's Plays*, ed., Eugene K. Bristow, (New York: W. W. Norton, 1977). Disagreements of this kind are far from unusual. The Dramatists Guild, in the United States, gives its members the right to approve the directors and casts of their scripts.

6. (p.11) Gorelik, "Brecht: I Am the Einstein of the New Dramatic Form," *(Theatre Arts*, March 1957).

7. (p.14) Robert Hethmon, *"The Annotated Hamlet,"* *(Drama Service*, Minneapolis, Spring 1982).

8. (p.16) *International Herald Tribune*, Paris, July 12/13, 1980.

9. (p.23) As late as 1970 a campus protest at Kent State University was answered by the Ohio National Guard killing four students and wounding nine others.

10. (p.75) Bircher: a member of the John Birch Society, generally regarded as a far-right group.

11. (p.75) Ben Gelman, *"Hey, Pops, Why did You Sell Out, Huh?"* *(Daily Southern Illinoisan)*, April 27, 1969.

12. (p.83) The Jewish population of Shchedrin, which included my Uncle Aaron and Aunt Rasha, no longer exists. In March 1942, Hitler's *Sonderkommandos*, with their anti-Communist Russian collaborators, lined

up all the inhabitants of this ghetto town — some 1200 women, children, and old men — in front of a mass grave and let loose with machine guns.

As the war ended, the butchers who had "Jew-cleaned" every settlement of the Byelorussian border regions were enlisted by top-secret U.S. agencies for the purpose of invading and overthrowing the Soviet regime. As documented by John Loftus in *The Belarus Secret* (New York: Knopf, 1982), this grandiose, no-expense-spared operation turned into a new sort of Gilbert & Sullivan extravaganza characterized by measureless deceit, cover-up, and incompetence — successful only in bringing its hundreds of proteges into safety, illegally, to the United States and South America. At least 300 beneficiaries of this interesting project, with American citizenship hastily conferred upon them, have been living here in modest retirement ever since.

13. (p.83) While the Inquisition is involved in *Andrus*, the issue is the universal one of humanism versus orthodoxy — a conflict that has acquired vast dimensions in our own period. The thirteenth century Church shared the primitiveness of its age; to the best of my knowledge its bigotry is not condoned by any living Catholic authority. (*The Modern Catholic Encyclopedia*, Washington, D.C., says the Inquisition "can only be classified as one of the darker chapters of the Church," and "as it evolved in practice, indefensible.") I am convinced that any good Catholic of today, including Pope John Paul II, would have been tried for heresy in the Middle Ages.

14. (p.137) O'Neal afterwards became president of the Actors Equity Association.

15. (p.203) George Abbott's letter was dated about 1967. Dan Sullivan, in *The Los Angeles Times* of January 2, 1982, quoted the cost of a Broadway "straight" play as $500,000 as recorded by the New York State Attorney General in May 1981, with musicals averaging $1.2 million. I have no figure for off-Broadway, but even at one-tenth the cost of a Broadway "straight" play, they would come to $50,000 each. Even the subsidized or partly subsidized community and academic playhouses face enormously increased expenses.

16. (p.341) *The Daily Egyptian*, (Southern Illinois University campus newspaper, 23 November, 1966).

17. (p.342) *The Saturday Review Magazine*, 31 December, 1966.

18. (p.344) *Daily Egyptian, supra*.

19. (p.345) Gorelik   "For a Theatre of Conscience, Not Consciousness," *(Dramatics Magazine*, Cincinnati, Ohio, September 1980).

20. (p.346) *New Theatre and Film, supra,* January 1936.

21. (p.348) Gorelik, "This Side Idolatry," *(Educational Theatre Journal,* 1951). The belief that Shakespeare is, above all, the most penetrating observer of human character will not bear too close study, "Misconceptions, barbarisms and violent prejudices were rampant in his lifetime: it is surprising, not that he had some, but that he was in so many ways far ahead of his time; that in fact he contributed mightily to the continuing liberation of the human mind. Shakespeare in his own era was a bringer of light; we can honor him most by seeing him clearly today.

22. (p.348) Chekhov himself, as a doctor, was socially aware, as shown by his ten-thousand-mile, three-month journey in 1890, across Siberia to look into the terrible conditions of the Tsarist prison camp on Sakhalin Island. See J. William Miller, *Modern Playwrights at Work* (N.Y.: Samuel French, Inc., 1968).

23. (p.349) Arthur Miller, "The Shadows of the Gods," *(Harper's Magazine,* August 1958).

24. (p.349) "Correspondence About *New Theatres for Old,"* *(Educational Theatre Journal,* March 1968).

25. (p.349) Antonin Artaud, *The Theatre and Its Double,* (New York: Grove Press, 1958).

26. (p.349) "The Gold Rush to Golgotha," *(Time Magazine,* 25 October, 1971).

27. (p.350) Alan Seymour and Mordecai Gorelik "Words and Music," *(Masque Magazine,* Sydney, Australia, August-September 1969).

28. (p.350) Martin Esslin, *The Theatre of the Absurd* (Garden City, N.Y.: Doubleday & Co., 1961).

29. (p.351) Bernard F. Dick, Iona College, New Rochelle, New York, in a letter to *The New York Times,* February 14, 1969: "The origins of tragedy out of the worship of Dionysos pose a serious artistic problem: can art arise from an orgy that was characterized by sexual frenzy and the dismemberment of a scapegoat? Even if one does accept such an origin of drama, how does it explain the *structure* of Greek tragedy? What Shechner has done in his production of *Dionysos in 69* (unwittingly, I would like to think) is to revert to the preliterary form of theatre, passing it off as 'Greek' and little realizing that it was a type of ritual, which most Athenians (the true theatregoers) would like to forget.

30. (p.351) Roderick Robertson, "A Theatre for the Absurd: The Passionate Equation," (*Drama Survey*, Spring 1962).

31. (p.351) Gorelik, "The Absurd Absurdists," (*N.Y. Times*, 8 August, 1965).

32. (p.352) Martin Esslin, *supra*.

33. (p.352) Gorelik, *supra*.

34. (p.352) Martin Esslin, "The Theatre of the Absurd Is Not Absurd At All," (*N.Y. Times*, 29 August, 1965).

35. (p.353) Eleanor Lester, "Richard Shechner: Professor of Dionysiac Theatre," *N.Y. Times*, 27 April, 1969.

36. (p.353) Jan Kott, *Shakespeare Our Contemporary* (Garden City, New York: Doubleday Anchor Books, 1966).

37. (p.354) I asked, "Does anyone suppose that President Johnson and Ho Chi Minh signed a contract to wage the Vietnam War using the rules of the stage?"

38. (p.355) Robert Brustein, "Drama in the Age of Einstein," (*New York Times*, 7 August, 1977).

39. (p.356) Roger Copeland, "Theatre in the Me Decade" (*New York Times*, 30 June, 1979).

40. (p.356) Margaret Croyden, "The Playwright Vanishes," (*New York Times*, 20 June, 1982).

41. (p.356) Walter Kerr, "The Spectacle of Cats, or Inflation Beyond Reason," (*New York Times*, 17 October, 1982).

42. (p.357) Norris Houghton, "Gorelik, Stavis, Corrigan, New ATA Fellows," (*Theatre News*, 14, No. 8, 1982).

43. (p.357) *Ibid*.

44. (p.357) Mordecai Gorelik, *New Theatres for Old*, (New York: Samuel French, 1940; New York, E.P. Dutton, 1962; London: Dennis Dobson, 1947).

45. (p.358) *Ibid*.

46. (p.359) *Ibid*.

47. (p.359) For a mini-version of Gorelik's proceedings and methods as teacher, see Gorelik, "The Scenic Imagination Seminar," *Theatre Crafts Magazine,* September 1978.

40. (p.360) Gorelik, "Theatre vs Drama," (*Dramatics Magazine,* Cincinnati, September/October 1978).

49. (p.360) James K. Lyon, Dr., *Bertolt Brecht in America* (Princeton, N.J.: Princeton University Press, 1980).

INDEX

A

Abbey Theatre, 350
Abbott, George, 203
Act 2 Community Theatre, ix
Actors Studio, viii, 137
Actors' Laboratory Theatre, viii,
  13, 137, 360
Agitprop, 8
Albee, Edward, 351
American National Theatre and
  Academy, 335
American Playwrights Theatre
  (APT), vii
American Repertory Theatre, 355
American Theatre Association, ix,
  358
American Theatre Association
  Fellowship, 359
Andreyev, Leonid, 5
Ansky, Sholom, 23
Anta, West, 131, 254
Antoine's Théatre Libre, 350
Aronson, Boris, 358
Arrabal, Fernaldo, 352
Artaud, Antonin, 349, 350
Arthur, Helen, 2
Asolo State Theatre, ix
Association of Music Publishers in
  Ireland, x

B

Baker, Walter, 137
Balch, Marston, Tufts University,
  337
Bard College (New York), 359
Basshe, Em Jo, 6
Beckett, Samuel, 348, 350, 352
Behan, Brendan, 254
Bel Geddes, Norman, vii, 358
Bell, Winifred, Lyric Players
  Theatre, Belfast 254
Berlau, Ruth, 137
Berlin, 4
Biarritz American University, 359
Billy Rose Theatre Collection, x

Bohnen, Roman (Bud), 13
Bottje, Will Gay, 14
Brecht, Bertolt, 10, 11, 137, 350,
  353, 360
Brecht's Epic Theatre, 14, 351
Brennan, Lorin, Los Angeles
  Lawyers for the Arts, x
Brigham Young University
  (Utah), 359
Brook, Peter, 351
Brustein, Robert, 355
Bunton, Norma D., Dr., ix

C

California State College
  (L.A.), 359
California State College (San
  Jose), viii
Carnovsky, Morris, 13, 203
Carrol, Dennis, University of
  Hawaii, 255
Casals, Pablo, 356
Central Florida University, ix
Chauve Souris, vii
Chekhov, Anton, 5, 348
Cleveland Playhouse, 131
Climenhaga, Joel, Dr., ix
Clurman, Harold, 7, 9, 346, 348
Coens, Sister Mary Xavier, 204
Colgate University, 138
Cook, George Cram, 2
Cook, Victor, 14
Cornish School, Seattle, 5, 359
Crawford, Cheryl, 9
Croyden, Margaret, 356
Curtiss, Thomas Quinn,
  International Herald Tribune, 16
Cusak, Dame Dymphna, 205

D

da Vinci, Leonardo, 81
Daily Egyptian, viii
Davidson, Gordon, 204
Deeter, Jasper, 5
Dessart, George, 204

367